Around the time this volume goes on sale in Japan, I'll be taking a short break. It'll be the longest break I've taken since *Toriko* began serialization over five years ago. I'm really looking forward to it. I kind of want to take it easy in Okinawa, but since I have so much to do, I don't know how much time I'll be able to devote to recharging my batteries. Anyway, I'm going to do my best to get some major R&R! (My current weight...69 kg!! Uh-oh, I've really got to focus if I want to run a full marathon!)

—Mitsutoshi Shimabukuro, 2014

Mitsutoshi Shimabukuro made his debut in **Weekly Shonen Jump** in 1996. He is best known for **Seikimatsu Leader Den Takeshi!** for which he won the 46th Shogakukan Manga Award for children's manga in 2001. His current series, **Toriko**, began serialization in Japan in 2008.

TORIKO VOL. 28
SHONEN JUMP Manga Edition

STORY AND ART BY **MITSUTOSHI SHIMABUKURO**

Translation/Christine Dashiell
Weekly Shonen Jump Lettering/Erika Terriquez
Graphic Novel Touch-Up Art & Lettering/Elena Diaz
Design/Matt Hinrichs
Editor/Hope Donovan

Printed in the U.S.A.

Published by VIZ Media, LLC
P.O. Box 77010
San Francisco, CA 94107

10 9 8 7 6 5 4 3 2 1
First printing, June 2015

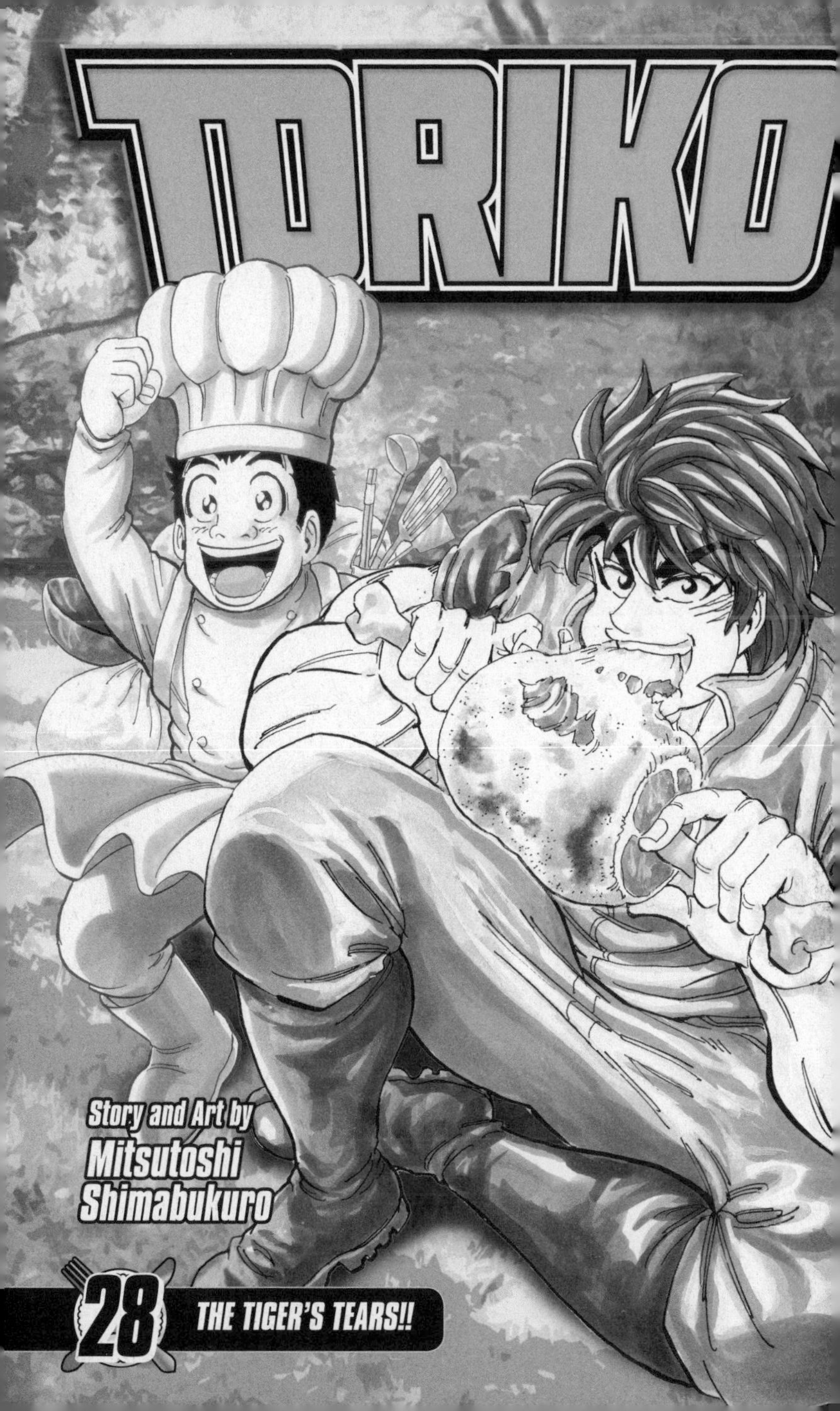
TORIKO
Story and Art by
Mitsutoshi Shimabukuro
28
THE TIGER'S TEARS!!

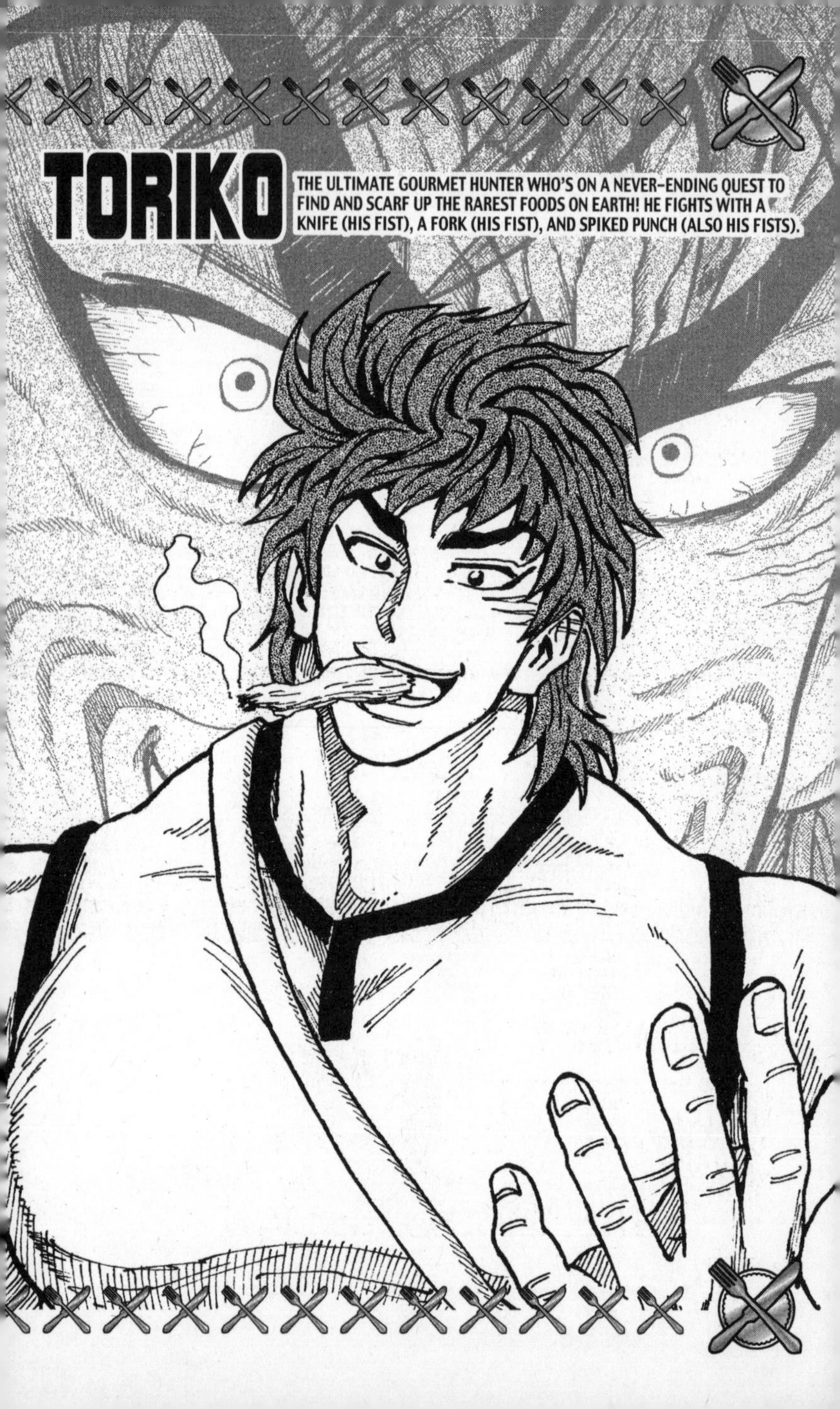
TORIKO
THE ULTIMATE GOURMET HUNTER WHO'S ON A NEVER-ENDING QUEST TO FIND AND SCARF UP THE RAREST FOODS ON EARTH! HE FIGHTS WITH A KNIFE (HIS FIST), A FORK (HIS FIST), AND SPIKED PUNCH (ALSO HIS FISTS).

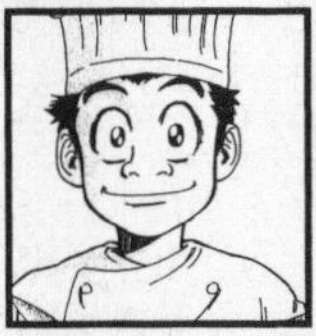

● KOMATSU
TALENTED IGO HOTEL CHEF AND TORIKO'S #1 FAN.

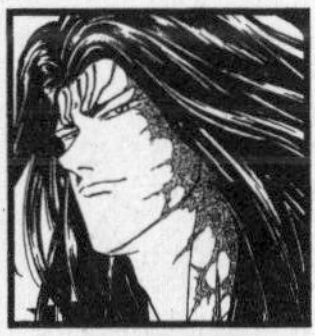

● STARJUN
ONE OF GOURMET CORP.'S THREE VICE-CHEFS. WANTS KOMATSU FOR HIS SKILLS.

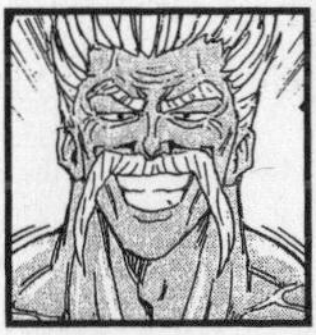

● ICHIRYU
HARDY IGO PRESIDENT AND DISCIPLE OF THE LATE GOURMET GOD ACACIA.

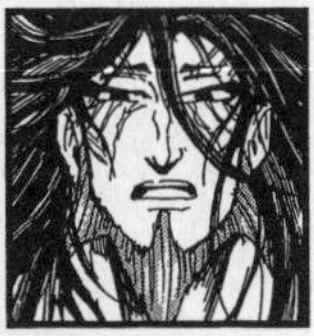

● MIDORA
BOSS OF GOURMET CORP. AND DISCIPLE OF ACACIA. LOOKING FOR GOD.

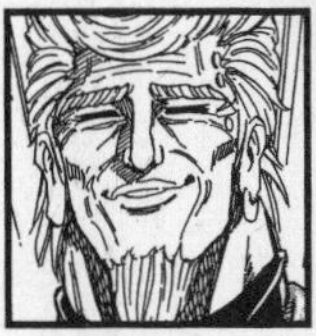

● JIRO
LEGENDARY GOURMET HUNGER WHO EARNED THE TITLE "KNOCKING MASTER." DISCIPLE OF ACACIA.

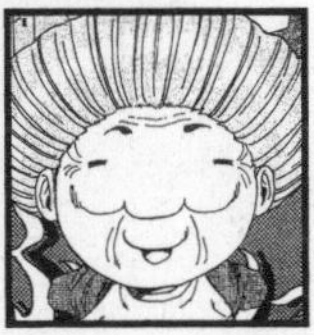

● SETSUNO
AKA GRANNY SETSU. FAMOUS CHEF AND GOURMET LIVING LEGEND.

WHAT'S FOR DINNER

IT'S THE AGE OF GOURMET! KOMATSU, THE HEAD CHEF AT THE HOTEL OWNED BY THE IGO (INTERNATIONAL GOURMET ORGANIZATION), BECAME FAST FRIENDS WITH THE LEGENDARY GOURMET HUNTER TORIKO WHILE GATOR HUNTING. NOW KOMATSU ACCOMPANIES TORIKO ON HIS LIFELONG QUEST TO CREATE THE PERFECT FULL-COURSE MEAL. THROUGH THEIR ADVENTURES, THEY FIND THEMSELVES ENTANGLED IN THE IGO'S RIVALRY WITH THE NEFARIOUS GOURMET CORP.

AT THE COOKING FESTIVAL, GOURMET CORP. ATTACKS! AT LAST, THE IGO ENGAGES GOURMET CORP. IN ALL-OUT WAR. TORIKO AND STARJUN BATTLE, WITH KOMATSU'S FATE HANGING IN THE BALANCE. THE BATTLE ENDS WITH TORIKO UNABLE TO FIGHT. MEANWHILE, SENSING GOURMET CORP.'S SINISTER ACTIONS, THE PRESIDENT OF THE IGO, ICHIRYU, SENDS HIS AGENTS TO GATHER ACACIA'S FULL-COURSE MEAL WHILE HE PERSONALLY FIGHTS GOURMET CORP.'S BOSS, MIDORA!

TO MAKE MATTERS MORE COMPLEX, A THIRD ORGANIZATION CALLED "NEO" EMERGES FROM THE SHADOWS, REVEALING DOUBLE AGENTS ON BOTH SIDES. SETSUNO SAYS THAT DARK CHEF JOIE IS BEHIND IT ALL, BUT WHEN JOIE SHOWS UP, SHE'S HOLDING THE KNIFE THAT ONCE BELONGED TO ACACIA'S PARTNER, GOD CHEF FROESE. AND SHE'S A DEAD RINGER FOR THE GOD CHEF TOO!

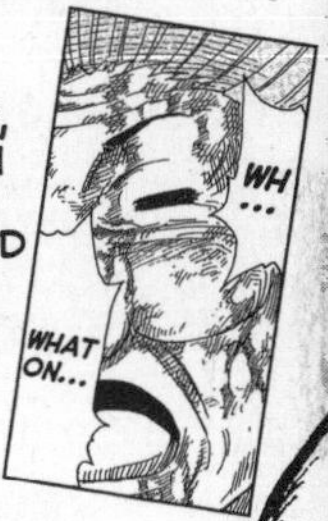
WH...
WHAT ON...

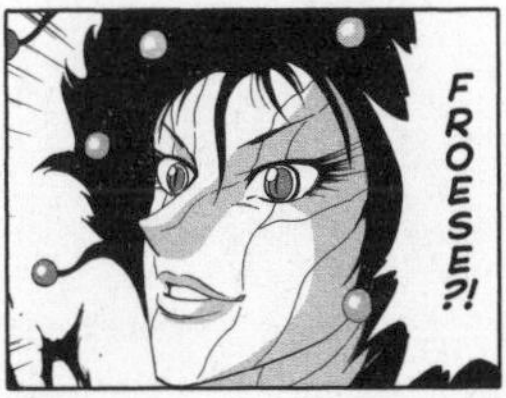
FROESE?!

Contents

TORIKO

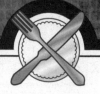

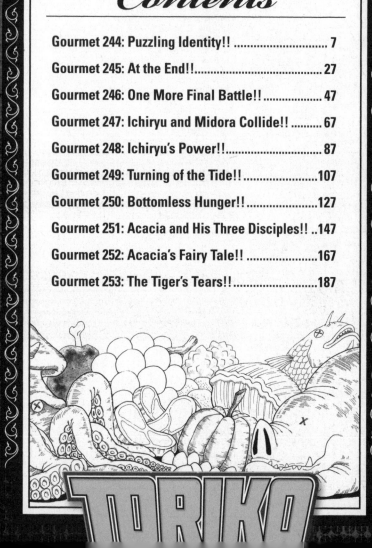

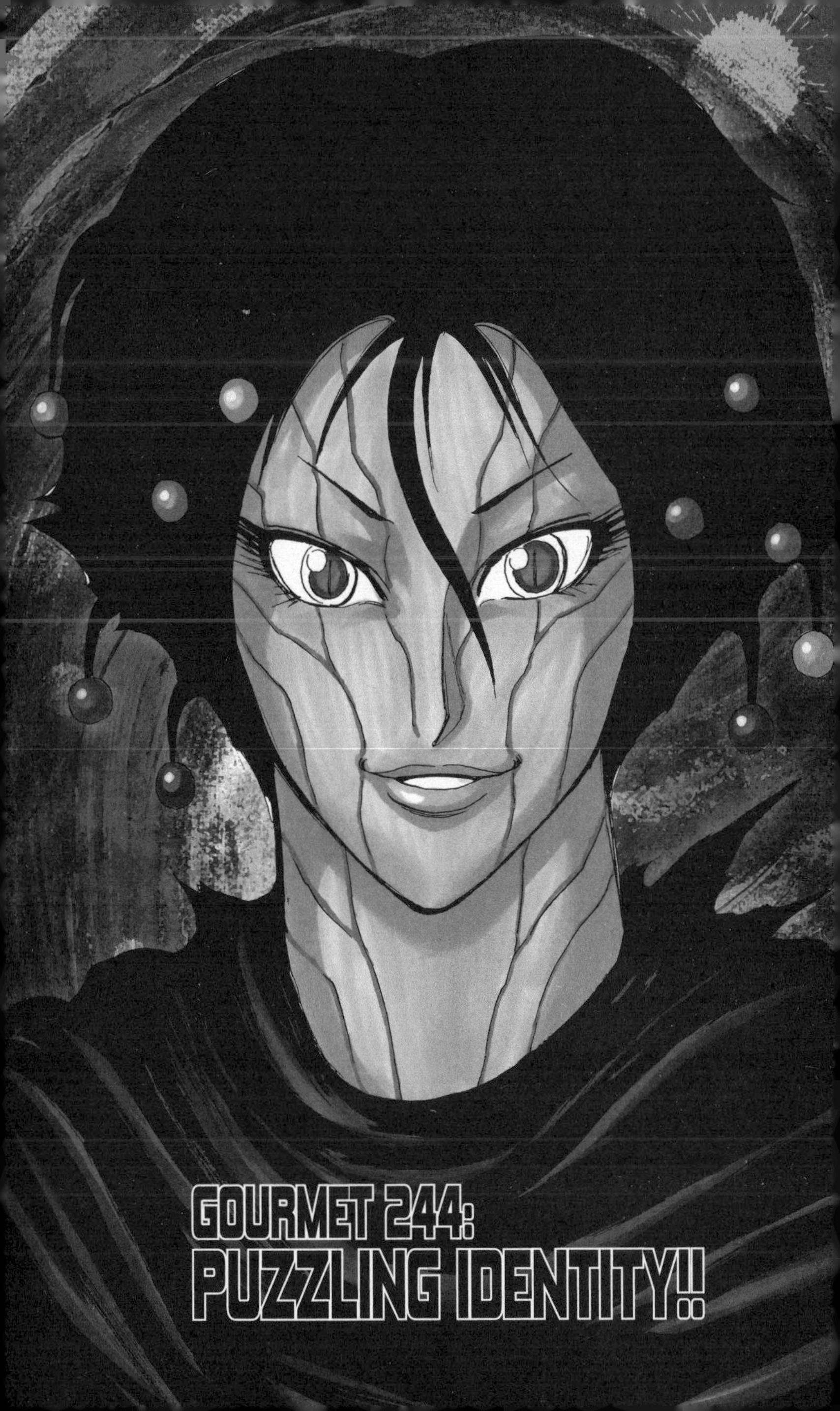
GOURMET 244:
PUZZLING IDENTITY!!

TORIKO

GOURMET CHECKLIST

Vol. 271

FLAVORED SNOW
(WEATHER)

CAPTURE LEVEL: LESS THAN 1

HABITAT: OCCURS UNDER SPECIFIC WEATHER CONDITIONS

SIZE: ---

HEIGHT: ---

WEIGHT: ---

PRICE: 1 KG / 300 YEN

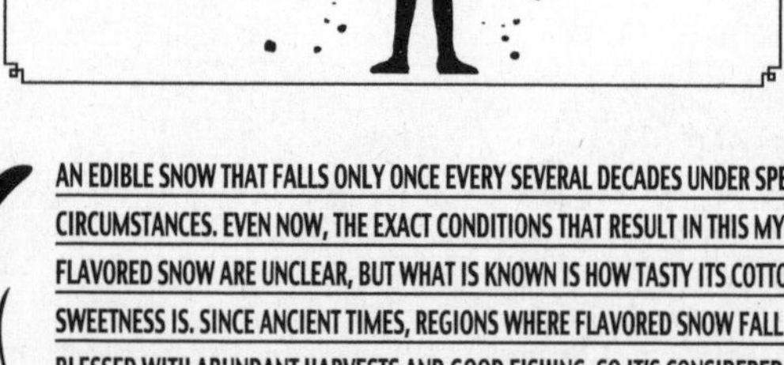

SCALE

AN EDIBLE SNOW THAT FALLS ONLY ONCE EVERY SEVERAL DECADES UNDER SPECIFIC CIRCUMSTANCES. EVEN NOW, THE EXACT CONDITIONS THAT RESULT IN THIS MYSTERIOUS FLAVORED SNOW ARE UNCLEAR, BUT WHAT IS KNOWN IS HOW TASTY ITS COTTON CANDY-LIKE SWEETNESS IS. SINCE ANCIENT TIMES, REGIONS WHERE FLAVORED SNOW FALL HAVE BEEN BLESSED WITH ABUNDANT HARVESTS AND GOOD FISHING, SO IT'S CONSIDERED GOOD LUCK.

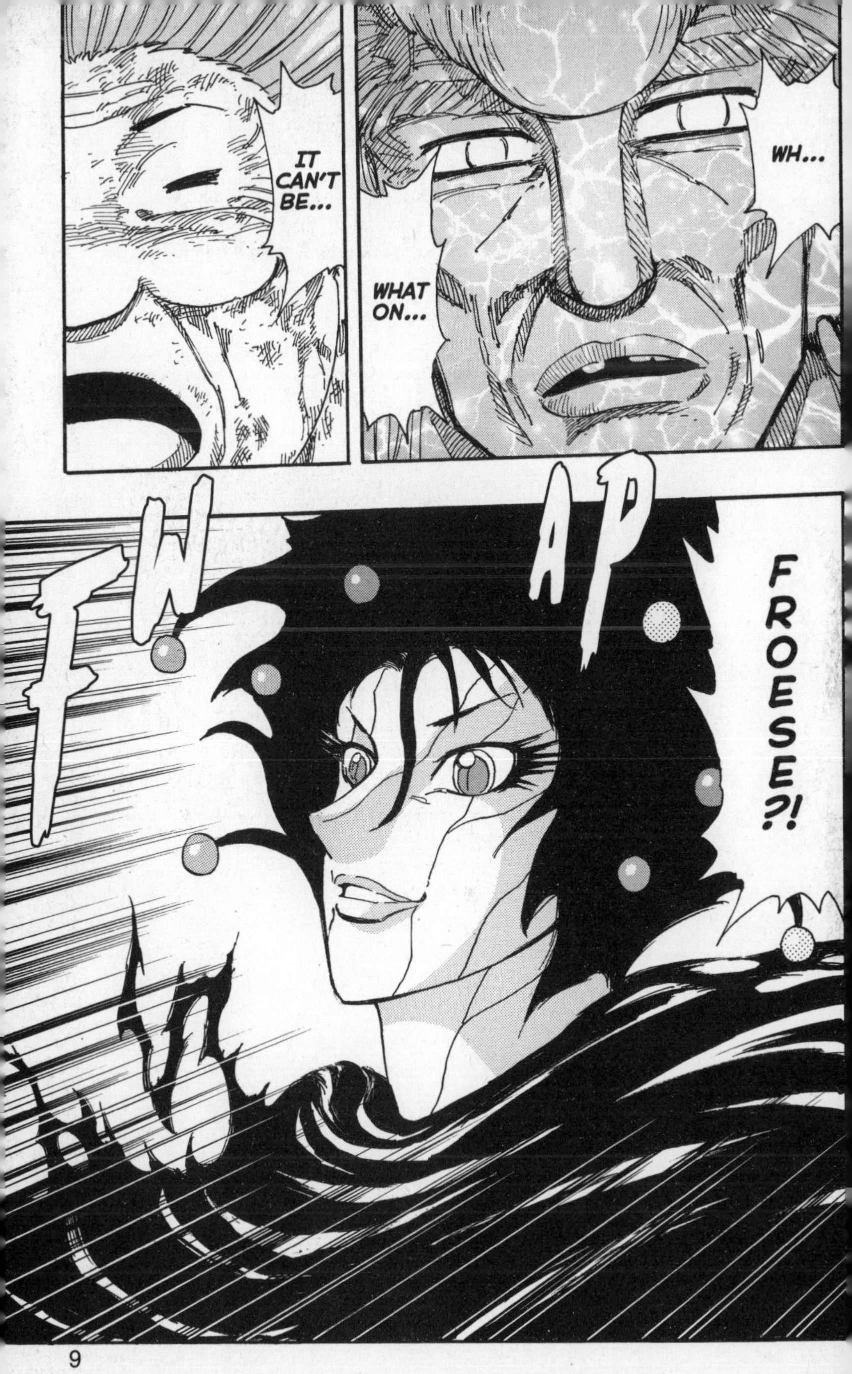
WH...
WHAT ON...
IT CAN'T BE...
FWAP
FROESE?!

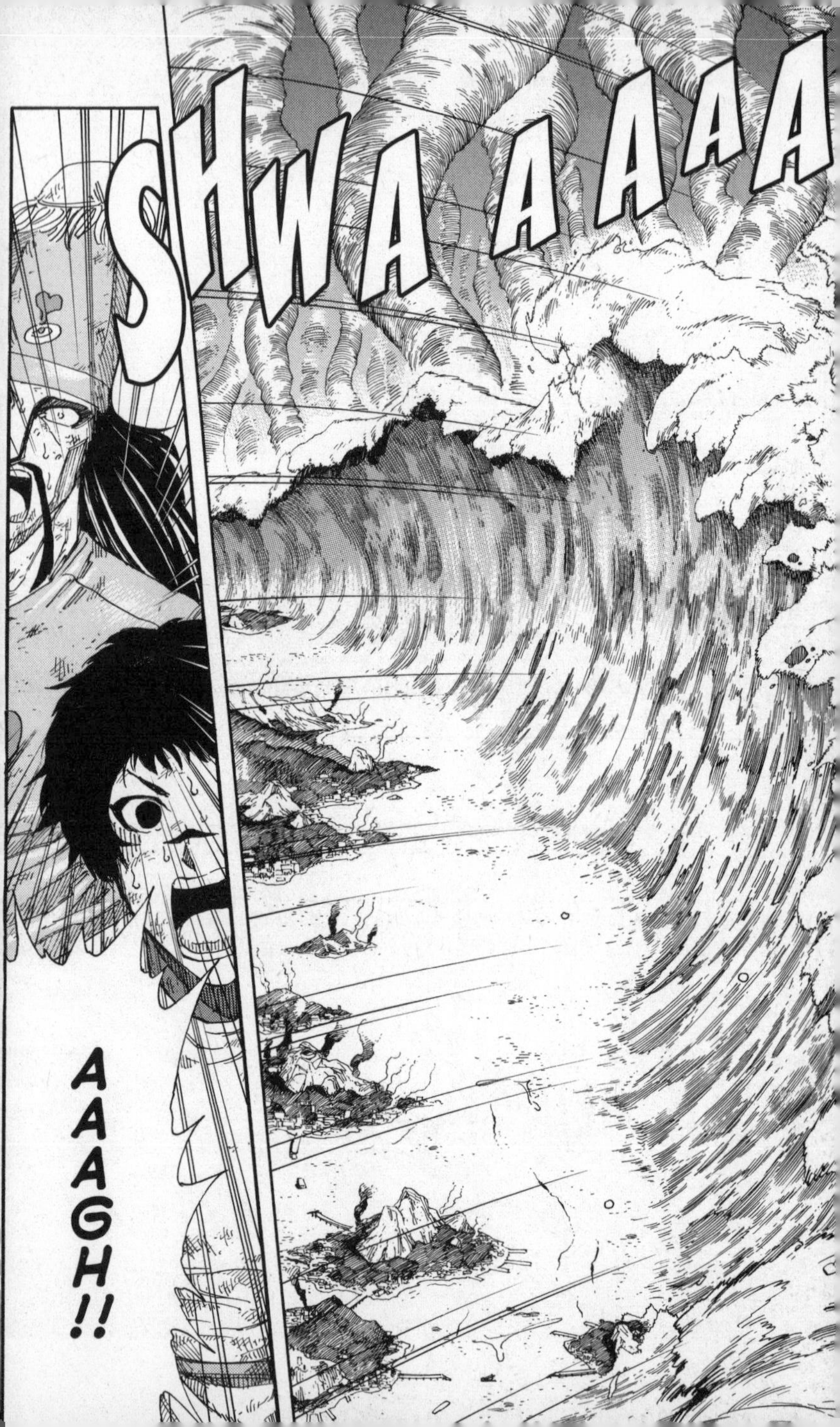
SHWAAAAA
AAAGH!!

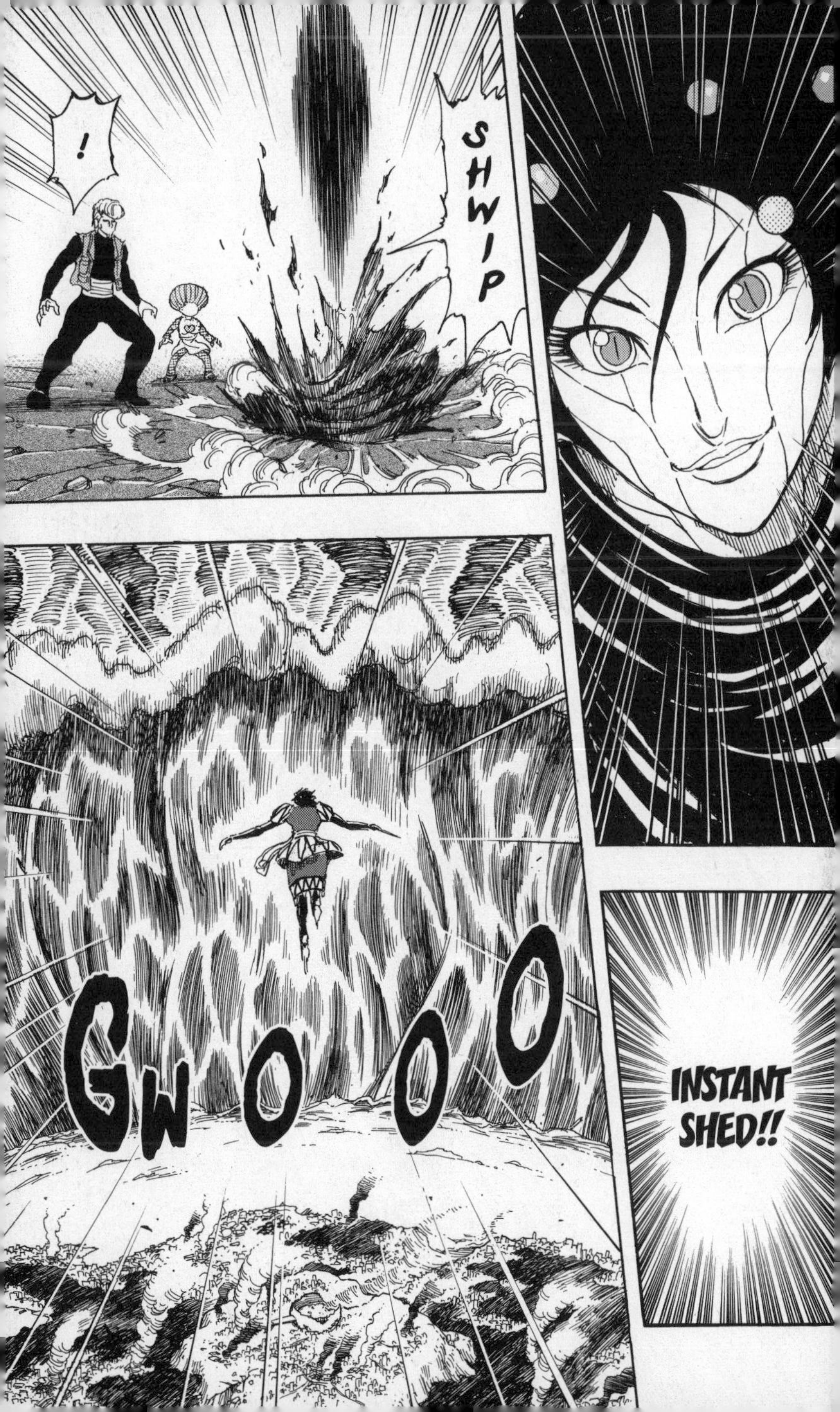
!
SHWIP
INSTANT SHED!!
GWOOOO

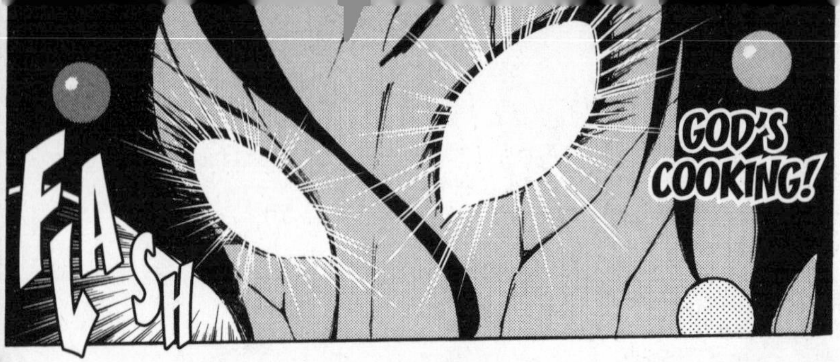
GOD'S COOKING!
FLASH
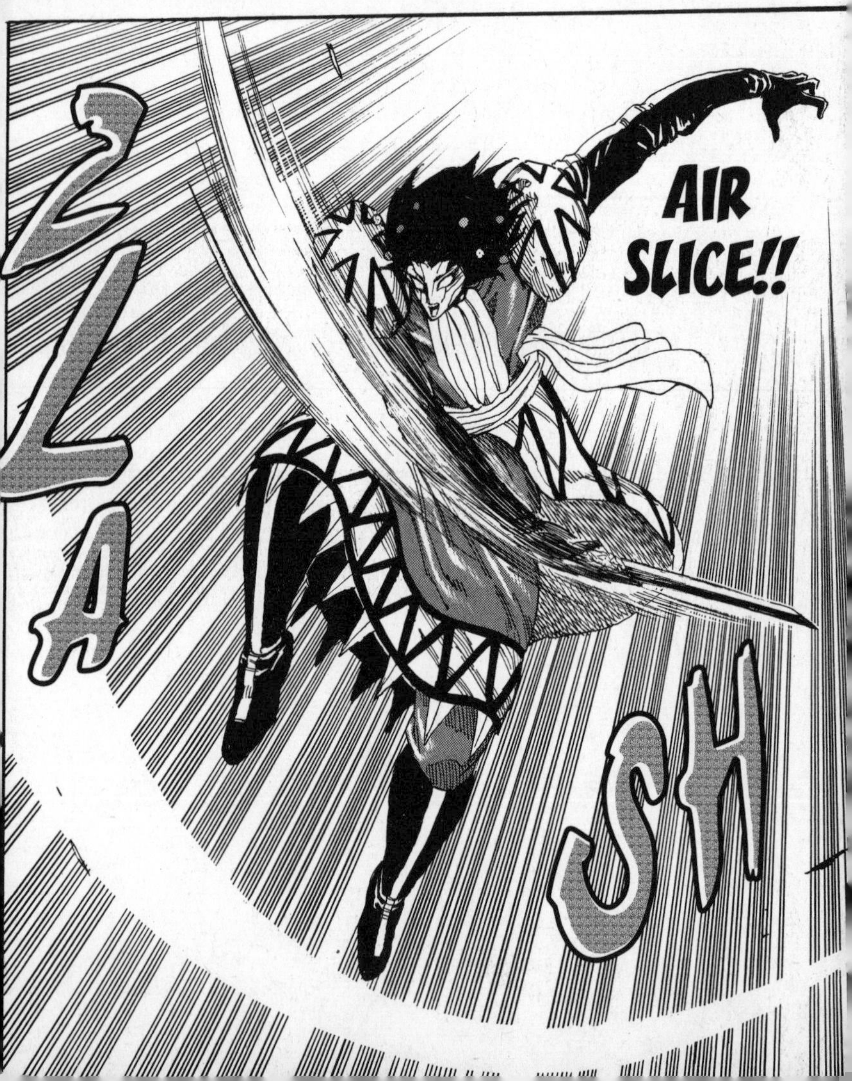
AIR SLICE!!
ZLASH

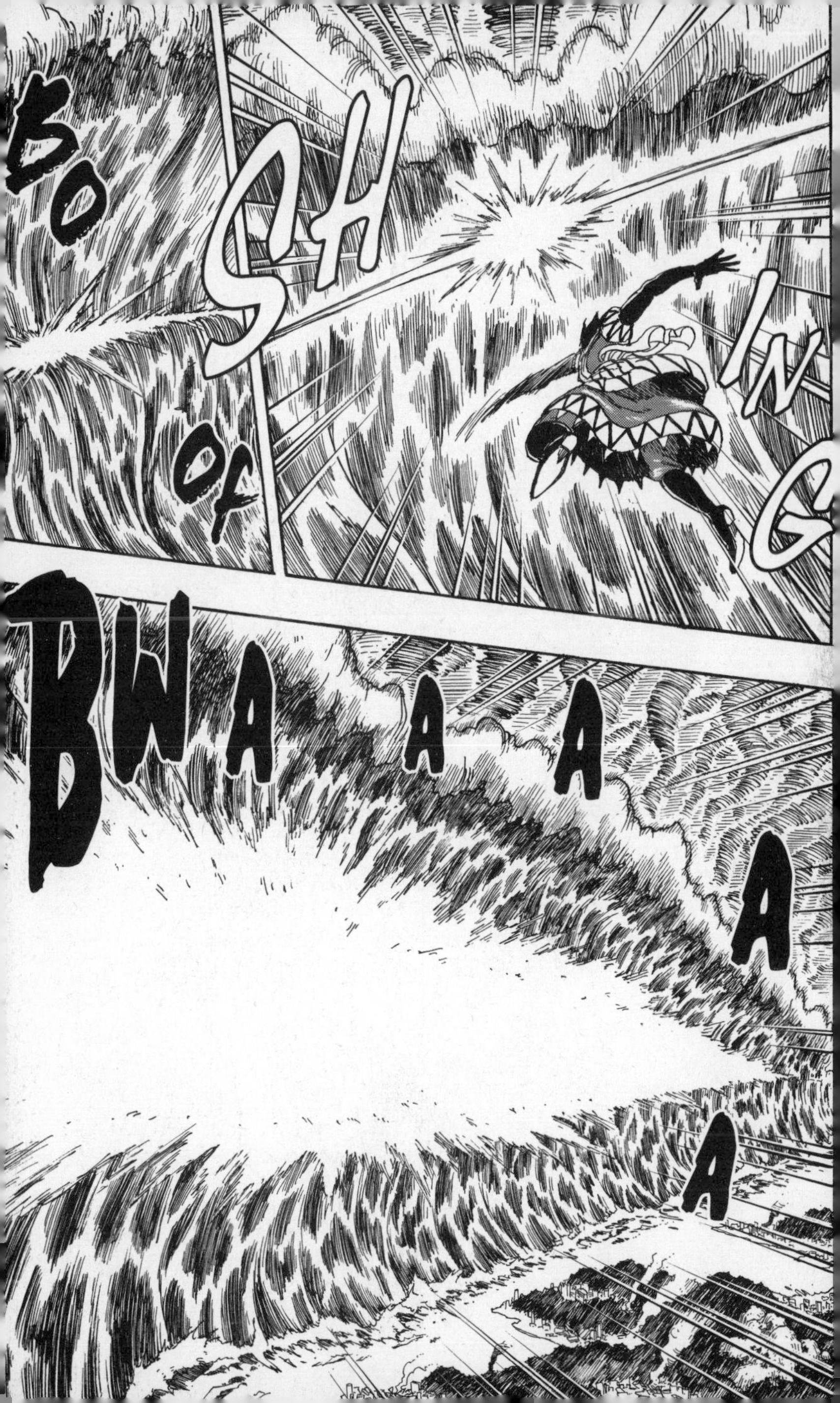
SH
ING
Bo
of
BWAAAAA

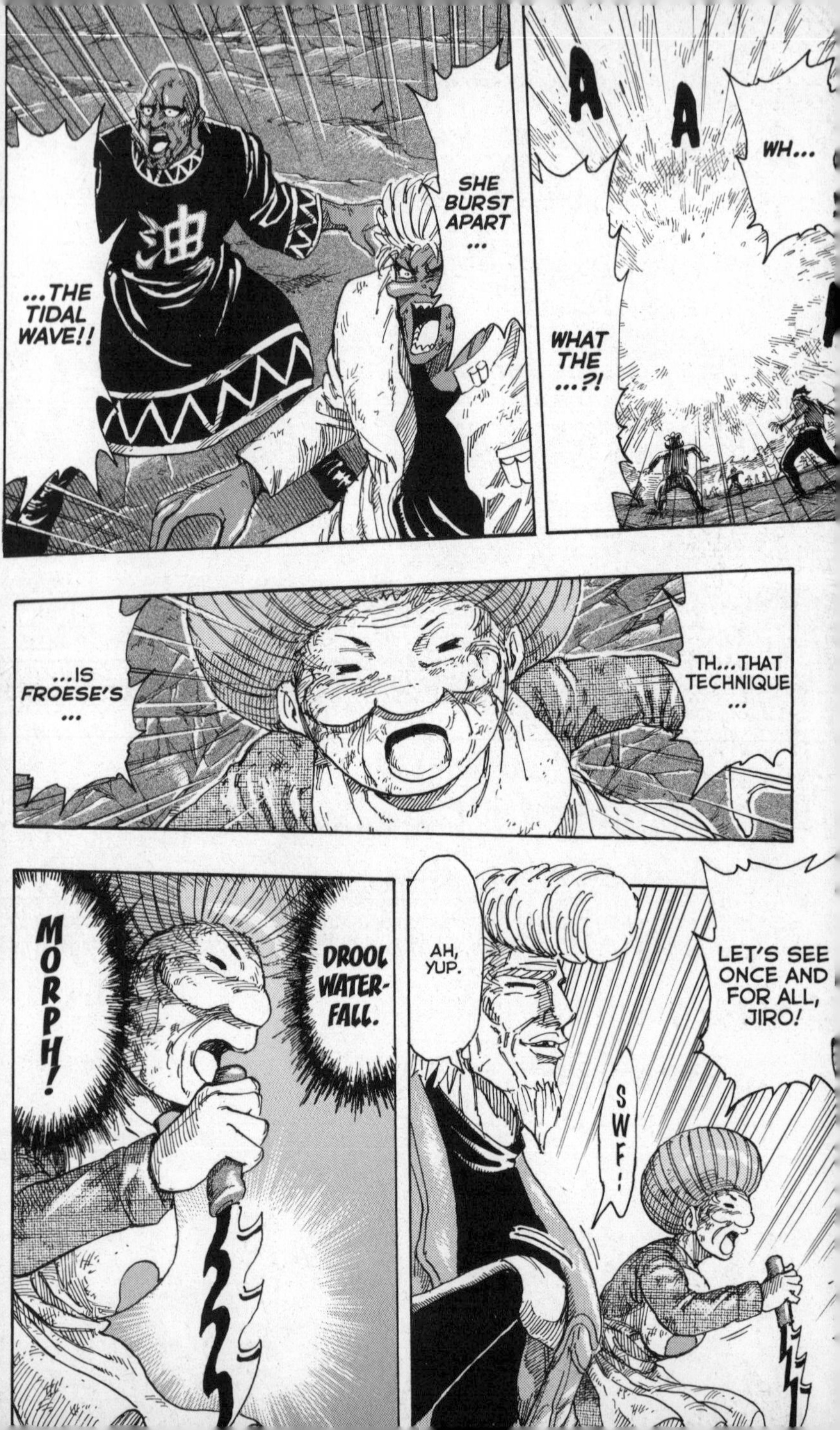
A A
WH...
WHAT THE ...?!
SHE BURST APART ...
...THE TIDAL WAVE!!
TH...THAT TECHNIQUE ...
...IS FROESE'S ...
LET'S SEE ONCE AND FOR ALL, JIRO!
SWF!
AH, YUP.
DROOL WATER-FALL.
MORPH!

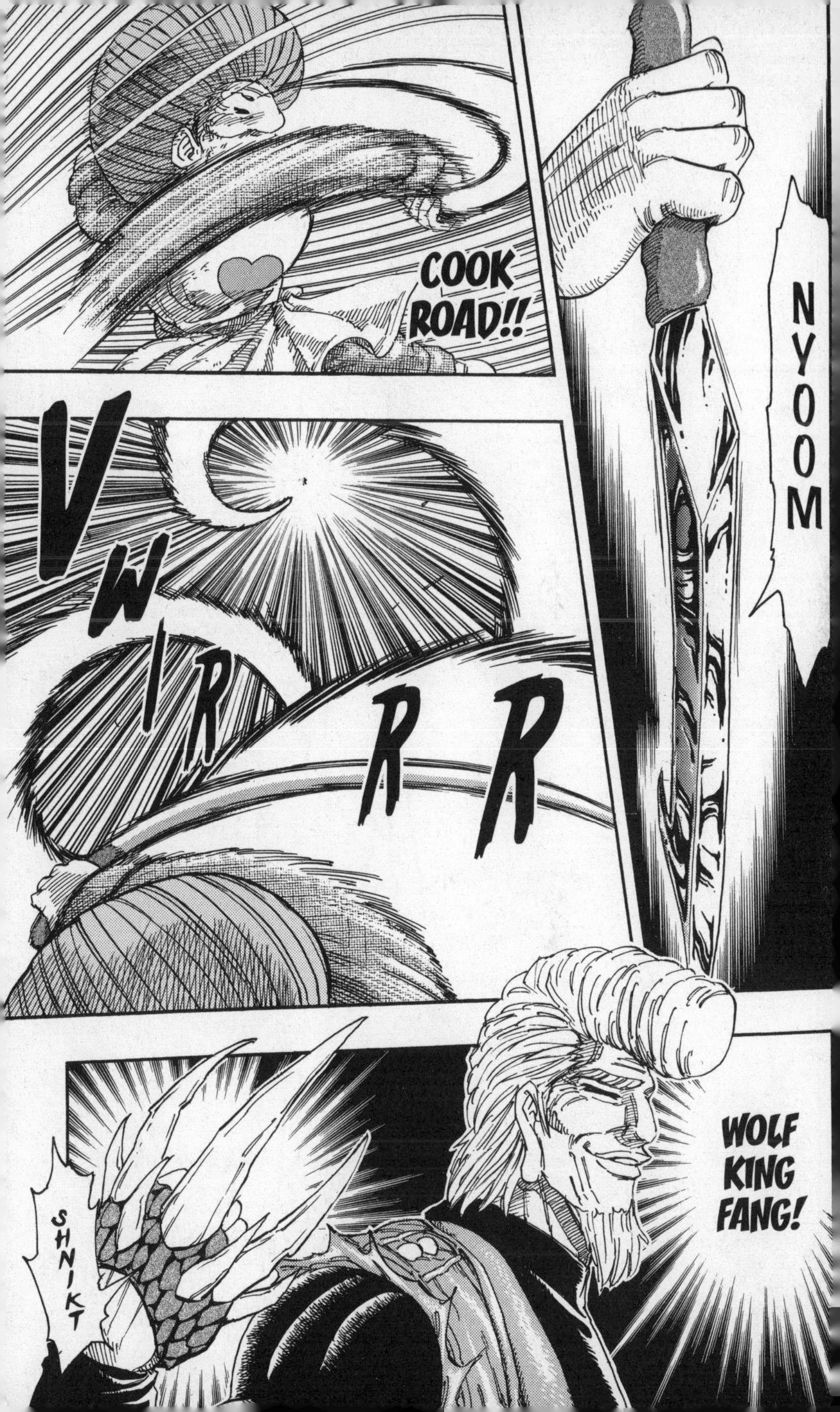
NYOOM
COOK ROAD!!
VWIRRR
WOLF KING FANG!
SHNIKT

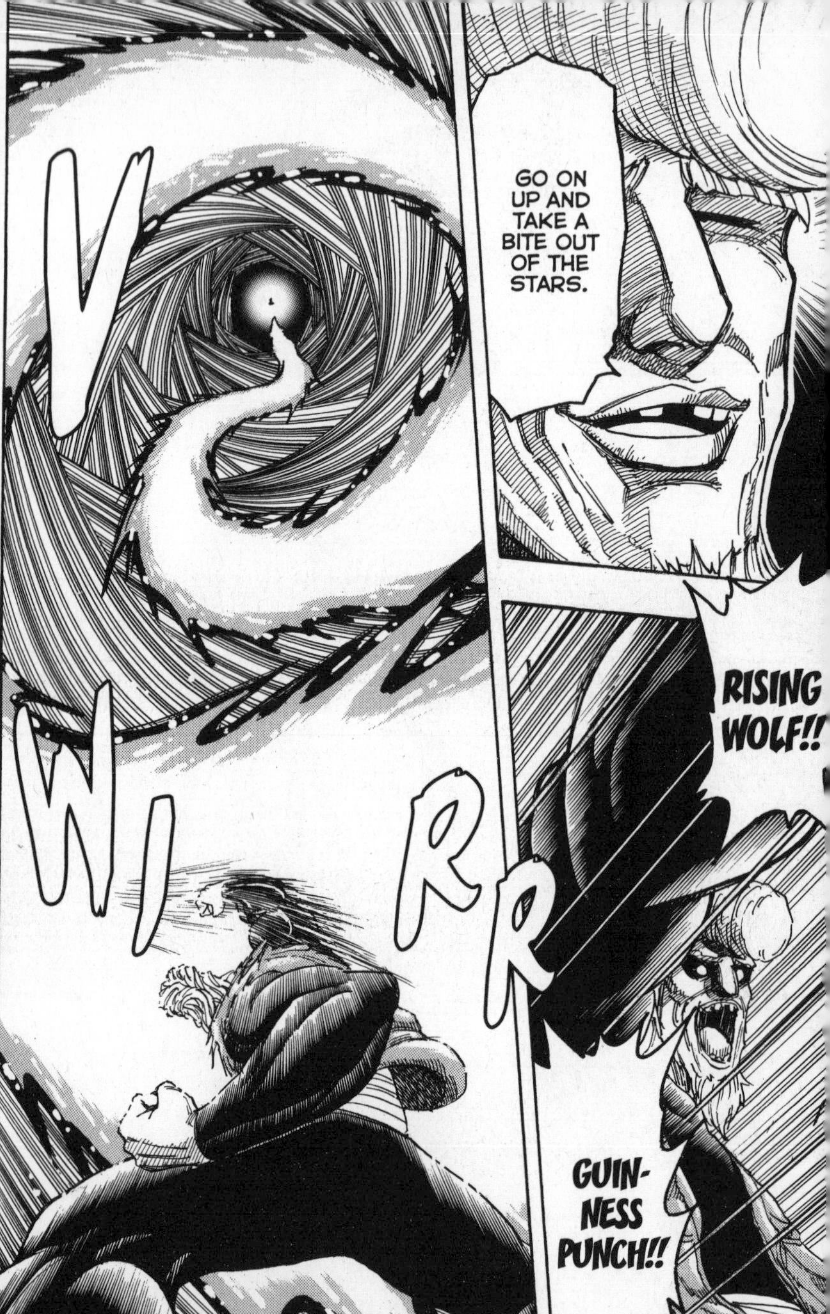
GO ON UP AND TAKE A BITE OUT OF THE STARS.
RISING WOLF!!
GUIN-NESS PUNCH!!
V
WI
RR

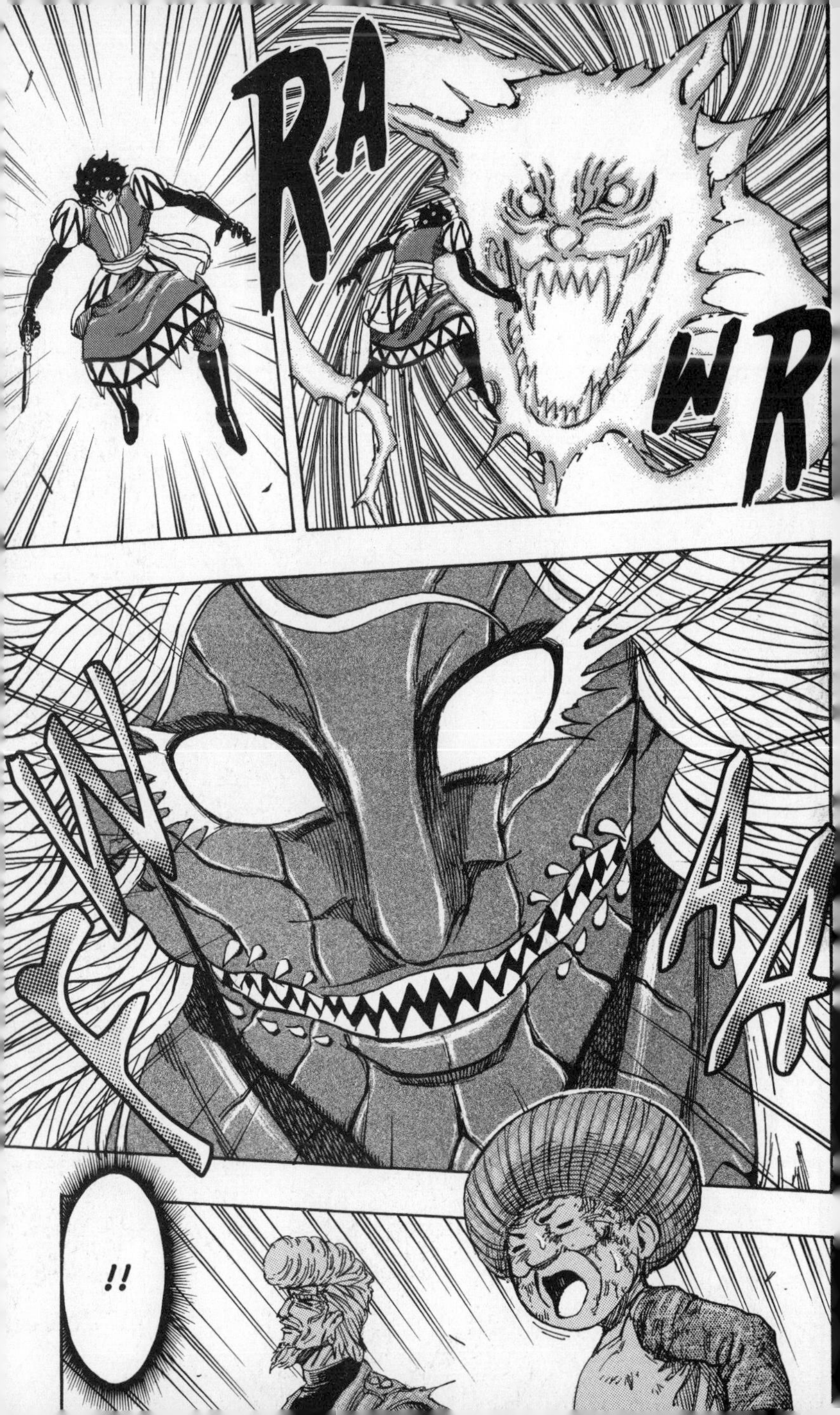

RAWR
WAAA
!!

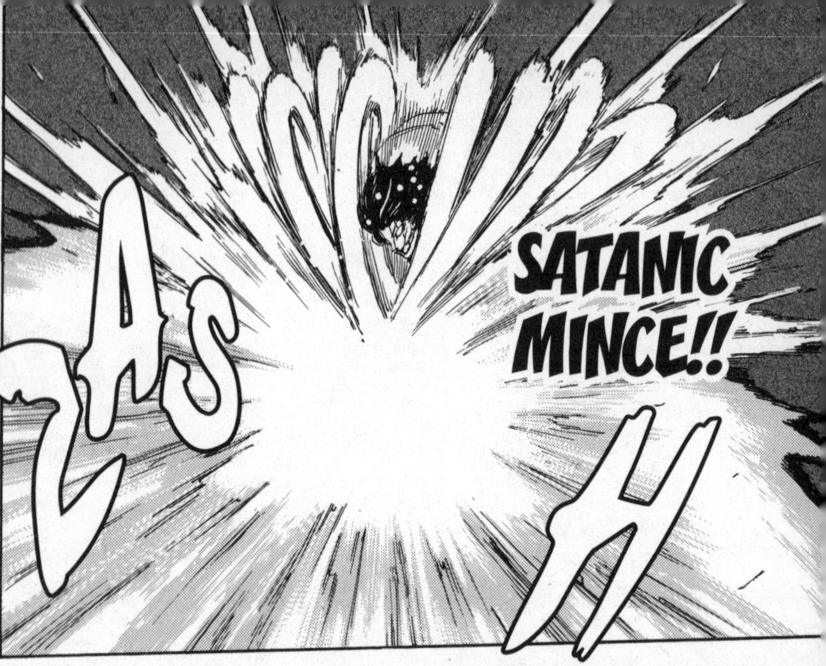
SATANIC MINCE!!
ZASH
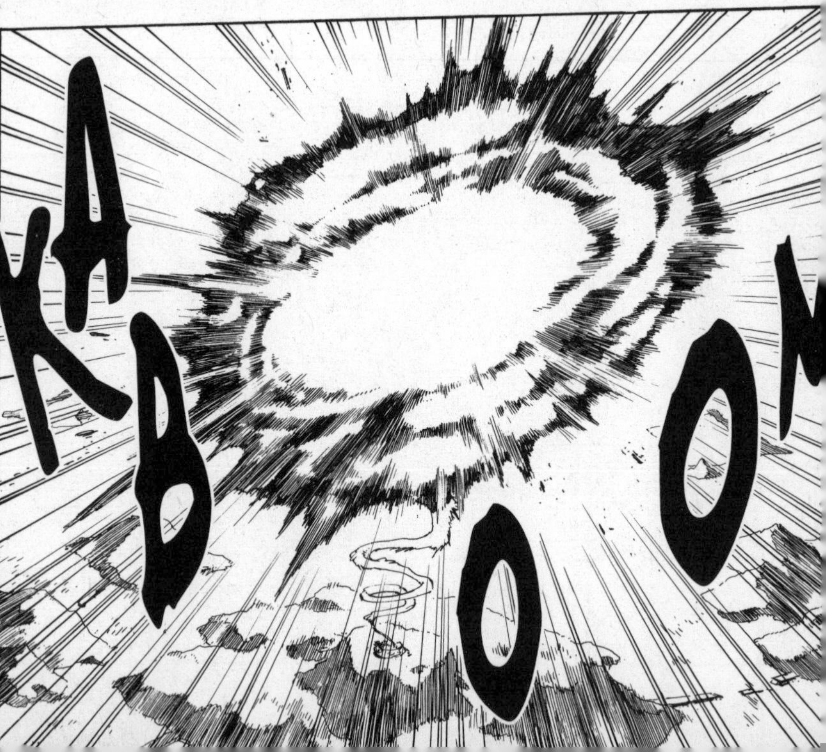
KABOOOM

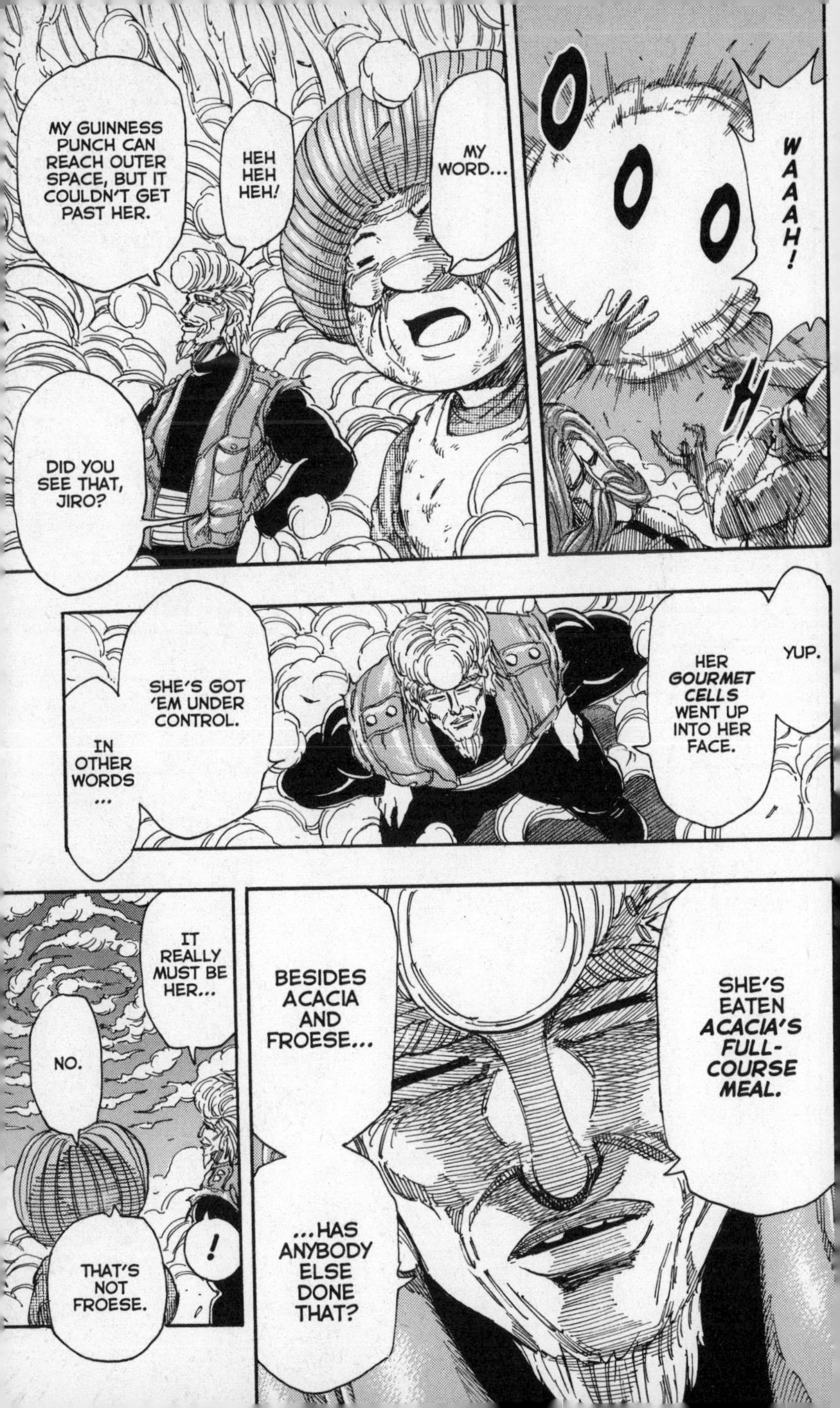
WAAAAH!
MY WORD...
HEH HEH HEH!
MY GUINNESS PUNCH CAN REACH OUTER SPACE, BUT IT COULDN'T GET PAST HER.
DID YOU SEE THAT, JIRO?
YUP.
HER *GOURMET CELLS* WENT UP INTO HER FACE.
SHE'S GOT 'EM UNDER CONTROL.
IN OTHER WORDS...
SHE'S EATEN *ACACIA'S FULL-COURSE MEAL.*
BESIDES ACACIA AND FROESE...
...HAS ANYBODY ELSE DONE THAT?
IT REALLY MUST BE HER...
NO.
!
THAT'S NOT FROESE.

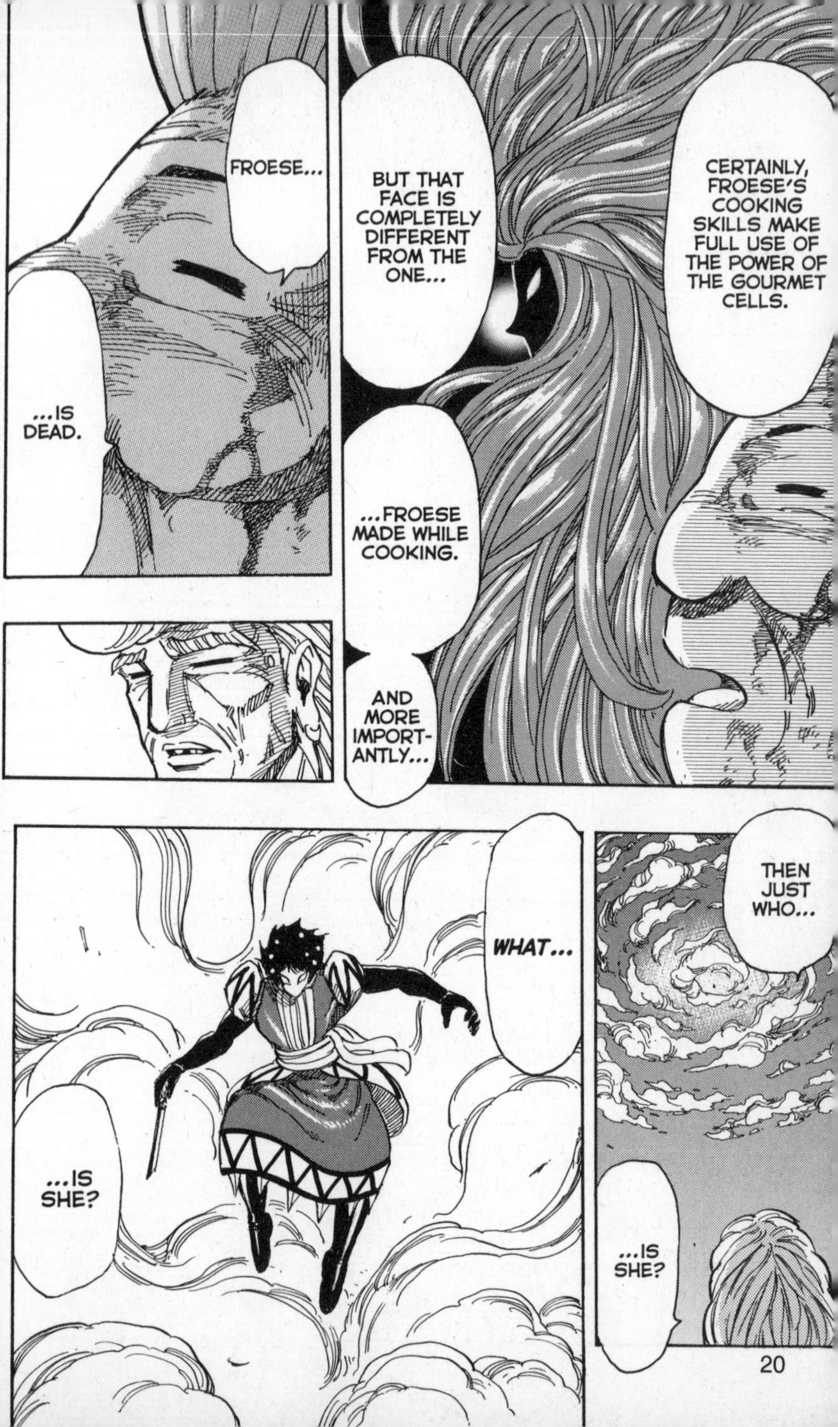
CERTAINLY, FROESE'S COOKING SKILLS MAKE FULL USE OF THE POWER OF THE GOURMET CELLS.
BUT THAT FACE IS COMPLETELY DIFFERENT FROM THE ONE...
...FROESE MADE WHILE COOKING.
AND MORE IMPORT-ANTLY...
FROESE...
...IS DEAD.
THEN JUST WHO...
...IS SHE?
WHAT...
...IS SHE?

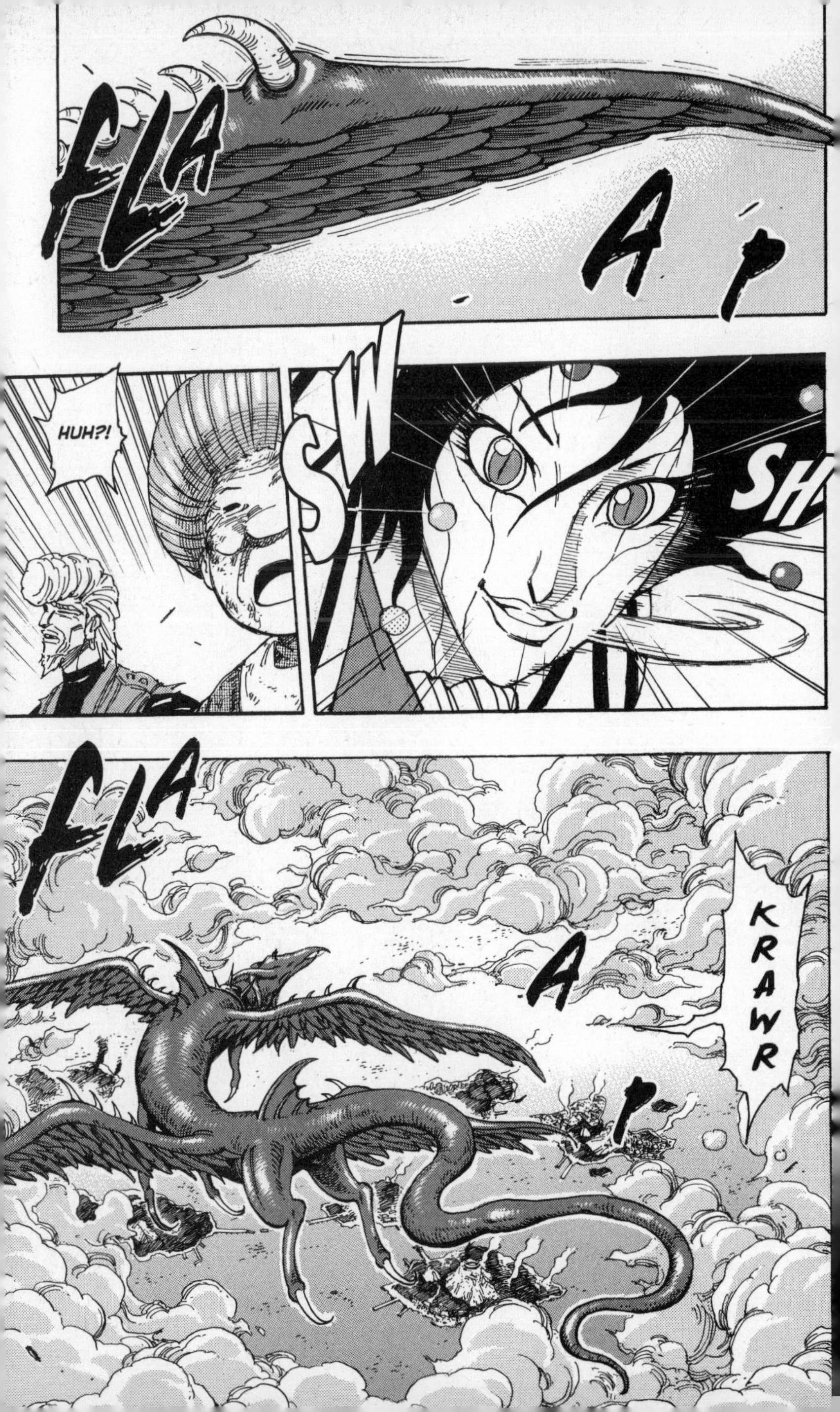
FLA
A
P
SH
SW
HUH?!
KRAWR
FLA
A
P

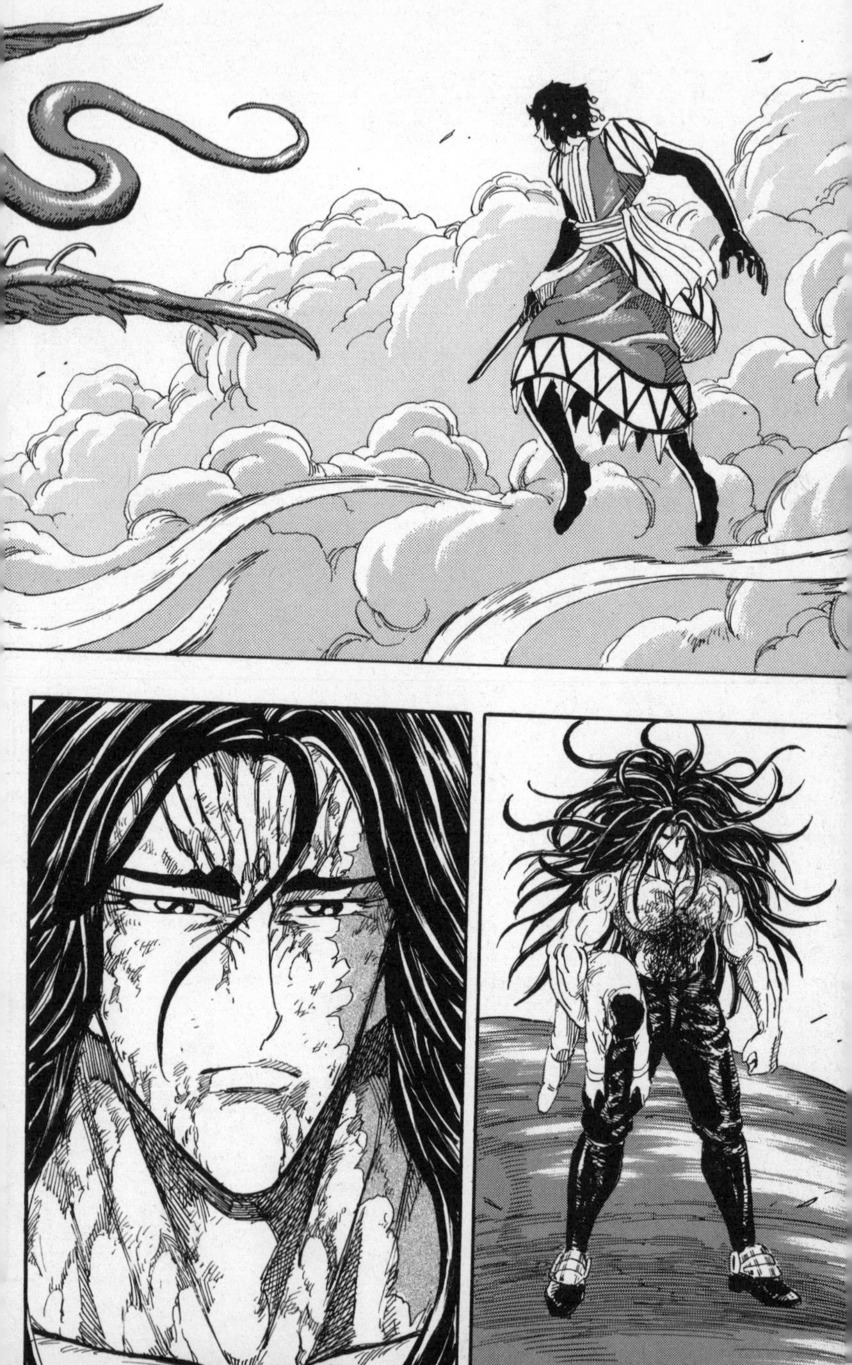

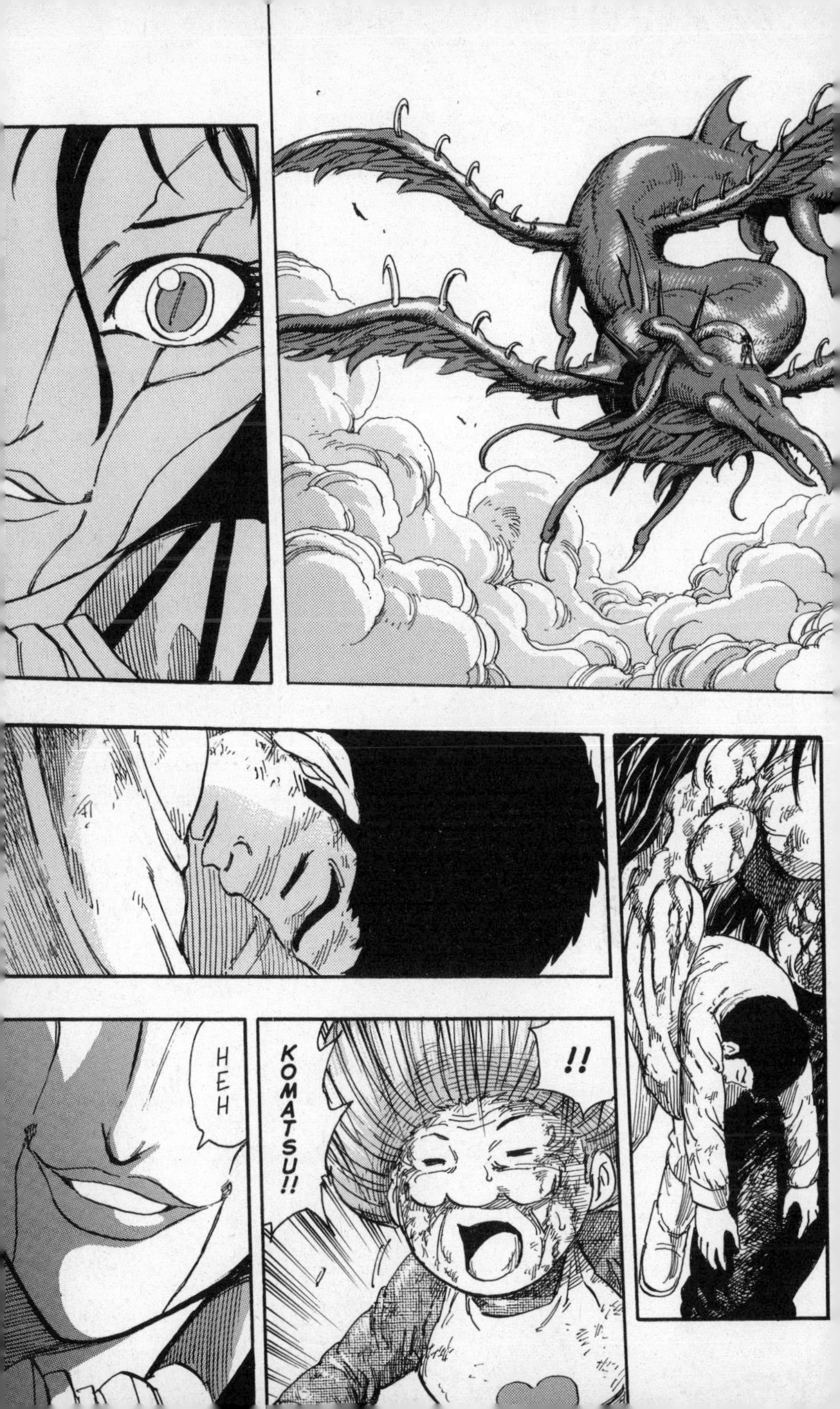
!!
KOMATSU!!
HEH

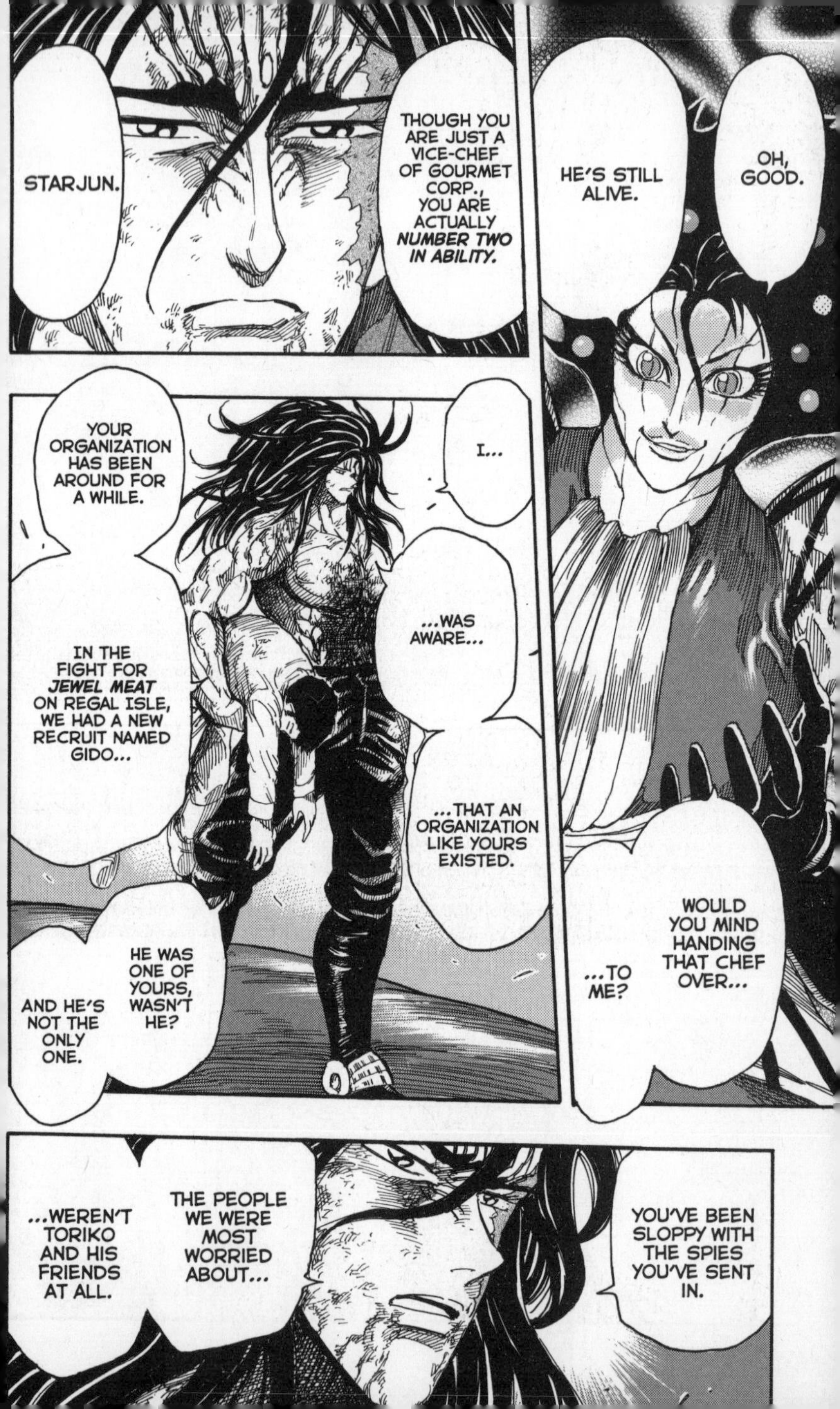
OH, GOOD.
HE'S STILL ALIVE.
WOULD YOU MIND HANDING THAT CHEF OVER...
...TO ME?
THOUGH YOU ARE JUST A VICE-CHEF OF GOURMET CORP., YOU ARE ACTUALLY *NUMBER TWO IN ABILITY.*
STARJUN.
I...
...WAS AWARE...
...THAT AN ORGANIZATION LIKE YOURS EXISTED.
YOUR ORGANIZATION HAS BEEN AROUND FOR A WHILE.
IN THE FIGHT FOR *JEWEL MEAT* ON REGAL ISLE, WE HAD A NEW RECRUIT NAMED GIDO...
HE WAS ONE OF YOURS, WASN'T HE?
AND HE'S NOT THE ONLY ONE.
YOU'VE BEEN SLOPPY WITH THE SPIES YOU'VE SENT IN.
THE PEOPLE WE WERE MOST WORRIED ABOUT...
...WEREN'T TORIKO AND HIS FRIENDS AT ALL.

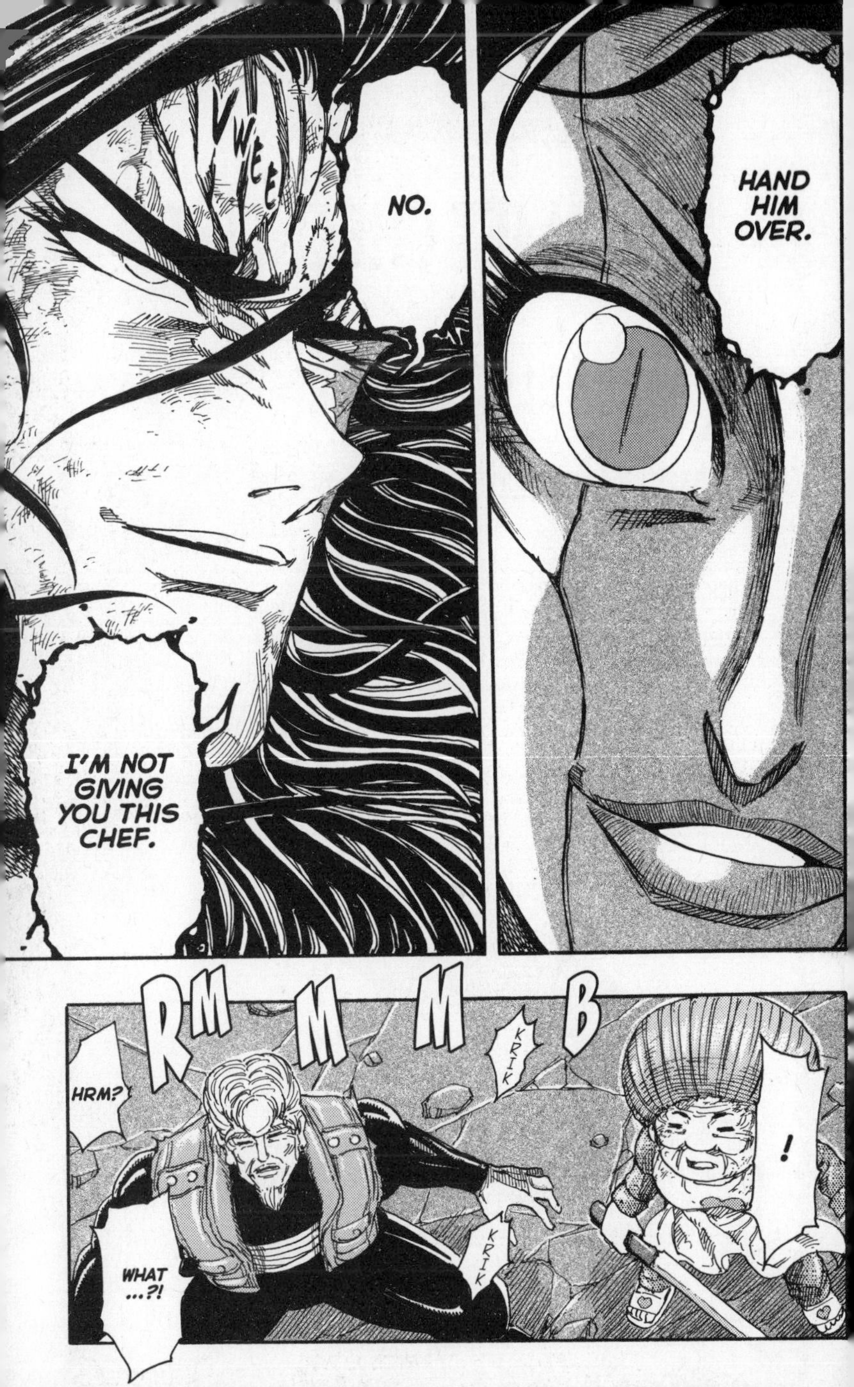
HAND HIM OVER.
VWEE
NO.
I'M NOT GIVING YOU THIS CHEF.
RMMMB
KRIK
!
HRM?
KRIK
WHAT ...?!

TORIKO

GOURMET CHECKLIST
Vol. 272

 ## SLUG WHALE
(MAMMAL)

CAPTURE LEVEL: 1 (15 IN WATER)
HABITAT: OCEANS
SIZE: 6 METERS
HEIGHT: ---
WEIGHT: 5 TONS
PRICE: 1 KG / 2,500 YEN

SCALE

THIS TIMID WHALE TYPICALLY LIVES ON LAND, BUT WILL RETREAT TO THE WATER WHEN HUNTING PREY OR THREATENED. THE SLUG WHALE HAS THE SAME SLIMY SKIN AS OTHER SLUGS, ENABLING IT TO EVADE MOST ATTACKS ON LAND. HOWEVER, UNLIKE OTHER SLUGS, SINCE IT LIVES IN THE OCEAN IT IS UNAFFECTED BY SALT.

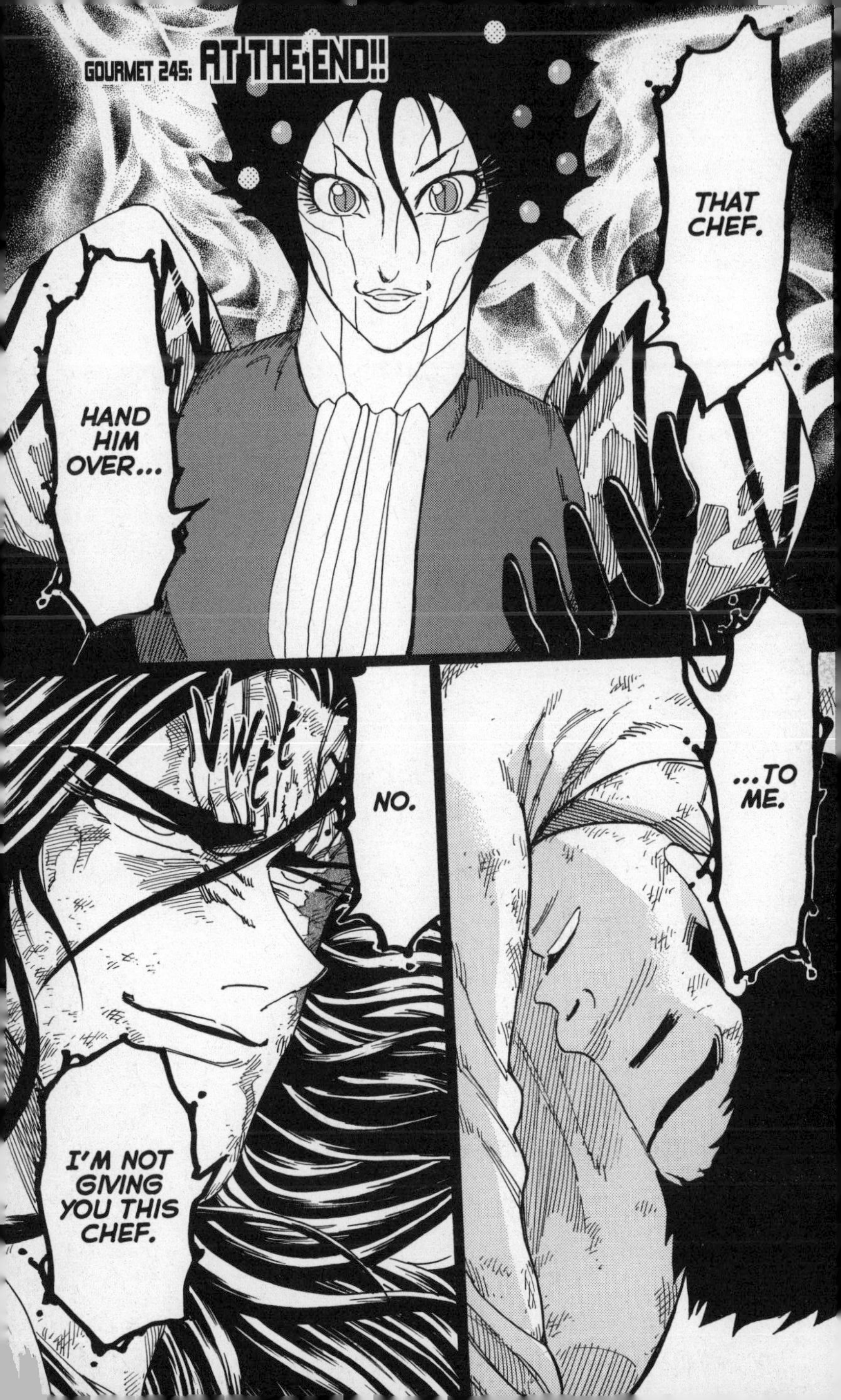
GOURMET 245: AT THE END!!
HAND HIM OVER...
THAT CHEF.
...TO ME.
NO.
I'M NOT GIVING YOU THIS CHEF.

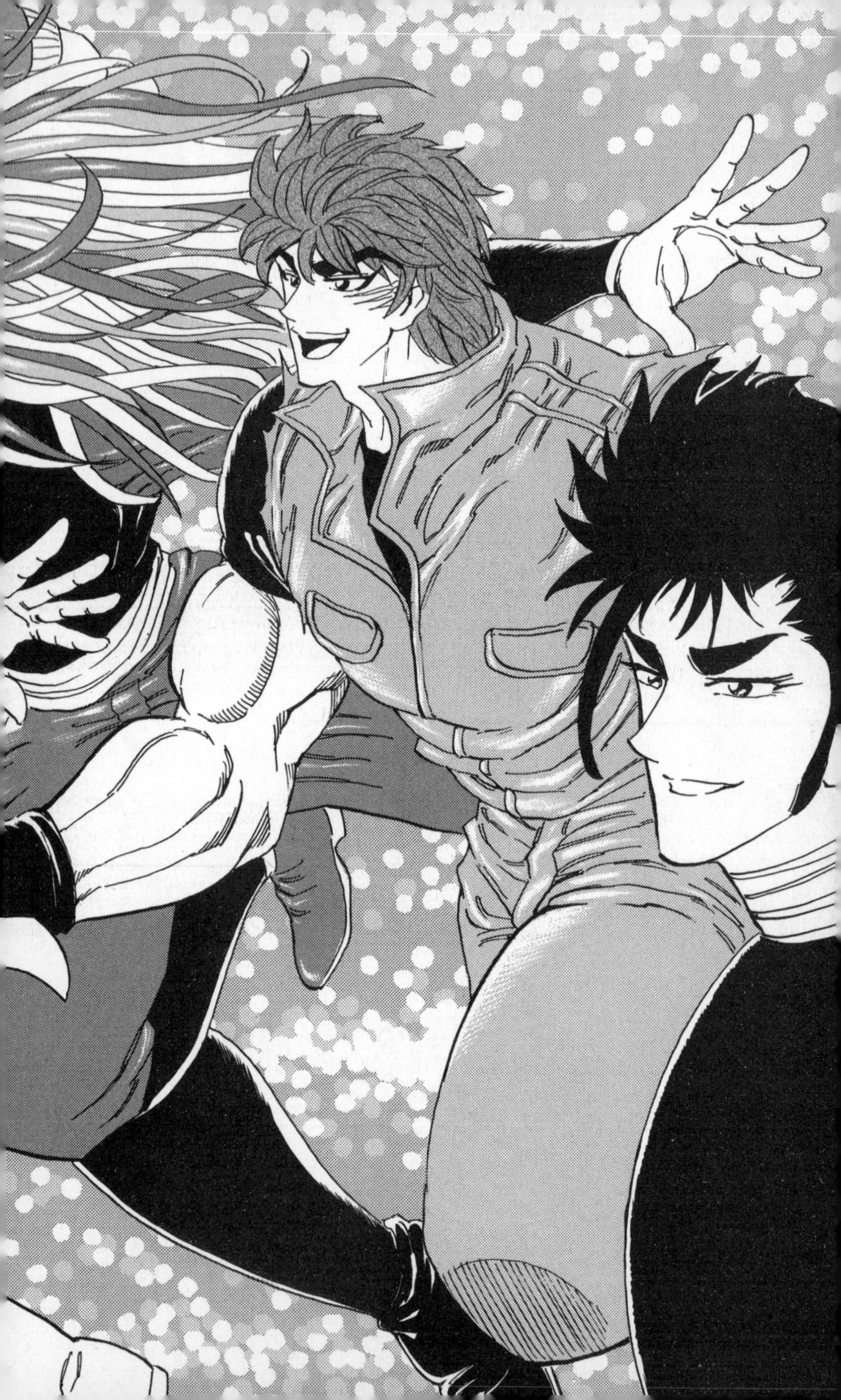

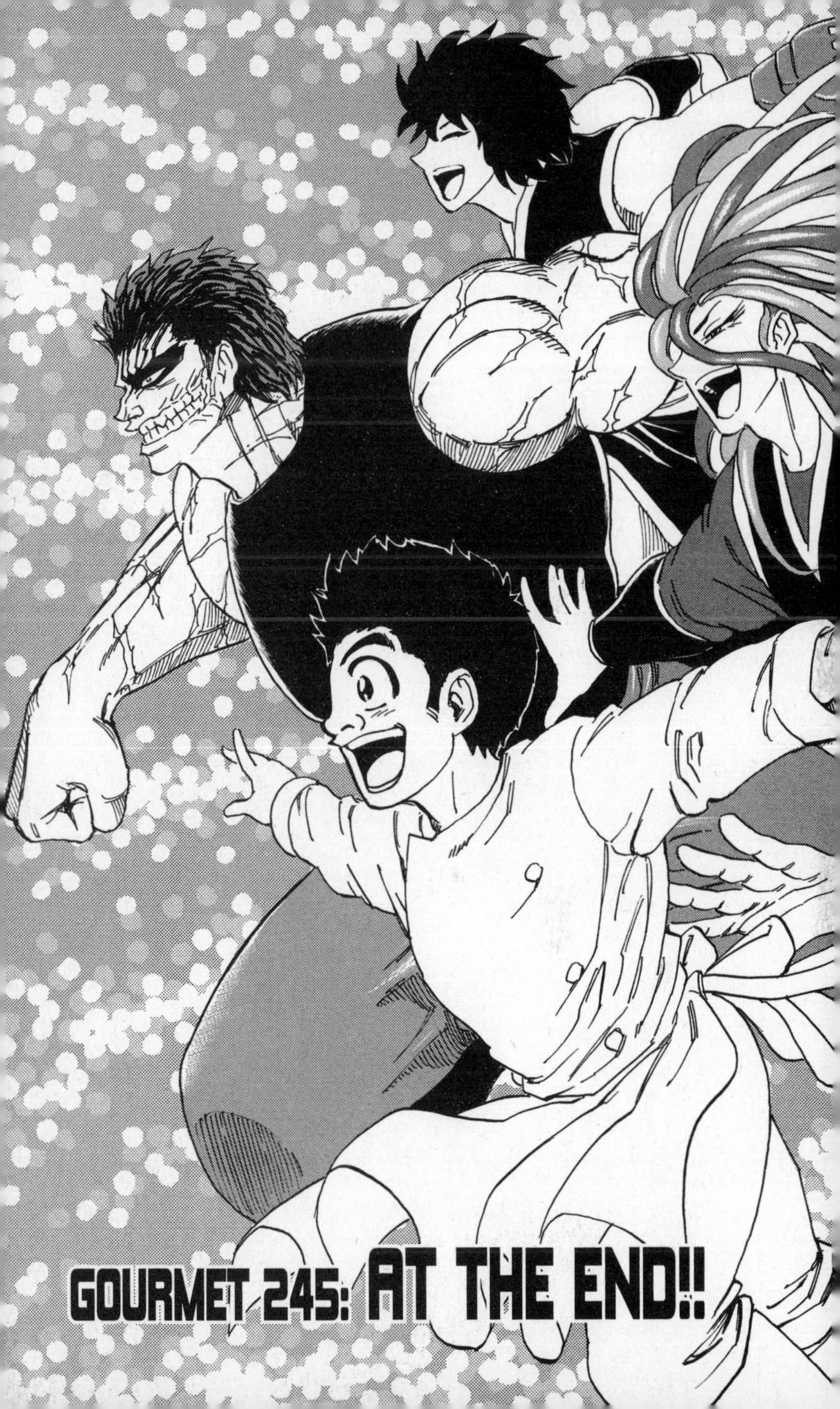
GOURMET 245: AT THE END!!

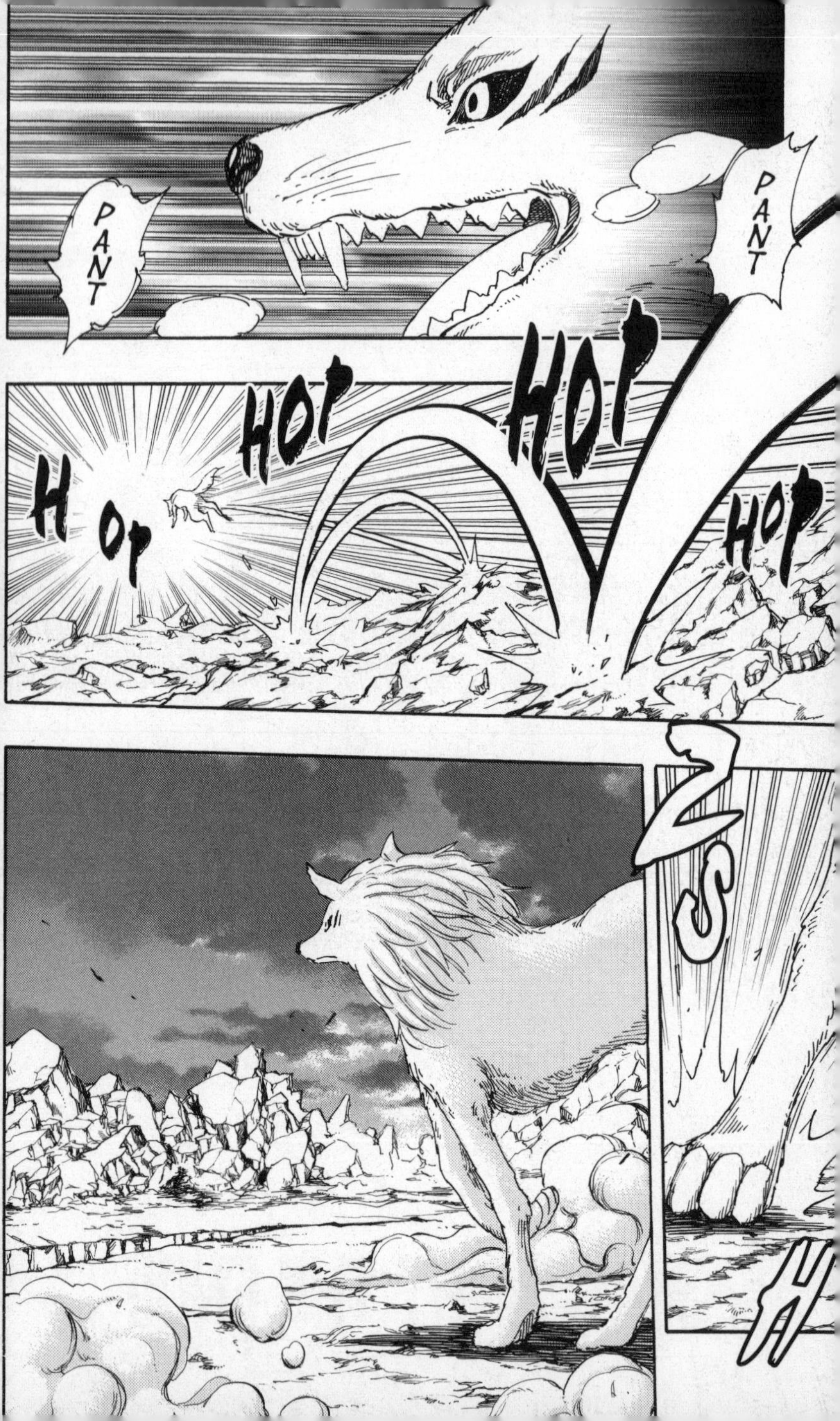
PANT
PANT
HOP
HOP
HOP
H
OP
ZUSH

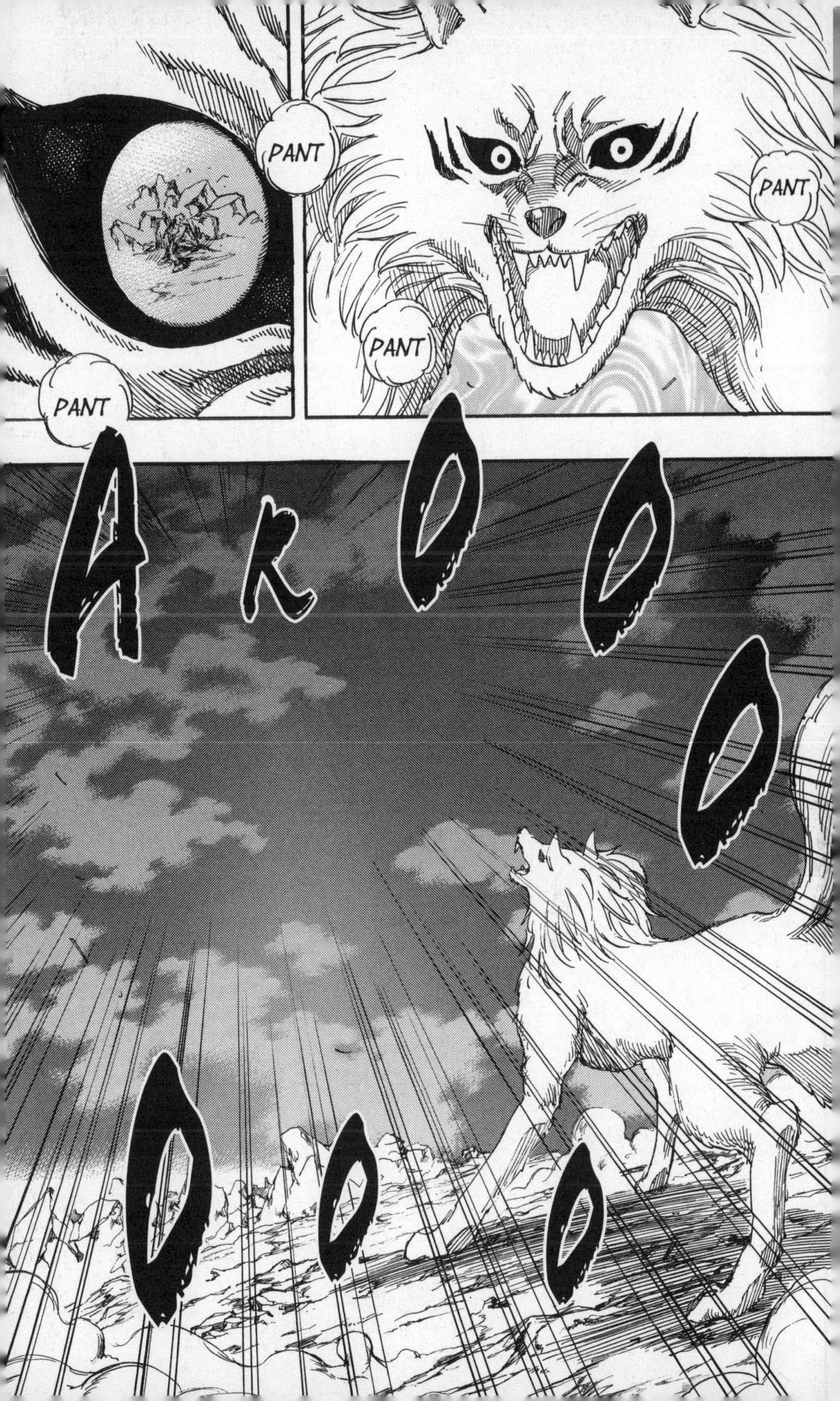
PANT
PANT
PANT
PANT
AROOO
OOO

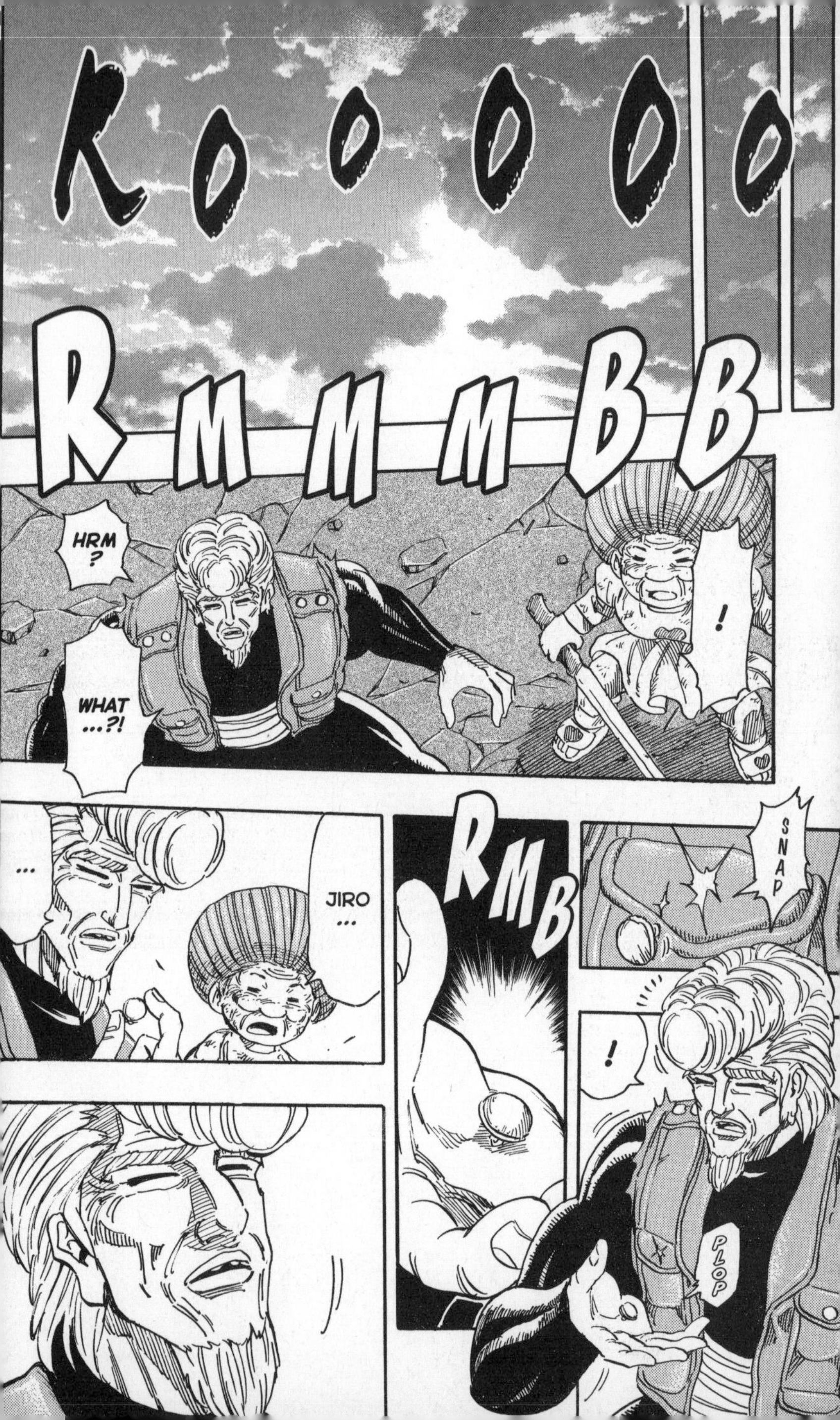
KOOOOO
RMMMMBB
!
HRM?
WHAT...?!
SNAP
!
PLOP
RMB
JIRO...
...

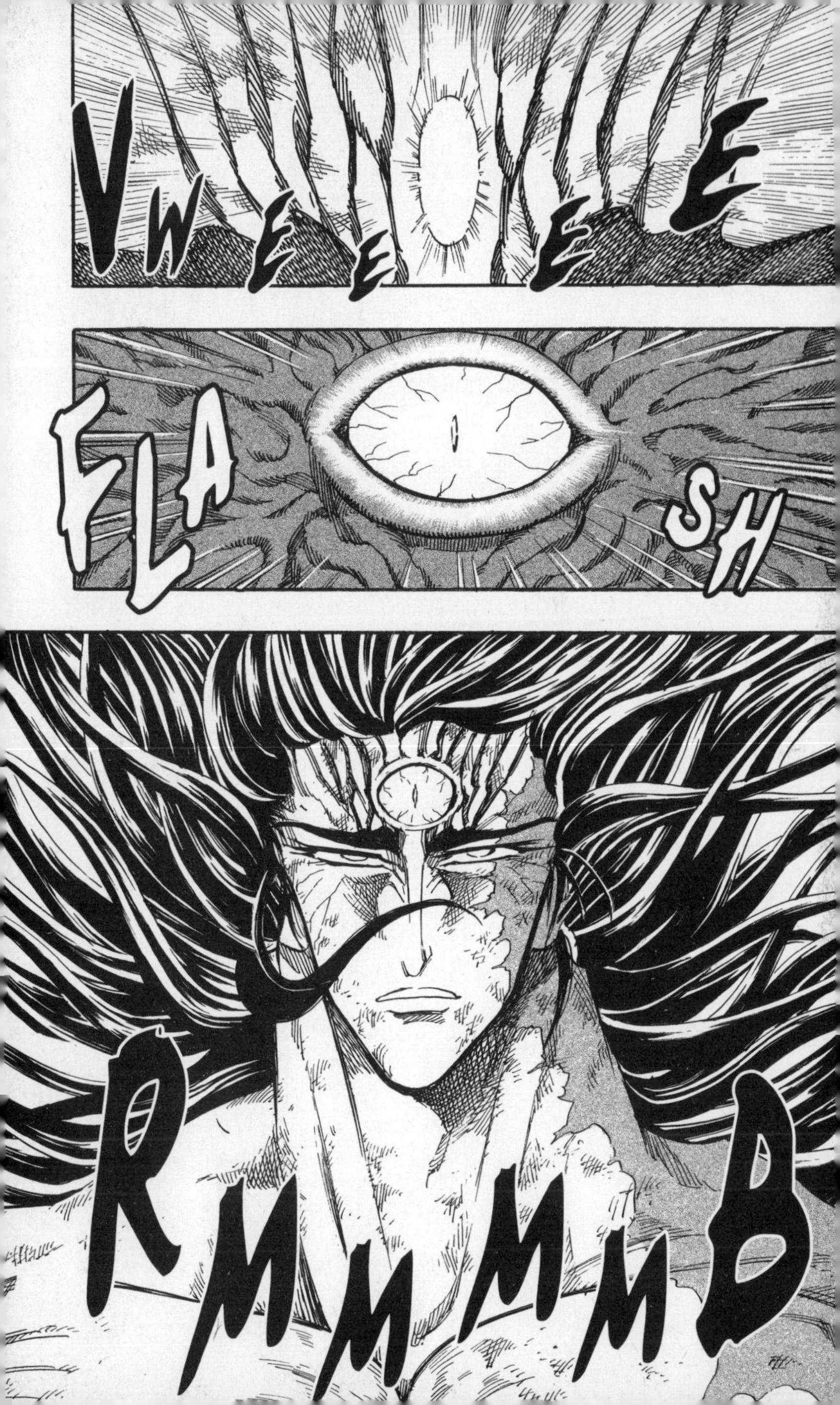
VWEEEEE
FLASH
RMMMMB

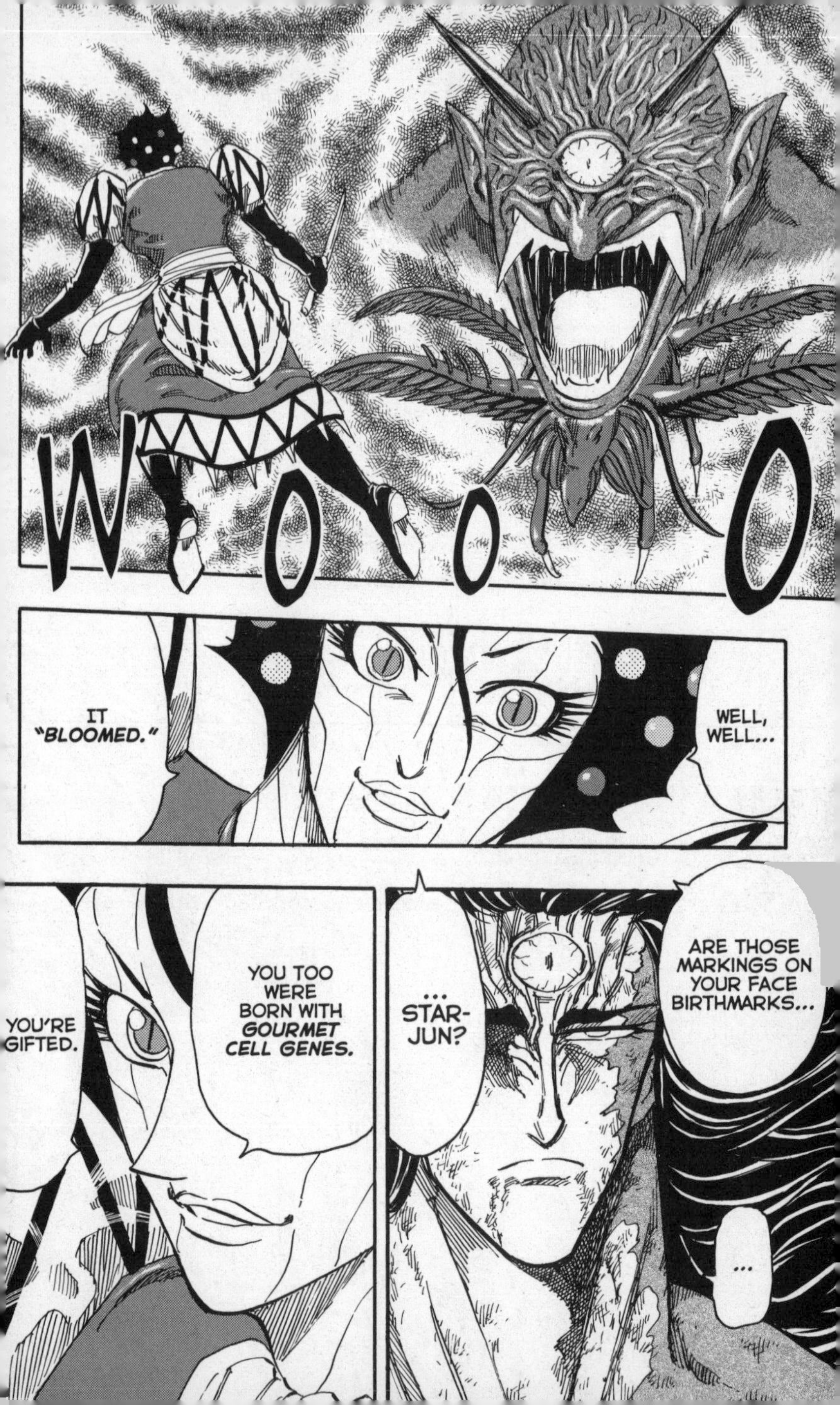
WOOO
WELL, WELL...
IT "BLOOMED."
ARE THOSE MARKINGS ON YOUR FACE BIRTHMARKS...
...STAR-JUN?
...
YOU TOO WERE BORN WITH GOURMET CELL GENES.
YOU'RE GIFTED.

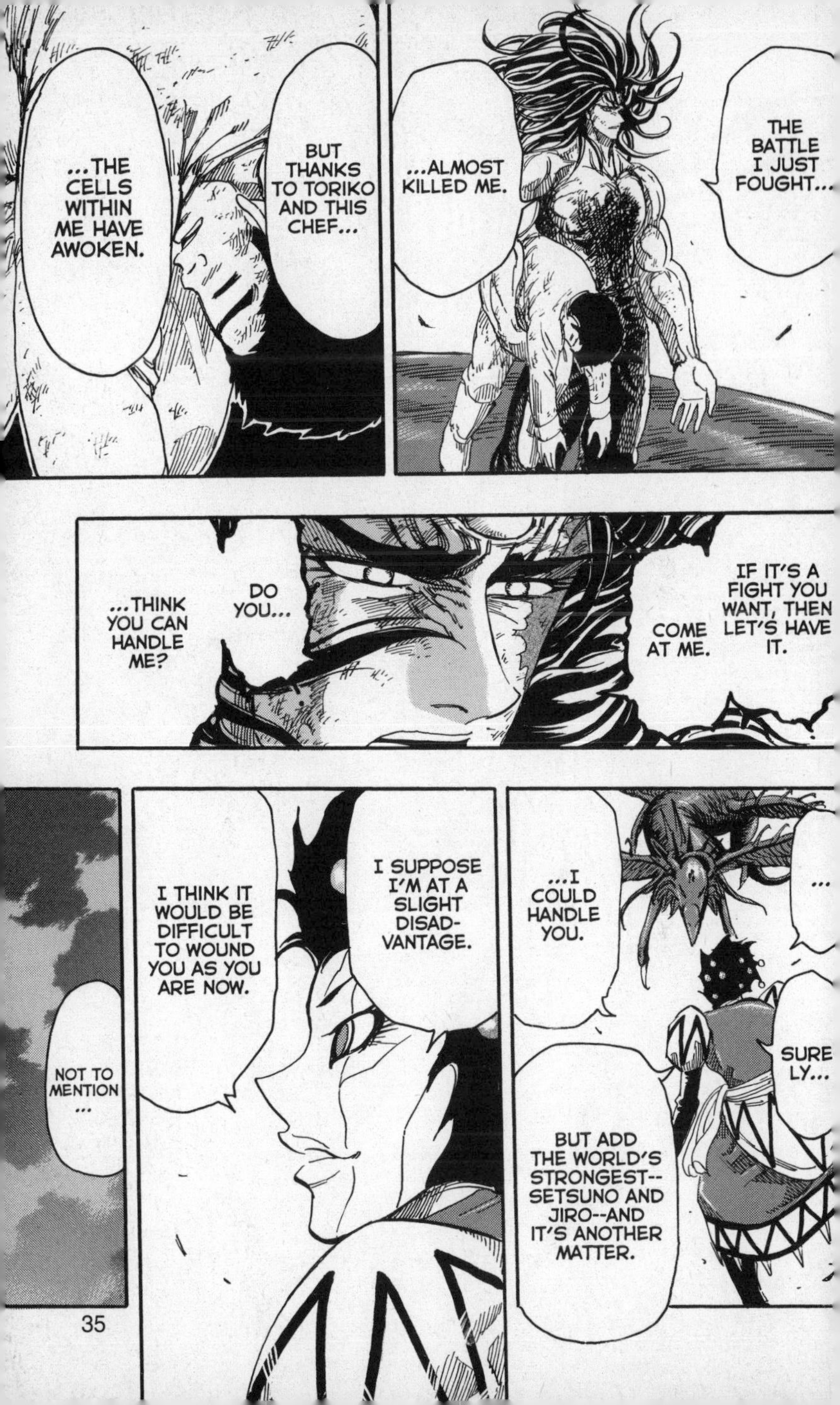
THE BATTLE I JUST FOUGHT...
...ALMOST KILLED ME.
BUT THANKS TO TORIKO AND THIS CHEF...
...THE CELLS WITHIN ME HAVE AWOKEN.
IF IT'S A FIGHT YOU WANT, THEN LET'S HAVE IT.
COME AT ME.
DO YOU...
...THINK YOU CAN HANDLE ME?
...
SURELY...
...I COULD HANDLE YOU.
BUT ADD THE WORLD'S STRONGEST--SETSUNO AND JIRO--AND IT'S ANOTHER MATTER.
I SUPPOSE I'M AT A SLIGHT DISADVANTAGE.
I THINK IT WOULD BE DIFFICULT TO WOUND YOU AS YOU ARE NOW.
NOT TO MENTION...

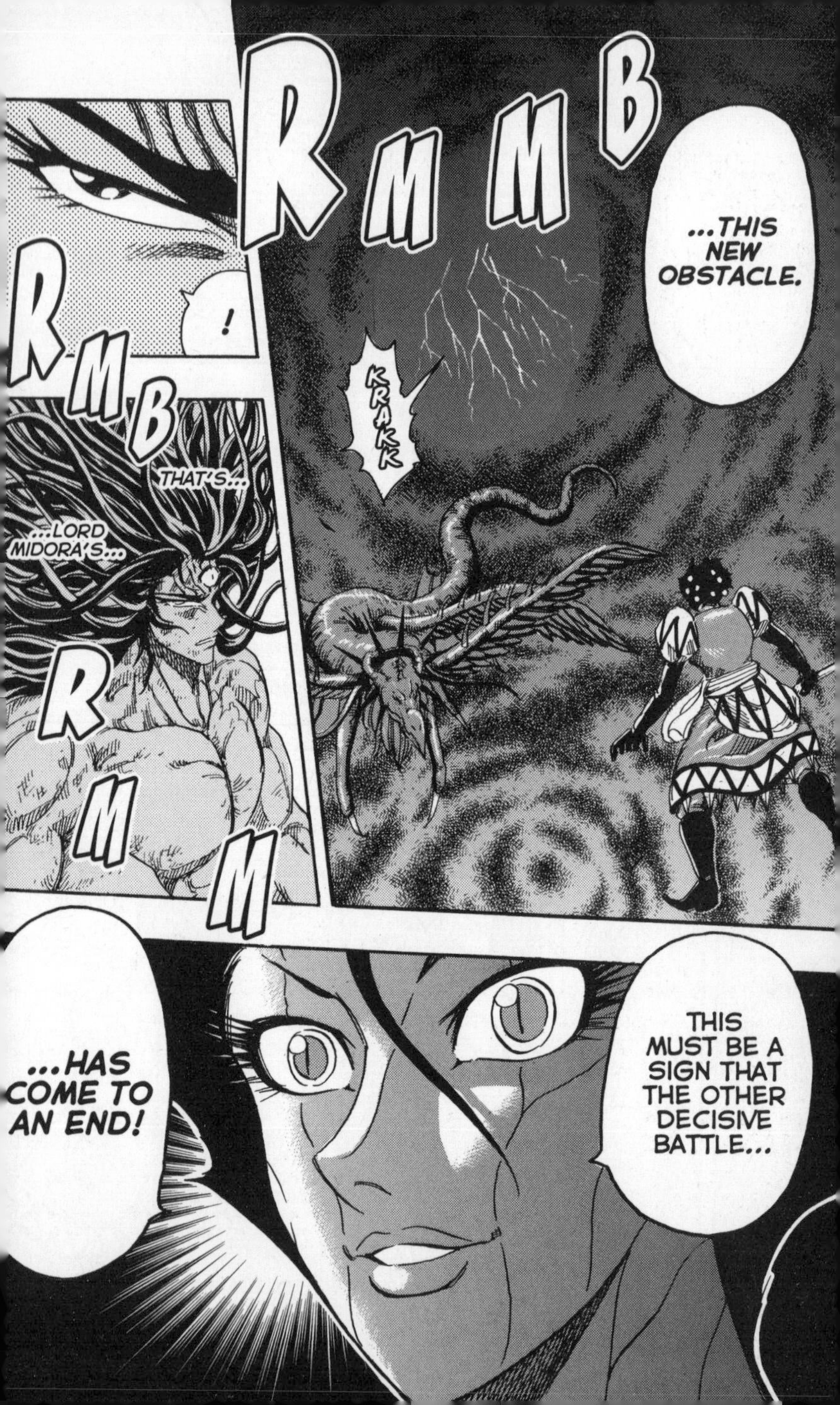
RMMB
...THIS NEW OBSTACLE.
KRAKK
!
RMB
THAT'S...
...LORD MIDORA'S...
RMMM
THIS MUST BE A SIGN THAT THE OTHER DECISIVE BATTLE...
...HAS COME TO AN END!

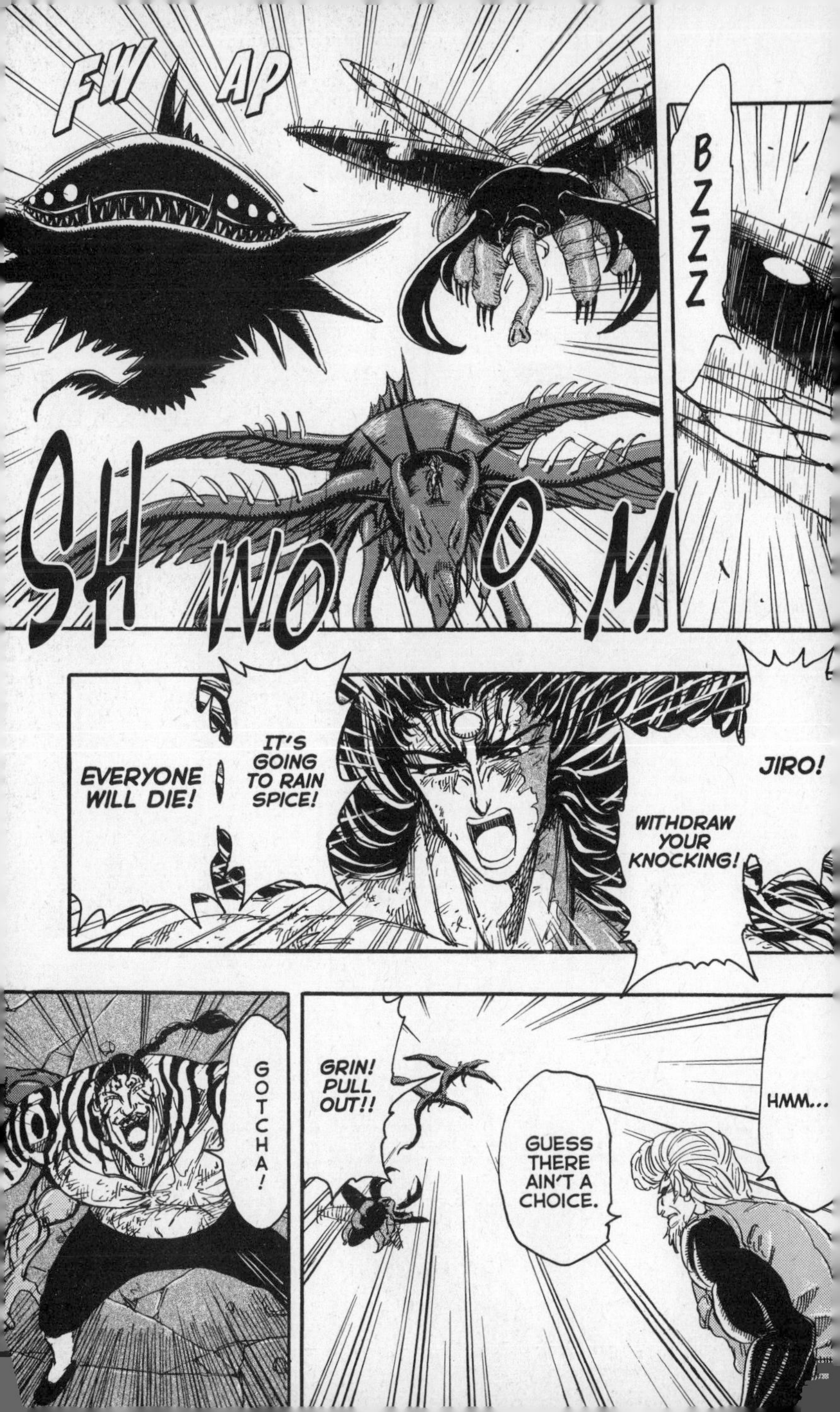
BZZZ
FW AP
SH WO O M
JIRO!
WITHDRAW YOUR KNOCKING!
IT'S GOING TO RAIN SPICE!
EVERYONE WILL DIE!
HMM...
GUESS THERE AIN'T A CHOICE.
GRIN! PULL OUT!!
GOTCHA!

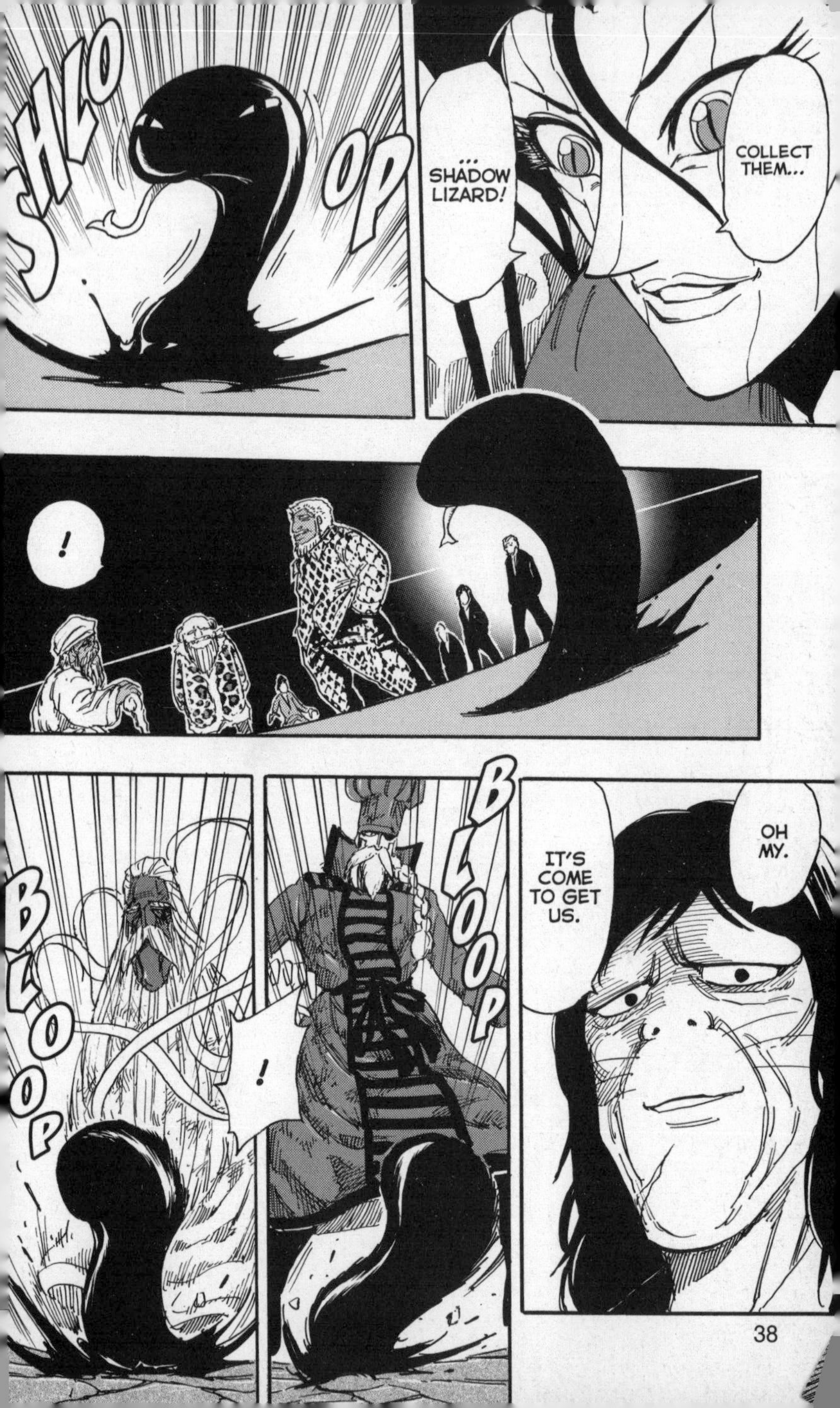
COLLECT THEM...
...SHADOW LIZARD!
SHLOOP
!
OH MY.
IT'S COME TO GET US.
BLOOP
!
BLOOP

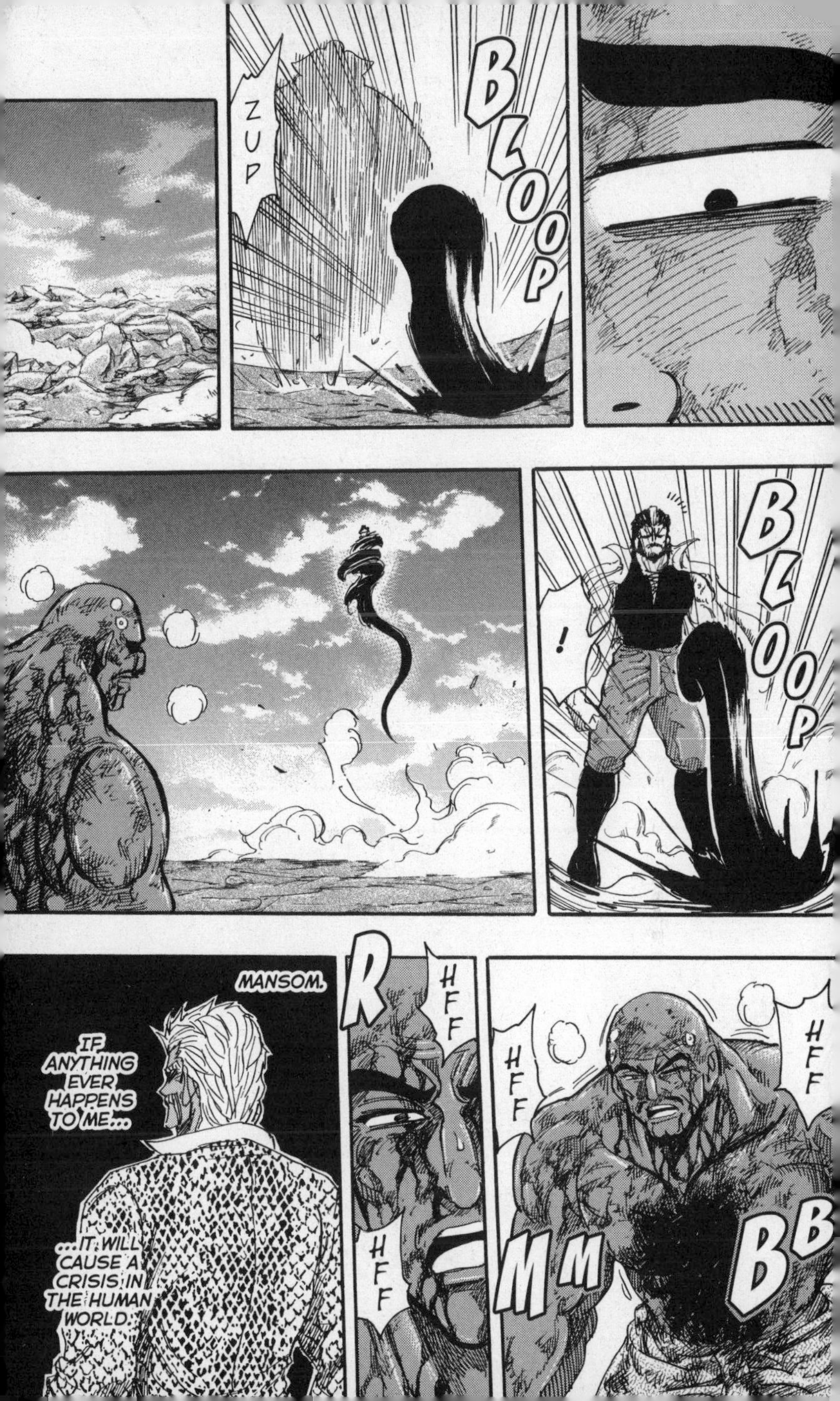
BLOOP
ZUP
BLOOP
!
HFF
HFF
BB
MM
R
HFF
HFF
MANSOM.
IF ANYTHING EVER HAPPENS TO ME...
...IT WILL CAUSE A CRISIS IN THE HUMAN WORLD.

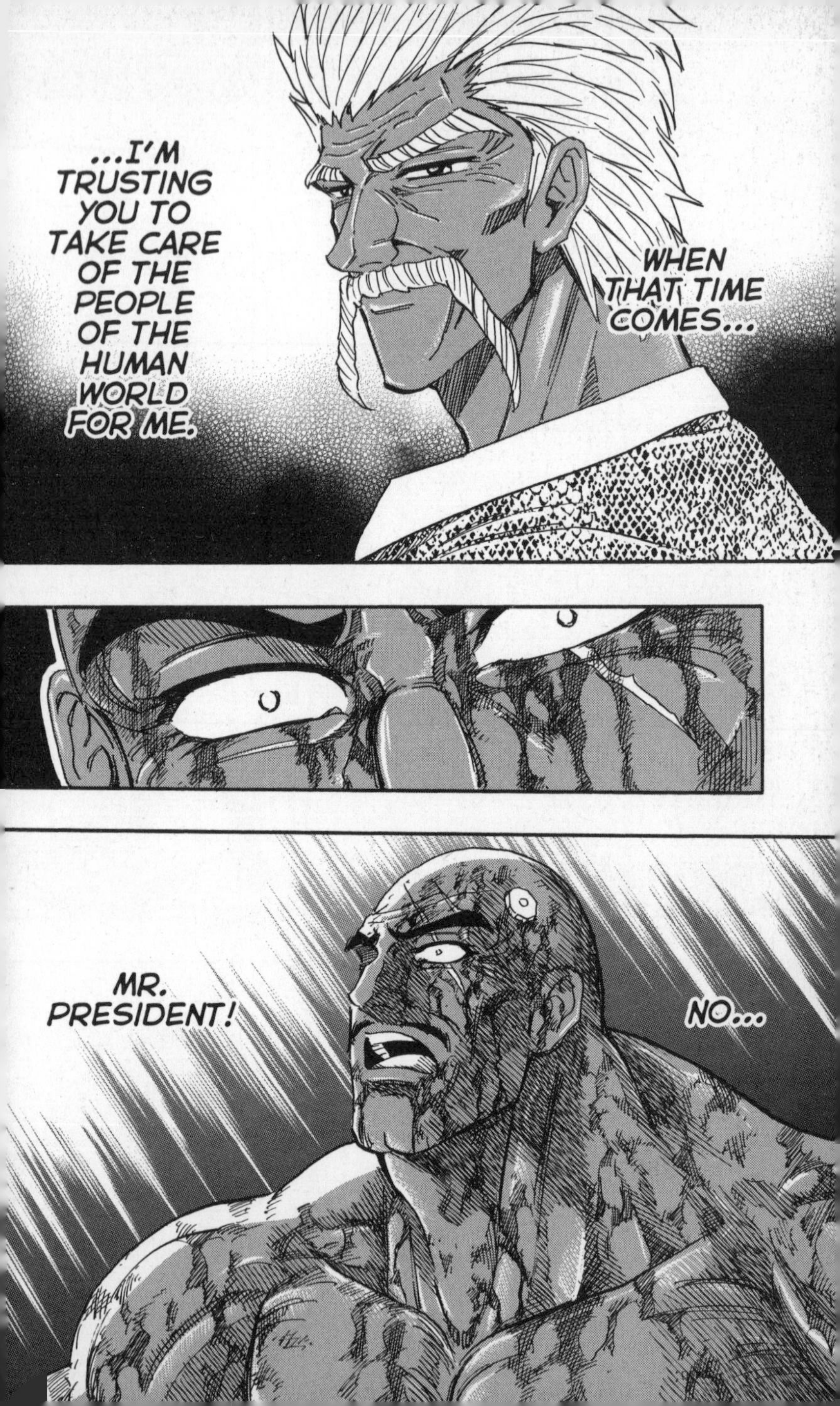
WHEN THAT TIME COMES...
...I'M TRUSTING YOU TO TAKE CARE OF THE PEOPLE OF THE HUMAN WORLD FOR ME.
NO...
MR. PRESIDENT!

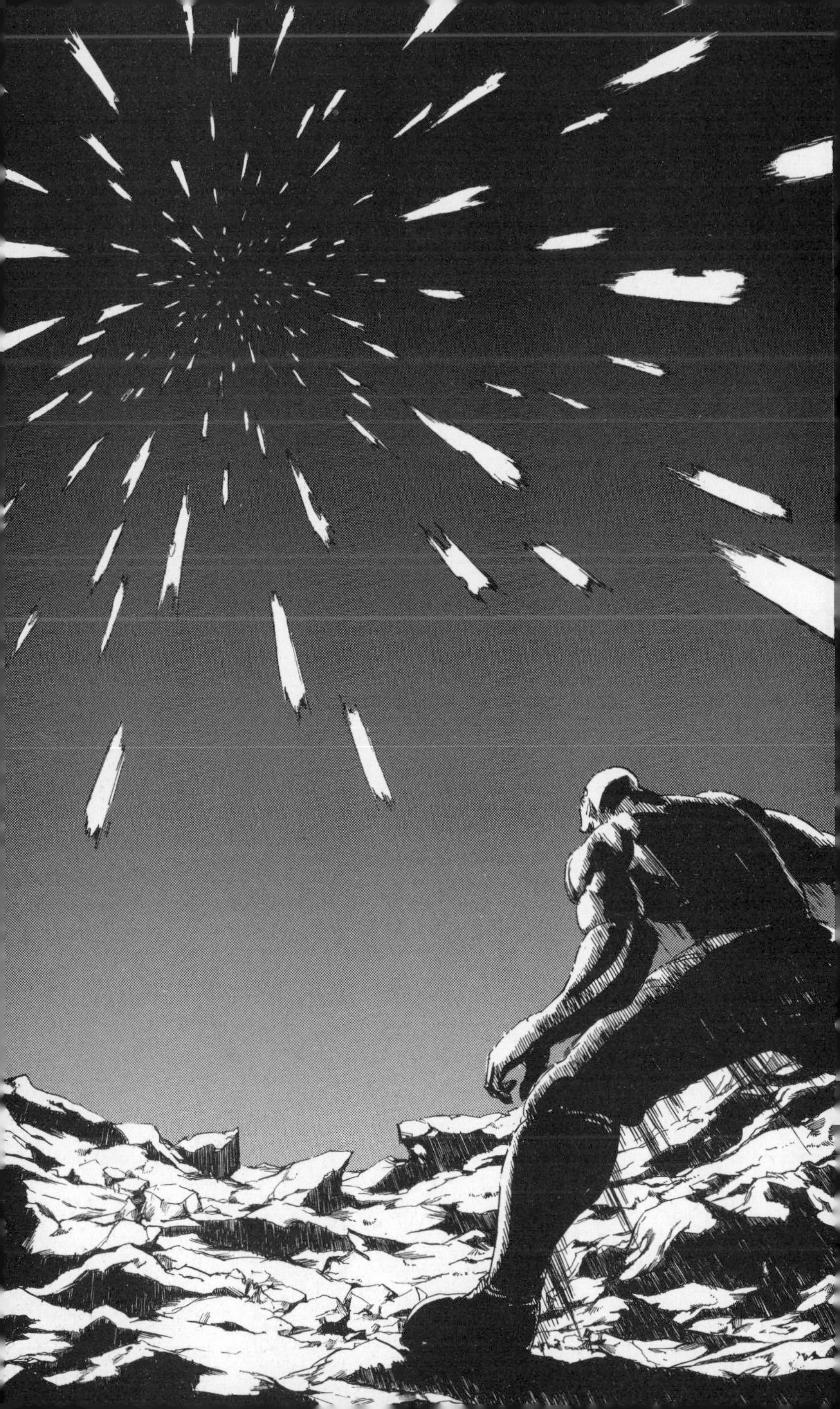

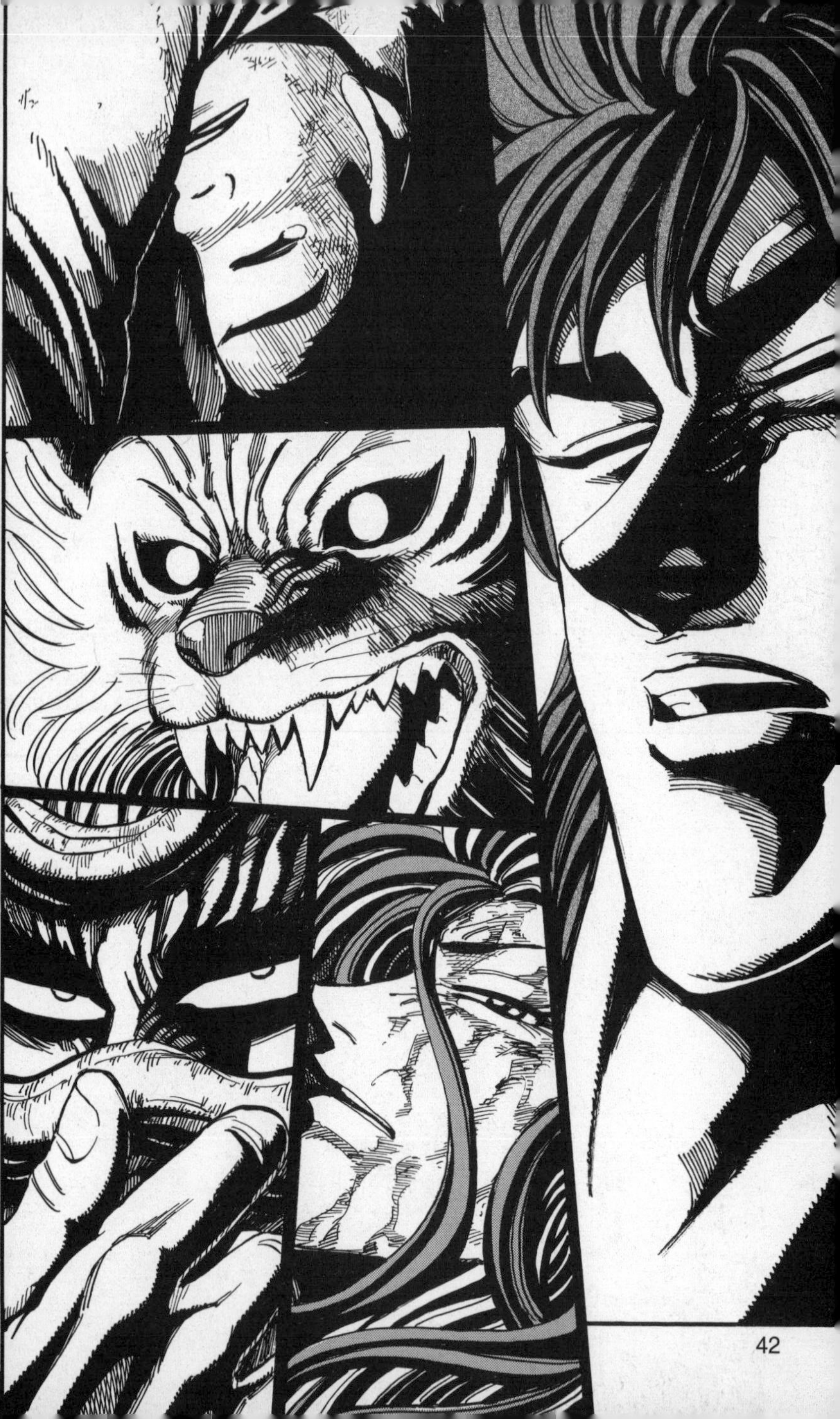

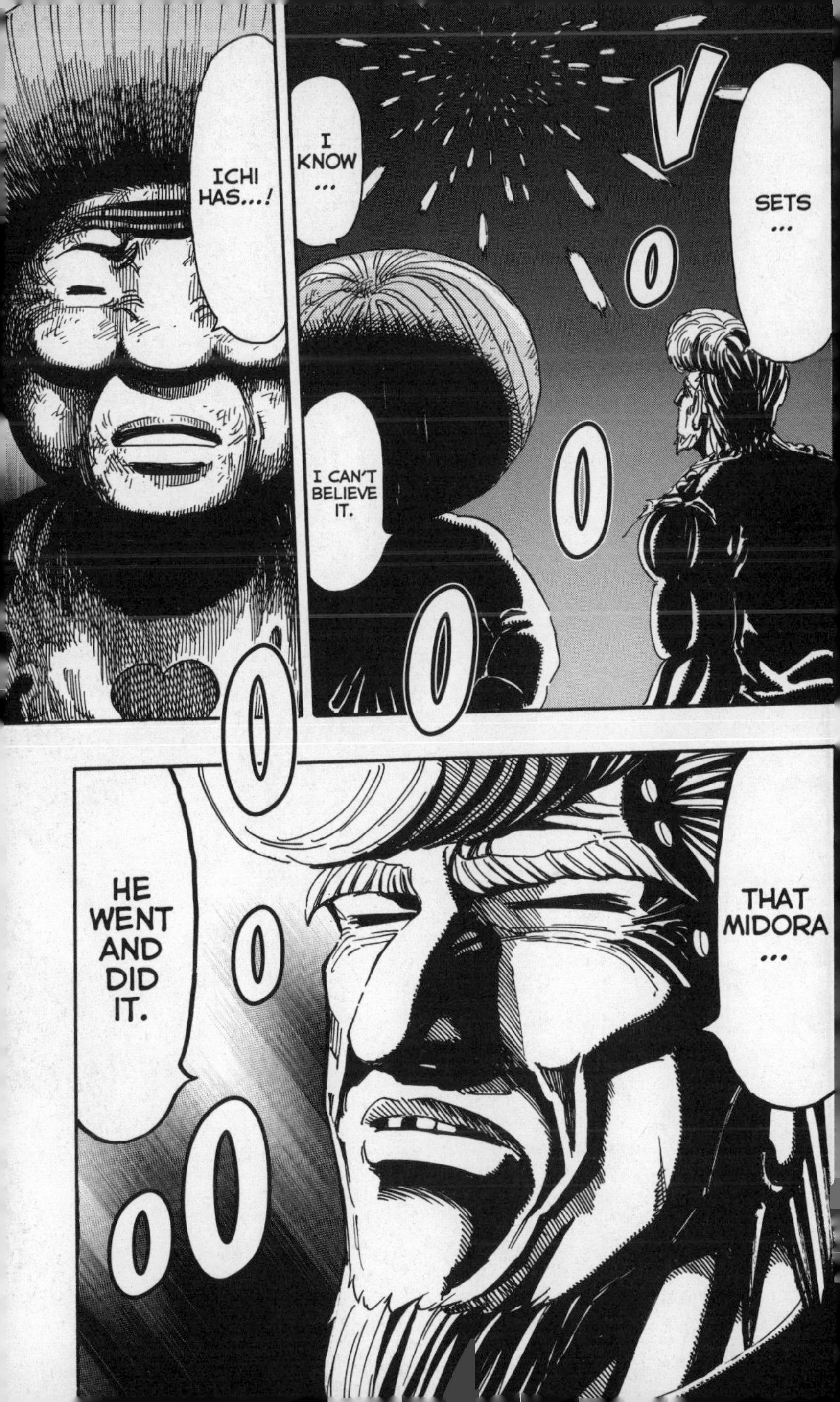
SETS...
I KNOW...
I CAN'T BELIEVE IT.
ICHI HAS...!
THAT MIDORA...
HE WENT AND DID IT.

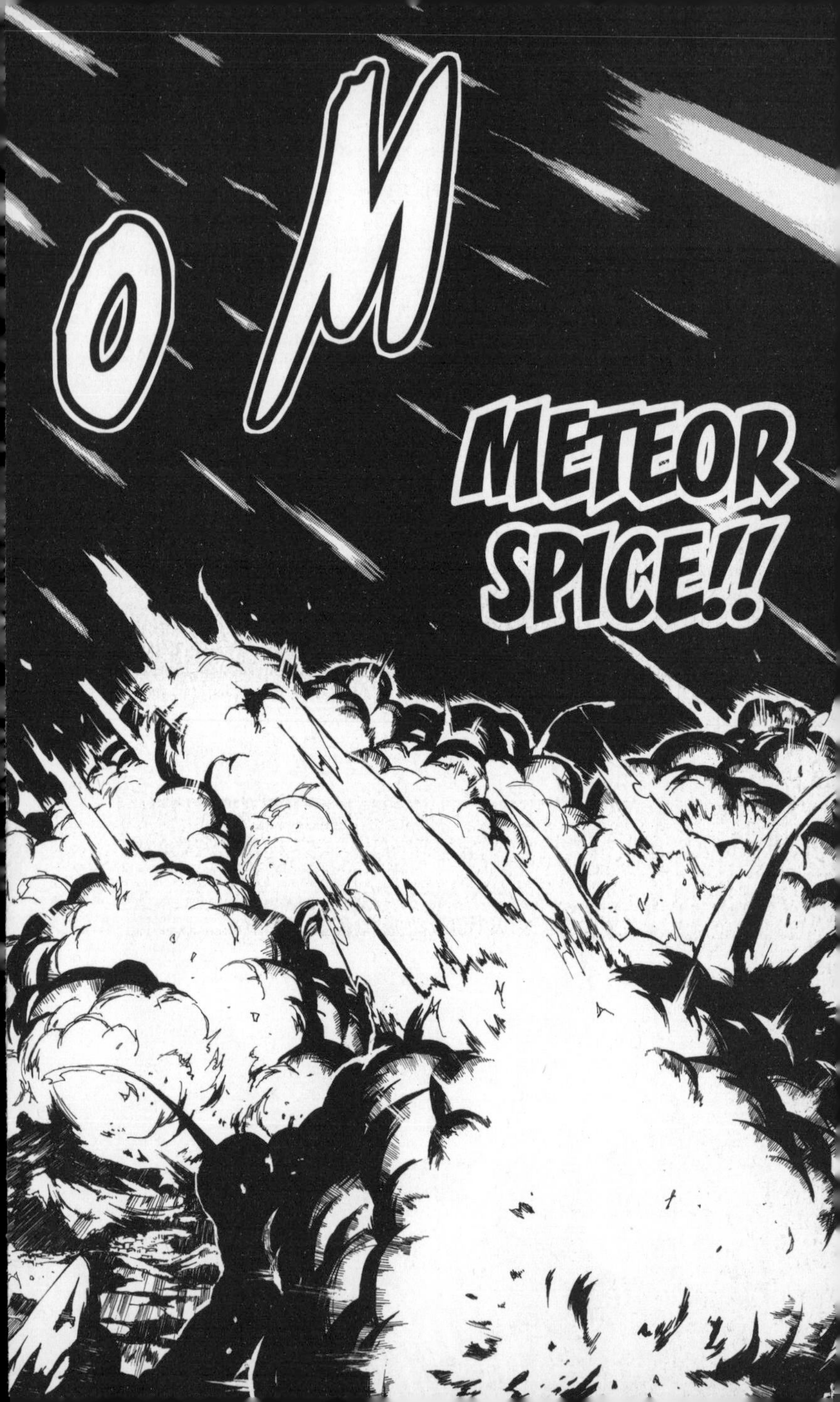
O M
METEOR SPICE!!

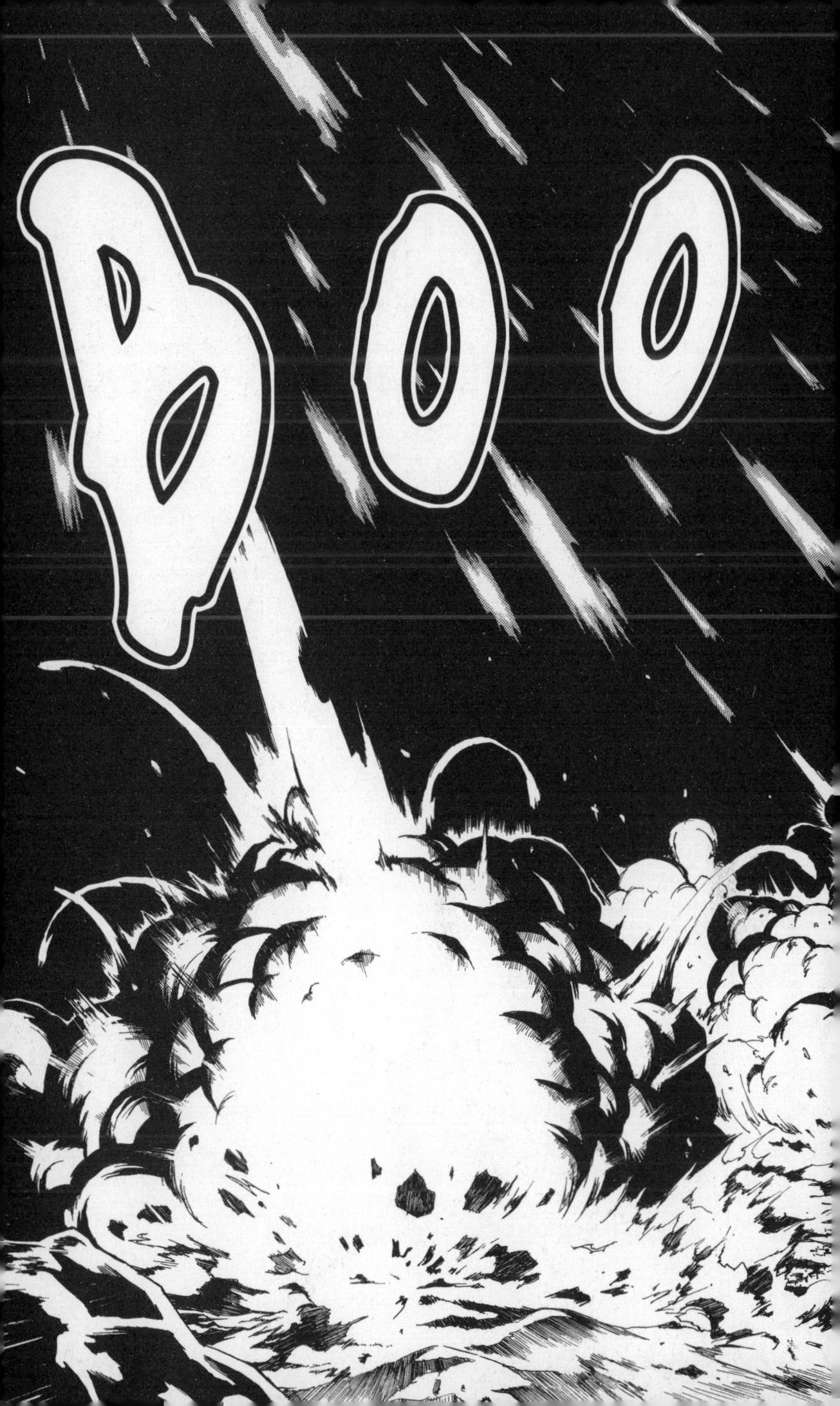
BOO

GOURMET CHECKLIST

Vol. 273

SEAWEED SNAKE

(REPTILE)

CAPTURE LEVEL: 29

HABITAT: STEW POND

SIZE: 1 METER

HEIGHT: ---

WEIGHT: 2 KG

PRICE: 7,000 YEN PER SNAKE

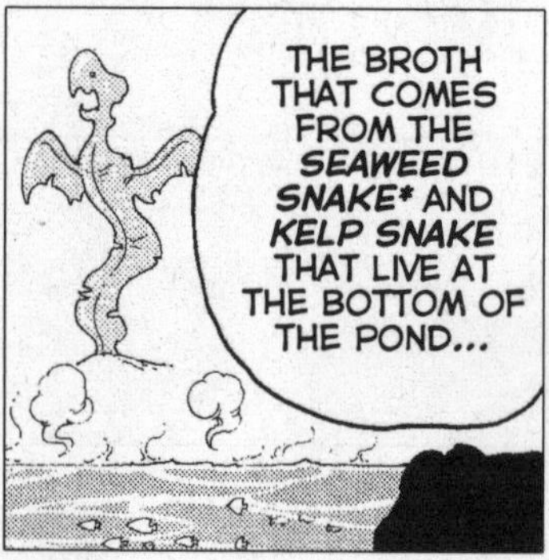
THE BROTH THAT COMES FROM THE *SEAWEED SNAKE** AND *KELP SNAKE* THAT LIVE AT THE BOTTOM OF THE POND...

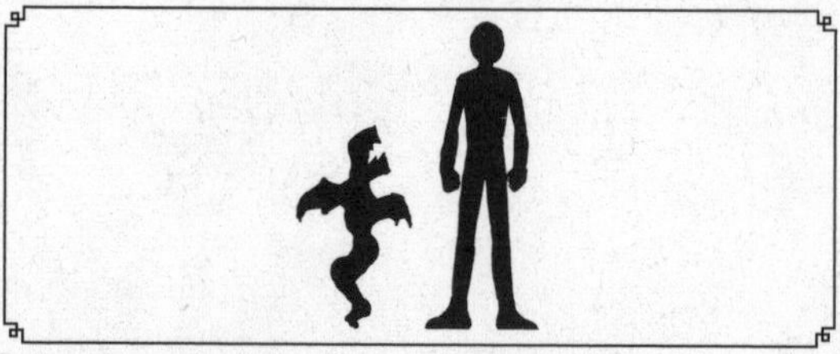

SCALE

A SNAKE THAT LIVES IN STEW POND, A LAKE THAT IS A CANDIDATE FOR A WORLD GOURMET HERITAGE SITE. WHEN HEATED, ITS BODY EXCRETES COMPONENTS COMPARABLE TO HIGH-QUALITY SEAWEED. BECAUSE OF THE HOT SPRINGS UNDERNEATH STEW POND, THE SEAWEED SNAKE IS CONSTANTLY PRODUCING BROTH. THAT DELICIOUS LIQUID SUPPORTS THE TASTY FISH OF STEW POND AND TURNS THE POND INTO THE STEW IT IS NAMED FOR.

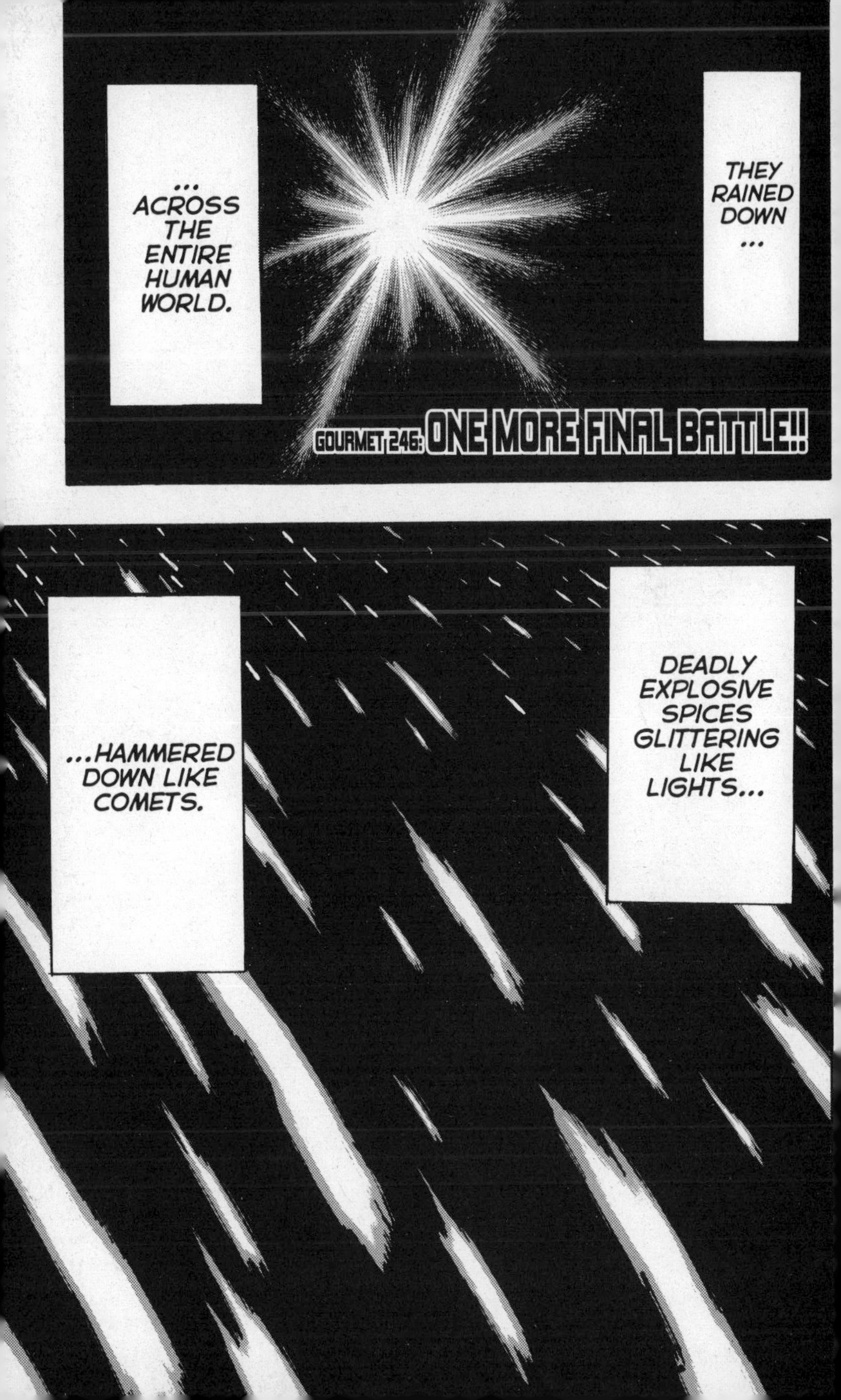
THEY RAINED DOWN...
...ACROSS THE ENTIRE HUMAN WORLD.
GOURMET 246: ONE MORE FINAL BATTLE!!
DEADLY EXPLOSIVE SPICES GLITTERING LIKE LIGHTS...
...HAMMERED DOWN LIKE COMETS.

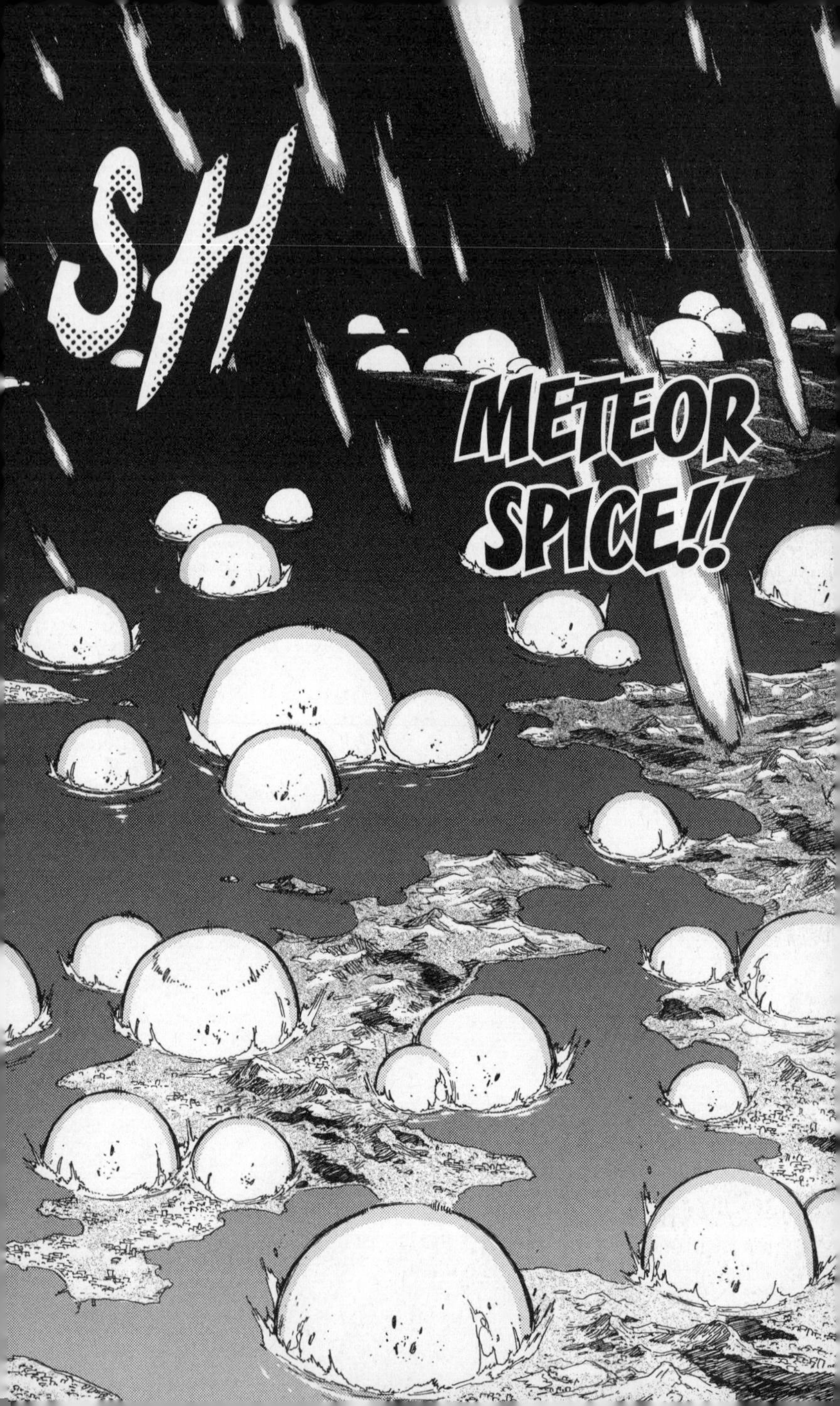
SH
METEOR SPICE!!

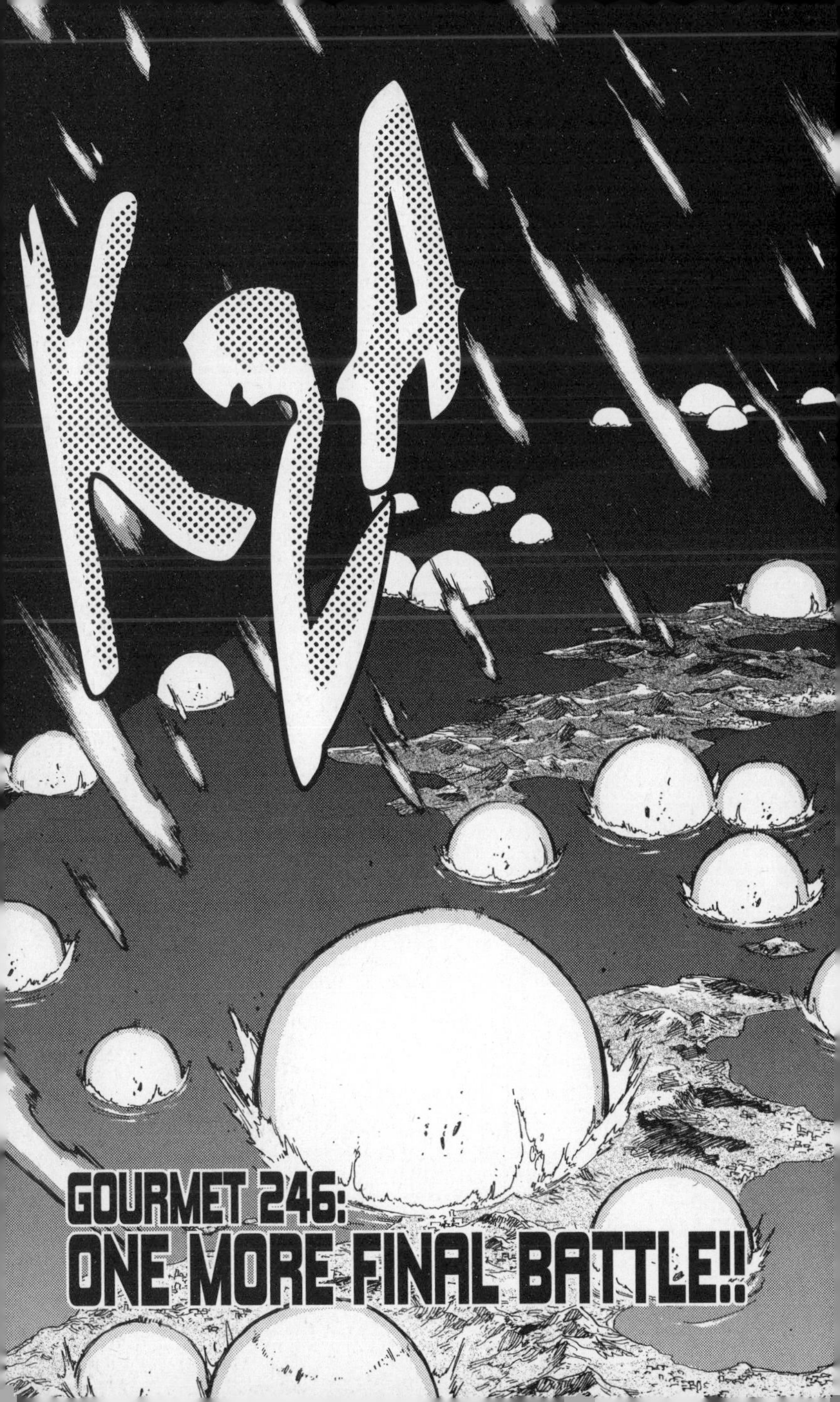

KZA
GOURMET 246:
ONE MORE FINAL BATTLE!!

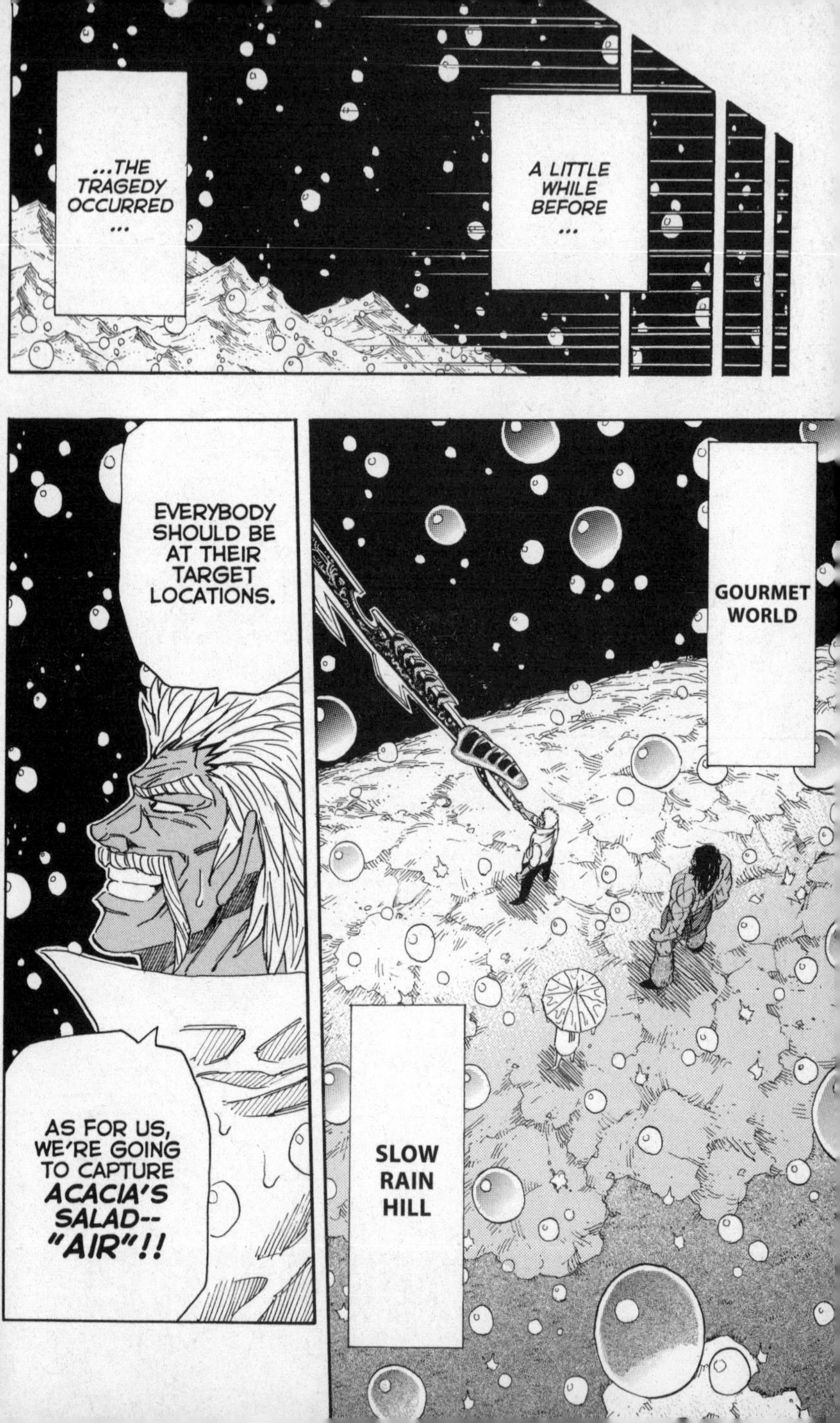
A LITTLE WHILE BEFORE ...
...THE TRAGEDY OCCURRED ...
GOURMET WORLD
SLOW RAIN HILL
EVERYBODY SHOULD BE AT THEIR TARGET LOCATIONS.
AS FOR US, WE'RE GOING TO CAPTURE ACACIA'S SALAD-- "AIR"!!

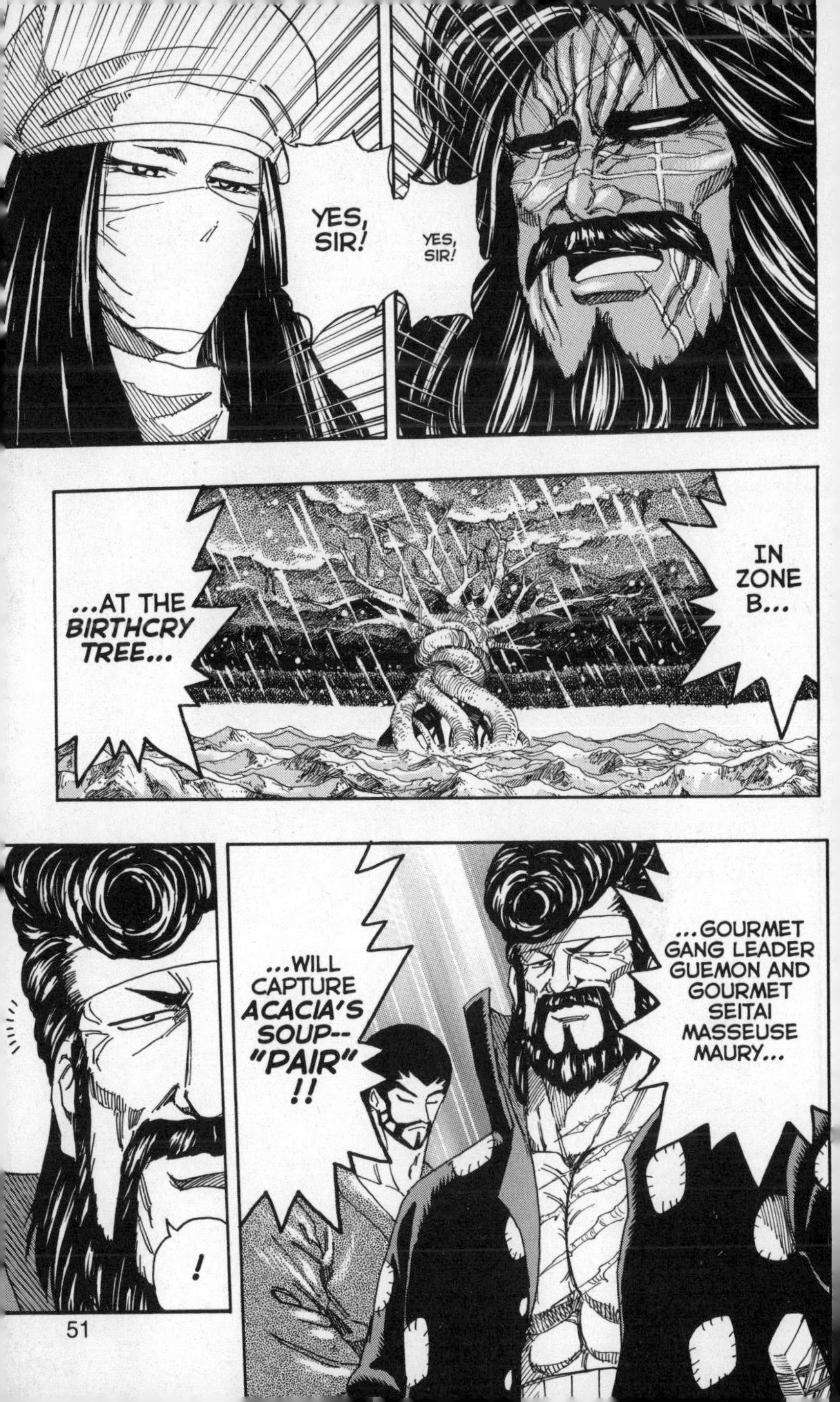
YES, SIR!
YES, SIR!
IN ZONE B...
...AT THE BIRTHCRY TREE...
...GOURMET GANG LEADER GUEMON AND GOURMET SEITAI MASSEUSE MAURY...
...WILL CAPTURE ACACIA'S SOUP-- "PAIR" !!
!

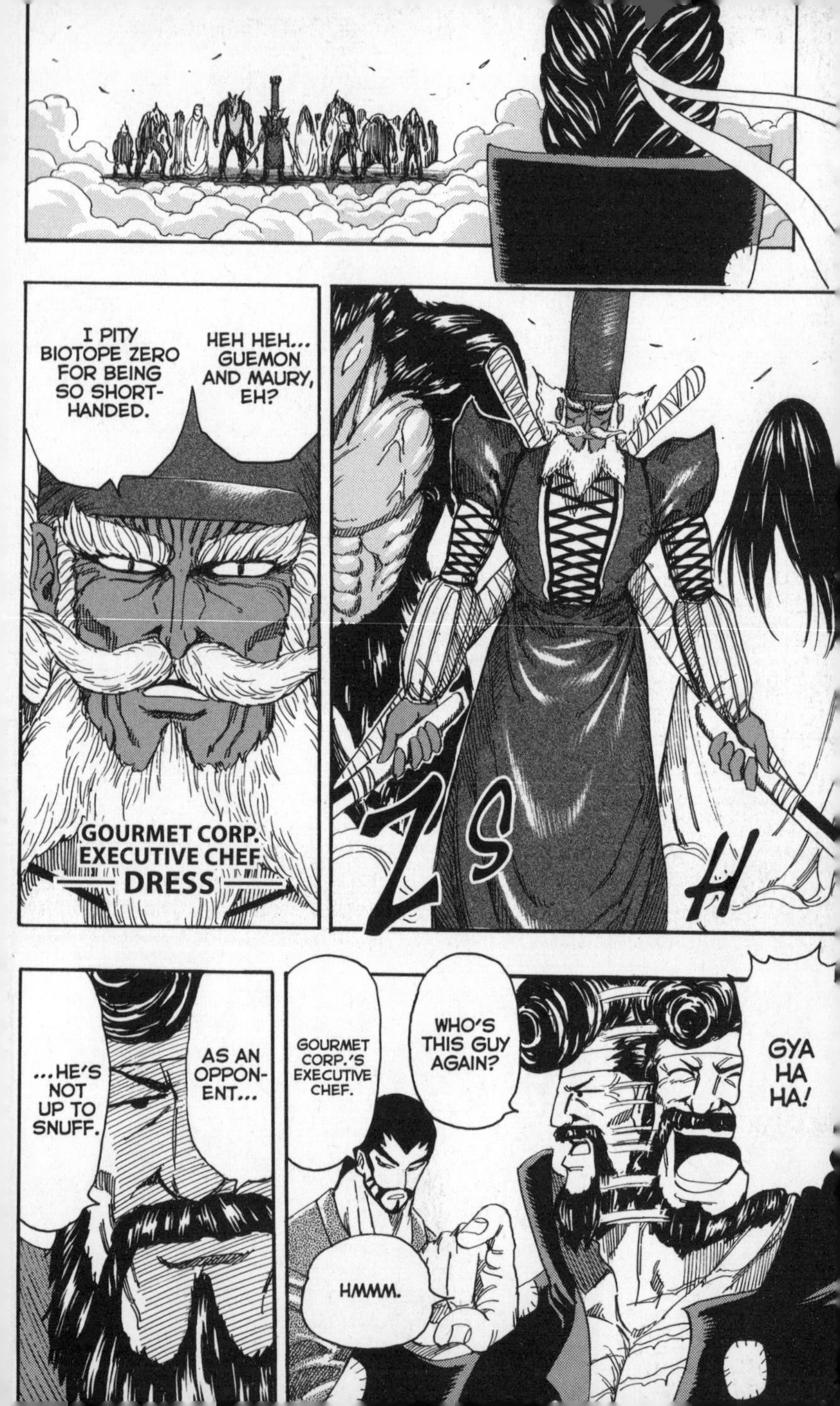
ZSH
HEH HEH... GUEMON AND MAURY, EH?
I PITY BIOTOPE ZERO FOR BEING SO SHORT-HANDED.
GOURMET CORP. EXECUTIVE CHEF
DRESS
GYA HA HA!
WHO'S THIS GUY AGAIN?
GOURMET CORP.'S EXECUTIVE CHEF.
HMMM.
AS AN OPPONENT...
...HE'S NOT UP TO SNUFF.

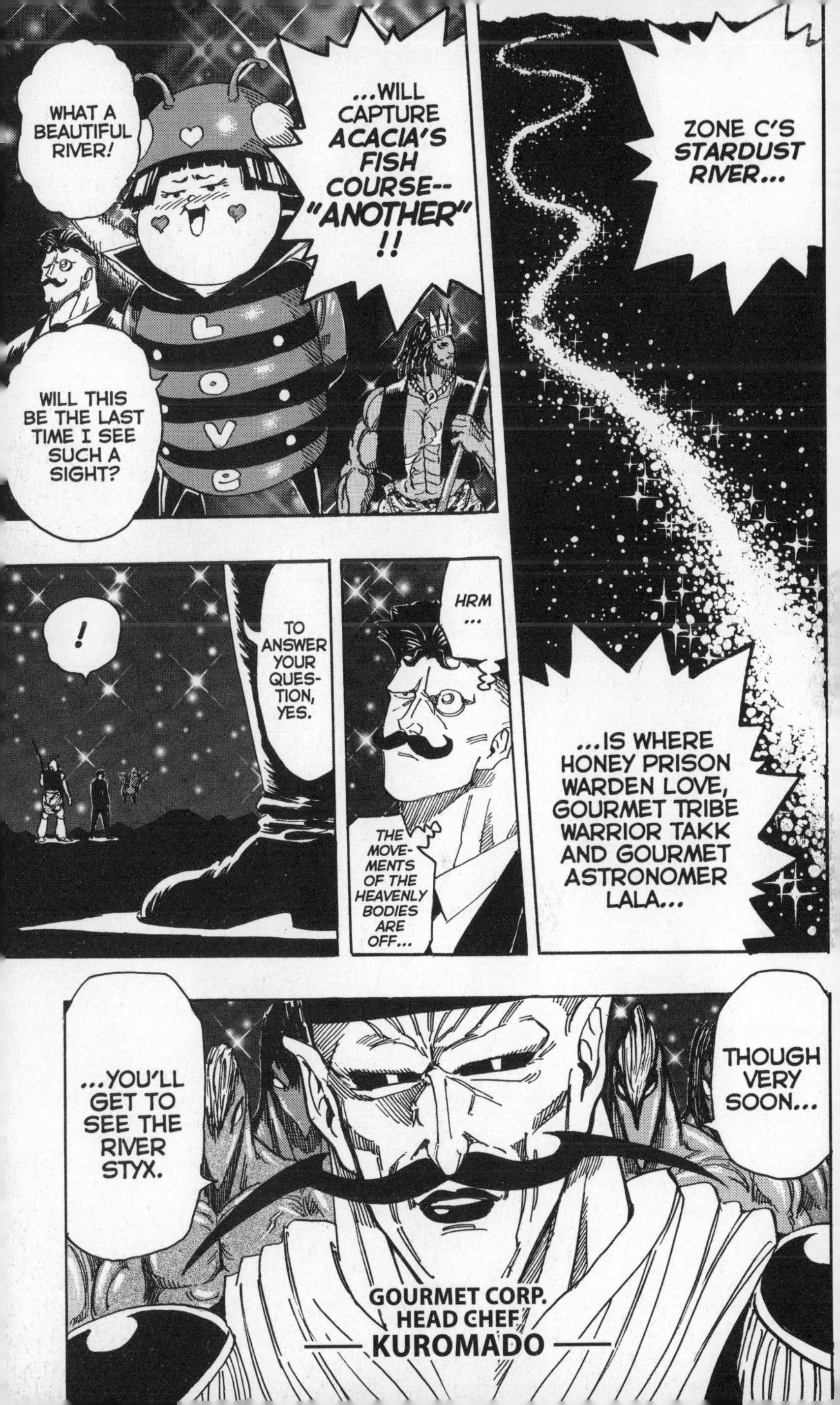
ZONE C'S STARDUST RIVER...
...IS WHERE HONEY PRISON WARDEN LOVE, GOURMET TRIBE WARRIOR TAKK AND GOURMET ASTRONOMER LALA...
...WILL CAPTURE ACACIA'S FISH COURSE-- "ANOTHER" !!
WHAT A BEAUTIFUL RIVER!
WILL THIS BE THE LAST TIME I SEE SUCH A SIGHT?
HRM...
THE MOVEMENTS OF THE HEAVENLY BODIES ARE OFF...
TO ANSWER YOUR QUESTION, YES.
!
THOUGH VERY SOON...
...YOU'LL GET TO SEE THE RIVER STYX.
GOURMET CORP. HEAD CHEF
—KUROMADO—

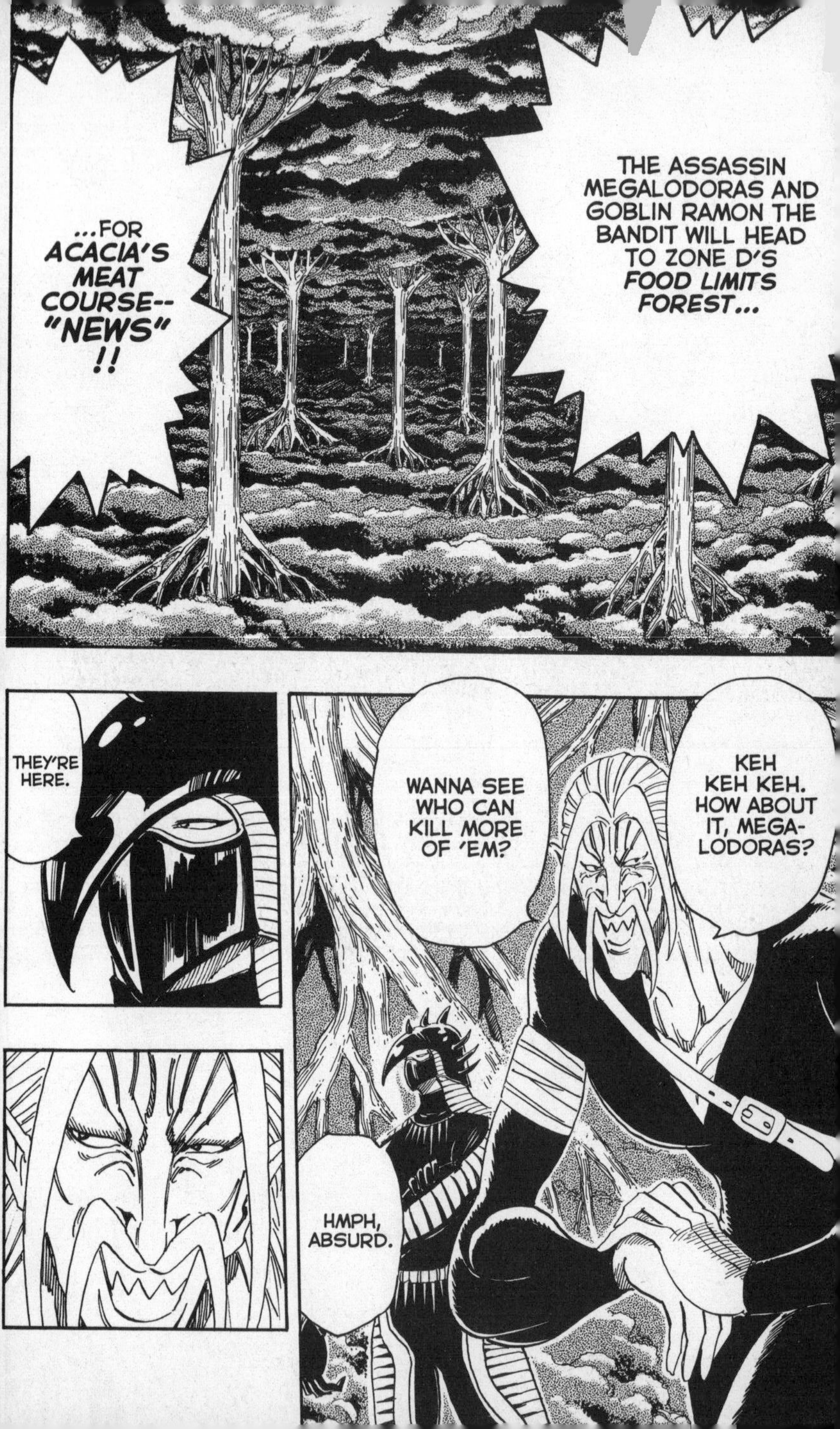
THE ASSASSIN MEGALODORAS AND GOBLIN RAMON THE BANDIT WILL HEAD TO ZONE D'S FOOD LIMITS FOREST...
...FOR ACACIA'S MEAT COURSE-- "NEWS" !!
KEH KEH KEH. HOW ABOUT IT, MEGA-LODORAS?
WANNA SEE WHO CAN KILL MORE OF 'EM?
HMPH, ABSURD.
THEY'RE HERE.

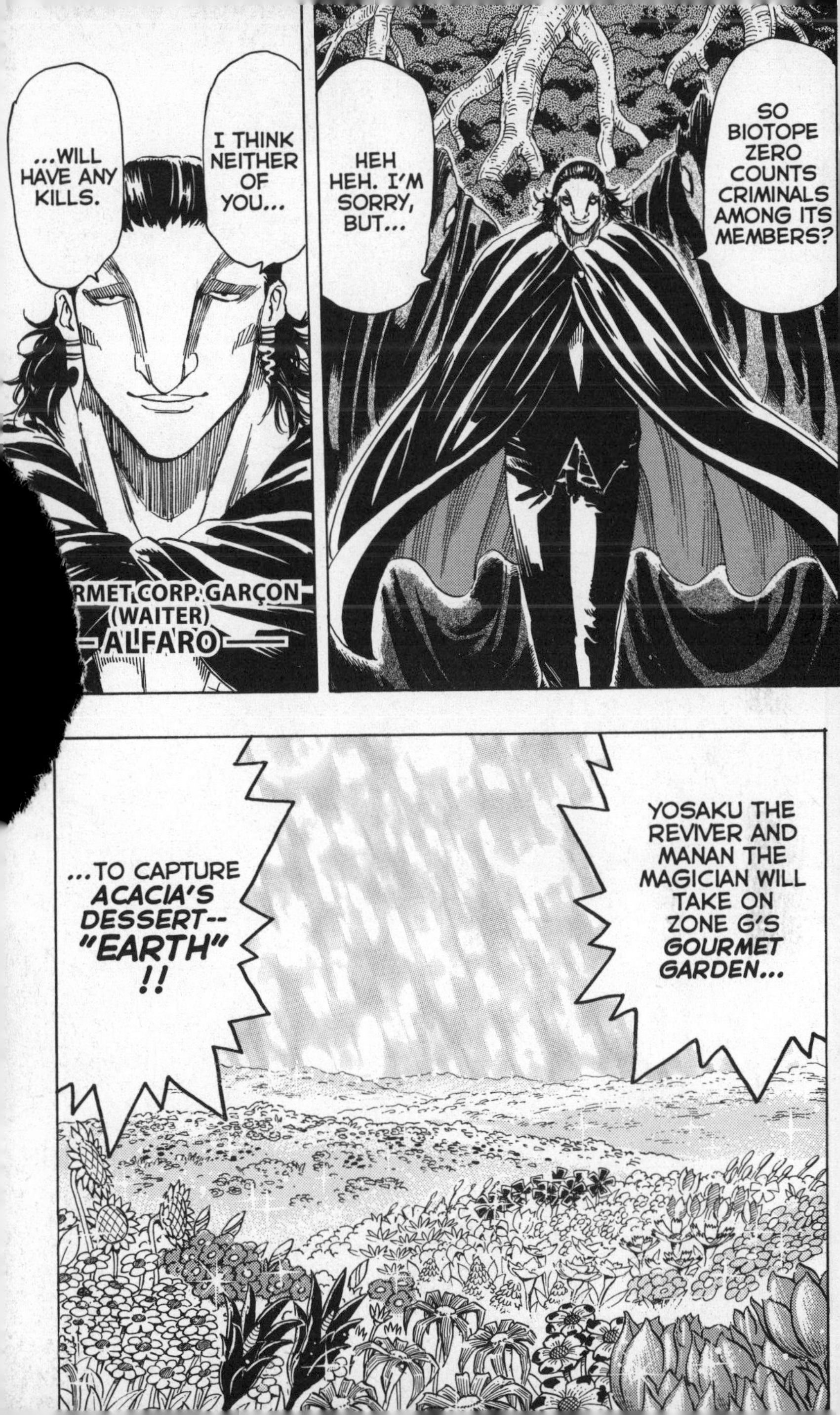
SO BIOTOPE ZERO COUNTS CRIMINALS AMONG ITS MEMBERS?
HEH HEH. I'M SORRY, BUT...
I THINK NEITHER OF YOU...
...WILL HAVE ANY KILLS.
RMET CORP. GARÇON (WAITER)
ALFARO
YOSAKU THE REVIVER AND MANAN THE MAGICIAN WILL TAKE ON ZONE G'S GOURMET GARDEN...
...TO CAPTURE ACACIA'S DESSERT-- "EARTH" !!

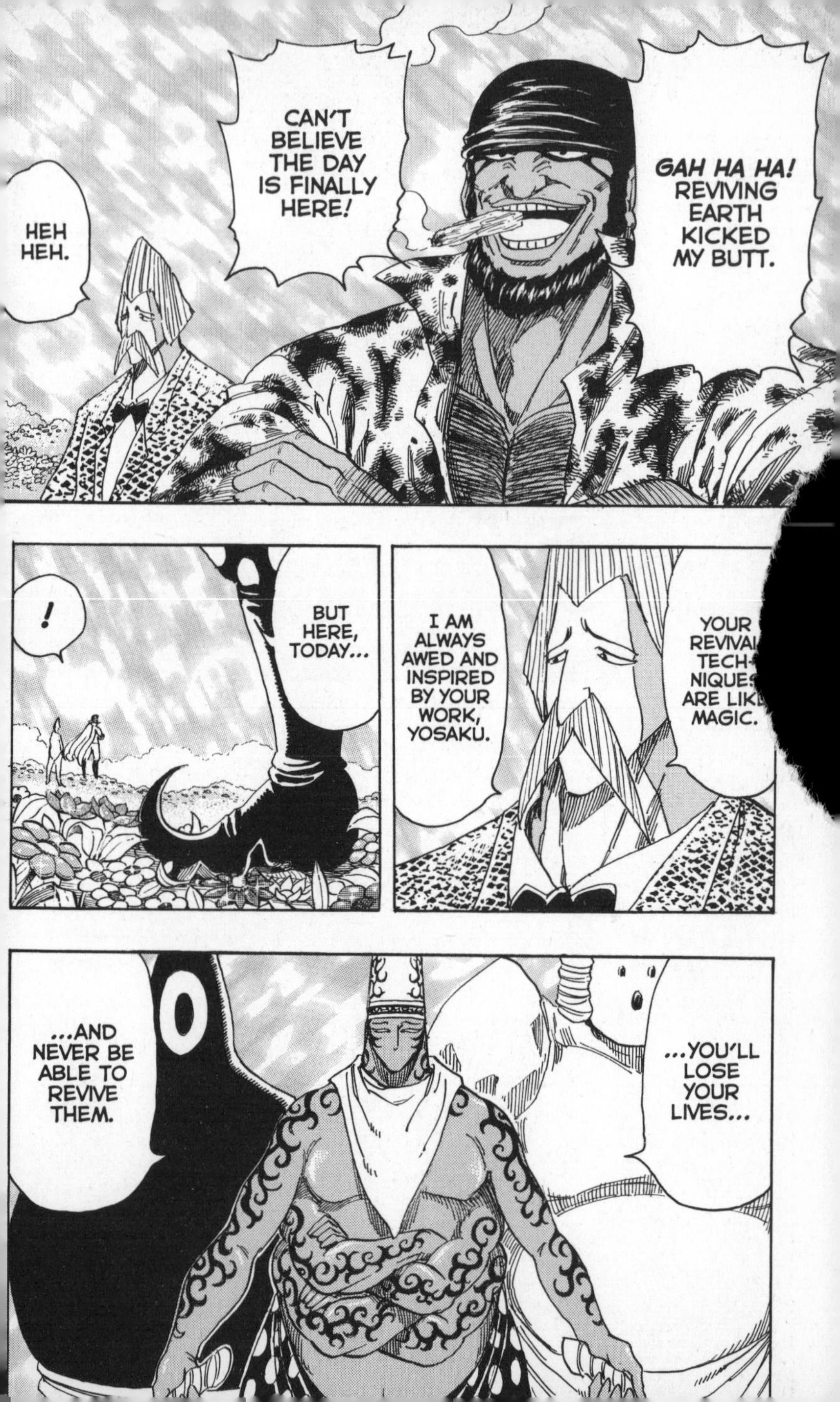
GAH HA HA! REVIVING EARTH KICKED MY BUTT.
CAN'T BELIEVE THE DAY IS FINALLY HERE!
HEH HEH.
YOUR REVIVAL TECH-NIQUES ARE LIKE MAGIC.
I AM ALWAYS AWED AND INSPIRED BY YOUR WORK, YOSAKU.
BUT HERE, TODAY...
!
...YOU'LL LOSE YOUR LIVES...
...AND NEVER BE ABLE TO REVIVE THEM.

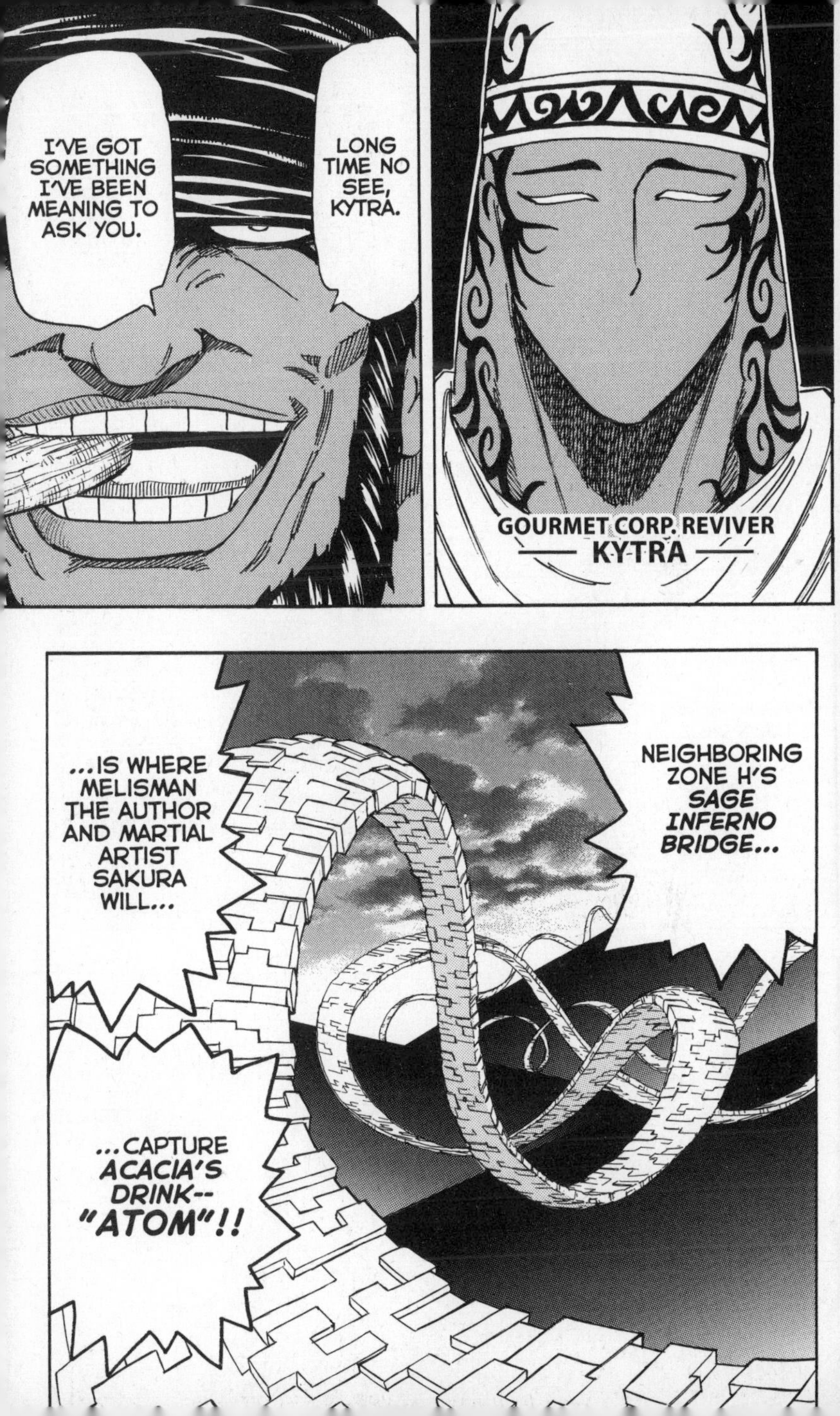
GOURMET CORP. REVIVER KYTRA
LONG TIME NO SEE, KYTRA.
I'VE GOT SOMETHING I'VE BEEN MEANING TO ASK YOU.
NEIGHBORING ZONE H'S SAGE INFERNO BRIDGE...
...IS WHERE MELISMAN THE AUTHOR AND MARTIAL ARTIST SAKURA WILL...
...CAPTURE ACACIA'S DRINK-- "ATOM"!!

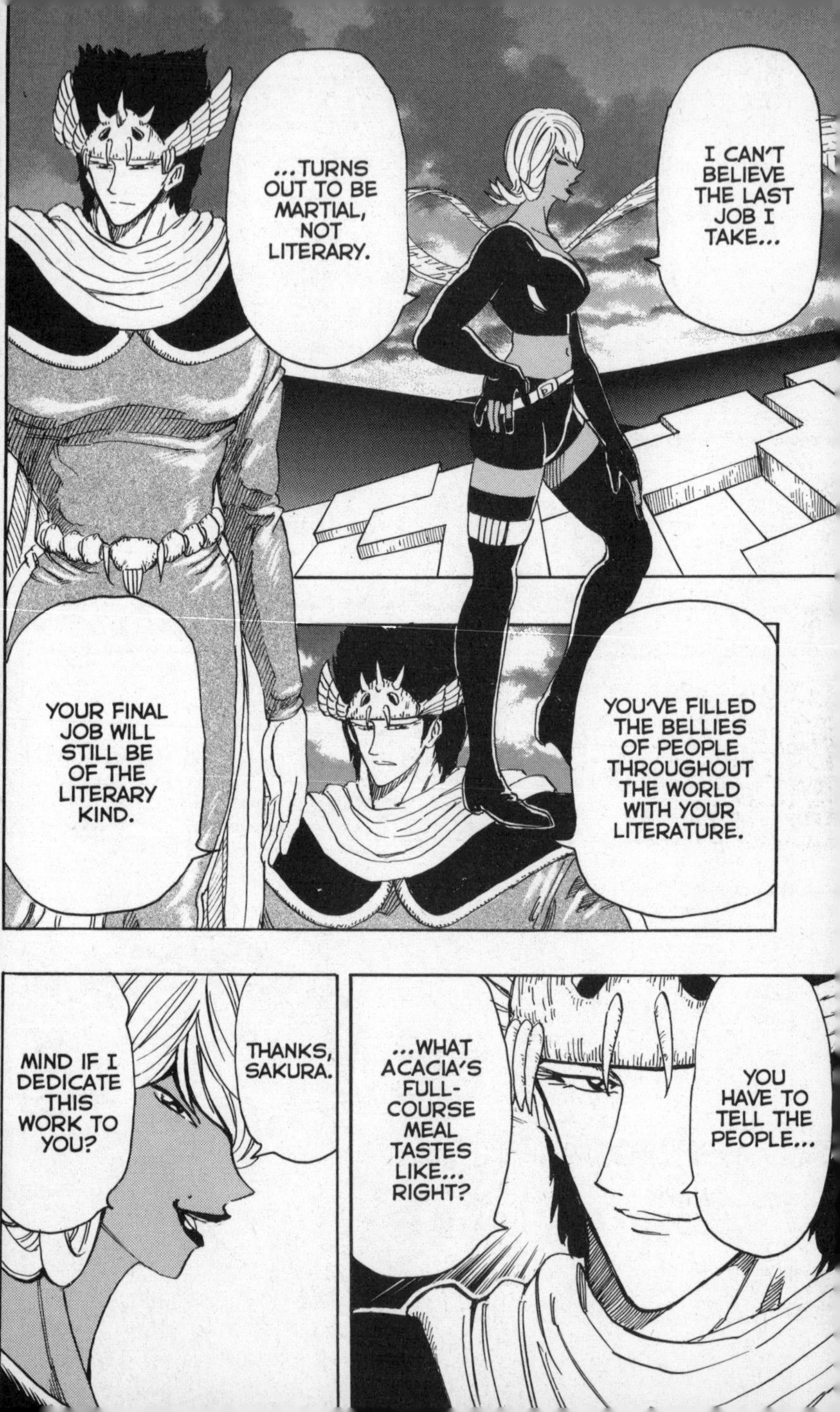
I CAN'T BELIEVE THE LAST JOB I TAKE...
...TURNS OUT TO BE MARTIAL, NOT LITERARY.
YOU'VE FILLED THE BELLIES OF PEOPLE THROUGHOUT THE WORLD WITH YOUR LITERATURE.
YOUR FINAL JOB WILL STILL BE OF THE LITERARY KIND.
YOU HAVE TO TELL THE PEOPLE...
...WHAT ACACIA'S FULL-COURSE MEAL TASTES LIKE... RIGHT?
THANKS, SAKURA.
MIND IF I DEDICATE THIS WORK TO YOU?

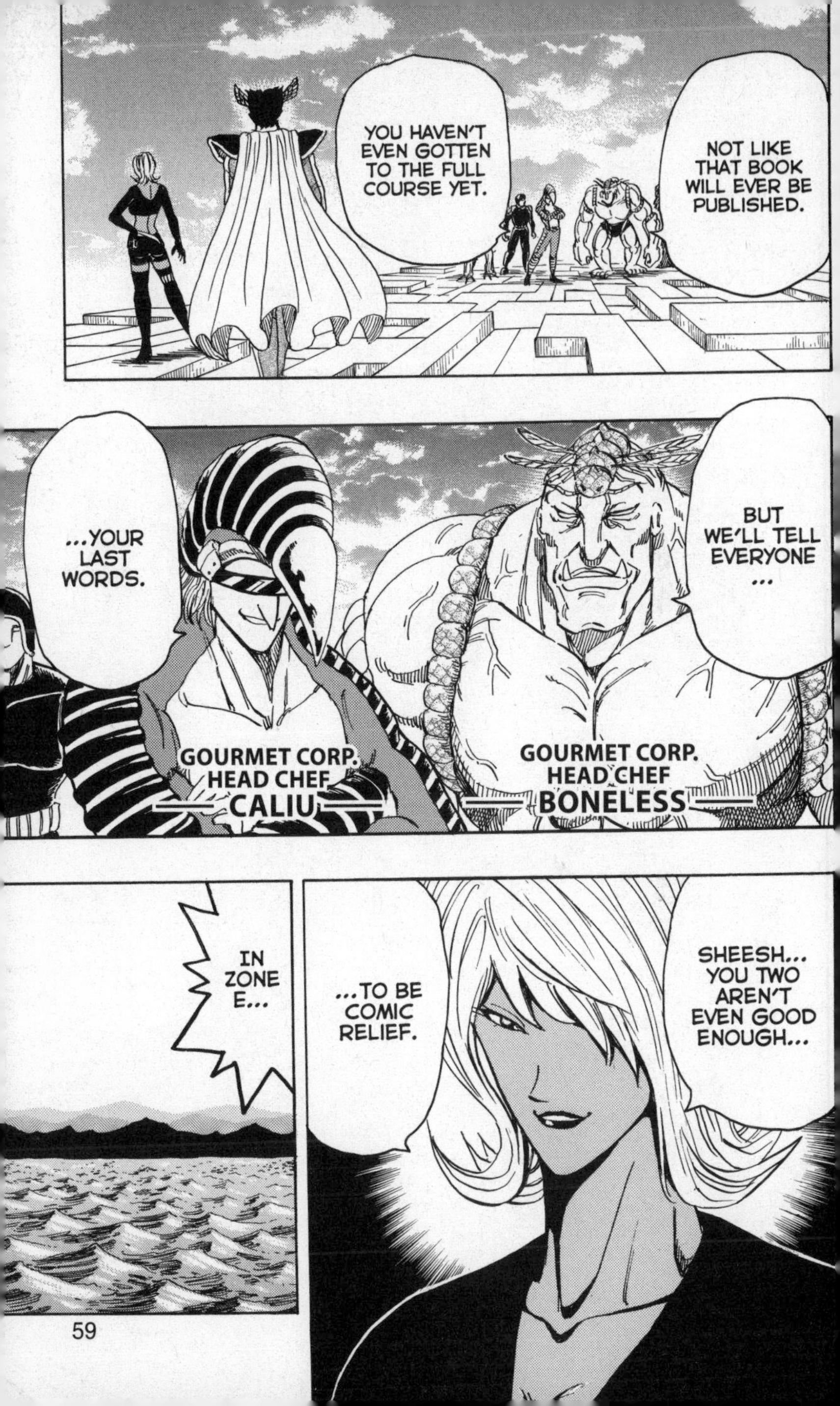
NOT LIKE THAT BOOK WILL EVER BE PUBLISHED.
YOU HAVEN'T EVEN GOTTEN TO THE FULL COURSE YET.
BUT WE'LL TELL EVERYONE ...
GOURMET CORP. HEAD CHEF BONELESS
...YOUR LAST WORDS.
GOURMET CORP. HEAD CHEF CALIU
SHEESH... YOU TWO AREN'T EVEN GOOD ENOUGH...
...TO BE COMIC RELIEF.
IN ZONE E...

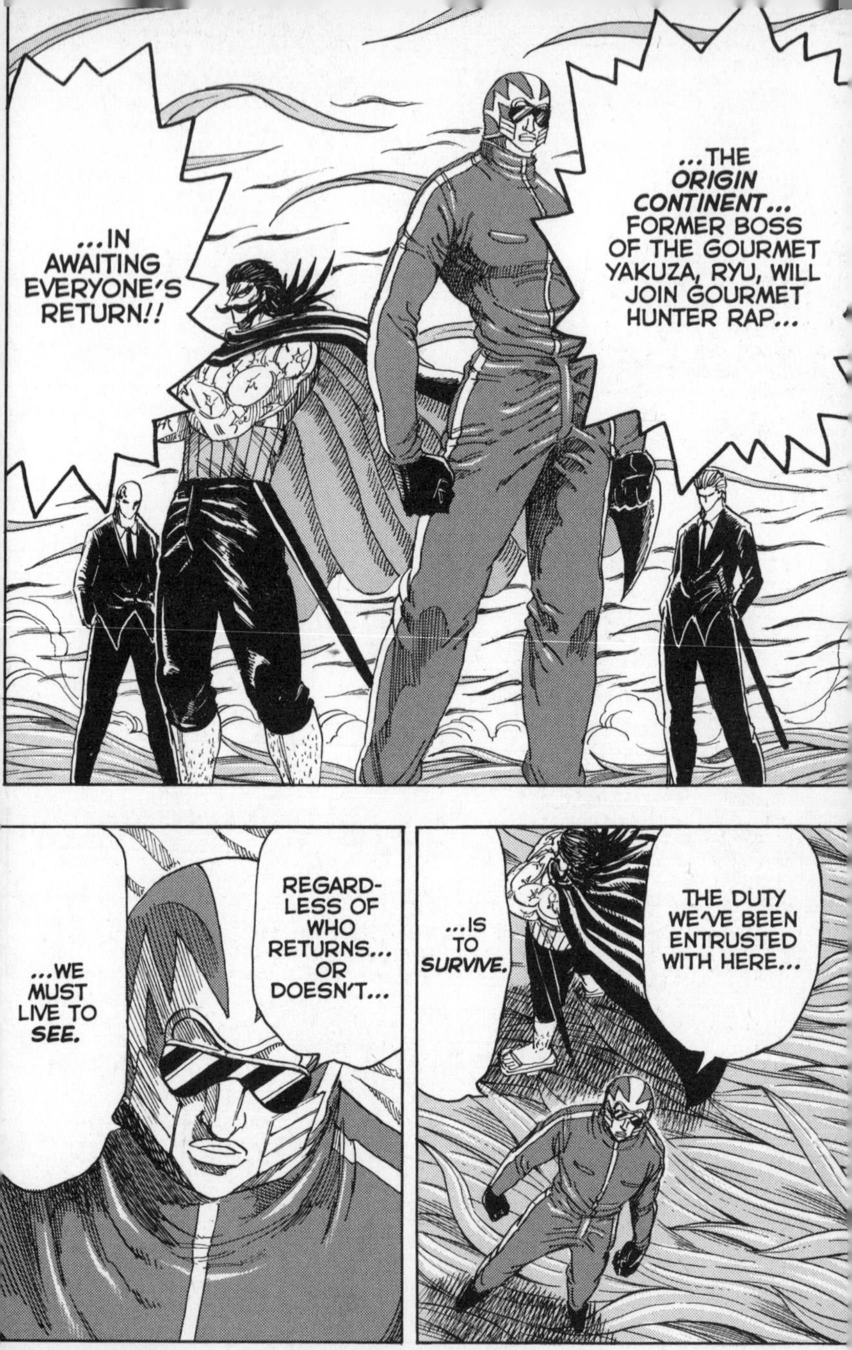
...THE *ORIGIN CONTINENT*... FORMER BOSS OF THE GOURMET YAKUZA, RYU, WILL JOIN GOURMET HUNTER RAP...
...IN AWAITING EVERYONE'S RETURN!!
THE DUTY WE'VE BEEN ENTRUSTED WITH HERE...
...IS TO *SURVIVE.*
REGARDLESS OF WHO RETURNS... OR DOESN'T...
...WE MUST LIVE TO *SEE.*

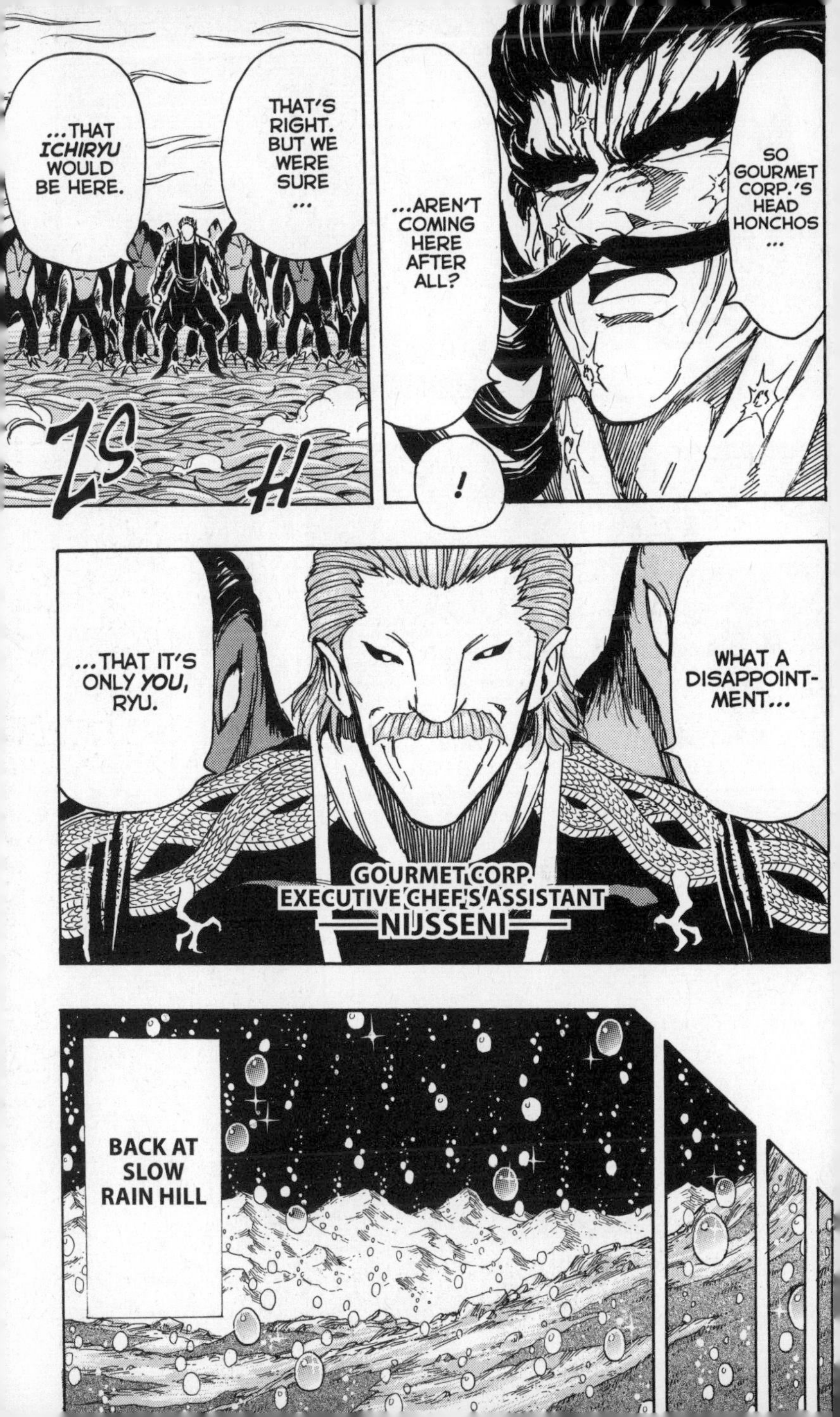
SO GOURMET CORP.'S HEAD HONCHOS...
...AREN'T COMING HERE AFTER ALL?
!
THAT'S RIGHT. BUT WE WERE SURE...
...THAT *ICHIRYU* WOULD BE HERE.
ZSH
WHAT A DISAPPOINTMENT...
...THAT IT'S ONLY *YOU*, RYU.
GOURMET CORP. EXECUTIVE CHEF'S ASSISTANT NIJSSENI
BACK AT SLOW RAIN HILL

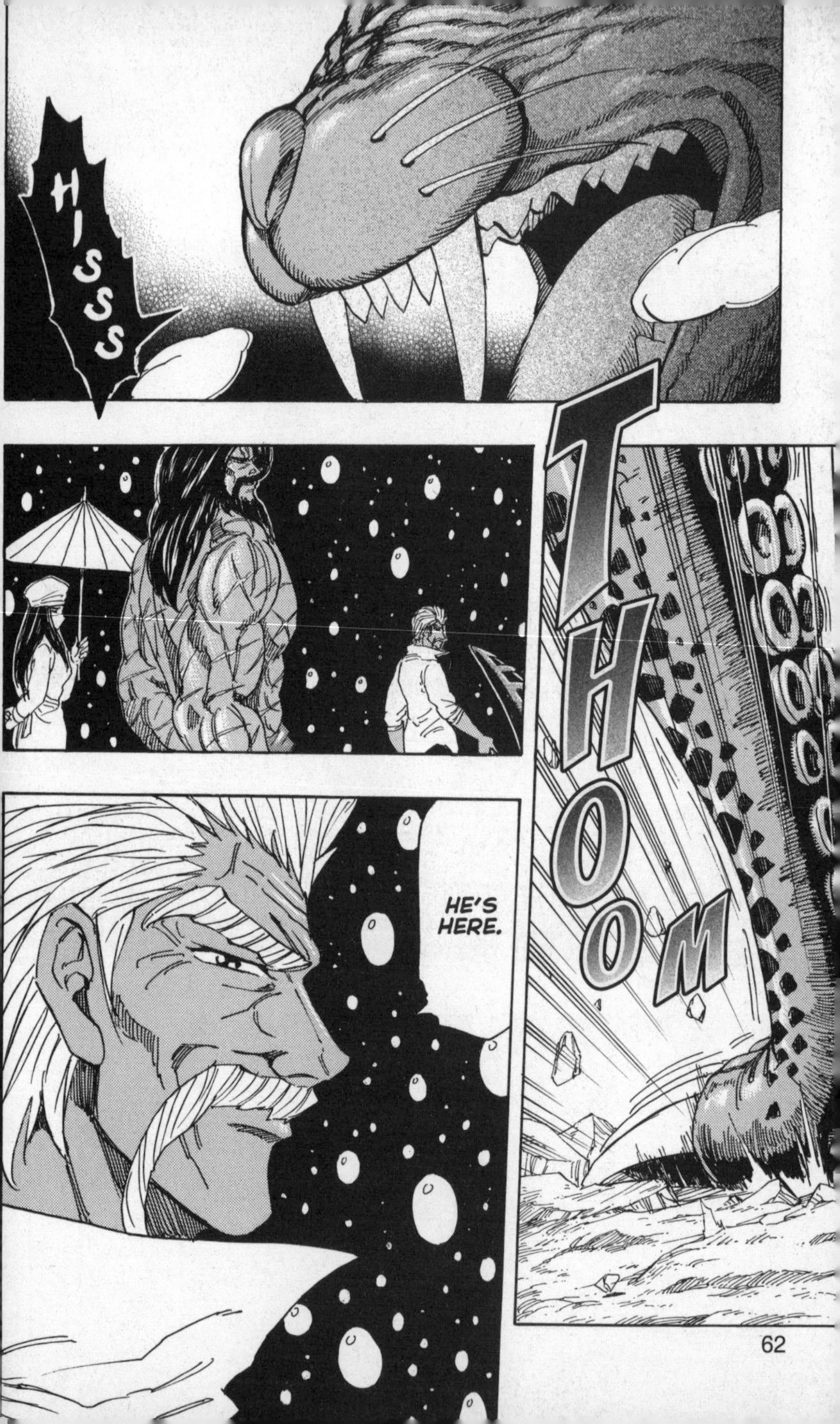
HISS
THOOM
HE'S HERE.

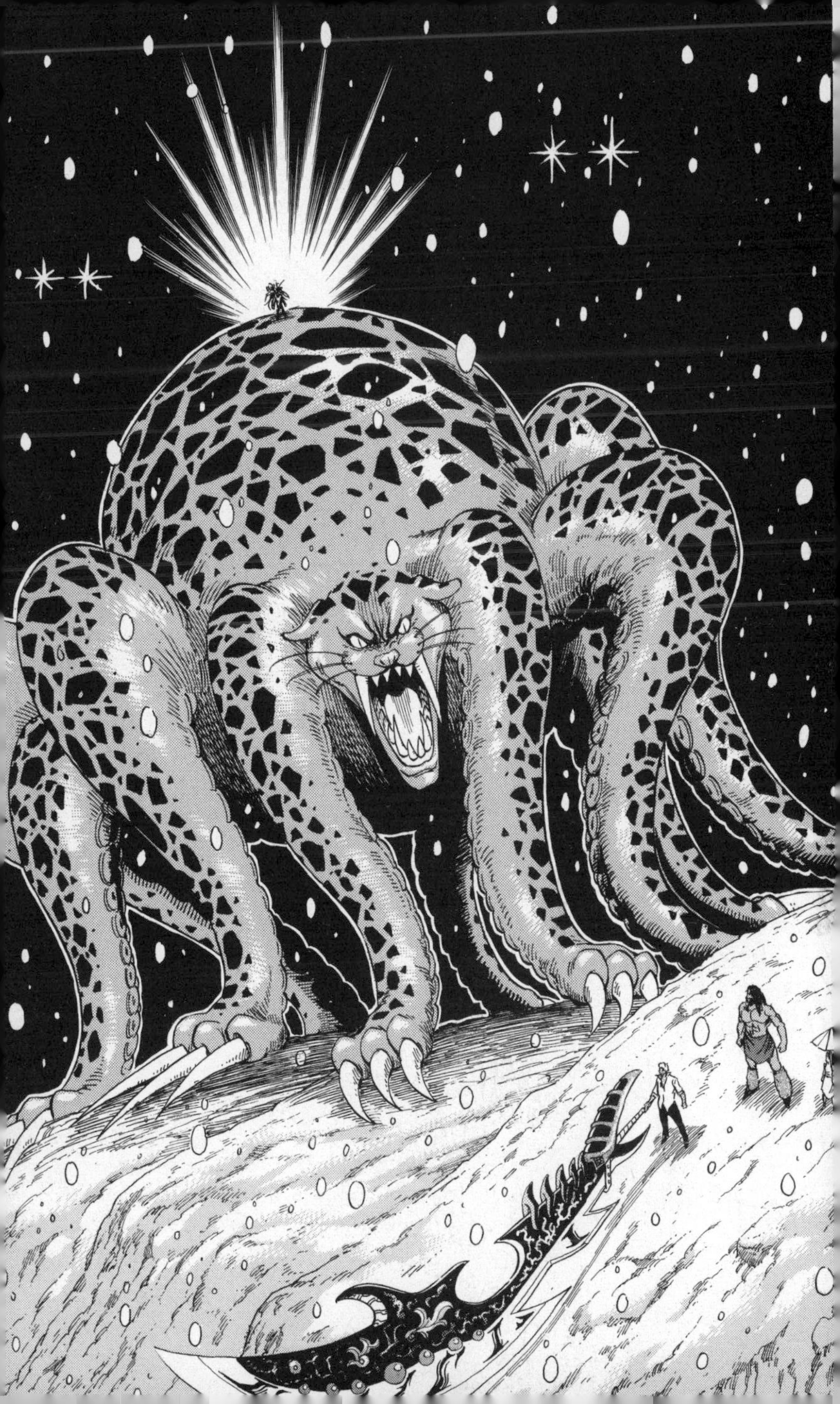

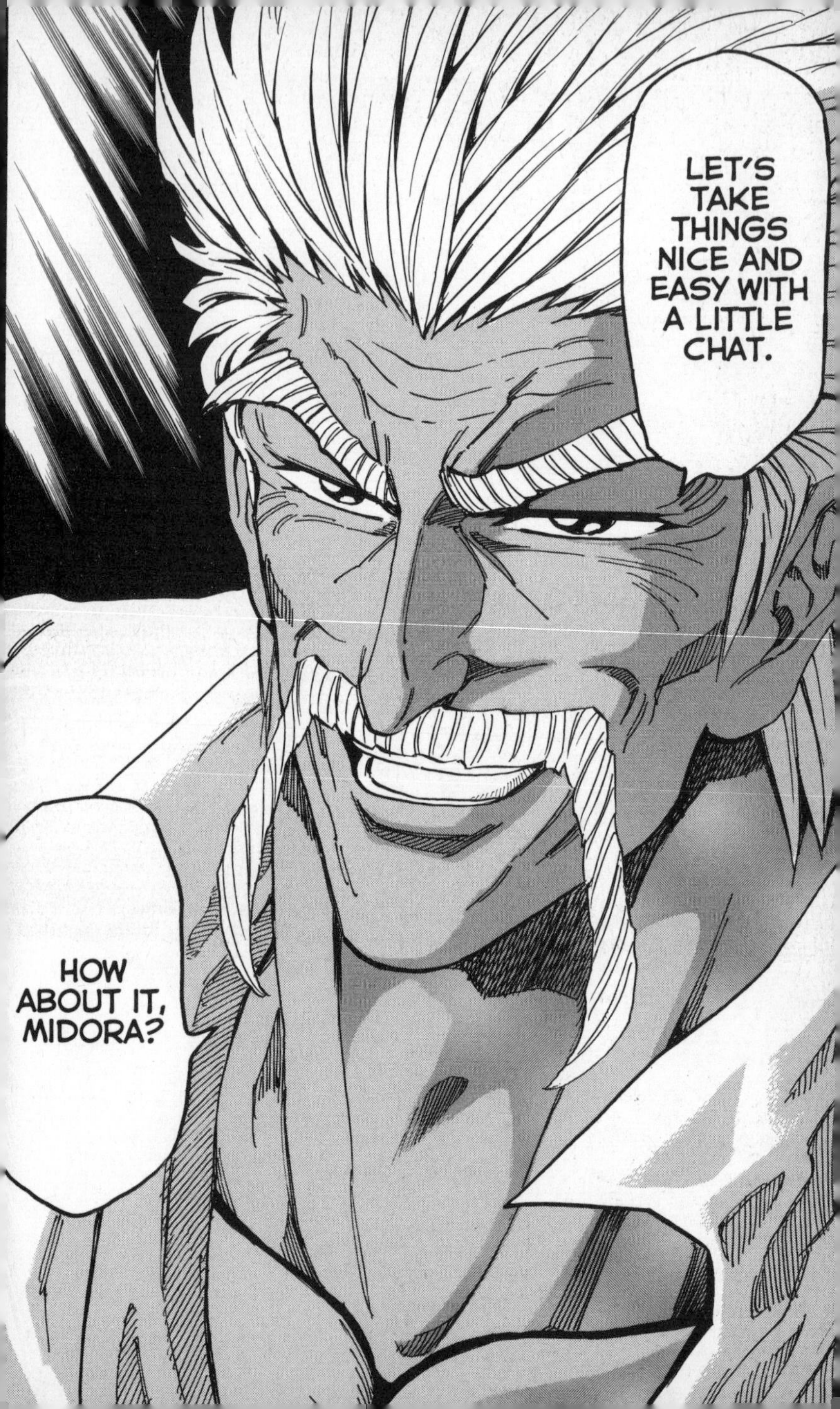
LET'S TAKE THINGS NICE AND EASY WITH A LITTLE CHAT.
HOW ABOUT IT, MIDORA?

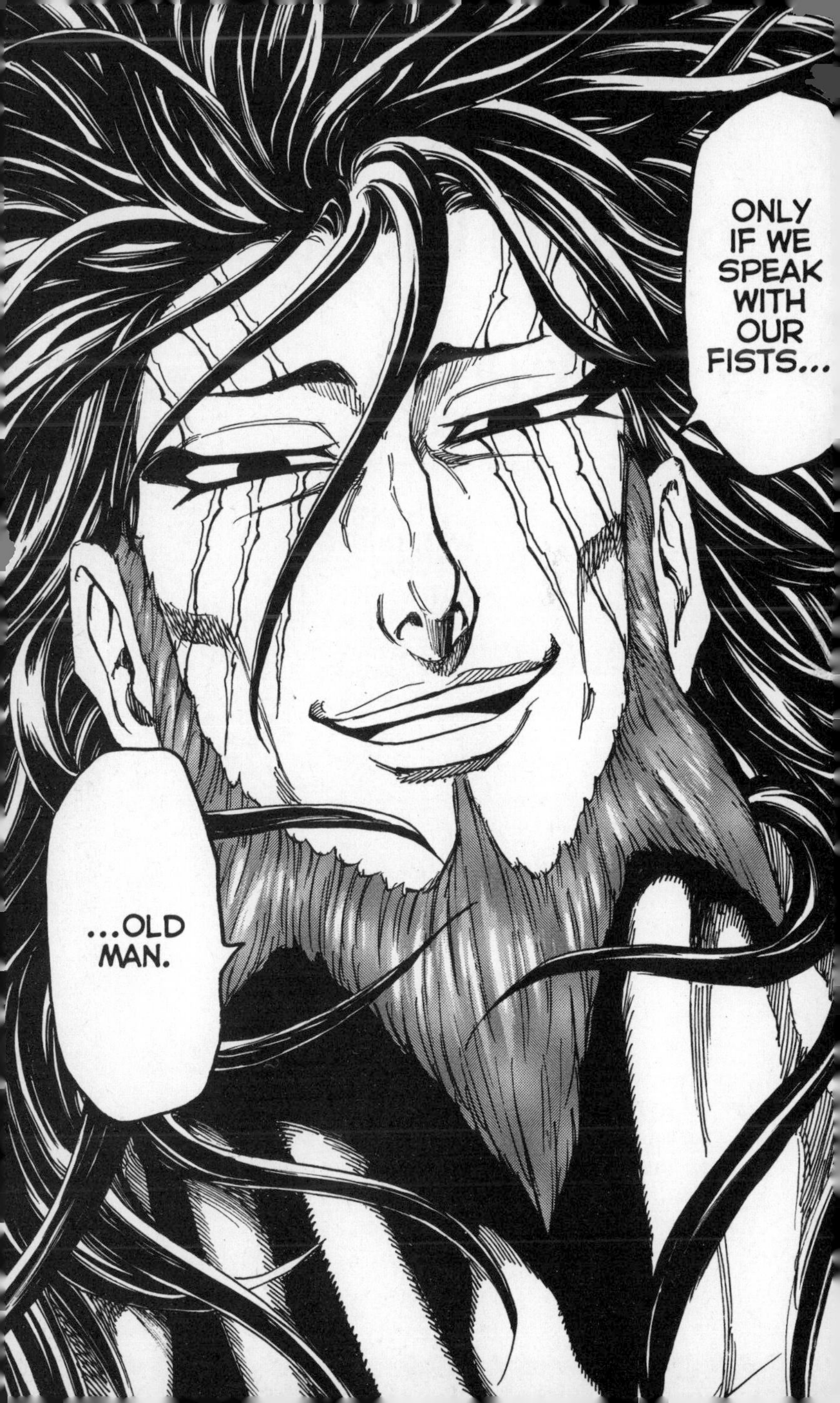
ONLY IF WE SPEAK WITH OUR FISTS...
...OLD MAN.

TORIKO

GOURMET CHECKLIST

Vol. 274

KELP SNAKE
(REPTILE)

CAPTURE LEVEL: 21
HABITAT: STEW POND
SIZE: 80 CM
HEIGHT: ---
WEIGHT: 1.5 KG
PRICE: 5,000 YEN PER SNAKE

...TURNS THE WATER INTO A NATURAL SOUP BROTH! IT'S LIKE THE ULTIMATE NABE STEW POT OF JAPANESE CUISINE.

SCALE

LIKE THE SEAWEED SNAKE IN THE PREVIOUS ENTRY, THIS SNAKE LIVES IN STEW POND, A LAKE THAT IS A CANDIDATE FOR A WORLD GOURMET HERITAGE SITE. WHEN HEATED, ITS BODY EXCRETES COMPONENTS THAT TASTE LIKE HIGH-QUALITY KELP. MORE OFTEN THAN NOT, KELP SNAKE IS USED AS A BROTH BASE RATHER THAN EATEN AS A FOOD ITSELF. KELP RAMEN IS A POPULAR LOCAL DISH IN TOWNS NEAR STEW POND.

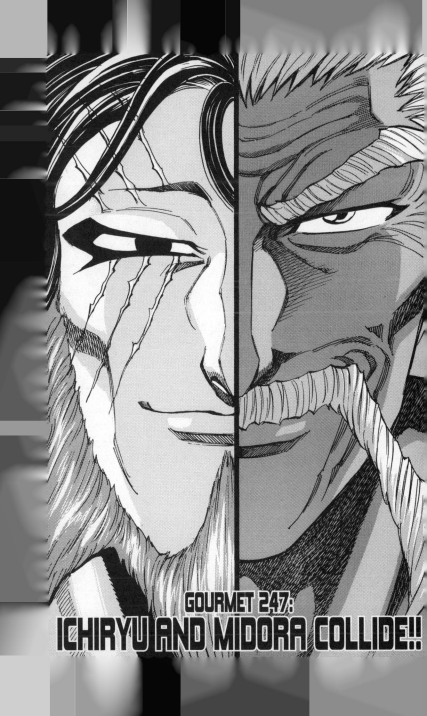

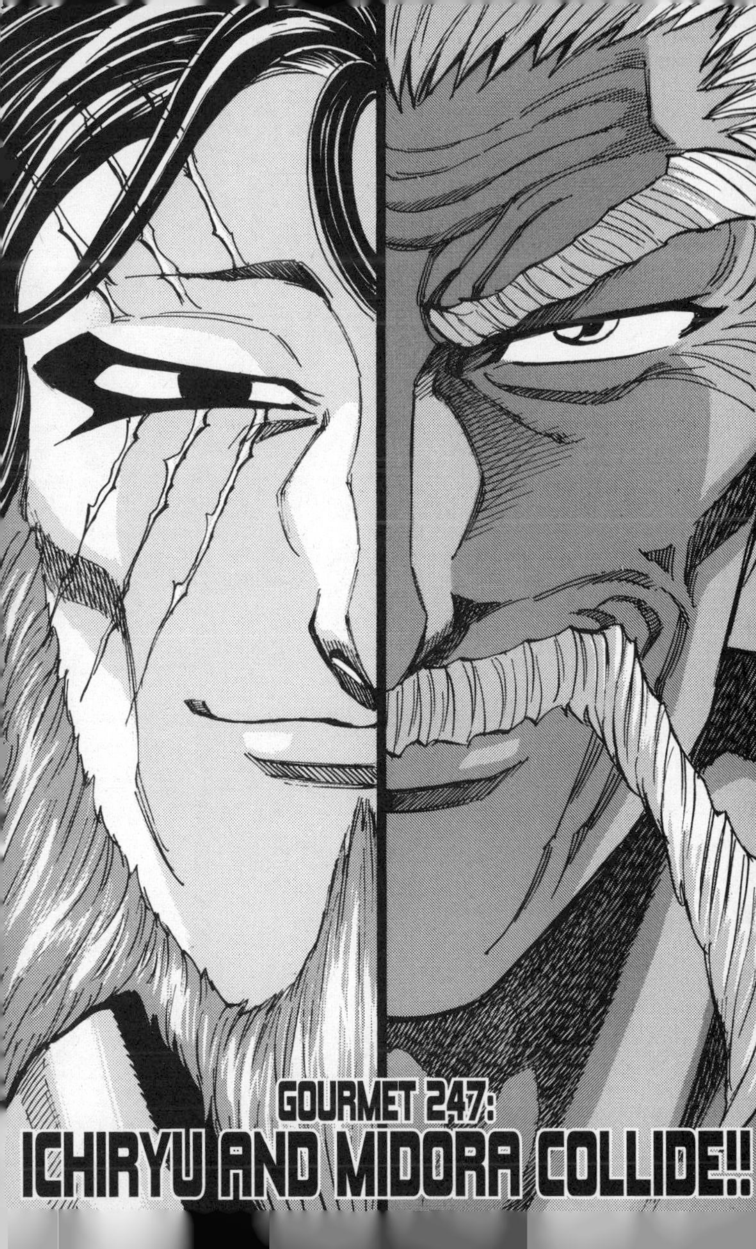
GOURMET 247:
ICHIRYU AND MIDORA COLLIDE!!

LET'S TAKE THINGS NICE AND EASY...

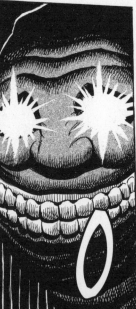

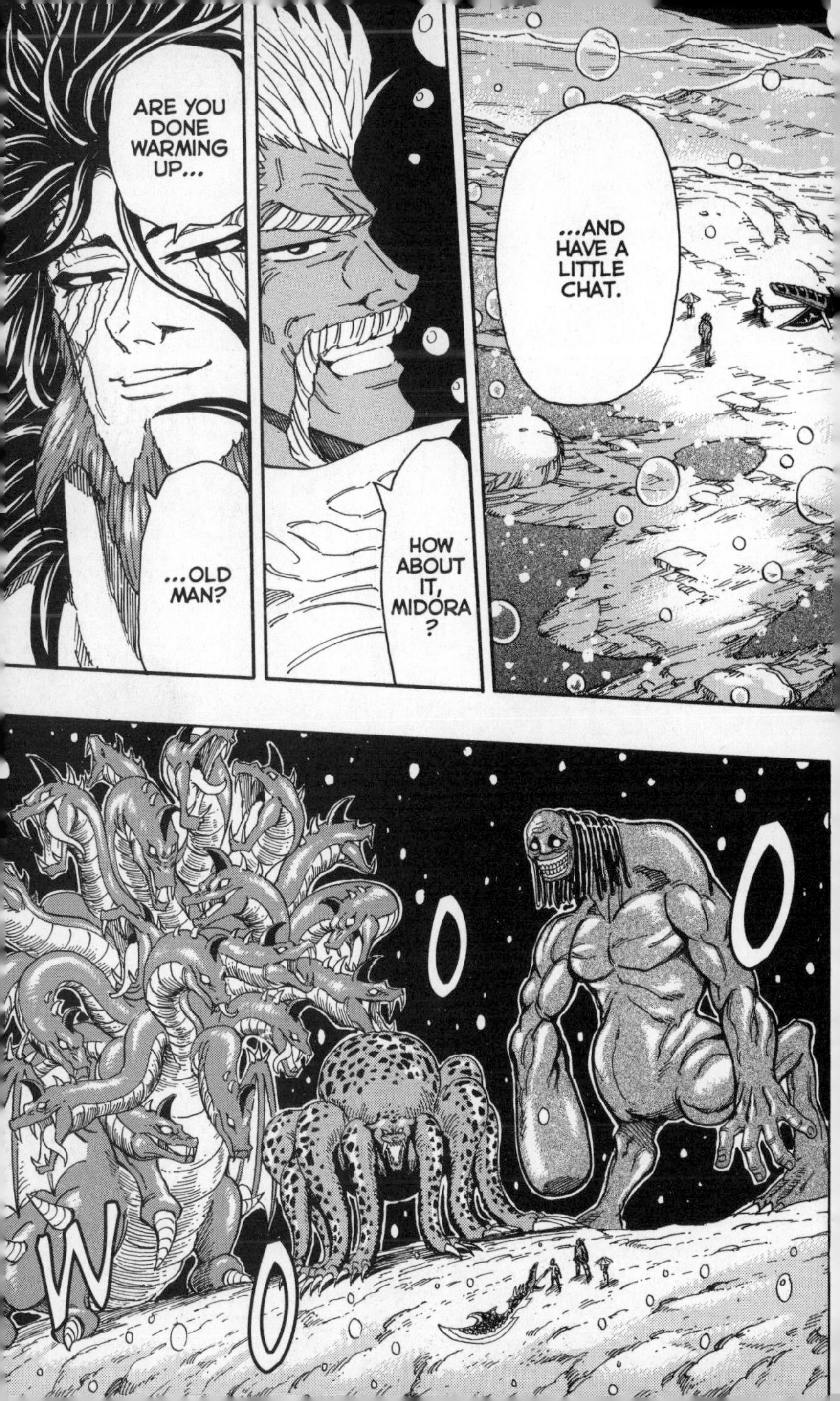
...AND HAVE A LITTLE CHAT.
HOW ABOUT IT, MIDORA?
ARE YOU DONE WARMING UP...
...OLD MAN?
WOOO

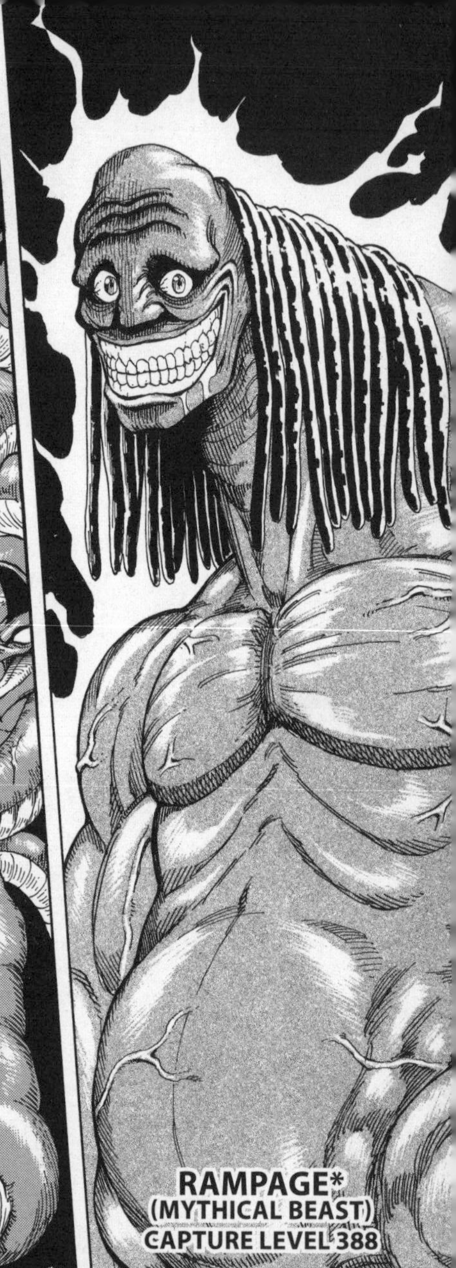
RAMPAGE*
(MYTHICAL BEAST)
CAPTURE LEVEL 388

*RAMPAGE SUBMITTED BY SURPRISED PERSON FROM TOKYO!

*TORNADO RADON SUBMITTED BY SAYUMI KATSUHARA FROM NAGANO!

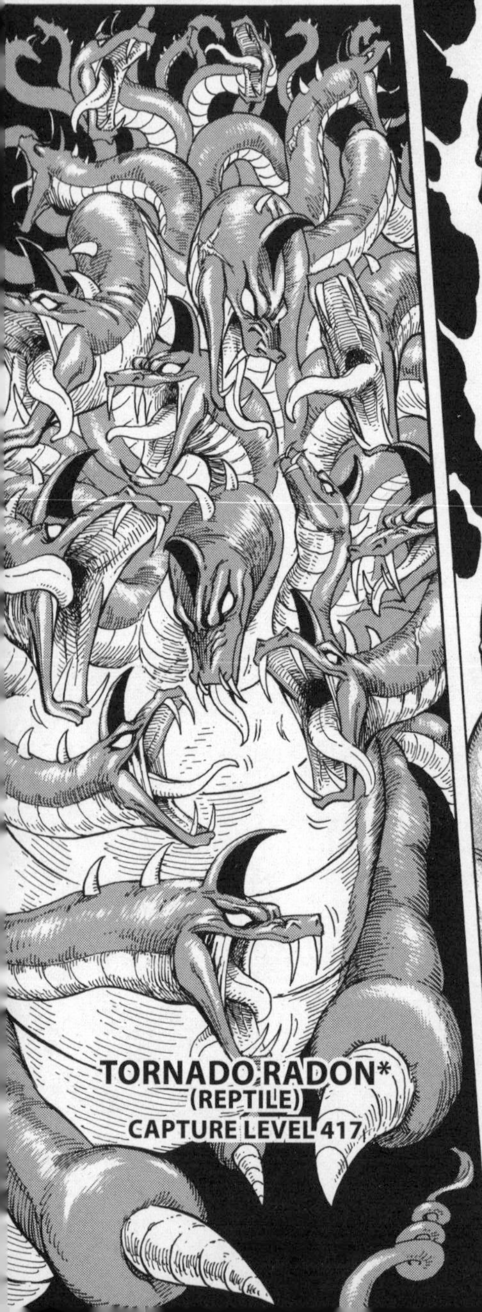
TORNADO RADON*
(REPTILE)
CAPTURE LEVEL 417

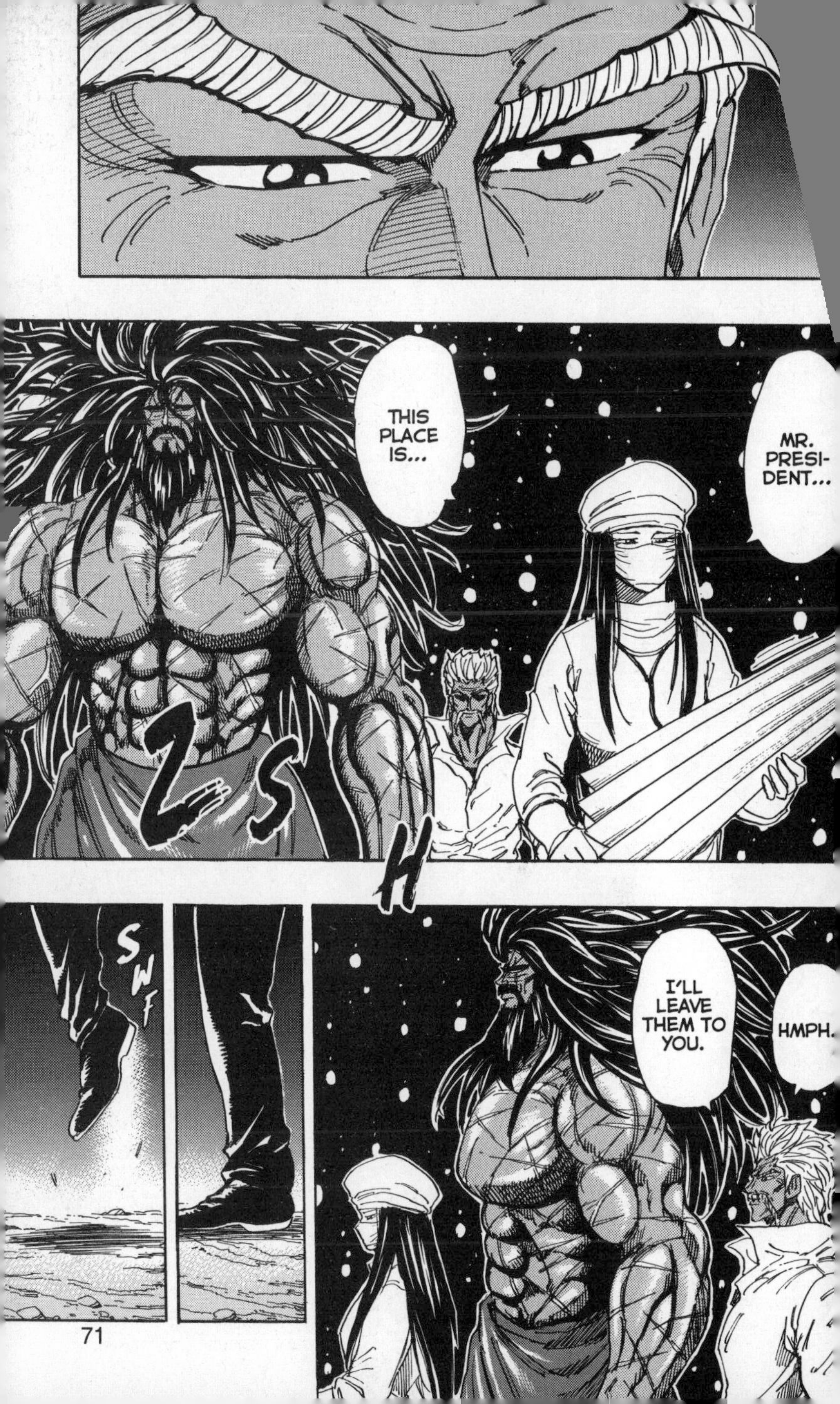

MR. PRESIDENT...
THIS PLACE IS...
ZSSH
HMPH.
I'LL LEAVE THEM TO YOU.
SWF

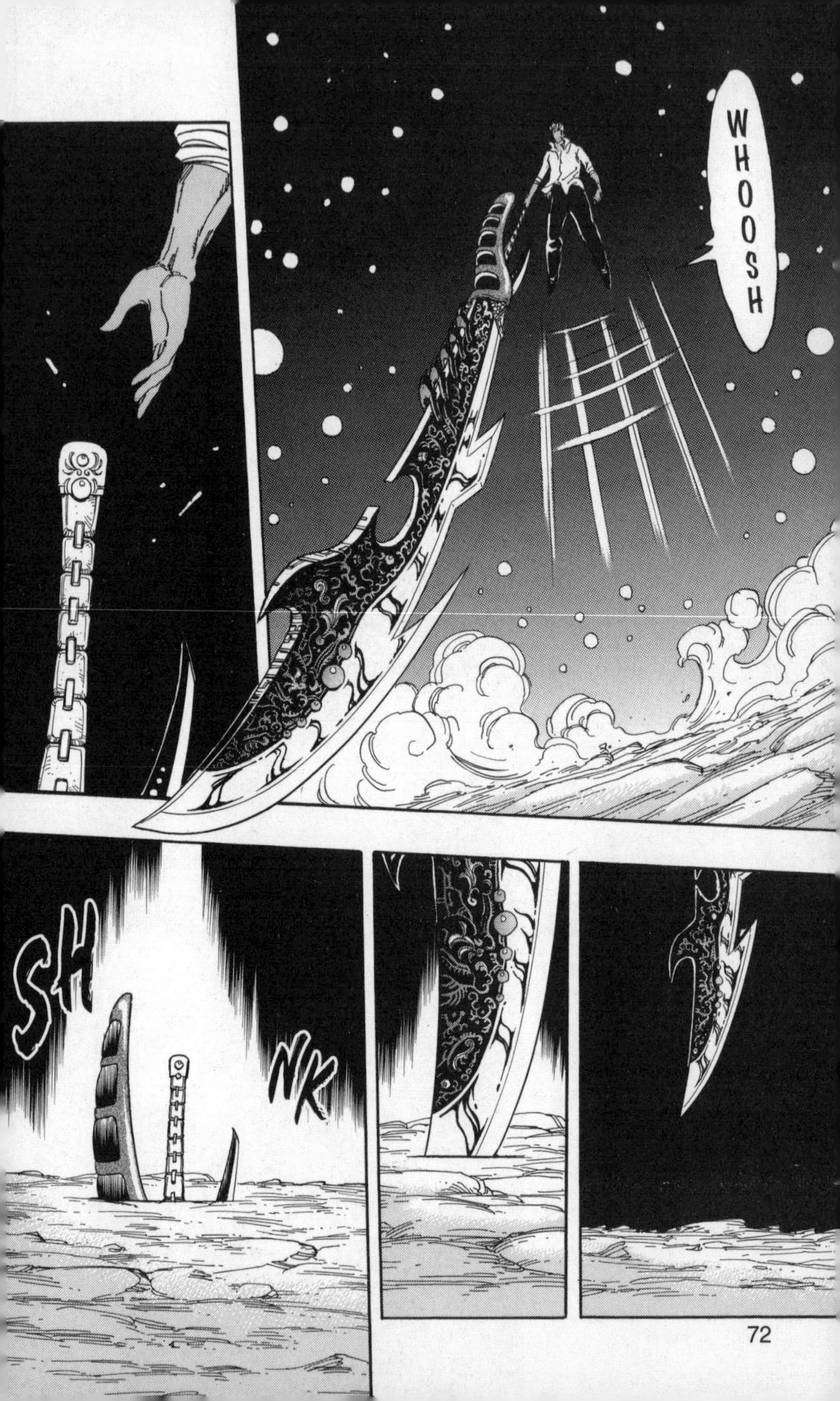
WHOOSH
SH NK

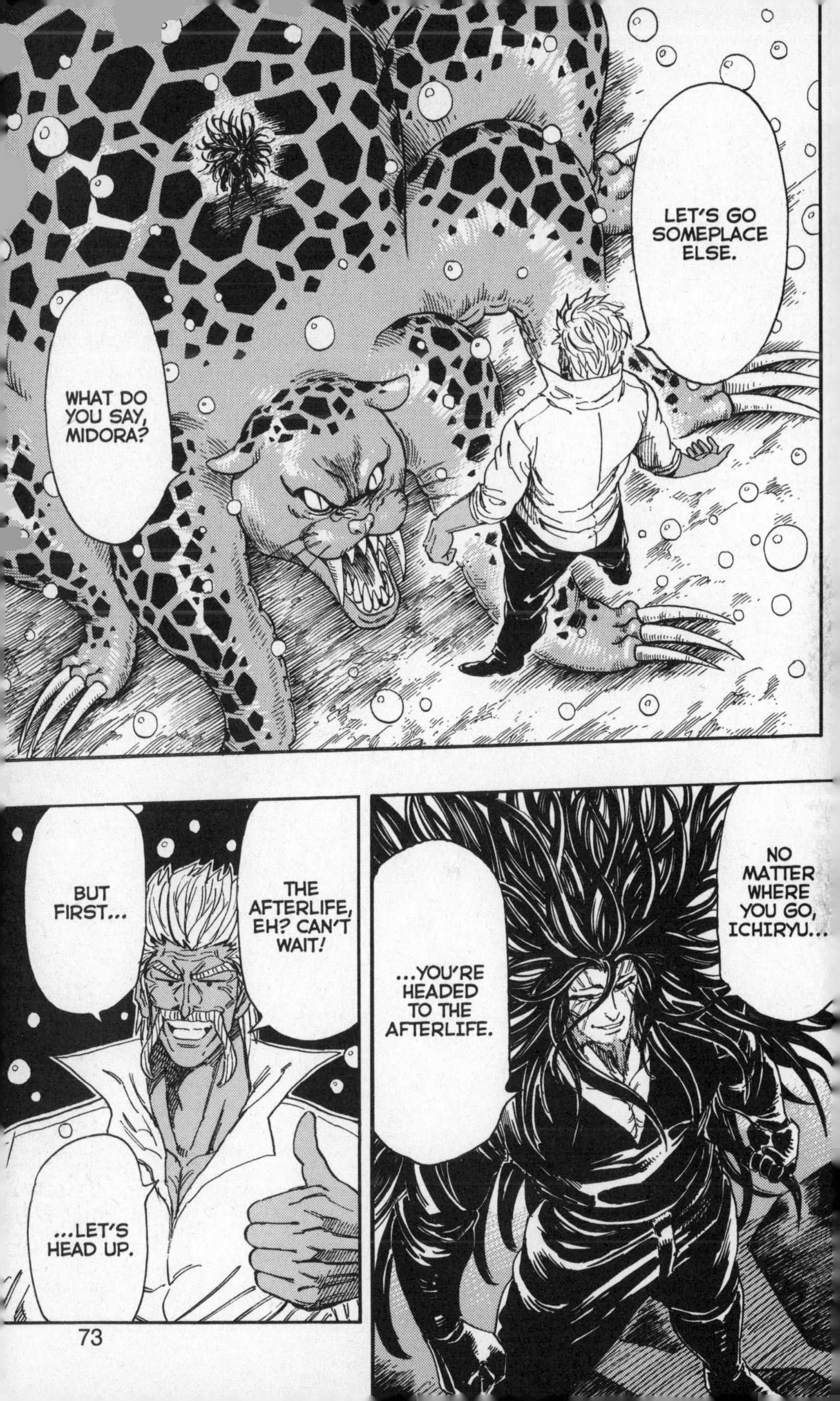
LET'S GO SOMEPLACE ELSE.
WHAT DO YOU SAY, MIDORA?
NO MATTER WHERE YOU GO, ICHIRYU...
...YOU'RE HEADED TO THE AFTERLIFE.
THE AFTERLIFE, EH? CAN'T WAIT!
BUT FIRST...
...LET'S HEAD UP.

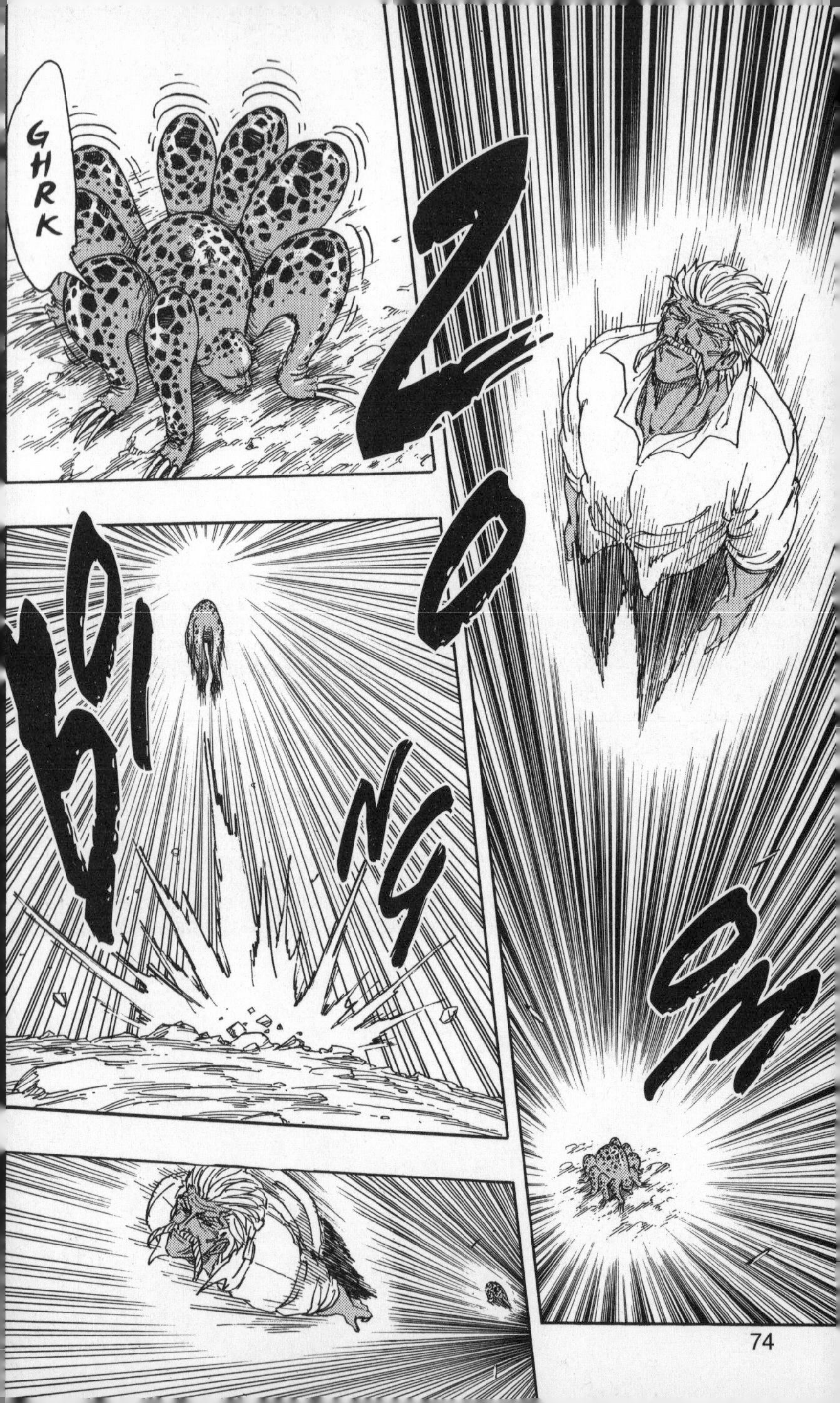
ZOOOM
GHRK
BOING

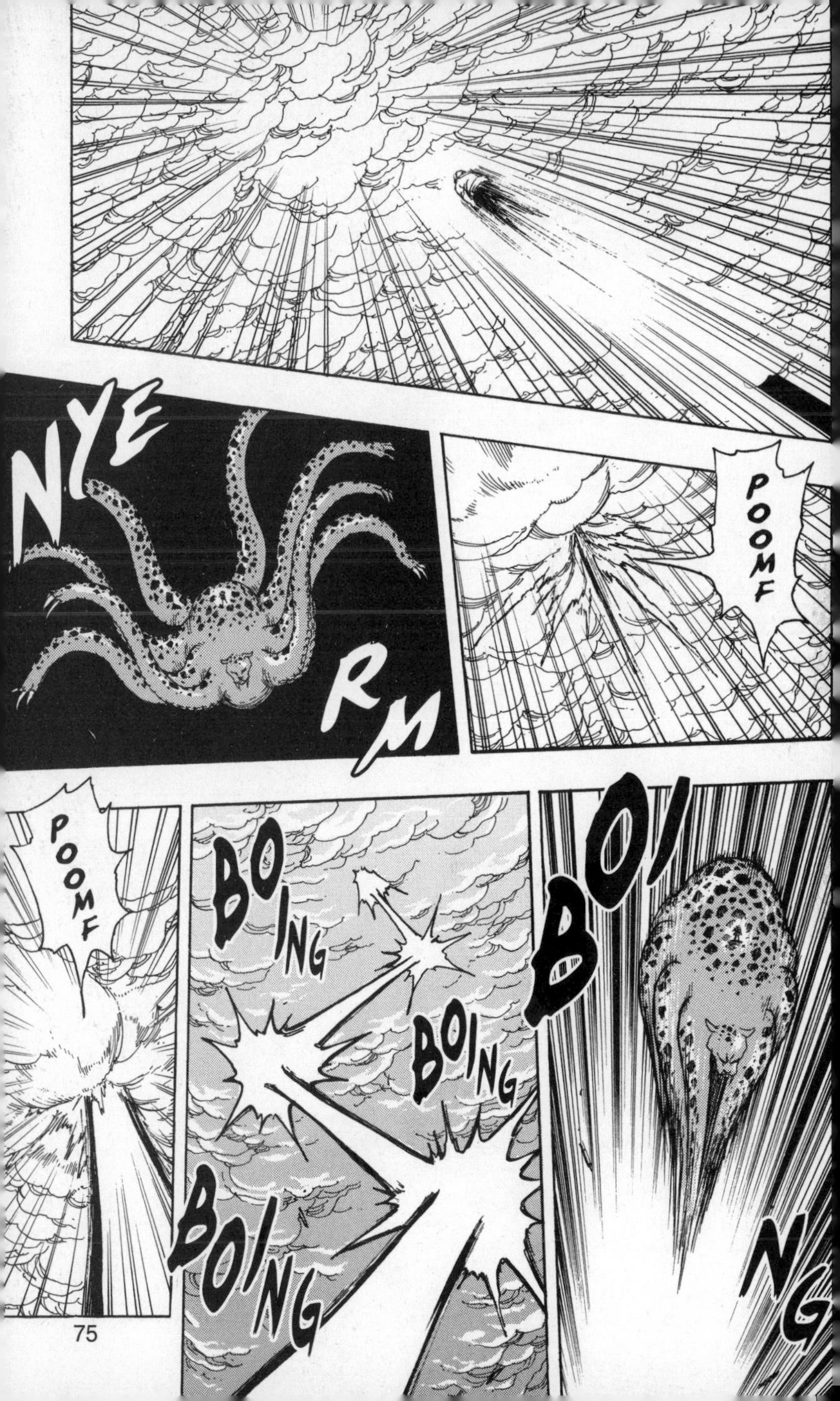
POOMF
NYERM
BOING
BOING
BOING
BOING
POOMF

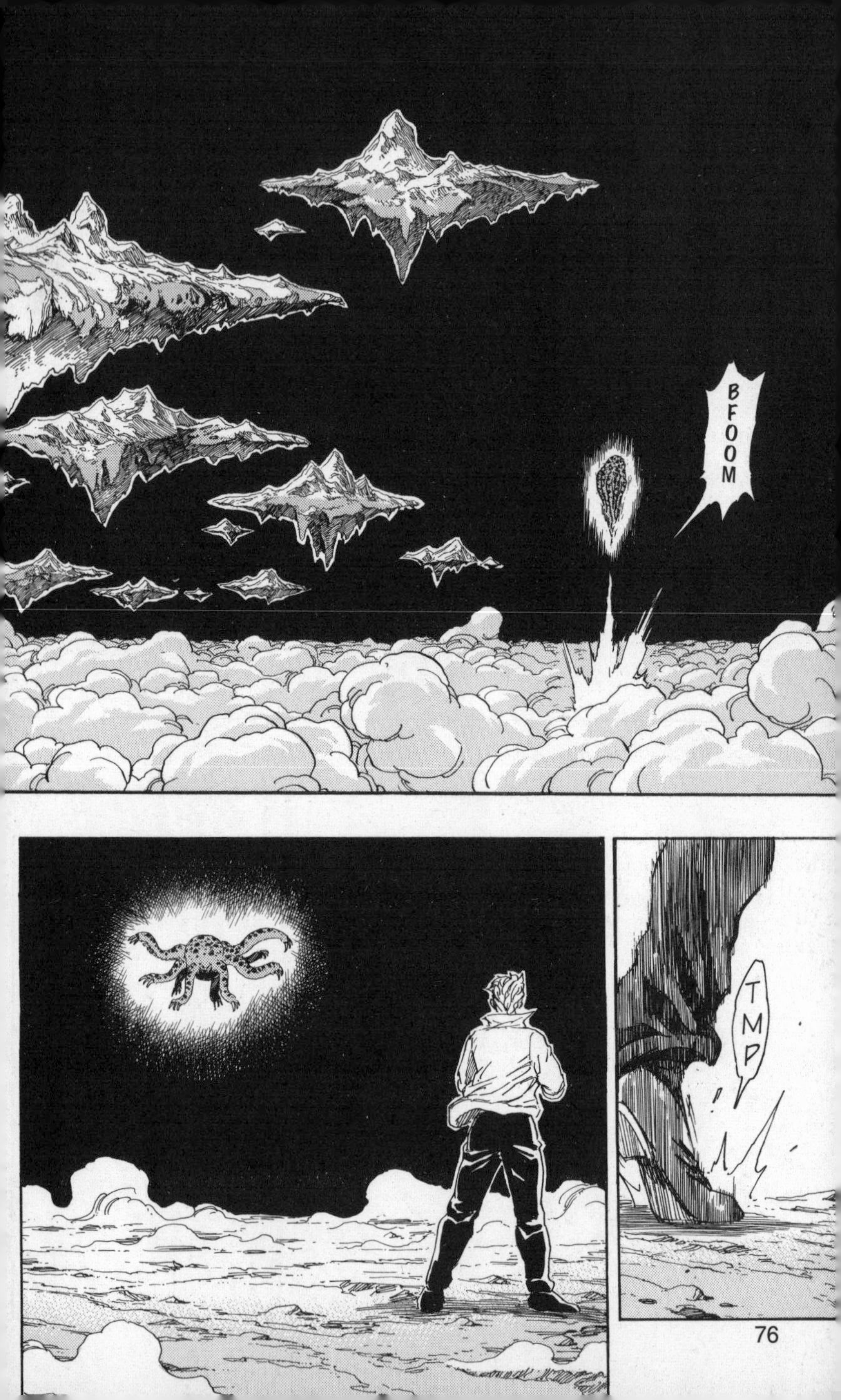
BFOOM
TMP

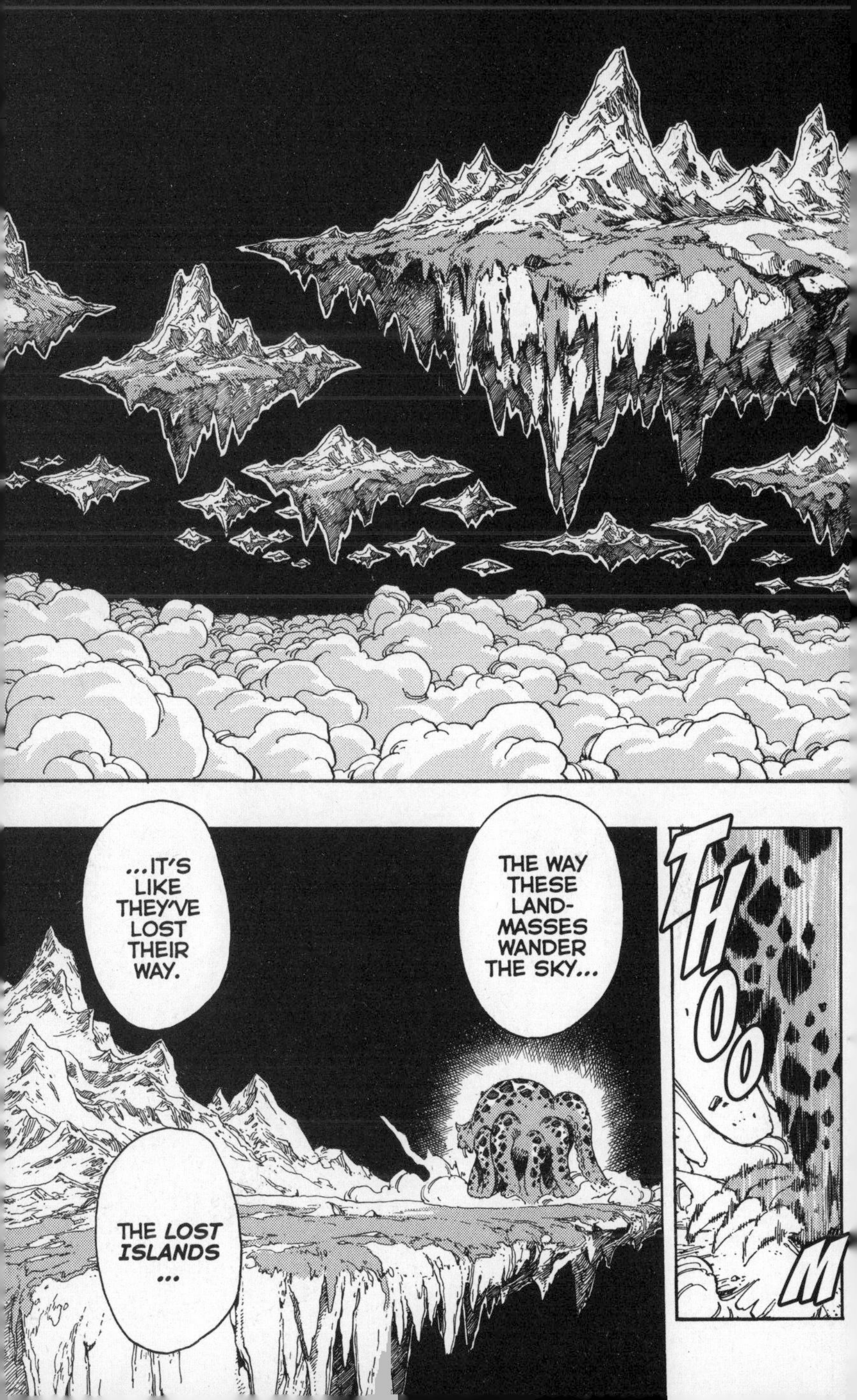
THOOOM
THE WAY THESE LANDMASSES WANDER THE SKY...
...IT'S LIKE THEY'VE LOST THEIR WAY.
THE *LOST ISLANDS*...

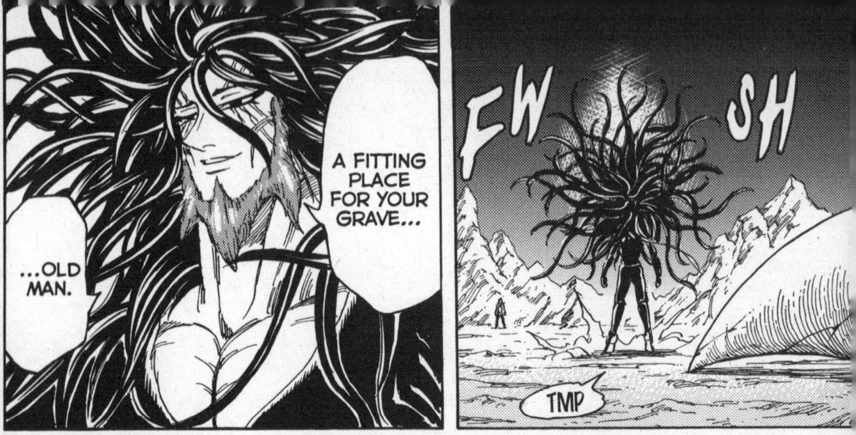
FW
SH
TMP
A FITTING PLACE FOR YOUR GRAVE...
...OLD MAN.

*GORON BEAST SUBMITTED BY TETSUYA YAMAOKA FROM HYOGO!

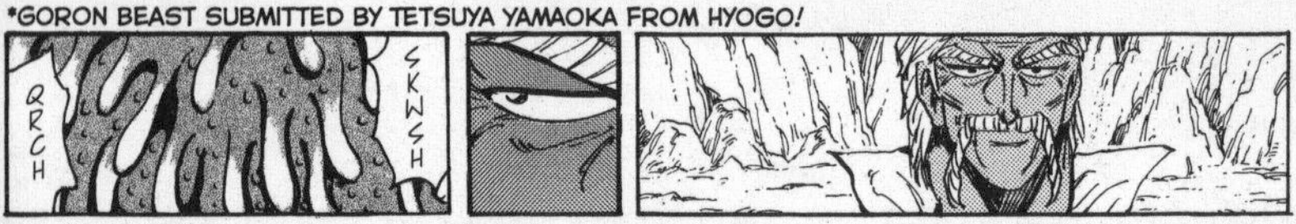
SKWSH
QRCH

*RIPPER THE FOX SUBMITTED BY YUSUKE YAOMURA FROM SHIZUOKA!

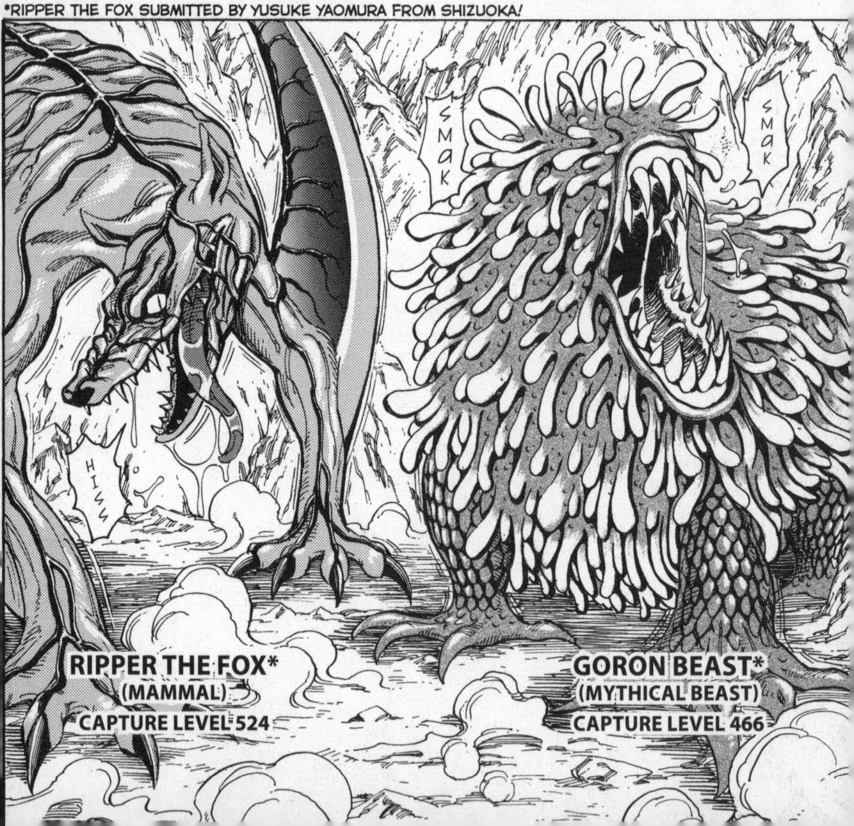
SMAK
SMAK
GORON BEAST*
(MYTHICAL BEAST)
CAPTURE LEVEL 466
HISS
RIPPER THE FOX*
(MAMMAL)
CAPTURE LEVEL 524

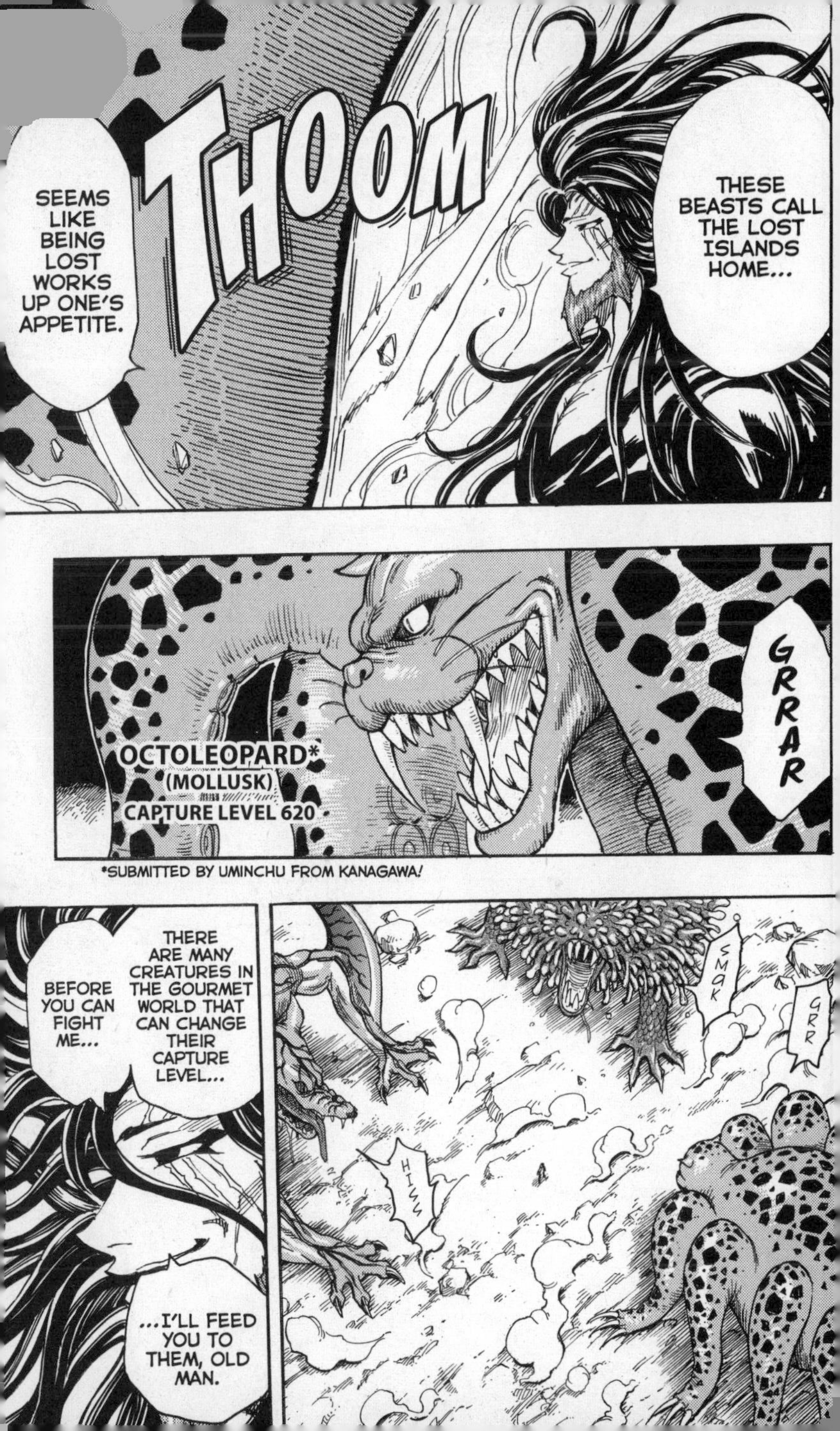
THESE BEASTS CALL THE LOST ISLANDS HOME...
THOOM
SEEMS LIKE BEING LOST WORKS UP ONE'S APPETITE.
GRRAR
OCTOLEOPARD*
(MOLLUSK)
CAPTURE LEVEL 620
*SUBMITTED BY UMINCHU FROM KANAGAWA!
SMAK
GRR
HISS
THERE ARE MANY CREATURES IN THE GOURMET WORLD THAT CAN CHANGE THEIR CAPTURE LEVEL...
BEFORE YOU CAN FIGHT ME...
...I'LL FEED YOU TO THEM, OLD MAN.

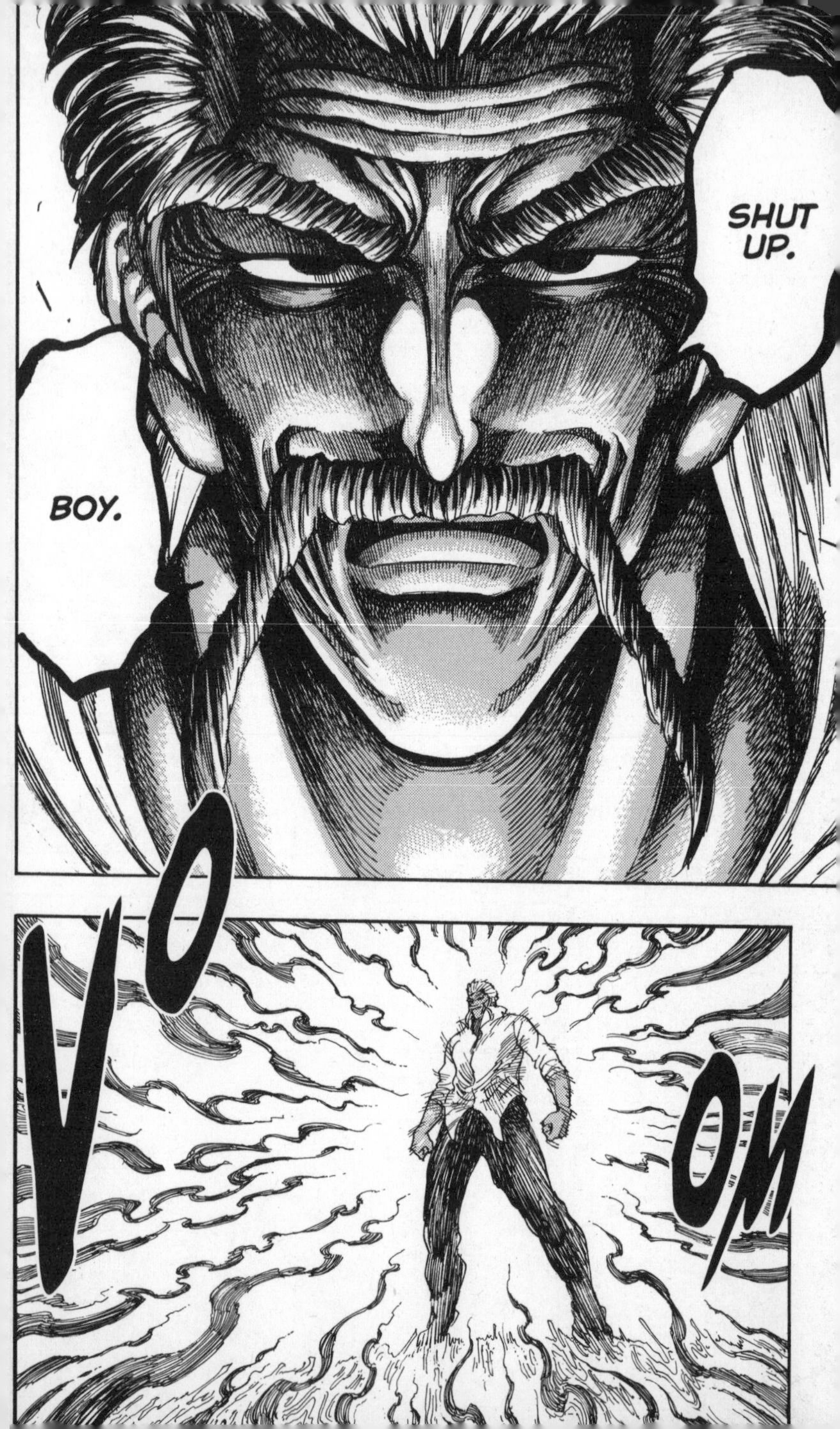
SHUT UP.
BOY.
VOOM

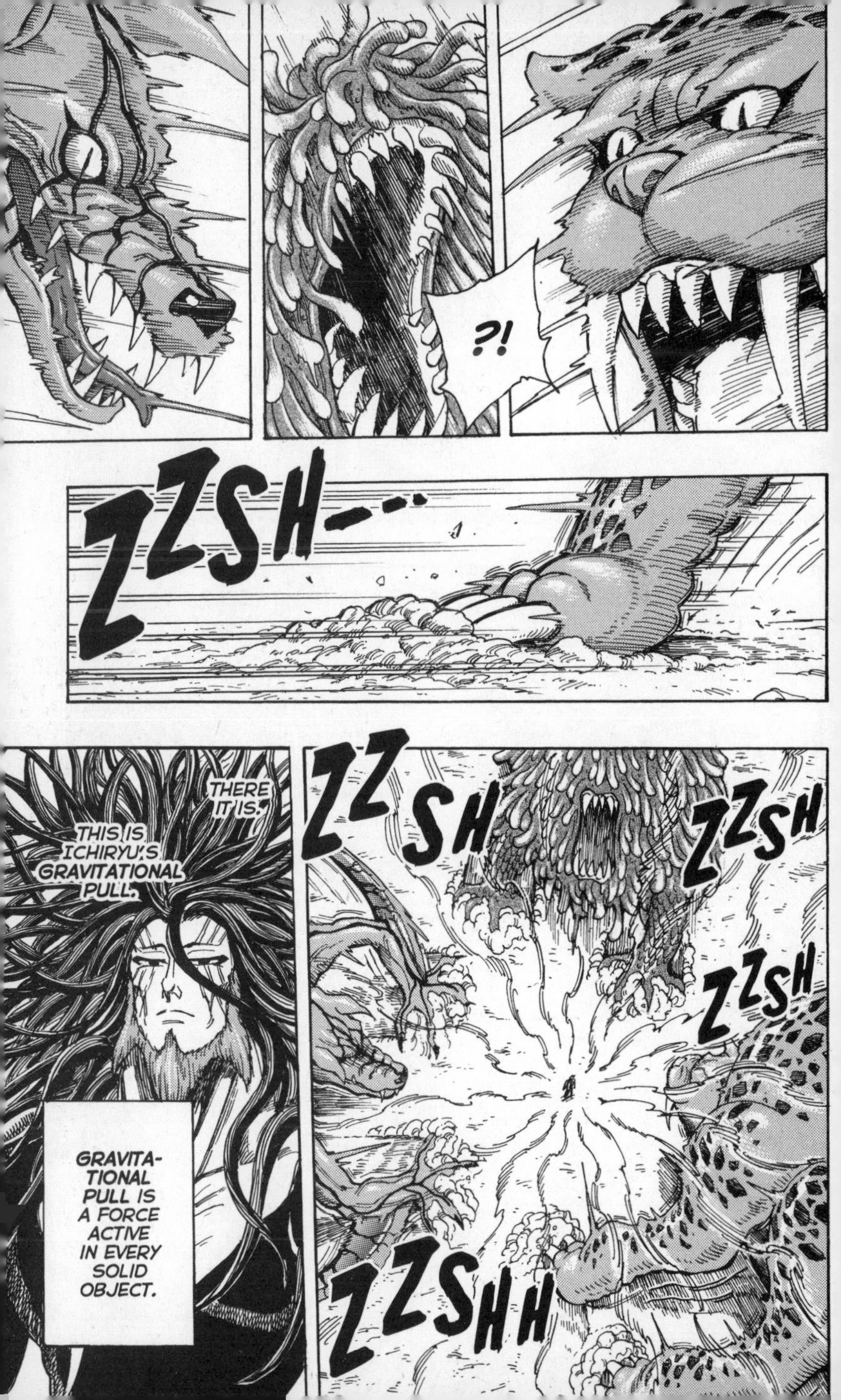
?!
ZZSH---
ZZSH
ZZSH
ZZSH
ZZSHH
THERE IT IS.
THIS IS ICHIRYU'S GRAVITATIONAL PULL.
GRAVITA-
TIONAL
PULL IS
A FORCE
ACTIVE
IN EVERY
SOLID
OBJECT.

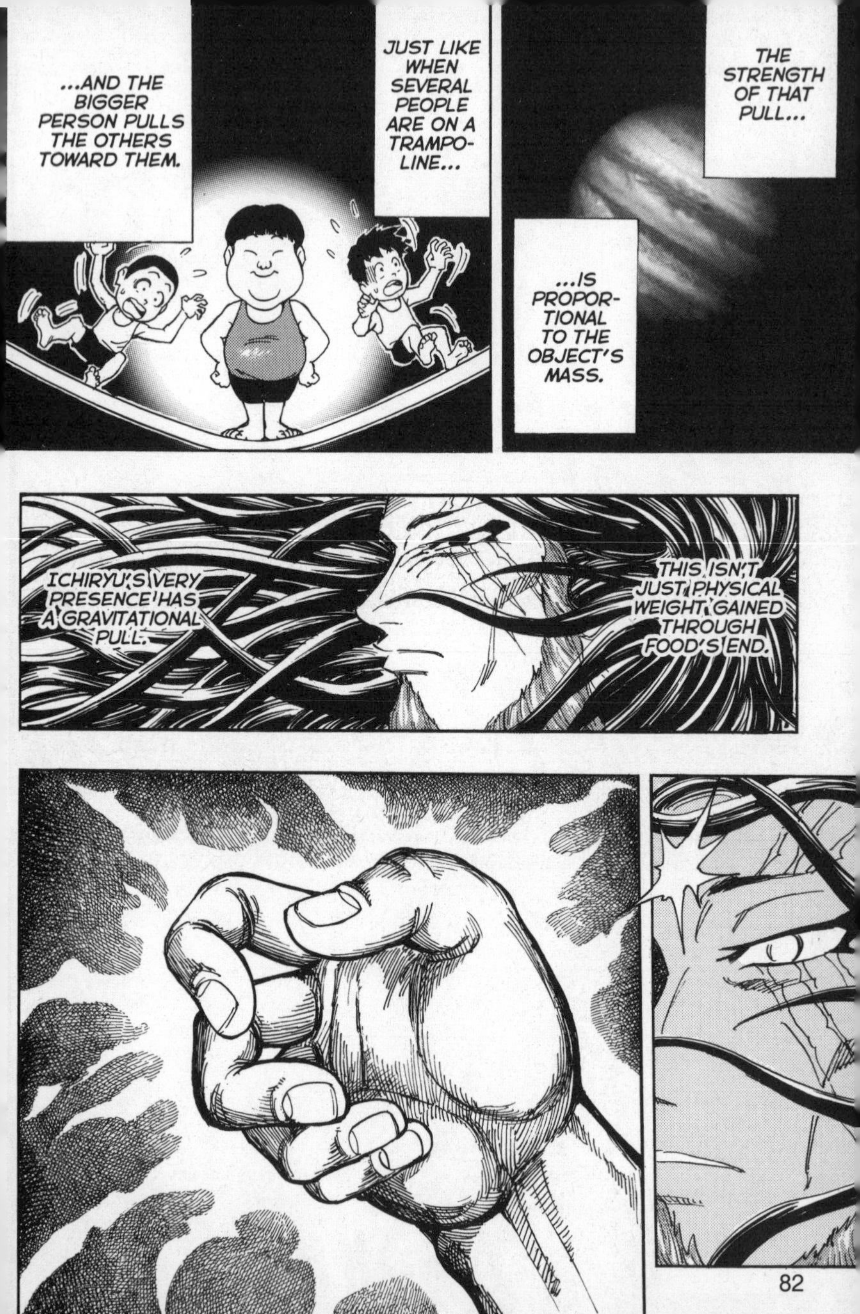
THE STRENGTH OF THAT PULL...
...IS PROPORTIONAL TO THE OBJECT'S MASS.
JUST LIKE WHEN SEVERAL PEOPLE ARE ON A TRAMPOLINE...
...AND THE BIGGER PERSON PULLS THE OTHERS TOWARD THEM.
THIS ISN'T JUST PHYSICAL WEIGHT GAINED THROUGH FOOD'S END.
ICHIRYU'S VERY PRESENCE HAS A GRAVITATIONAL PULL.

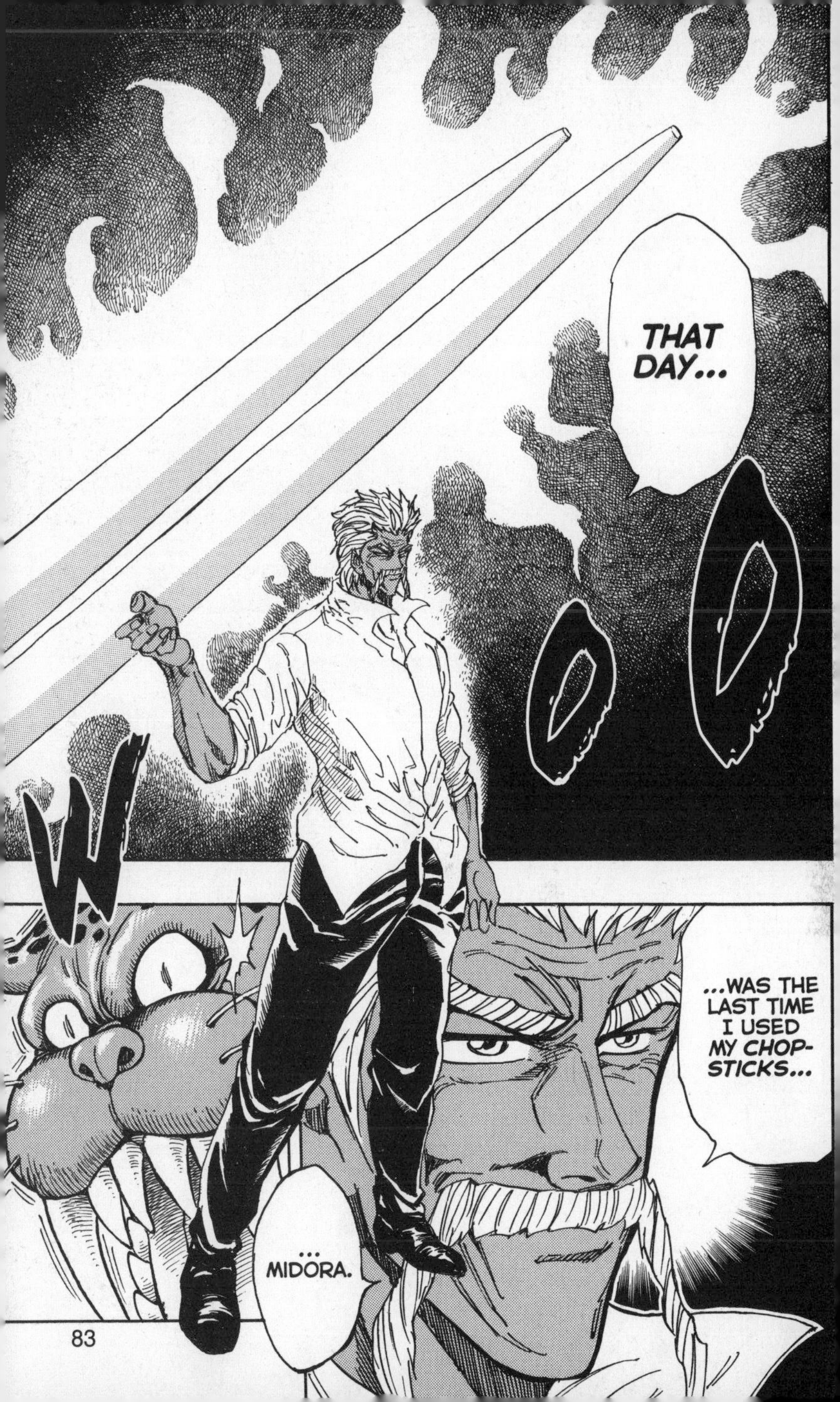
THAT DAY...
...WAS THE LAST TIME I USED MY CHOP-STICKS...
... MIDORA.

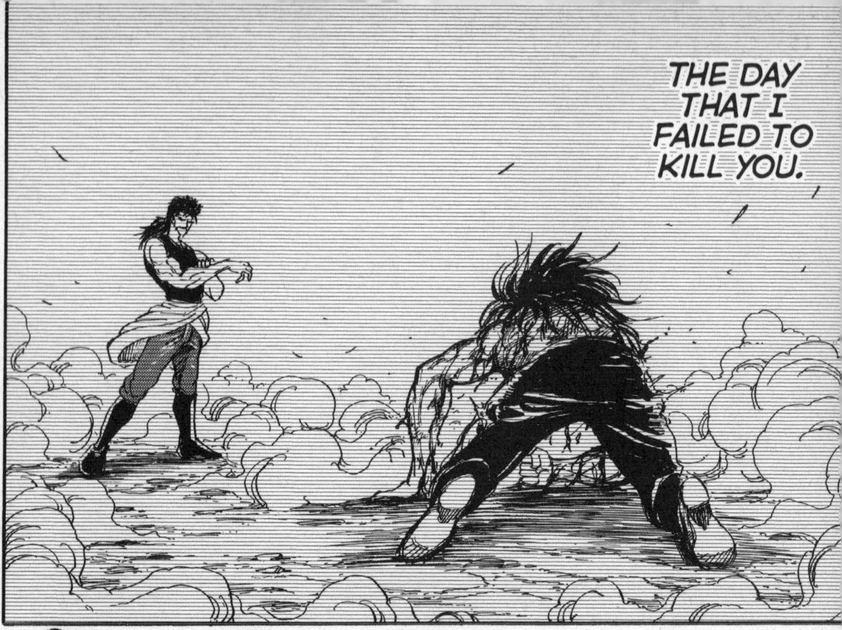
THE DAY THAT I FAILED TO KILL YOU.
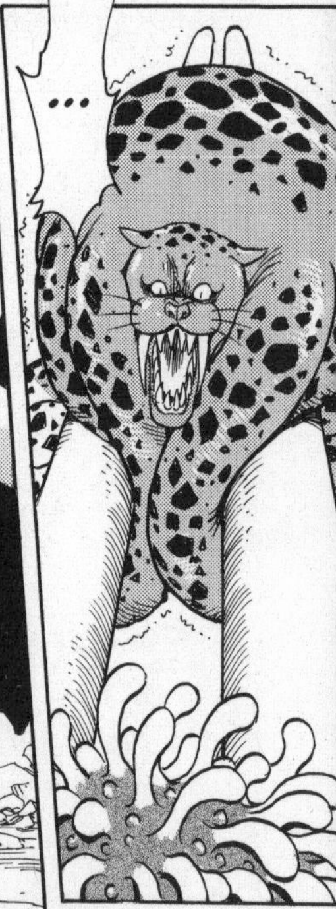
...
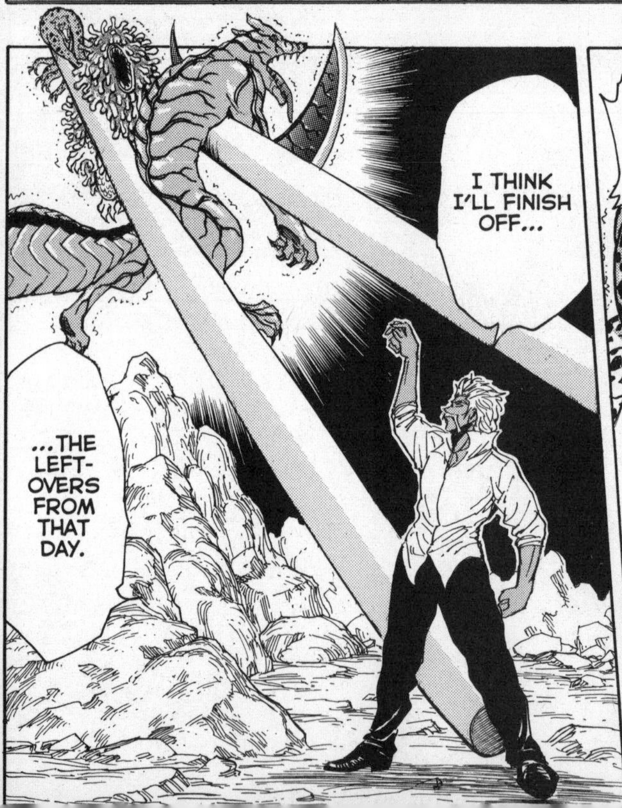
I THINK I'LL FINISH OFF...
...THE LEFT-OVERS FROM THAT DAY.

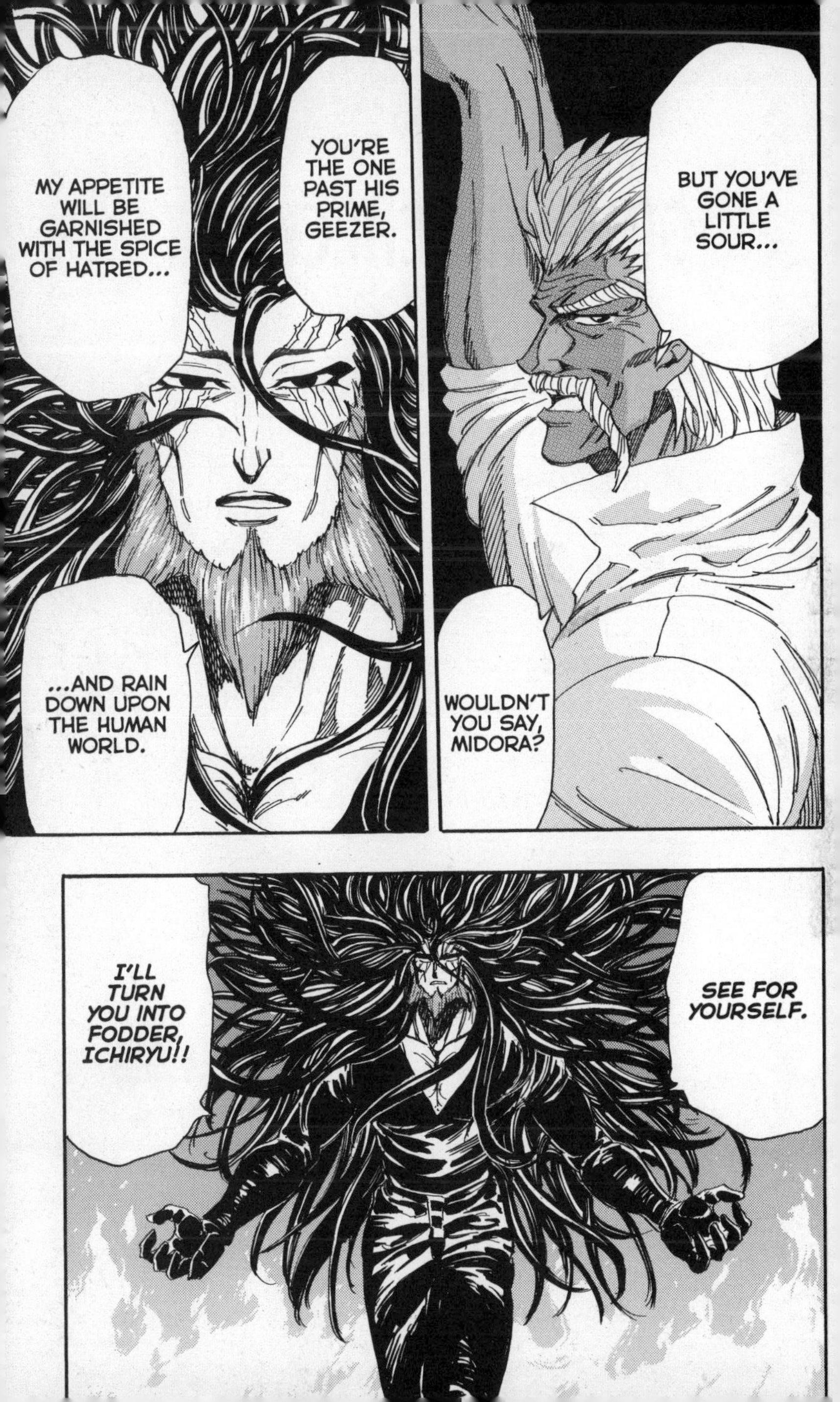
BUT YOU'VE GONE A LITTLE SOUR...
WOULDN'T YOU SAY, MIDORA?
YOU'RE THE ONE PAST HIS PRIME, GEEZER.
MY APPETITE WILL BE GARNISHED WITH THE SPICE OF HATRED...
...AND RAIN DOWN UPON THE HUMAN WORLD.
SEE FOR YOURSELF.
I'LL TURN YOU INTO FODDER, ICHIRYU!!

TORIKO

GOURMET CHECKLIST

Vol. 275

TASTY WORM

(ANNELID)

CAPTURE LEVEL: LESS THAN 1

HABITAT: FERTILE SOIL

SIZE: 7 CM

HEIGHT: ---

WEIGHT: 5 G

PRICE: 30 YEN PER WORM

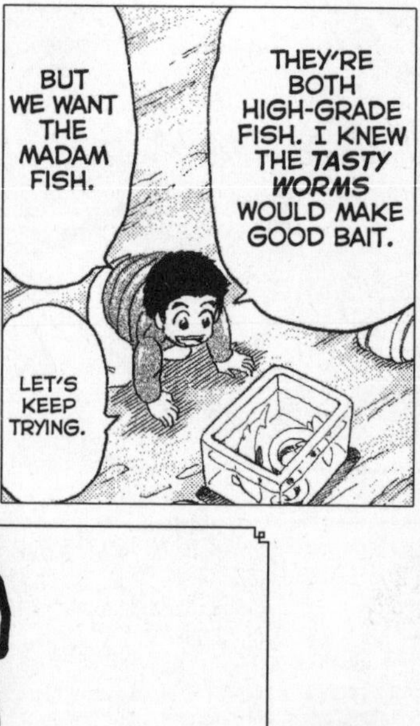
THEY'RE BOTH HIGH-GRADE FISH. I KNEW THE TASTY WORMS WOULD MAKE GOOD BAIT.
BUT WE WANT THE MADAM FISH.
LET'S KEEP TRYING.

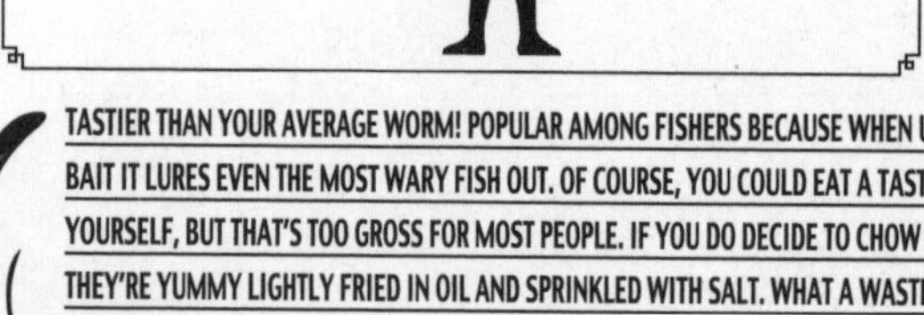

SCALE

TASTIER THAN YOUR AVERAGE WORM! POPULAR AMONG FISHERS BECAUSE WHEN USED AS BAIT IT LURES EVEN THE MOST WARY FISH OUT. OF COURSE, YOU COULD EAT A TASTY WORM YOURSELF, BUT THAT'S TOO GROSS FOR MOST PEOPLE. IF YOU DO DECIDE TO CHOW DOWN, THEY'RE YUMMY LIGHTLY FRIED IN OIL AND SPRINKLED WITH SALT. WHAT A WASTE TO FEED TO FISH!

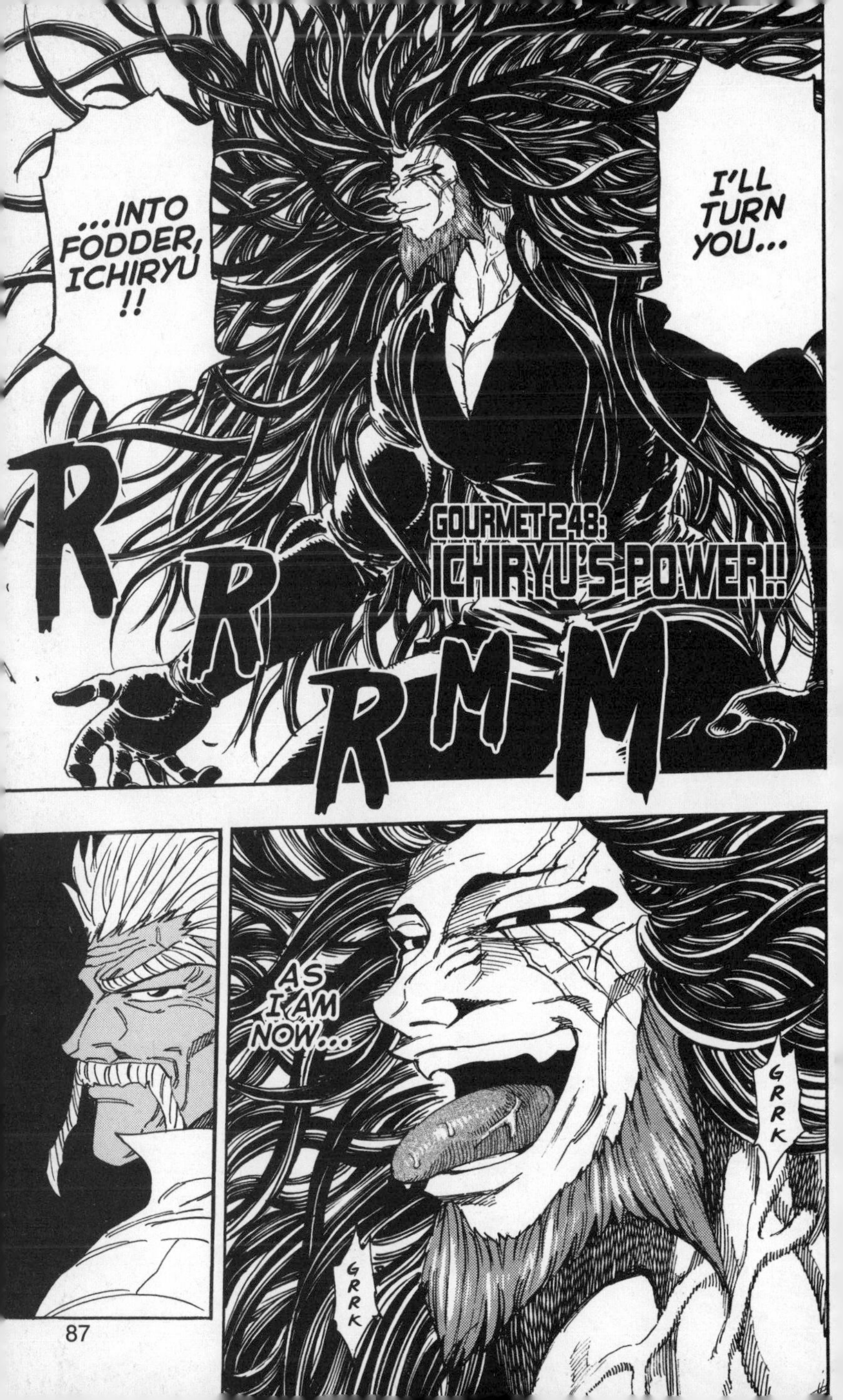
I'LL TURN YOU...
...INTO FODDER, ICHIRYU!!
GOURMET 248: ICHIRYU'S POWER!!
RRRMM
AS I AM NOW...
GRRK
GRRK

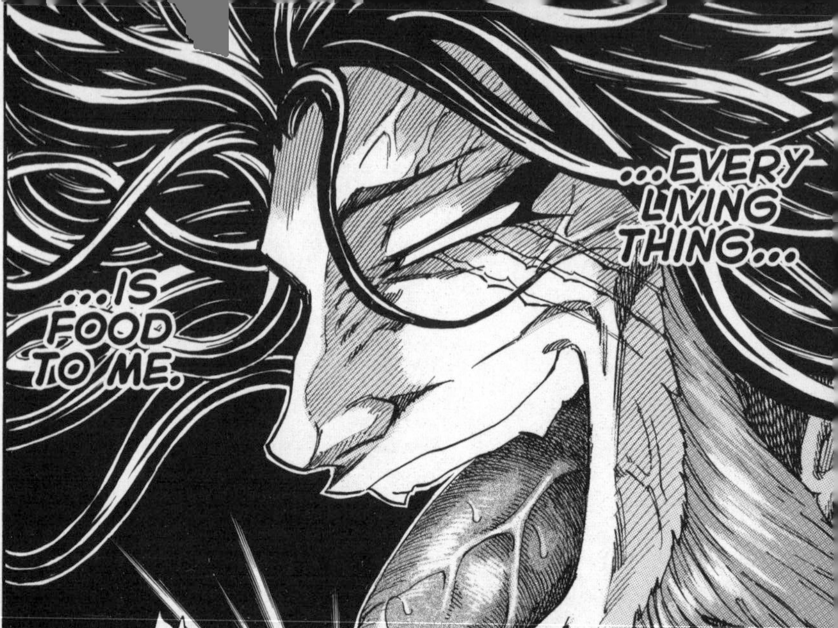
...EVERY LIVING THING...
...IS FOOD TO ME.
BLORNG

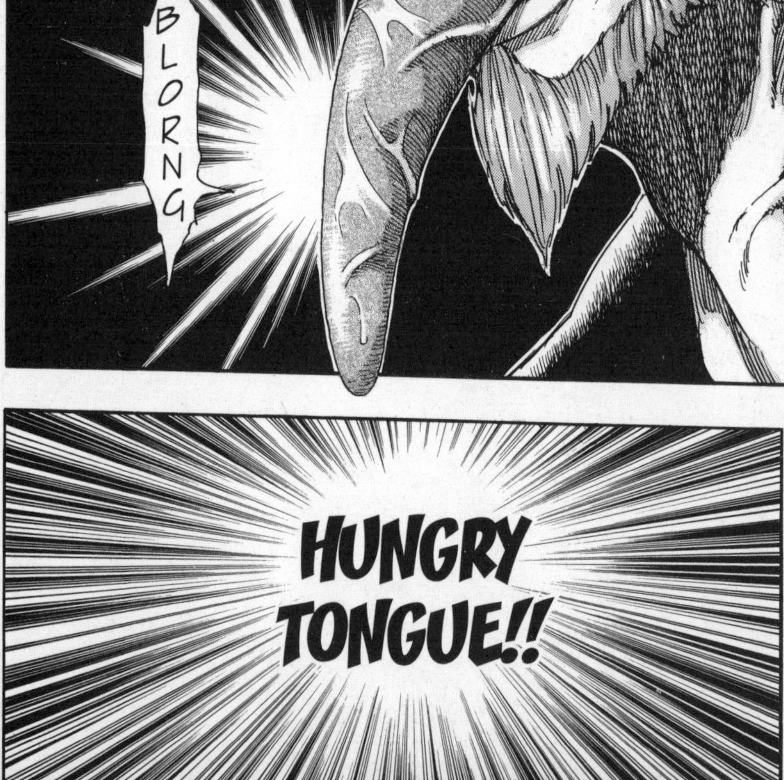
HUNGRY TONGUE!!

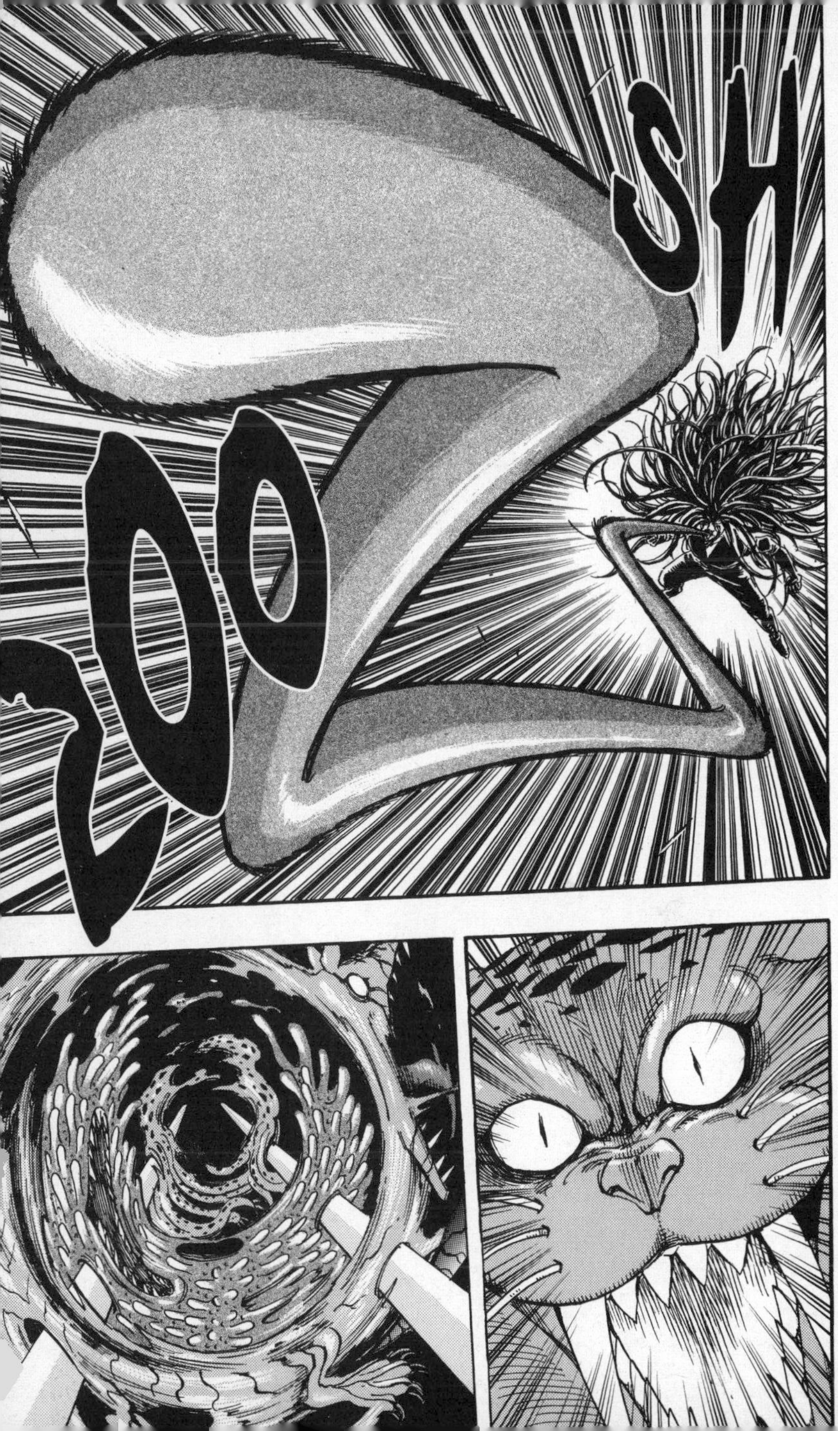
ZOOOSH

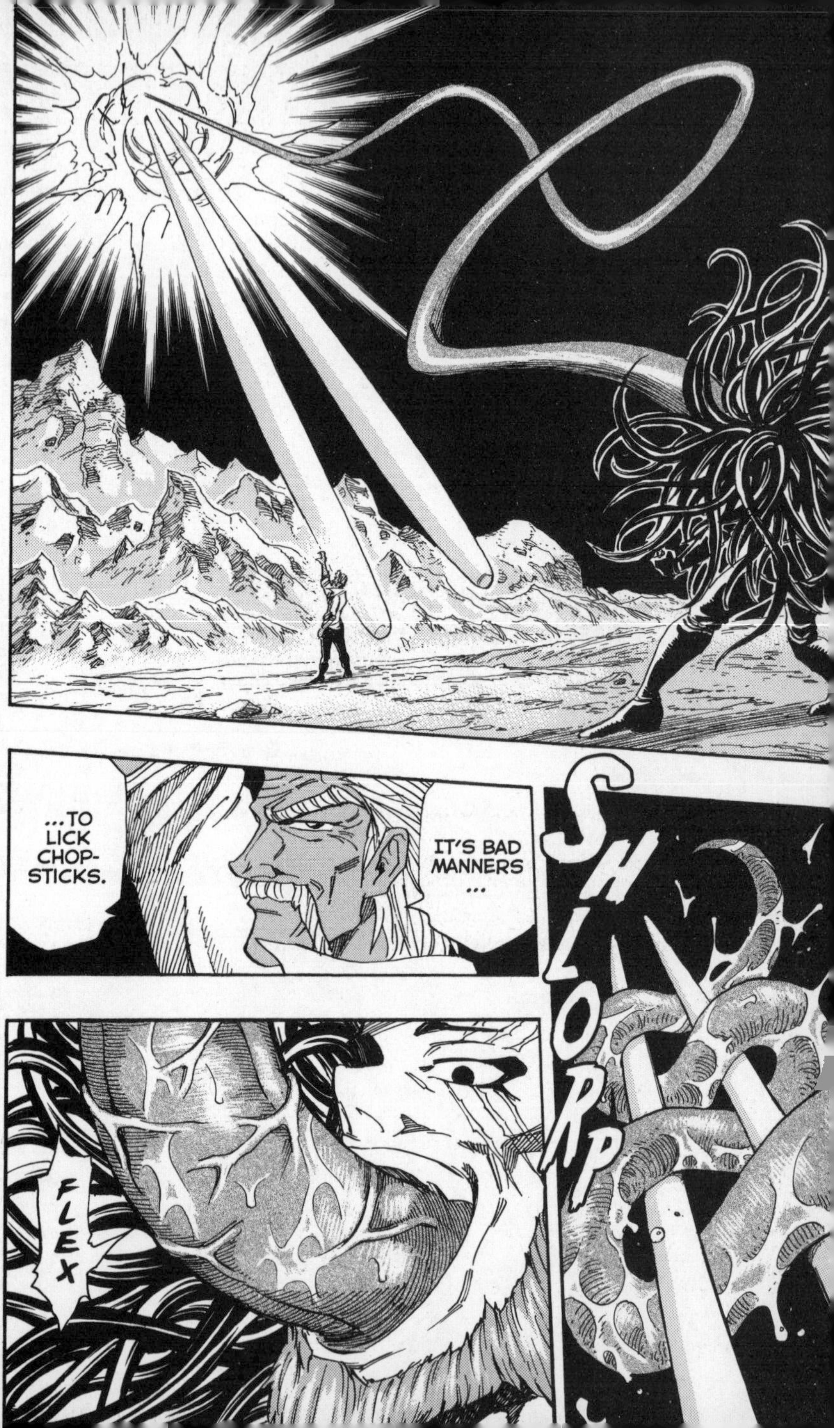
SHLORP
IT'S BAD MANNERS ...
...TO LICK CHOP-STICKS.
FLEX

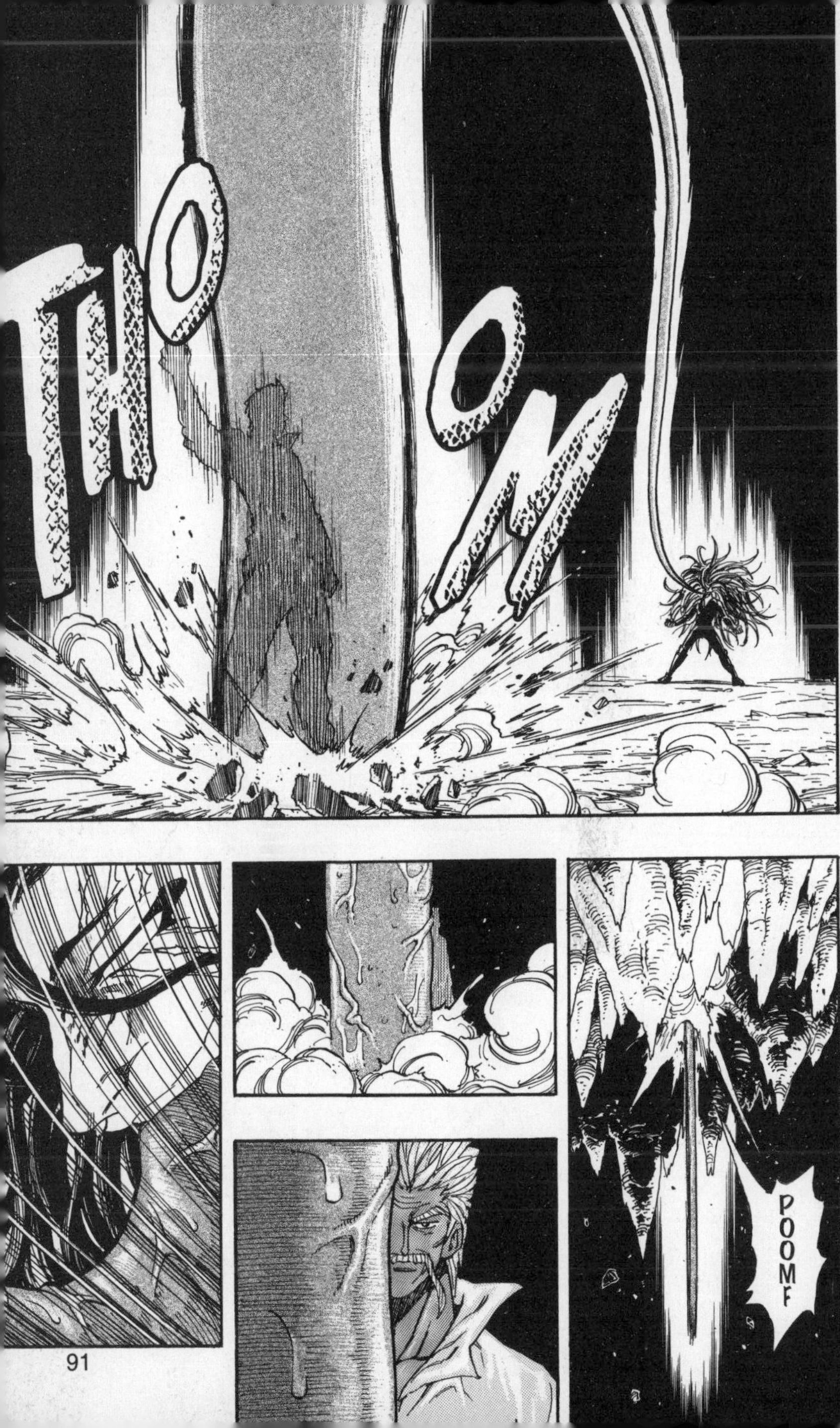
THOOM
POOMF

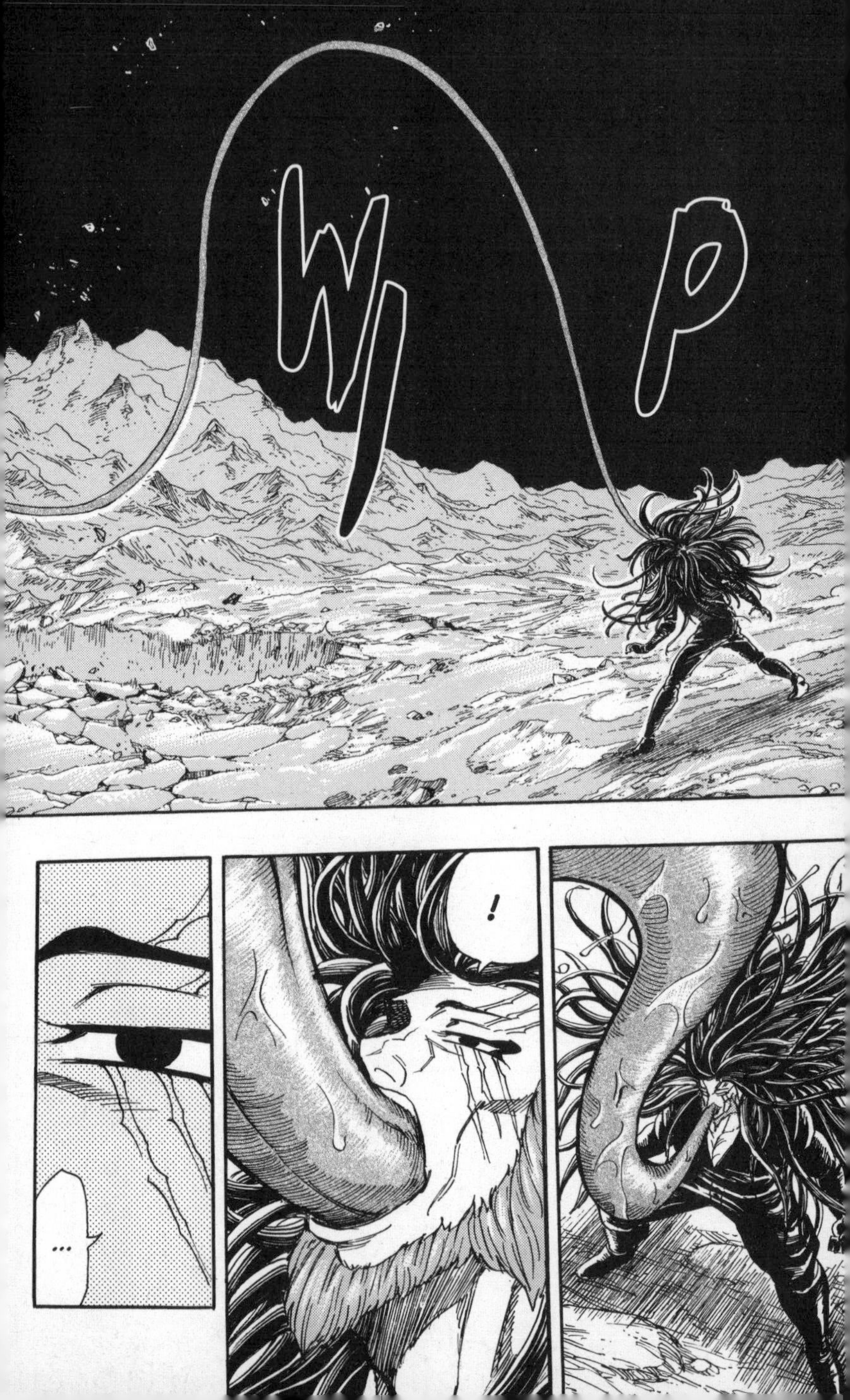
WIP
!
...

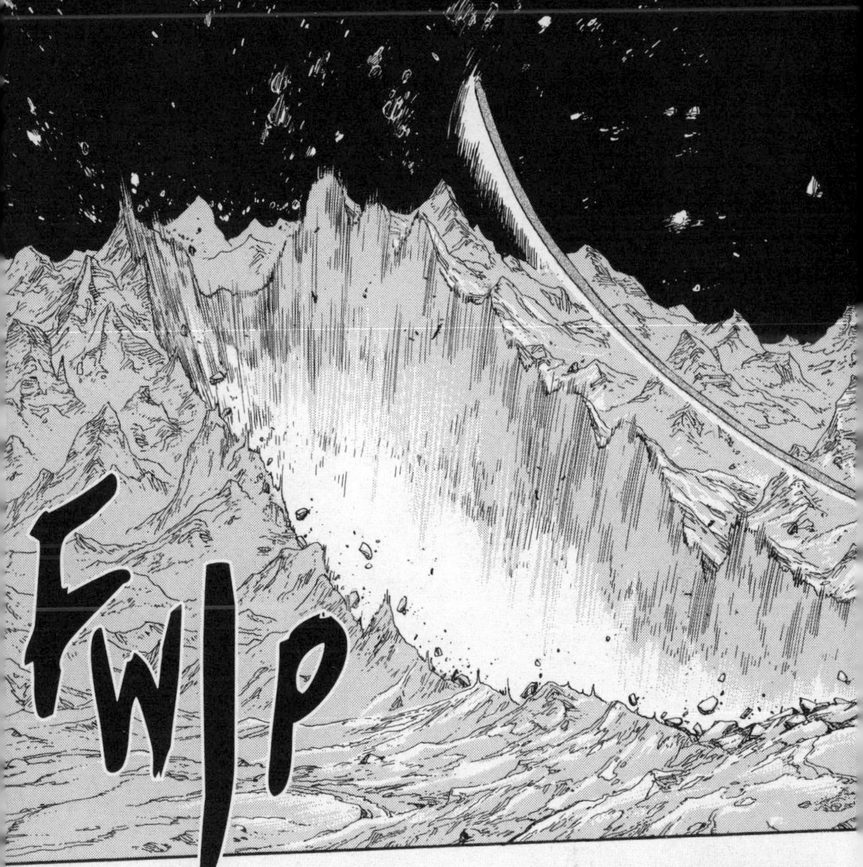
FWIP

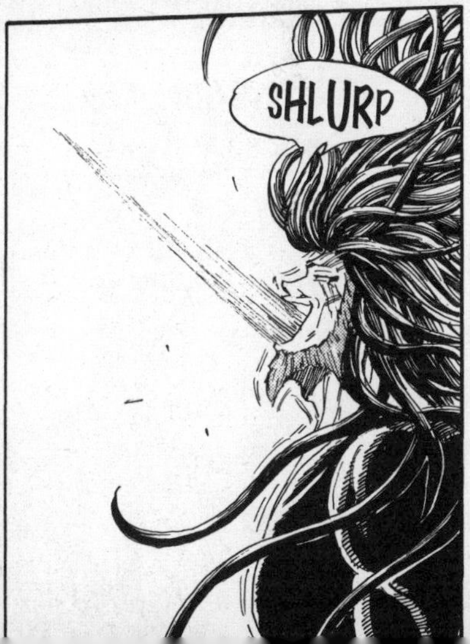
SHLURP

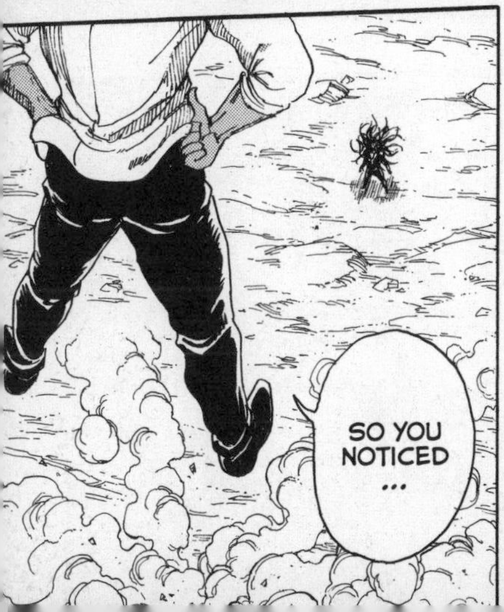
SO YOU NOTICED ...

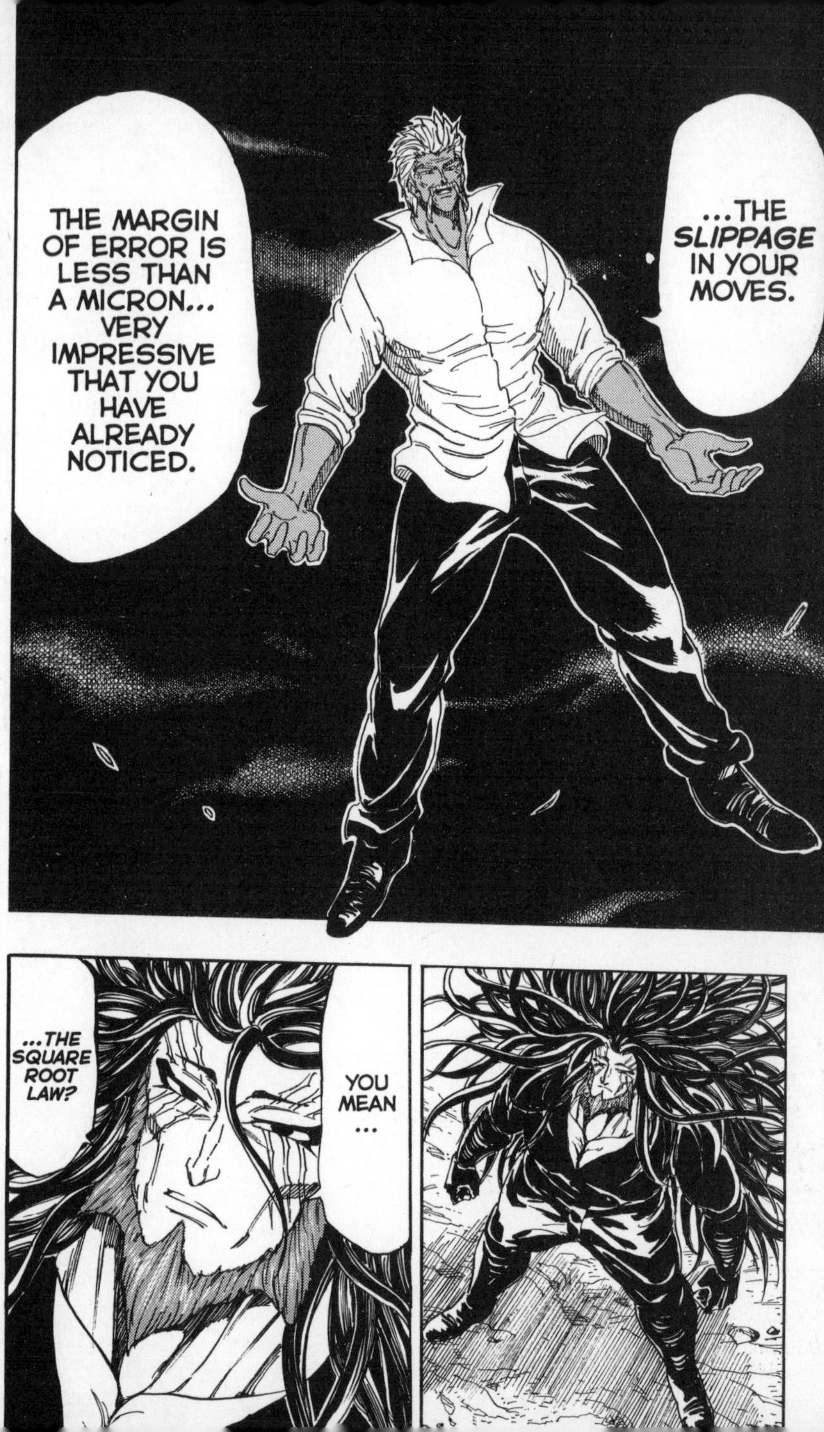
...THE SLIPPAGE IN YOUR MOVES.
THE MARGIN OF ERROR IS LESS THAN A MICRON... VERY IMPRESSIVE THAT YOU HAVE ALREADY NOTICED.
YOU MEAN ...
...THE SQUARE ROOT LAW?

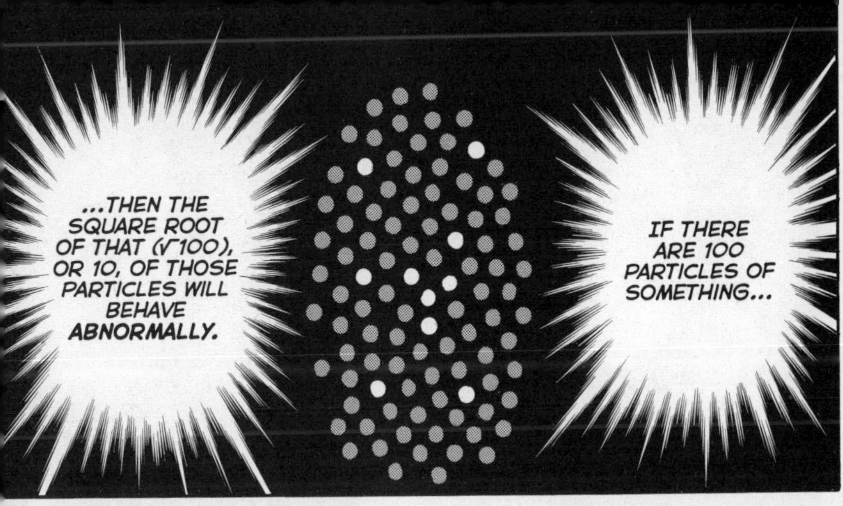
IF THERE ARE 100 PARTICLES OF SOMETHING...
...THEN THE SQUARE ROOT OF THAT (√100), OR 10, OF THOSE PARTICLES WILL BEHAVE ABNORMALLY.

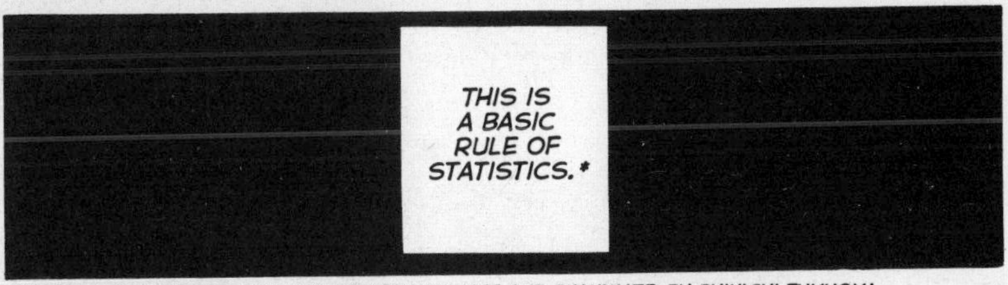
THIS IS A BASIC RULE OF STATISTICS.*

*REFERENCE MATERIAL: *THE LINE BETWEEN ANIMATE AND INANIMATE*, BY SHINICHI FUKUOKA

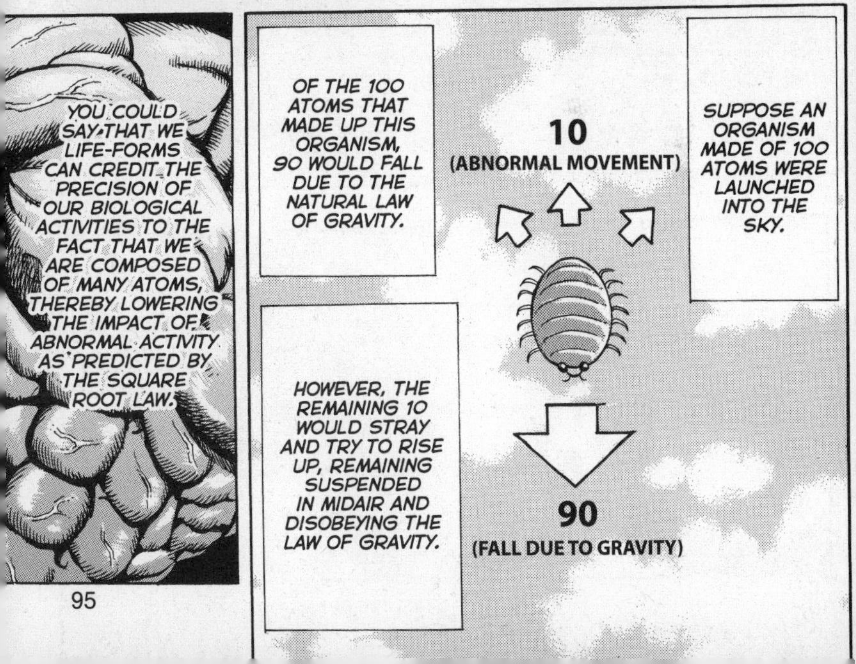
SUPPOSE AN ORGANISM MADE OF 100 ATOMS WERE LAUNCHED INTO THE SKY.
10
(ABNORMAL MOVEMENT)
OF THE 100 ATOMS THAT MADE UP THIS ORGANISM, 90 WOULD FALL DUE TO THE NATURAL LAW OF GRAVITY.
90
(FALL DUE TO GRAVITY)
HOWEVER, THE REMAINING 10 WOULD STRAY AND TRY TO RISE UP, REMAINING SUSPENDED IN MIDAIR AND DISOBEYING THE LAW OF GRAVITY.
YOU COULD SAY THAT WE LIFE-FORMS CAN CREDIT THE PRECISION OF OUR BIOLOGICAL ACTIVITIES TO THE FACT THAT WE ARE COMPOSED OF MANY ATOMS, THEREBY LOWERING THE IMPACT OF ABNORMAL ACTIVITY AS PREDICTED BY THE SQUARE ROOT LAW.

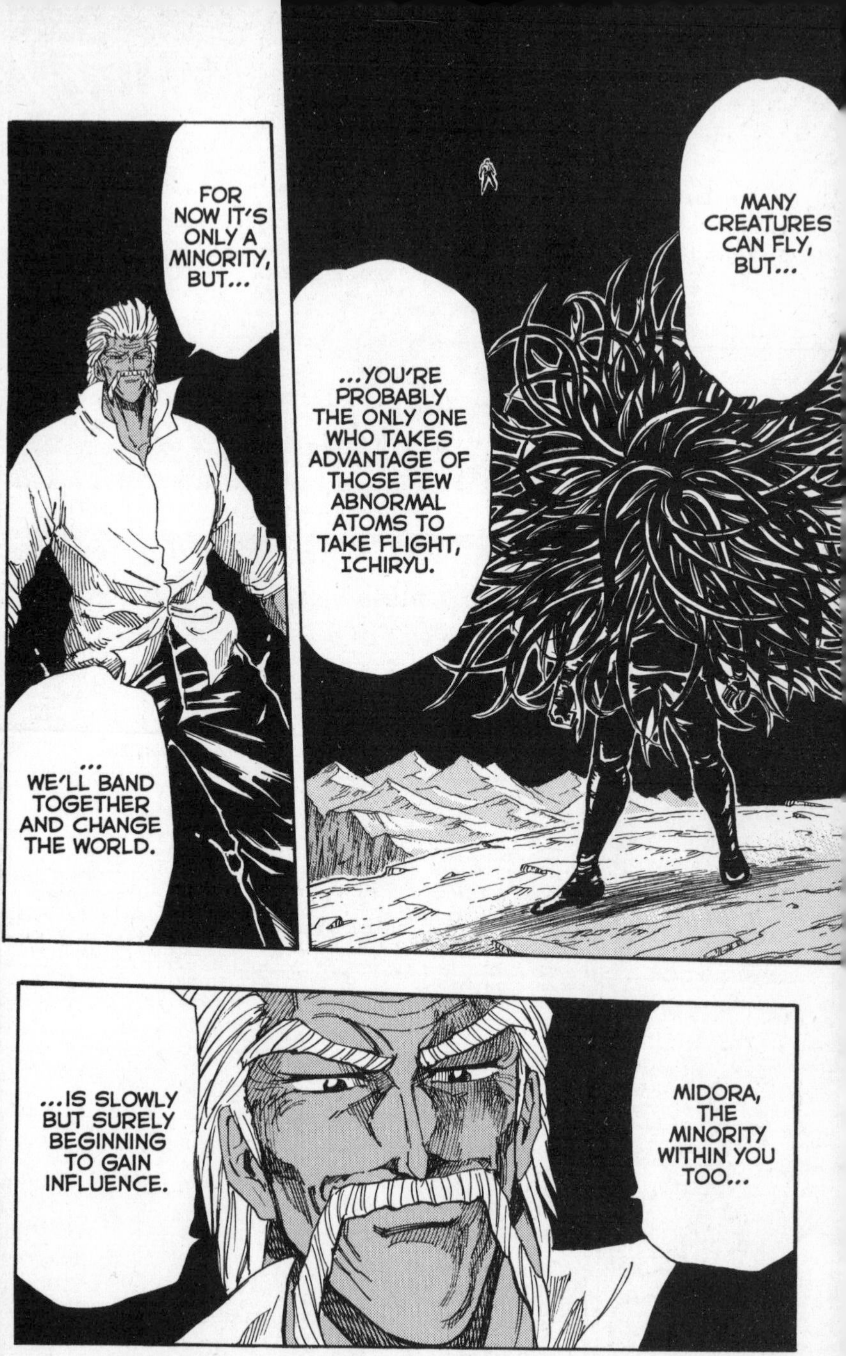
MANY CREATURES CAN FLY, BUT...
...YOU'RE PROBABLY THE ONLY ONE WHO TAKES ADVANTAGE OF THOSE FEW ABNORMAL ATOMS TO TAKE FLIGHT, ICHIRYU.
FOR NOW IT'S ONLY A MINORITY, BUT...
...WE'LL BAND TOGETHER AND CHANGE THE WORLD.
MIDORA, THE MINORITY WITHIN YOU TOO...
...IS SLOWLY BUT SURELY BEGINNING TO GAIN INFLUENCE.

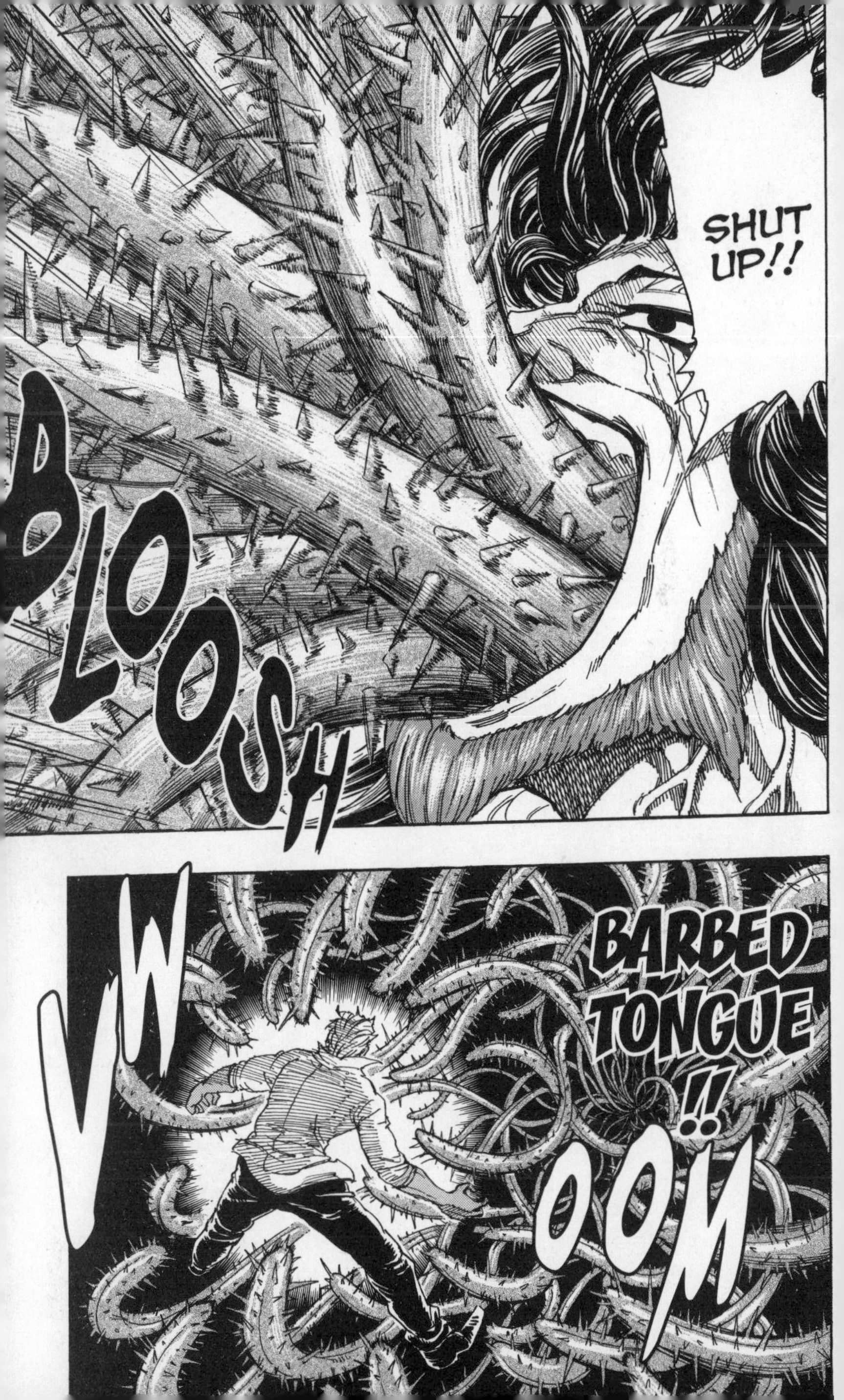
SHUT UP!!
BLOOSH
BARBED TONGUE!!
VWOOM

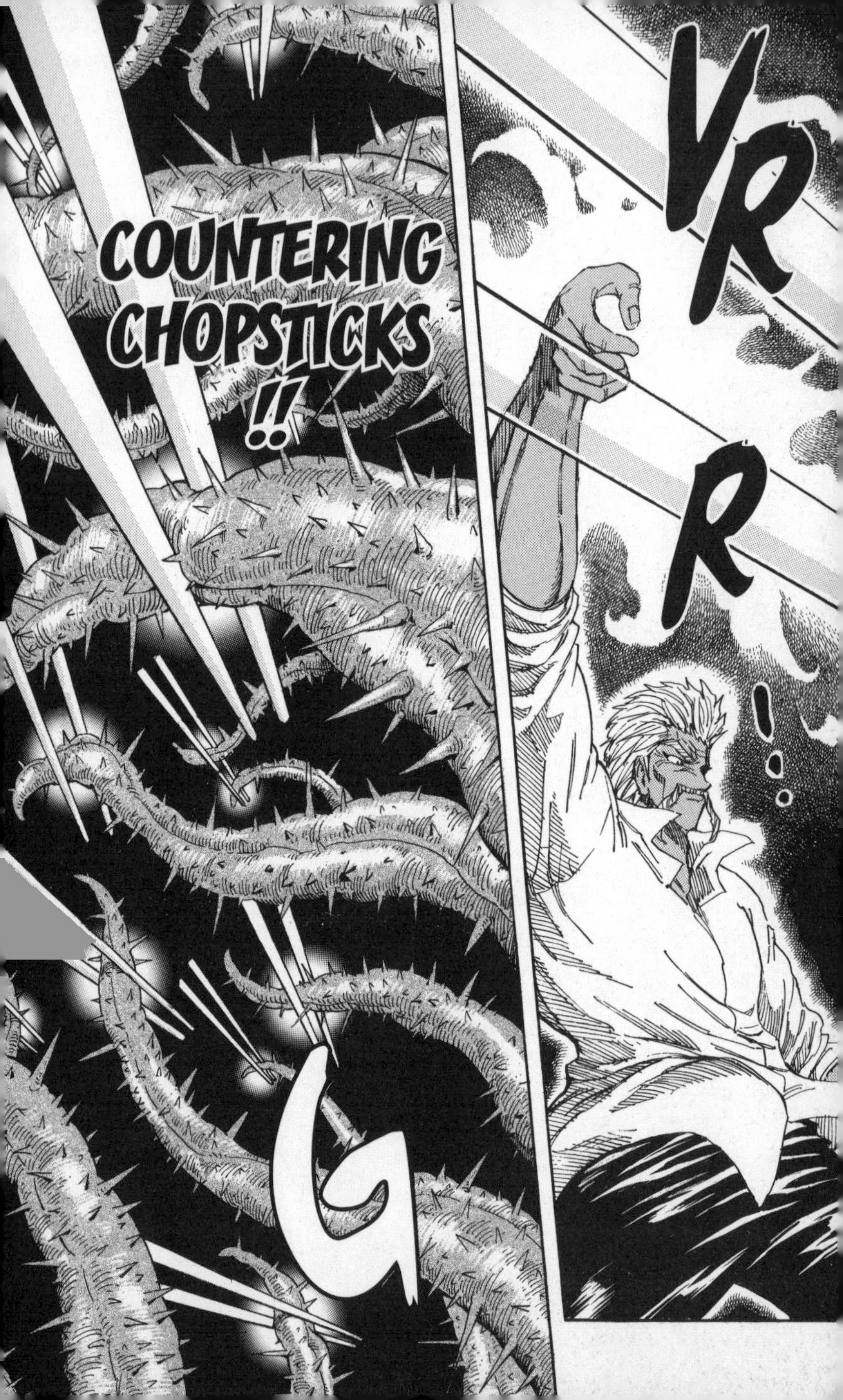
VRR!!
COUNTERING CHOPSTICKS!!
G

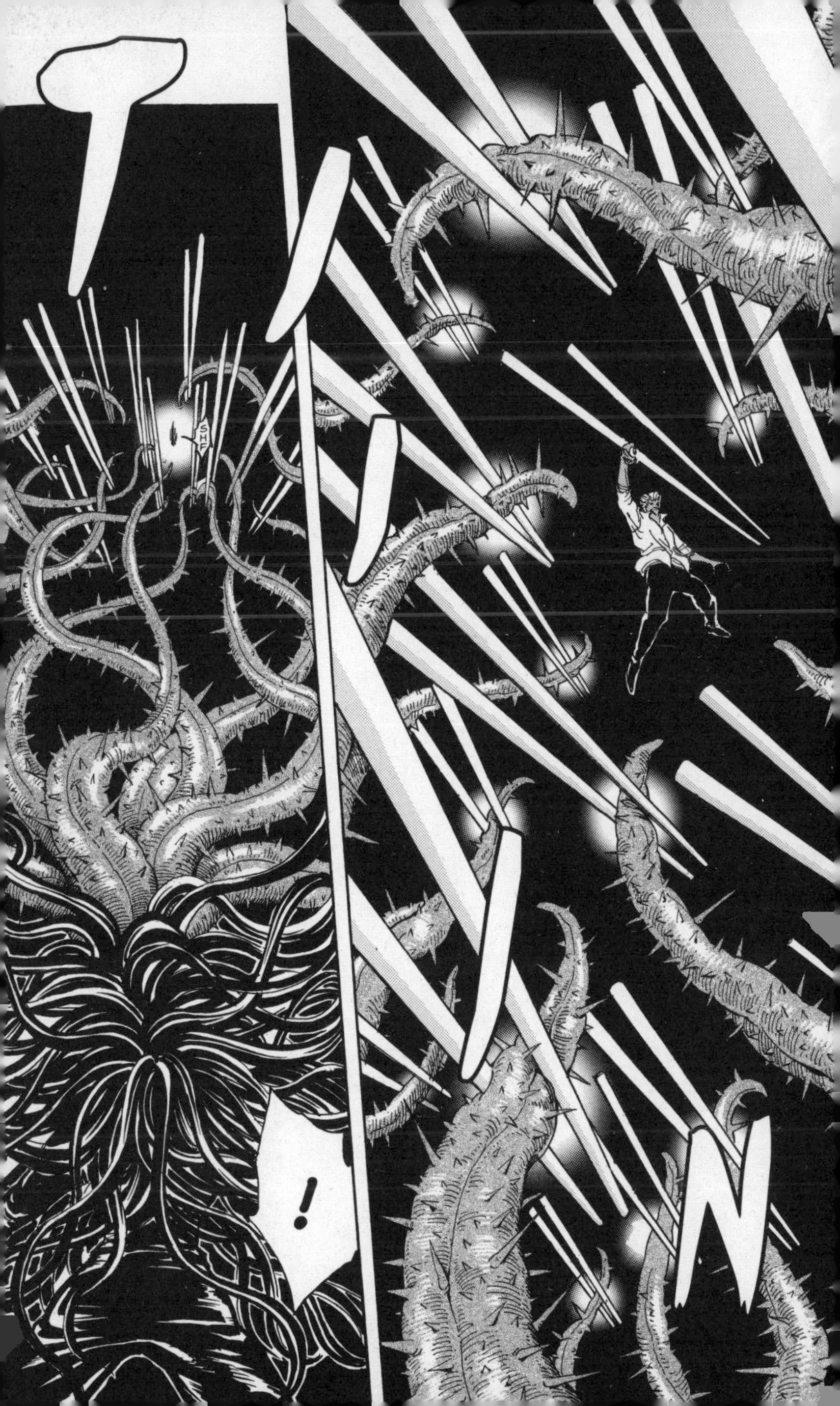
SHF
!

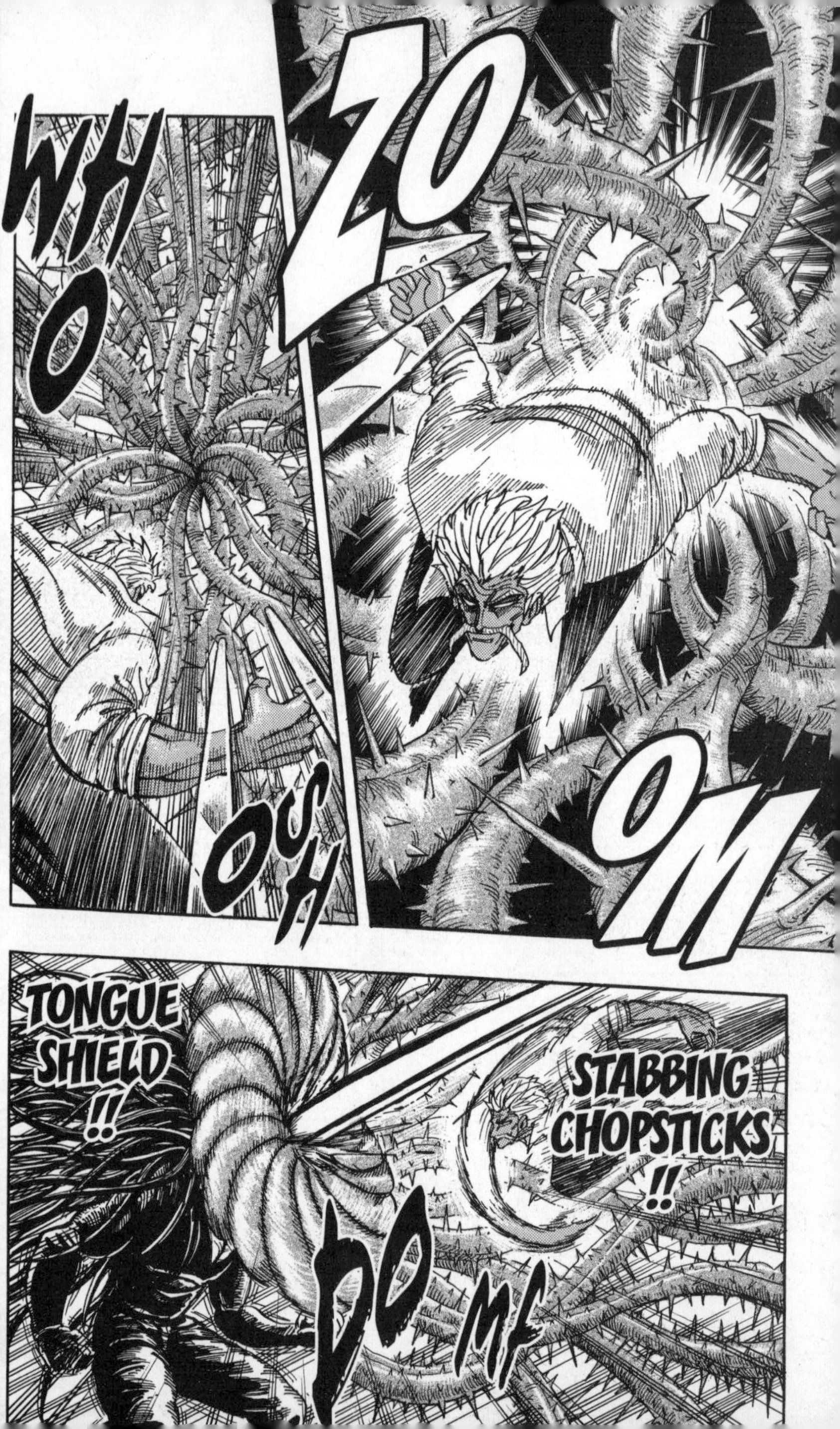
ZOOM
WHOOSH
STABBING CHOPSTICKS!!
TONGUE SHIELD!!
DOMF

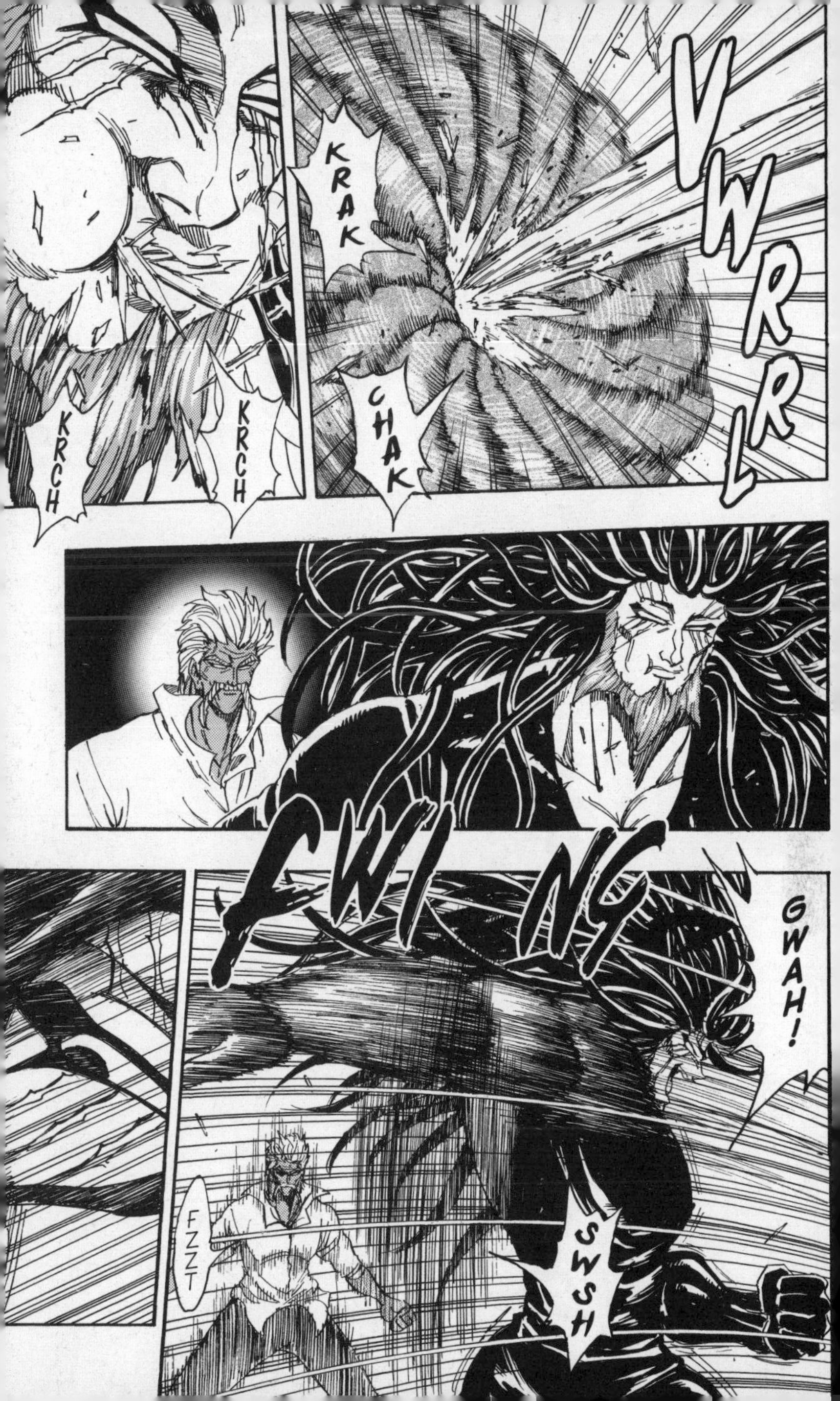
VWRRLL
KRAK
CHAK
KRCH
KRCH
FWING
GWAH!
SWSH
FZZT

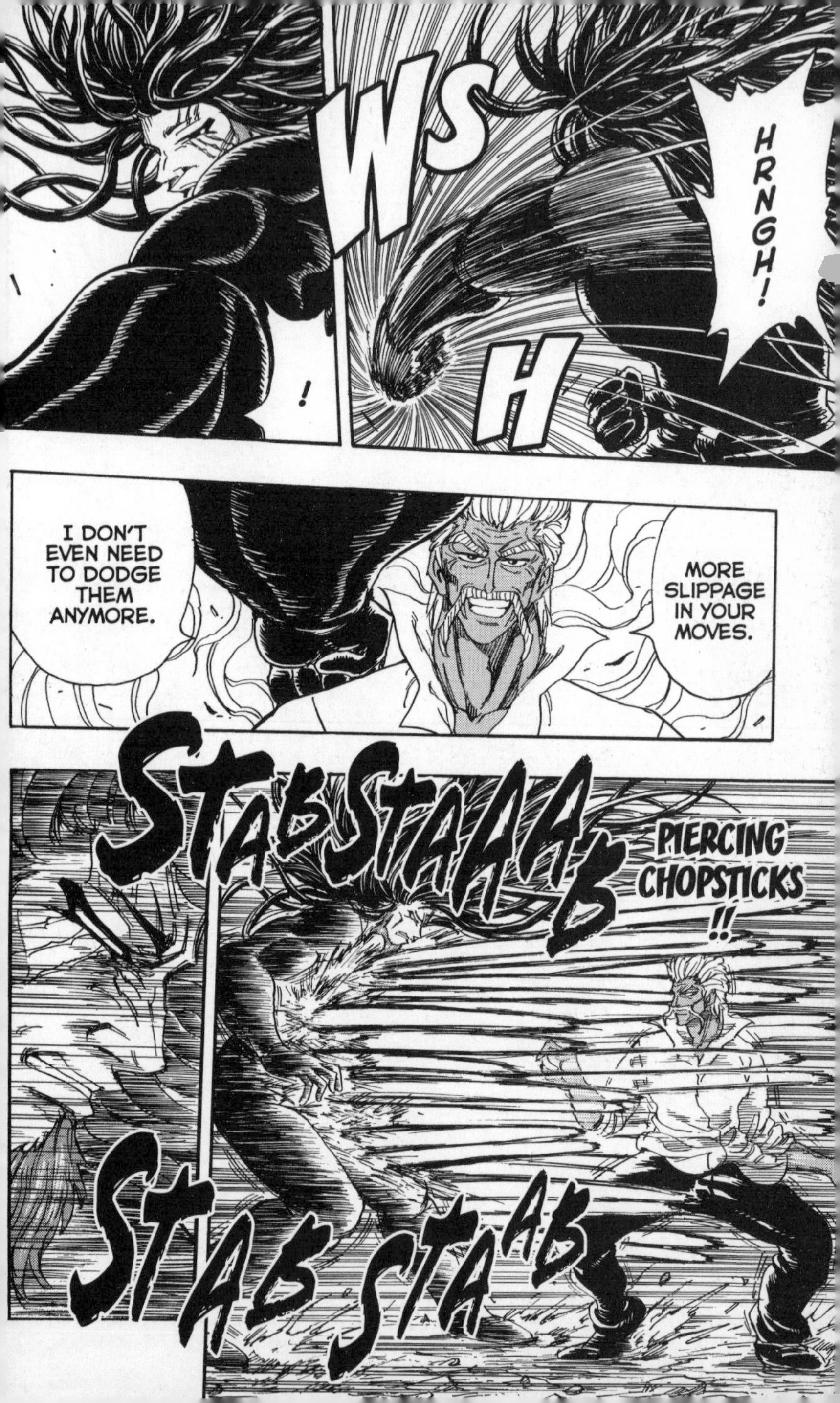
HRNGH!
WSH
!
MORE SLIPPAGE IN YOUR MOVES.
I DON'T EVEN NEED TO DODGE THEM ANYMORE.
STAB STAAAB
PIERCING CHOPSTICKS!!
STAB STAAB

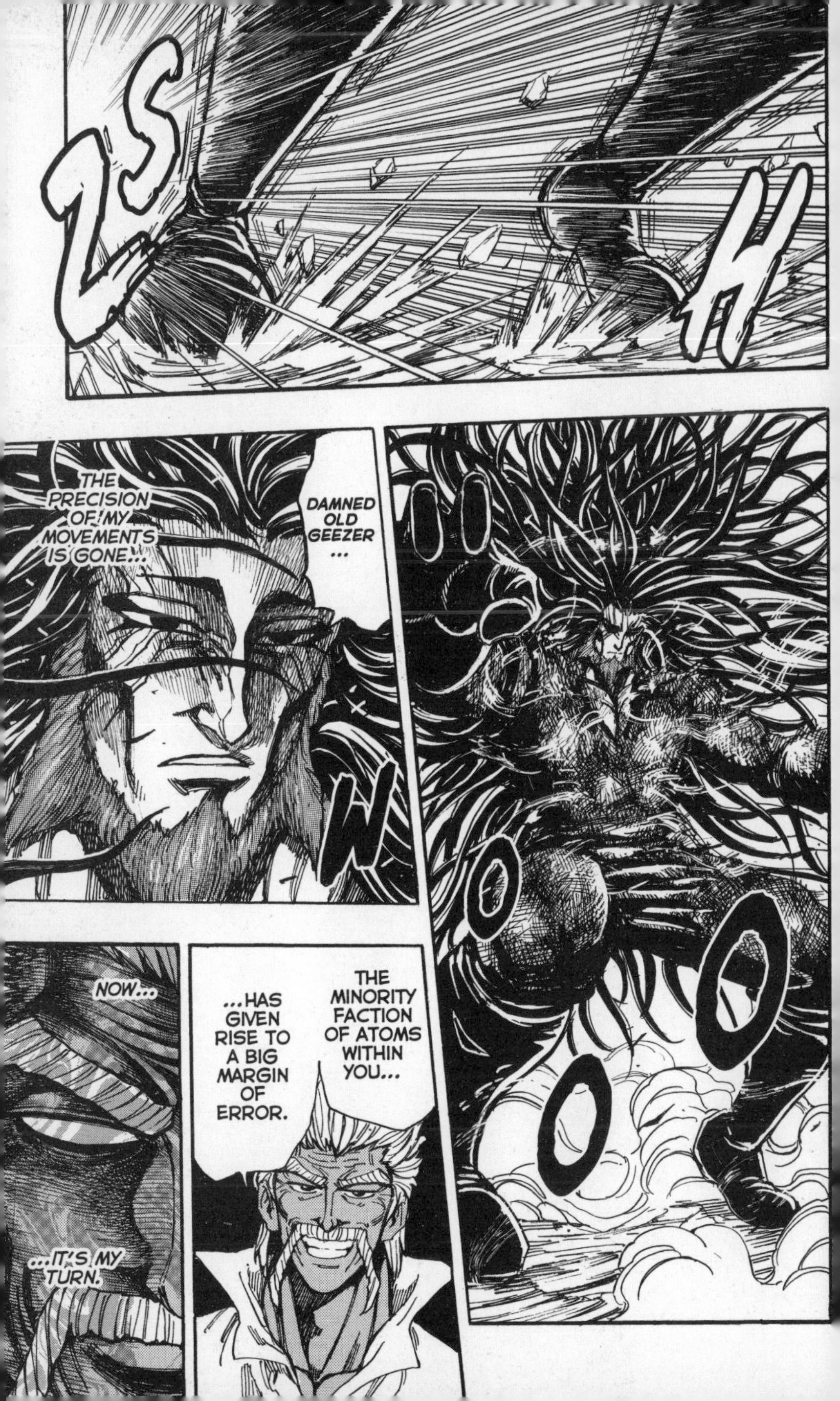
ZS
H
WOOOO
DAMNED OLD GEEZER...
THE PRECISION OF MY MOVEMENTS IS GONE...
THE MINORITY FACTION OF ATOMS WITHIN YOU...
...HAS GIVEN RISE TO A BIG MARGIN OF ERROR.
NOW...
...IT'S MY TURN.

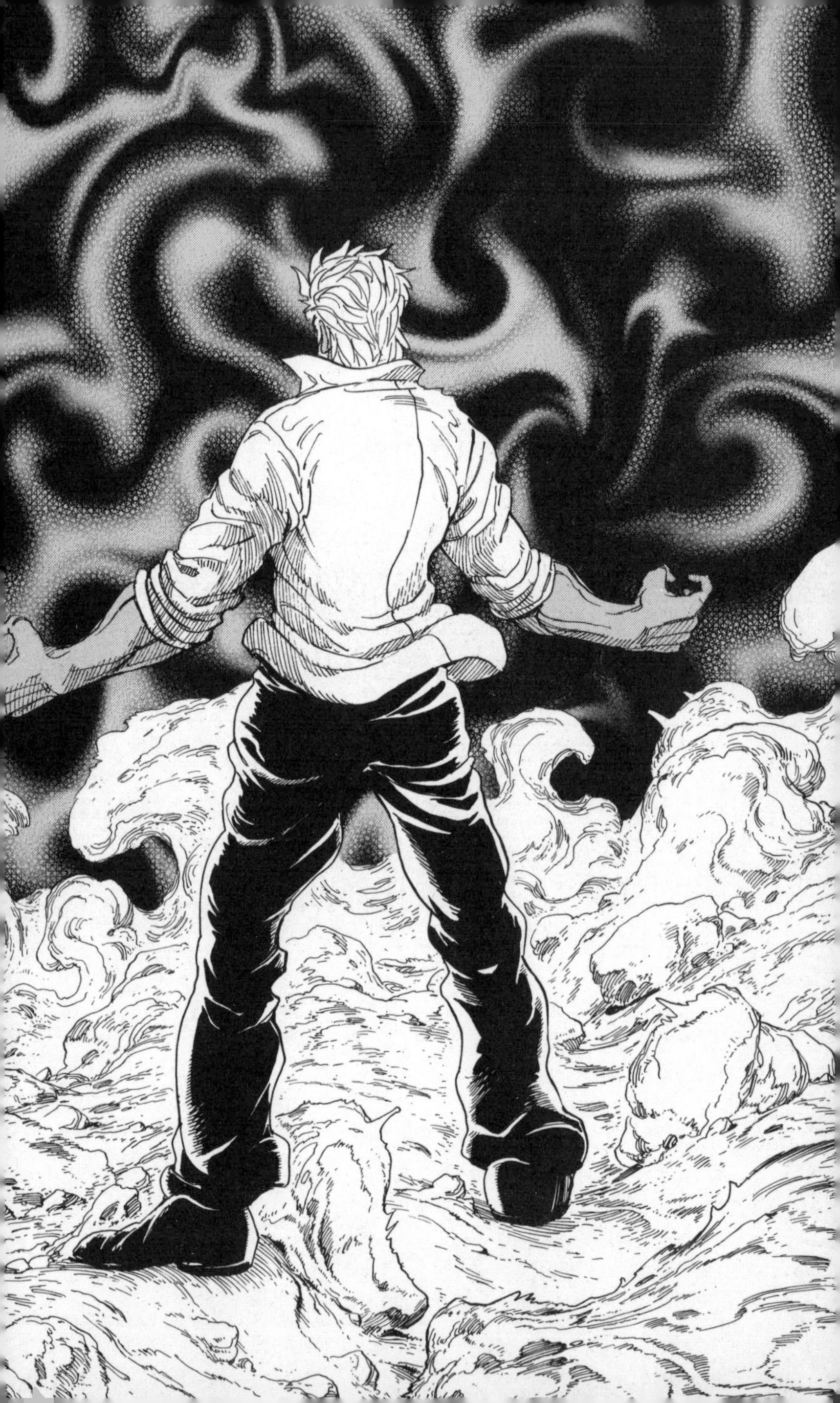

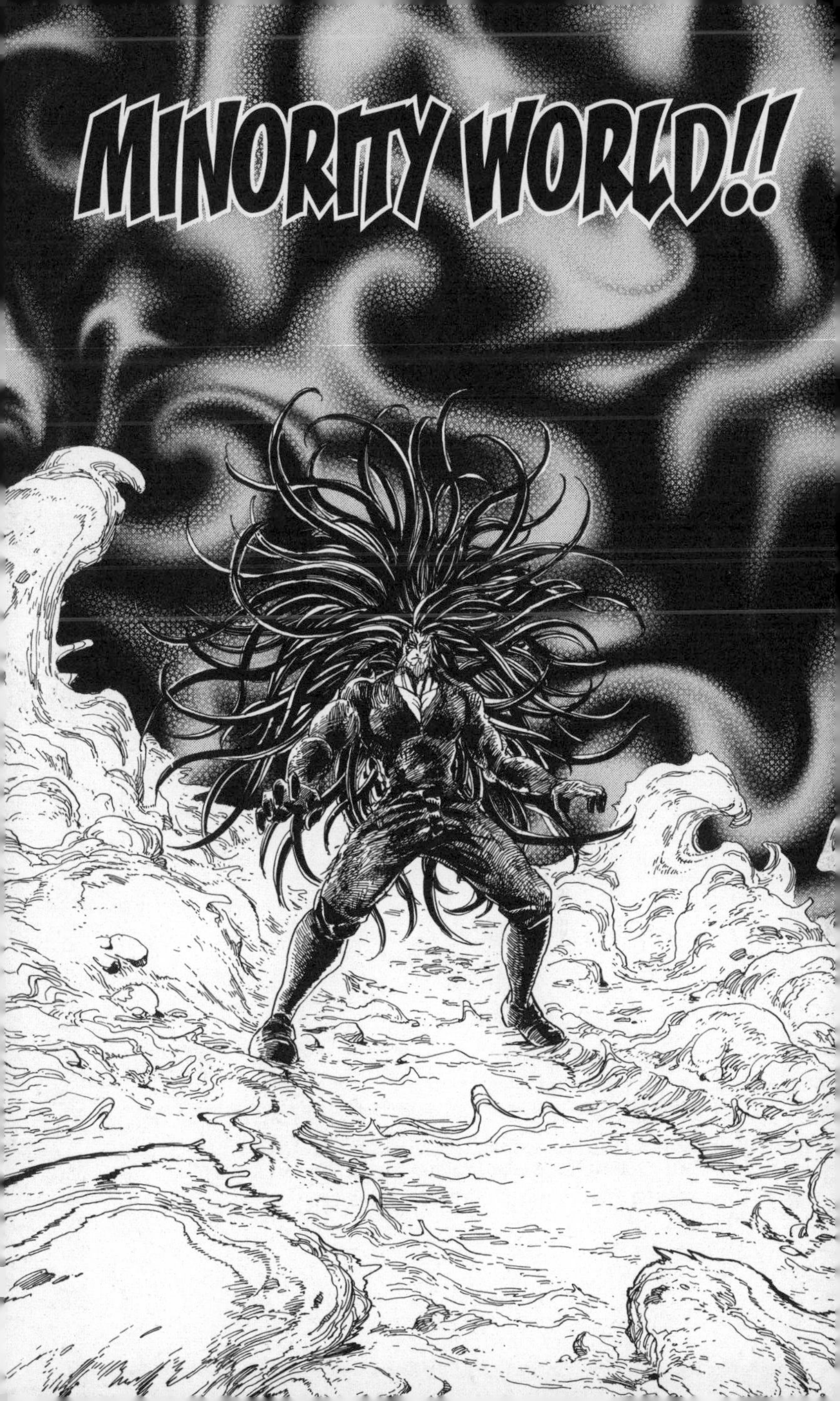
MINORITY WORLD!!

TORIKO

GOURMET CHECKLIST
Vol. 276

 ## ELEPHANT SHRIMP
(CRUSTACEAN)

CAPTURE LEVEL: 35
HABITAT: STEW POND
SIZE: 7 METERS
HEIGHT: ---
WEIGHT: 3 TONS
PRICE: 1 KG / 6,000 YEN

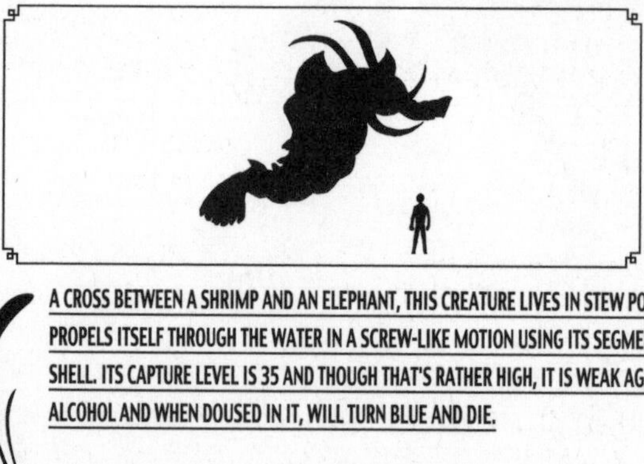

SCALE

A CROSS BETWEEN A SHRIMP AND AN ELEPHANT, THIS CREATURE LIVES IN STEW POND. IT PROPELS ITSELF THROUGH THE WATER IN A SCREW-LIKE MOTION USING ITS SEGMENTED SHELL. ITS CAPTURE LEVEL IS 35 AND THOUGH THAT'S RATHER HIGH, IT IS WEAK AGAINST ALCOHOL AND WHEN DOUSED IN IT, WILL TURN BLUE AND DIE.

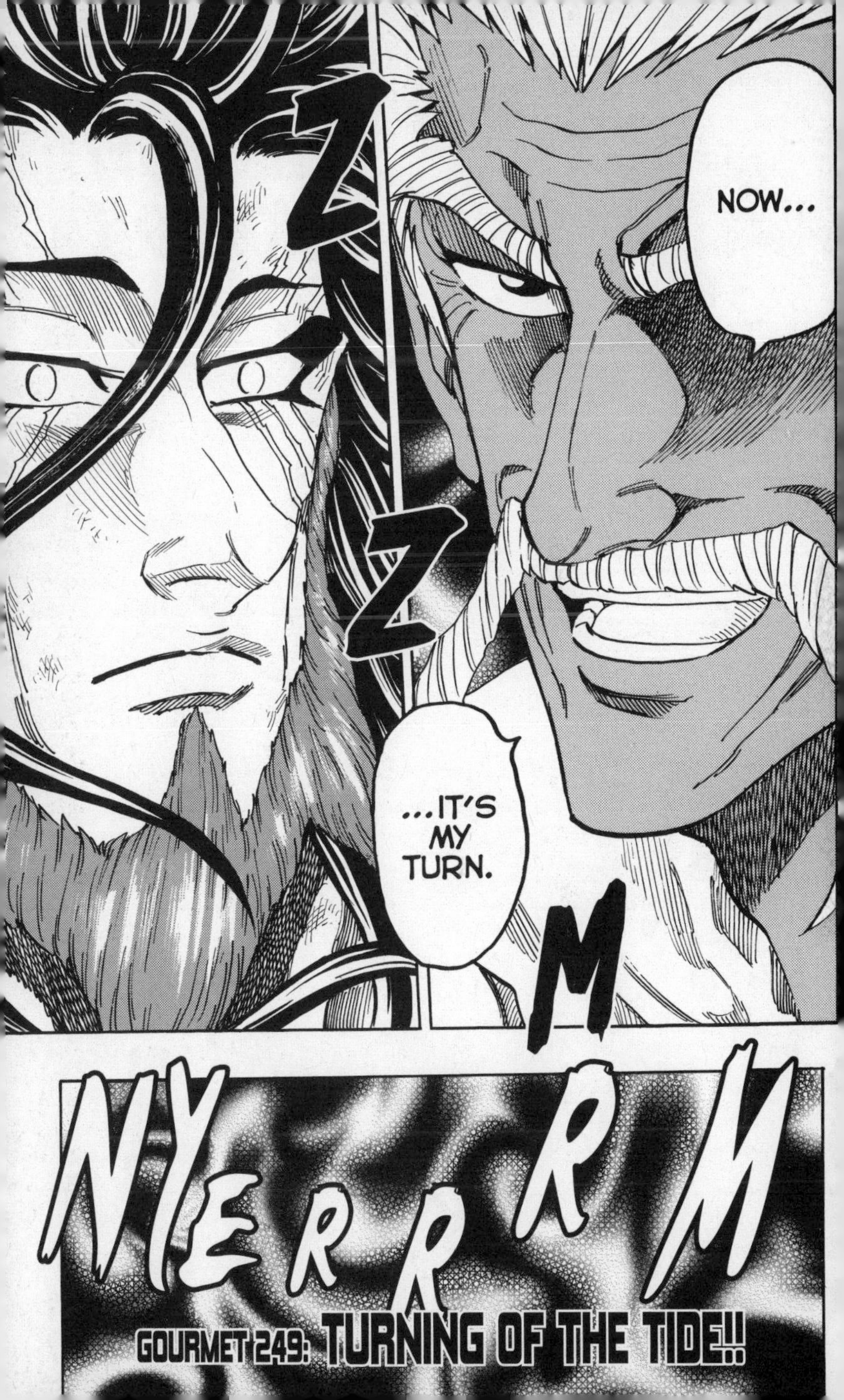
NOW...
...IT'S MY TURN.
ZZ
M
NYERRRM
GOURMET 249: TURNING OF THE TIDE!!

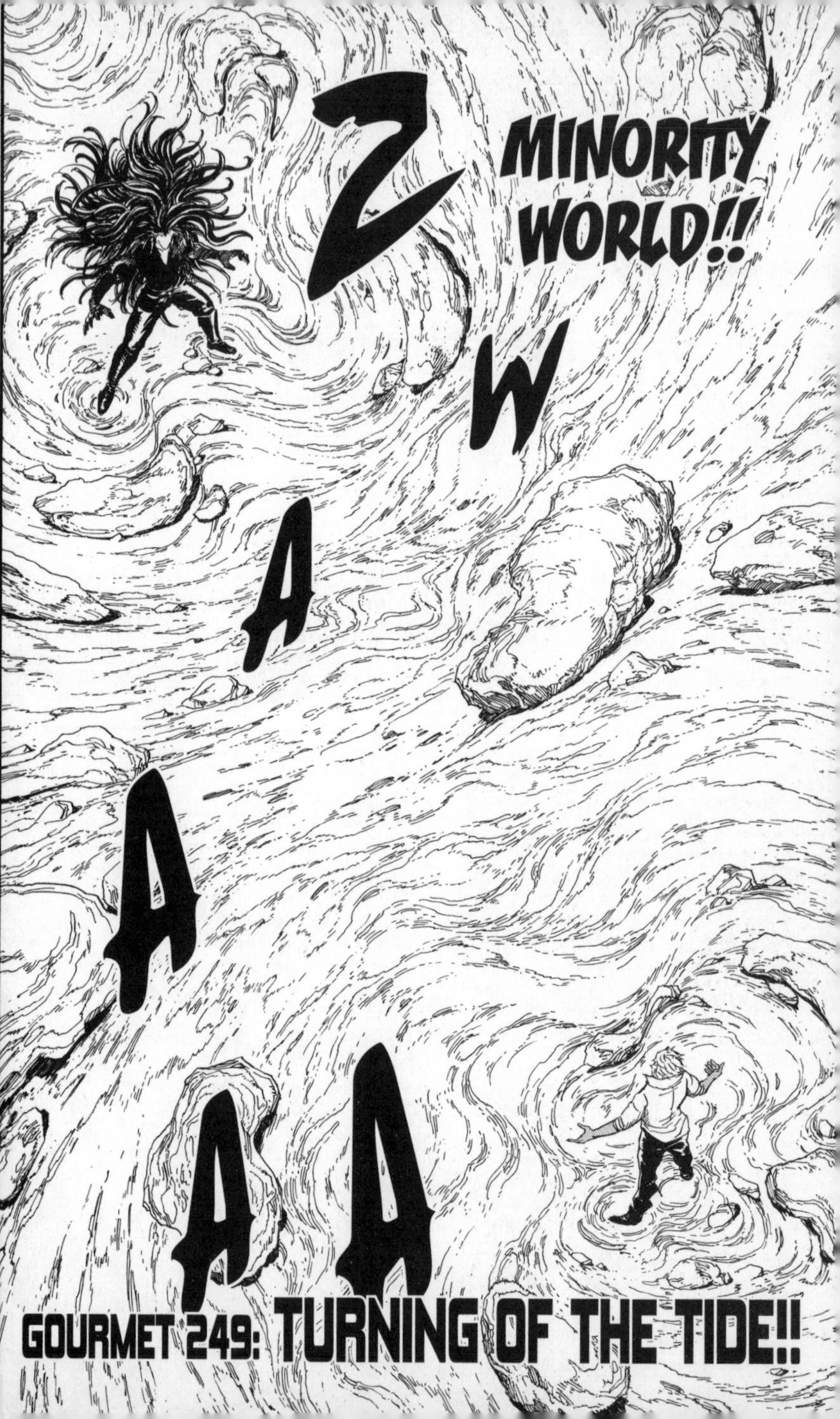
MINORITY WORLD!!
ZWAAAAA
GOURMET 249: TURNING OF THE TIDE!!

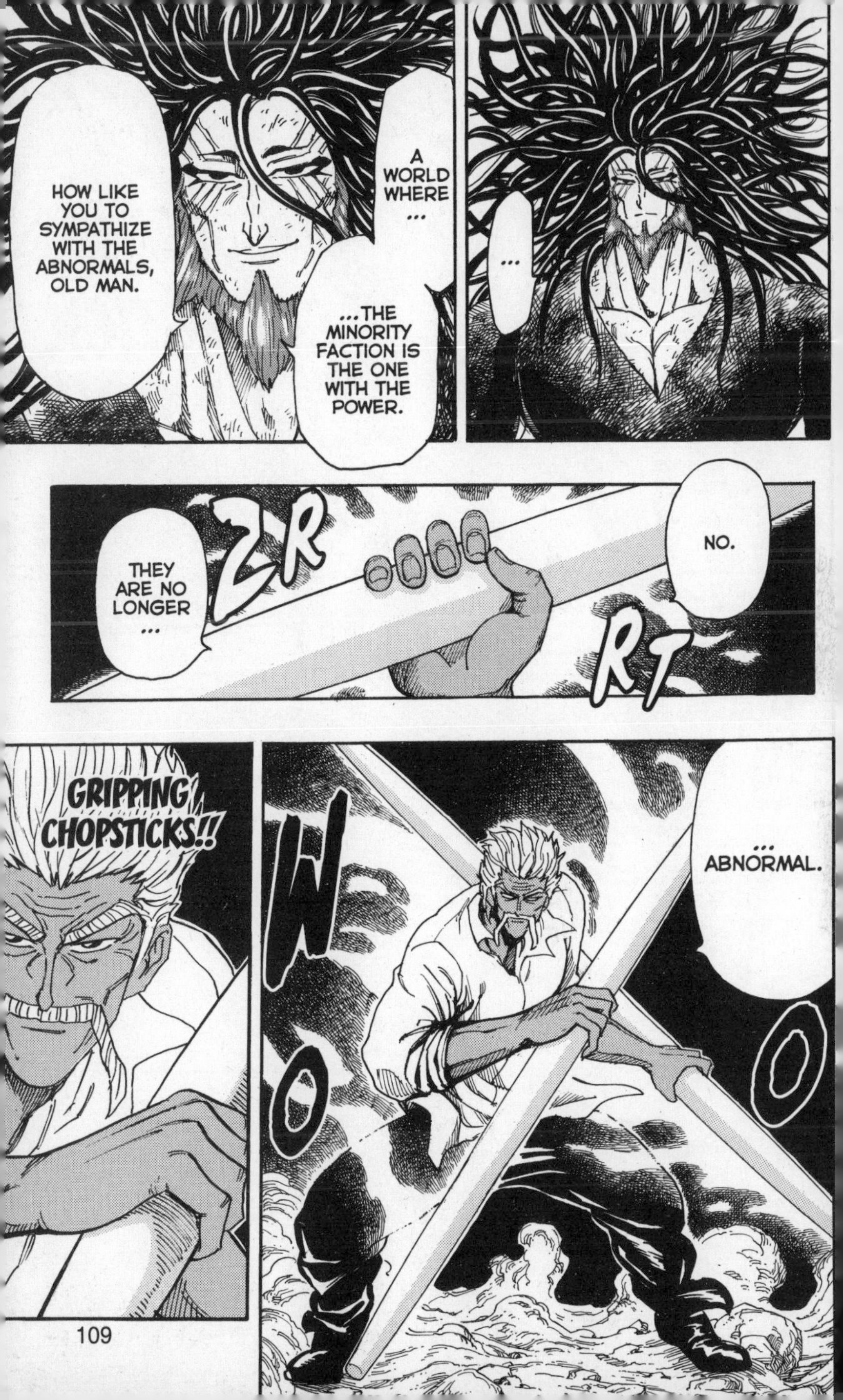
...
A WORLD WHERE ...
...THE MINORITY FACTION IS THE ONE WITH THE POWER.
HOW LIKE YOU TO SYMPATHIZE WITH THE ABNORMALS, OLD MAN.
NO.
ZRRT
THEY ARE NO LONGER ...
... ABNORMAL.
WOOO
GRIPPING CHOPSTICKS!!

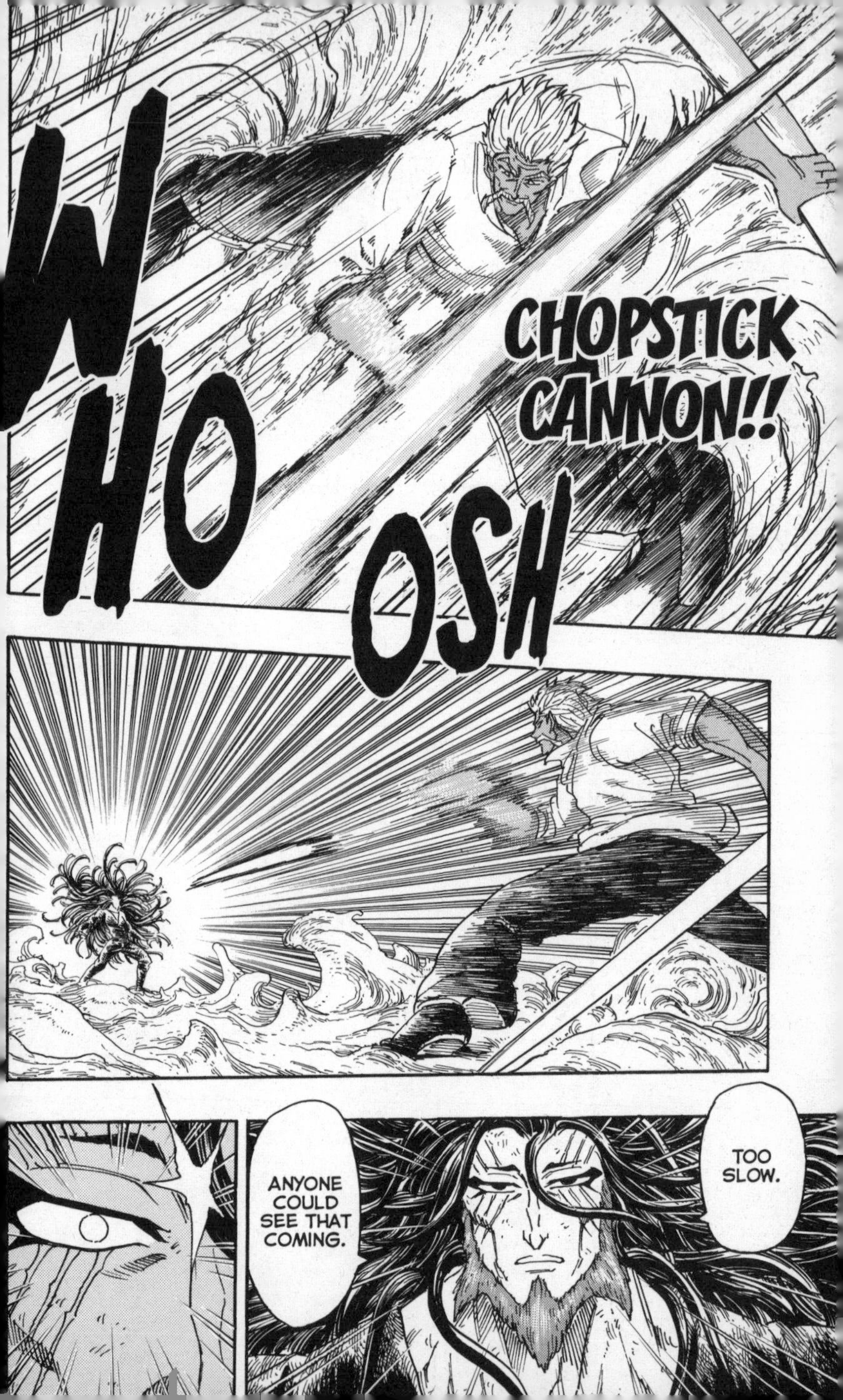
CHOPSTICK CANNON!!
WHOOSH
TOO SLOW.
ANYONE COULD SEE THAT COMING.

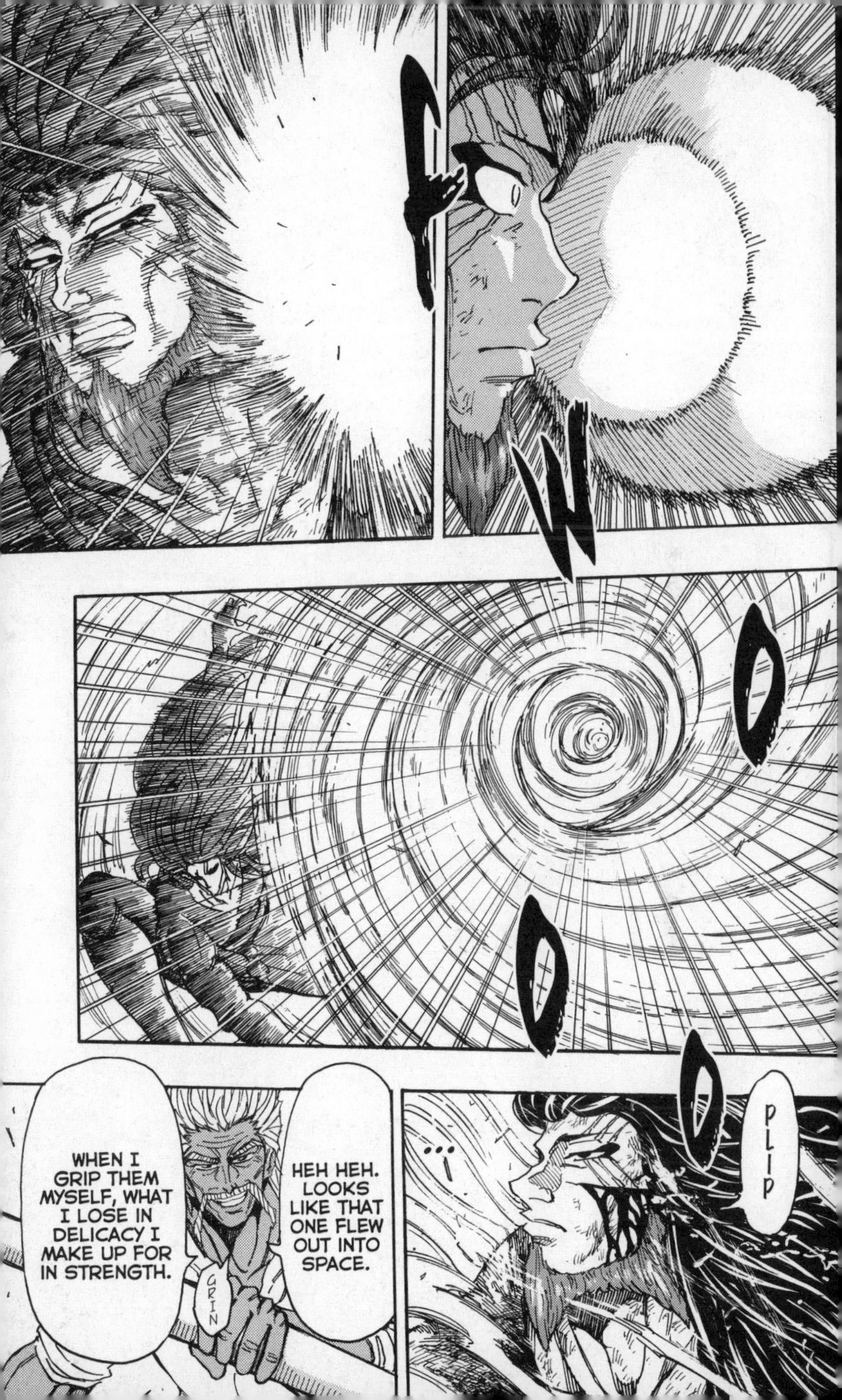
PLIP
...!
HEH HEH. LOOKS LIKE THAT ONE FLEW OUT INTO SPACE.
GRIN
WHEN I GRIP THEM MYSELF, WHAT I LOSE IN DELICACY I MAKE UP FOR IN STRENGTH.

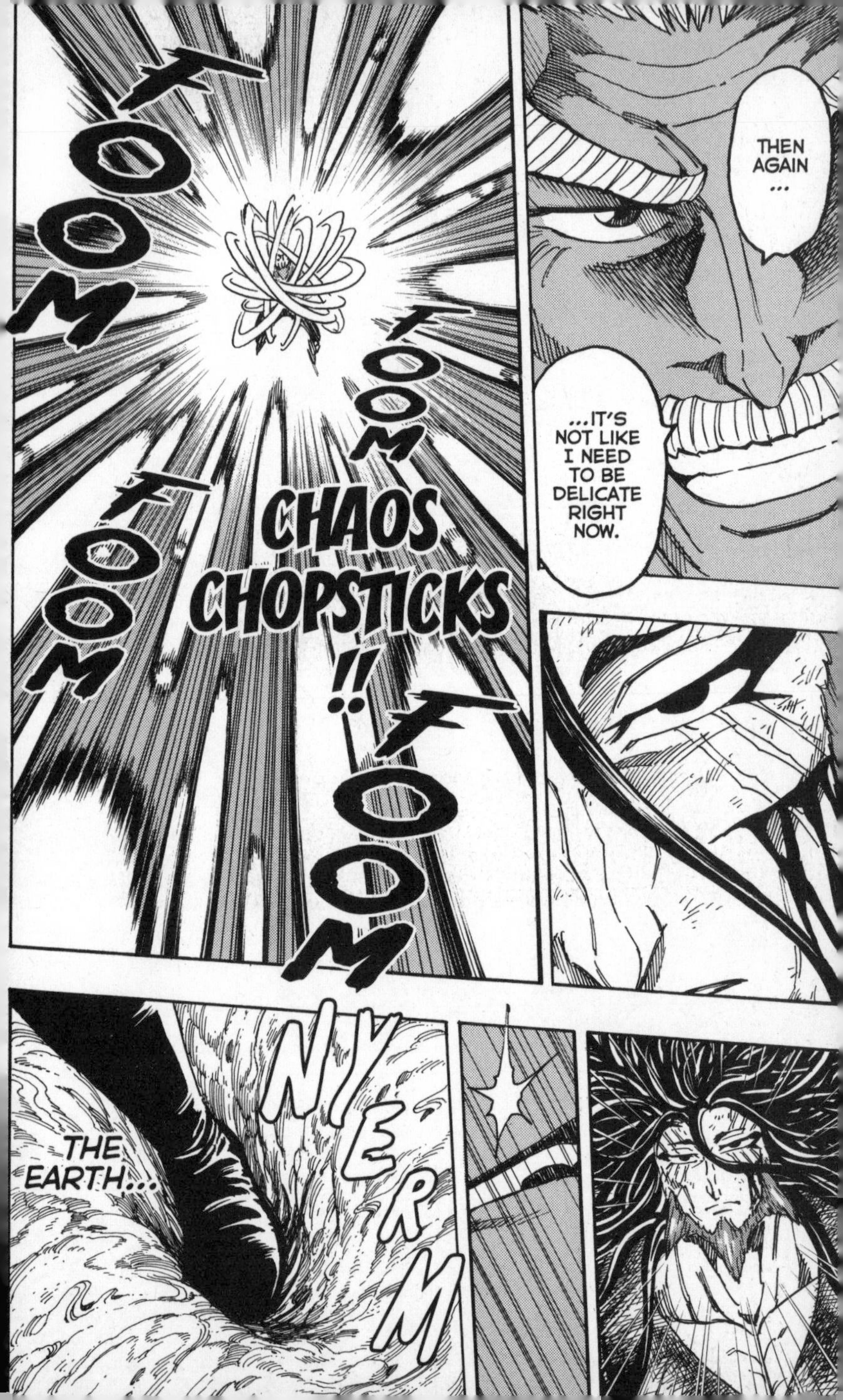
THEN AGAIN ...
...IT'S NOT LIKE I NEED TO BE DELICATE RIGHT NOW.
FOOOM
FOOOM
FOOOM
CHAOS CHOPSTICKS!!
FOOOM
NYERM
THE EARTH...

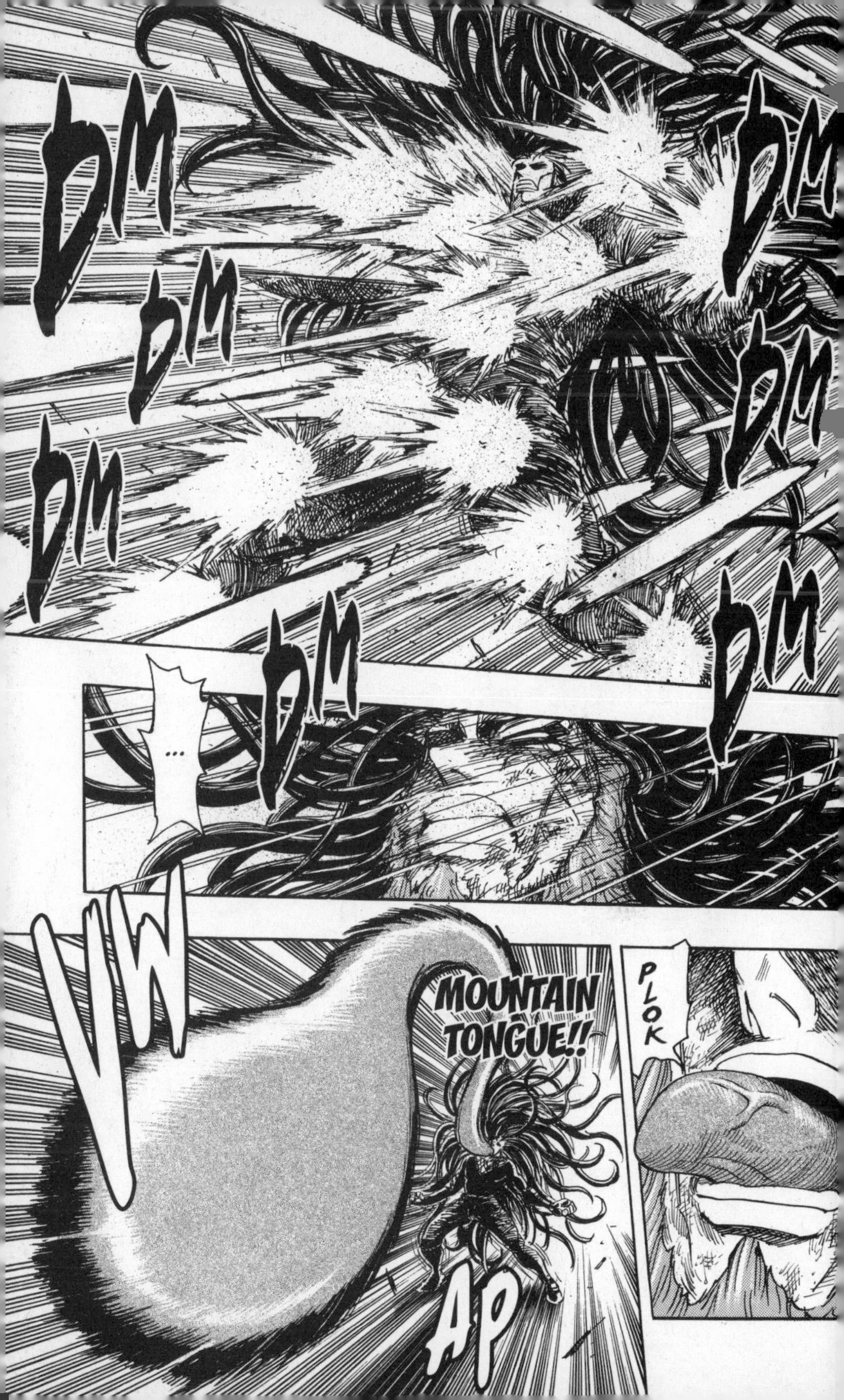
DM
DM
DM
DM
DM
DM
DM
DM
...
PLOK
MOUNTAIN TONGUE!!
VWN
AP

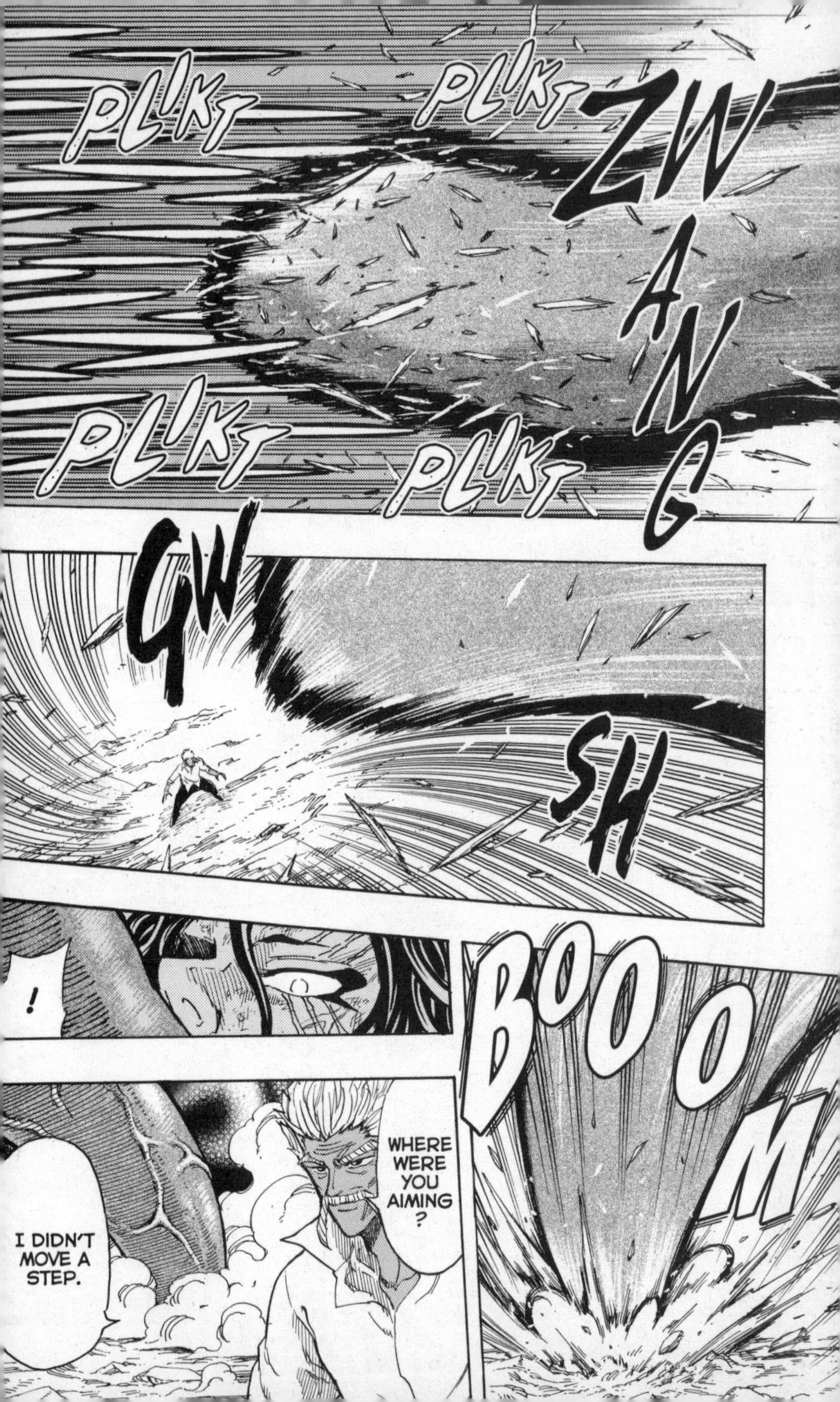
ZWANG
PLINKT
PLINKT
PLINKT
PLINKT
GW
SH
BOOOM
!
WHERE WERE YOU AIMING?
I DIDN'T MOVE A STEP.

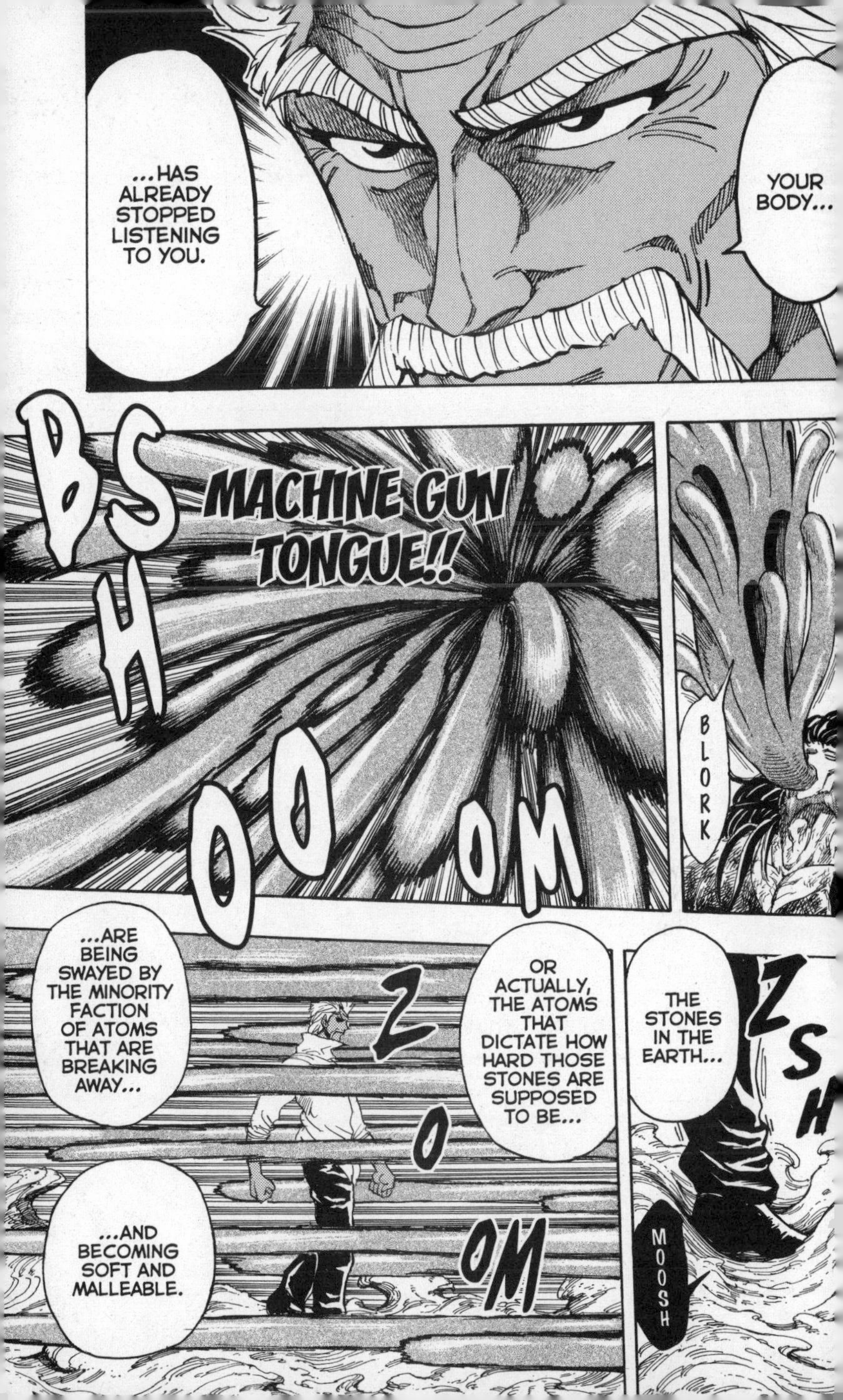
YOUR BODY...
...HAS ALREADY STOPPED LISTENING TO YOU.
BLORK
BSHOOOM
MACHINE GUN TONGUE!!
ZSH
MOOSH
THE STONES IN THE EARTH...
OR ACTUALLY, THE ATOMS THAT DICTATE HOW HARD THOSE STONES ARE SUPPOSED TO BE...
ZOOOM
...ARE BEING SWAYED BY THE MINORITY FACTION OF ATOMS THAT ARE BREAKING AWAY...
...AND BECOMING SOFT AND MALLEABLE.

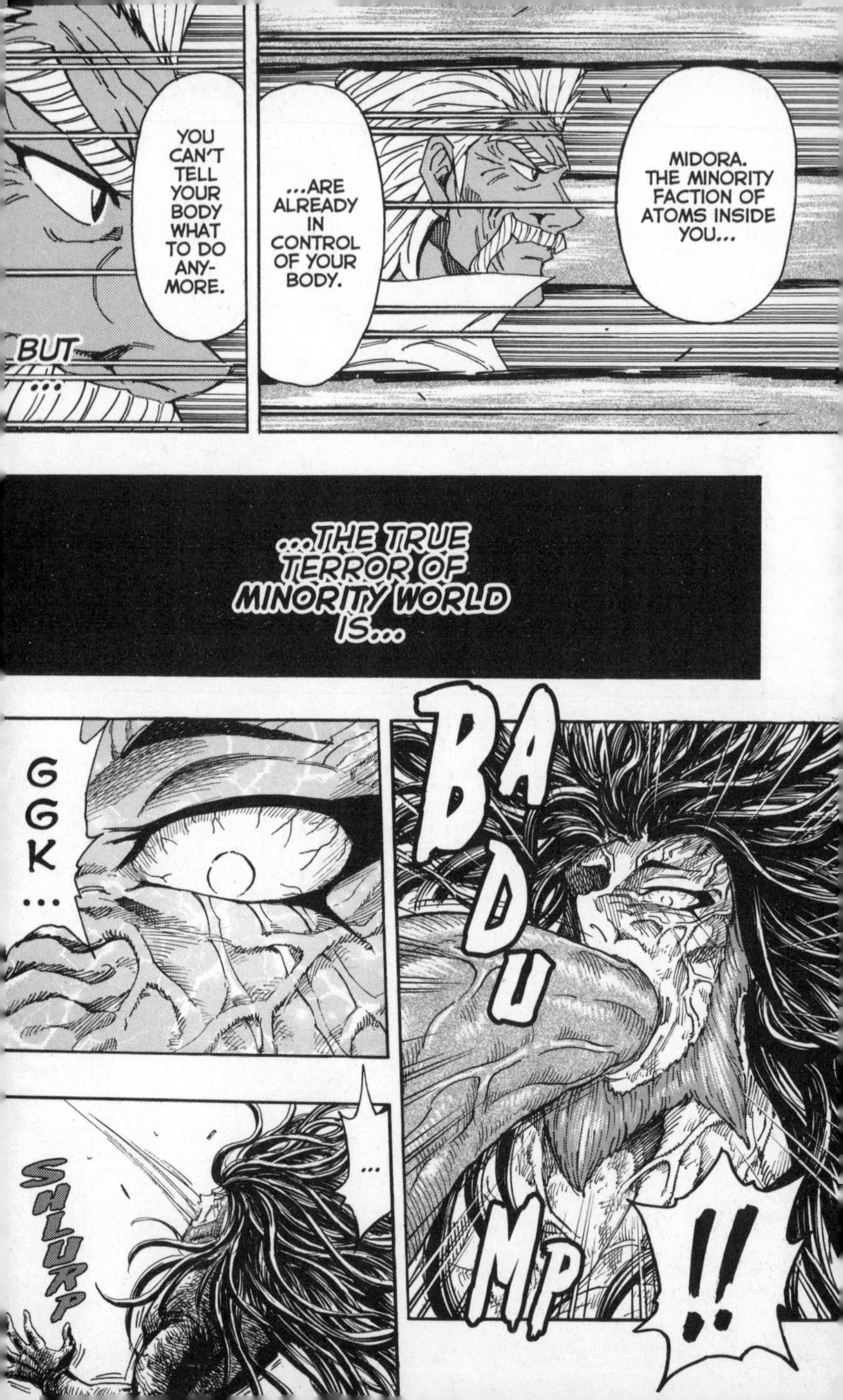
MIDORA. THE MINORITY FACTION OF ATOMS INSIDE YOU...
...ARE ALREADY IN CONTROL OF YOUR BODY.
YOU CAN'T TELL YOUR BODY WHAT TO DO ANYMORE.
BUT...
...THE TRUE TERROR OF MINORITY WORLD IS...
BADUMP!!
GGK...
...
SHLURP

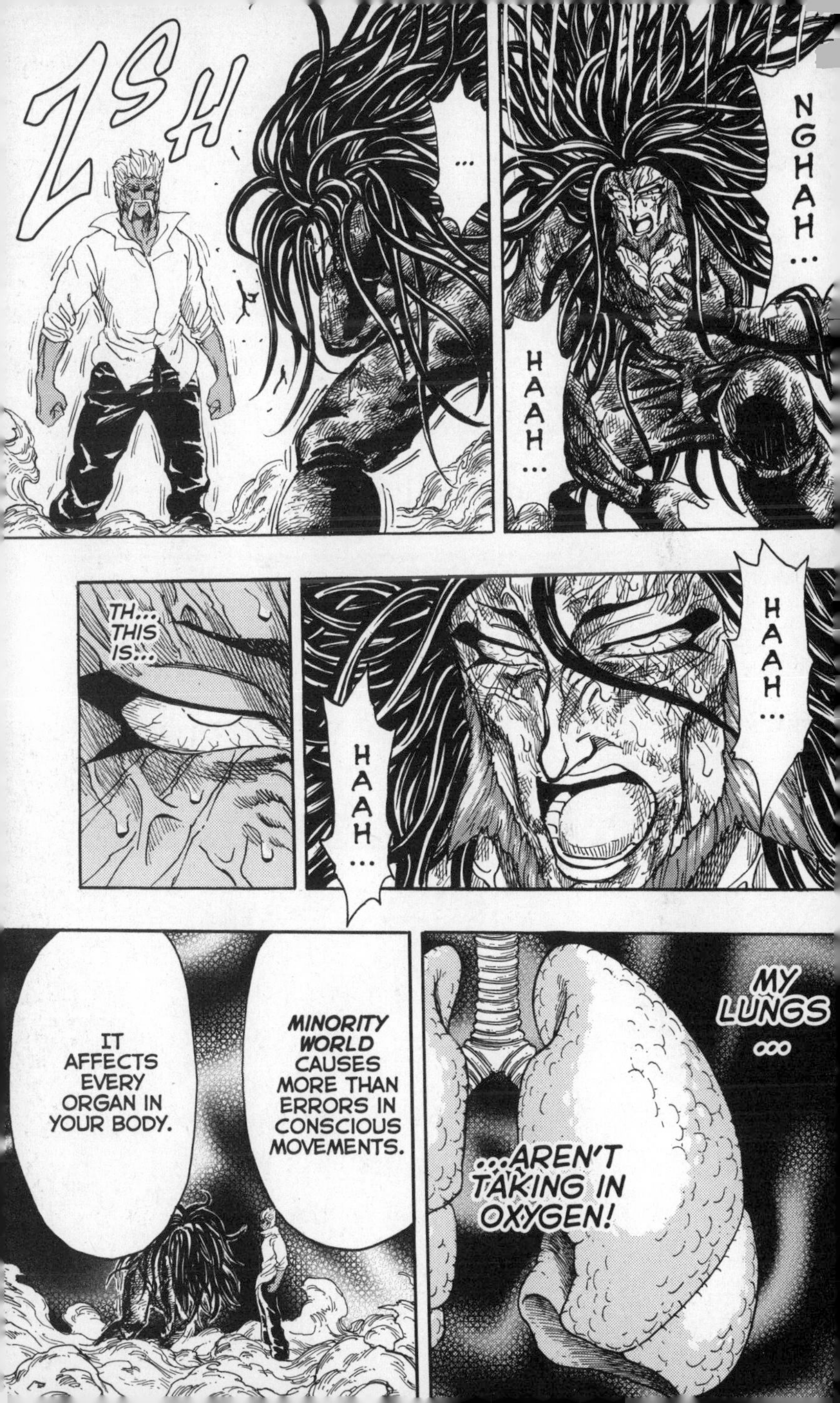
NGHAH...
HAAH...
...
ZSH
HAAH...
HAAH...
TH... THIS IS...
MY LUNGS...
...AREN'T TAKING IN OXYGEN!
MINORITY WORLD CAUSES MORE THAN ERRORS IN CONSCIOUS MOVEMENTS.
IT AFFECTS EVERY ORGAN IN YOUR BODY.

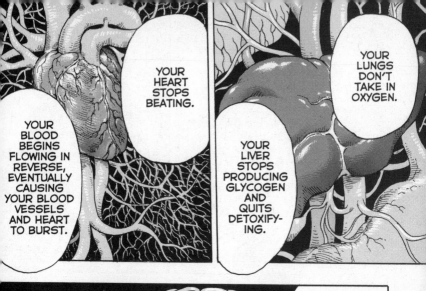

YOUR LUNGS DON'T TAKE IN OXYGEN.
YOUR LIVER STOPS PRODUCING GLYCOGEN AND QUITS DETOXIFY-ING.
YOUR HEART STOPS BEATING.
YOUR BLOOD BEGINS FLOWING IN REVERSE, EVENTUALLY CAUSING YOUR BLOOD VESSELS AND HEART TO BURST.
YOUR BRAIN HAS ALREADY STOPPED TRANSMITTING INFORMATION THROUGH YOUR NERVOUS SYSTEM.
ALL THE SYSTEMS THAT KEEP YOU "ALIVE"...
...ARE HEADING IN THE OPPOSITE DIRECTION...
...TO YOUR "DEATH."
HAAH...
HAAH...

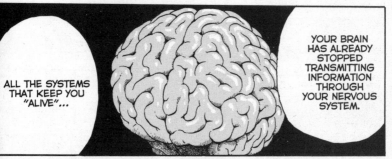

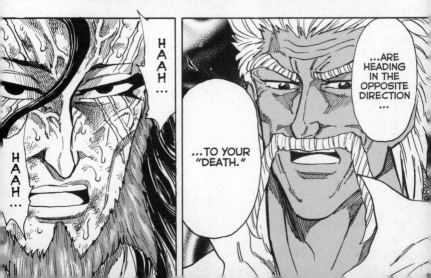

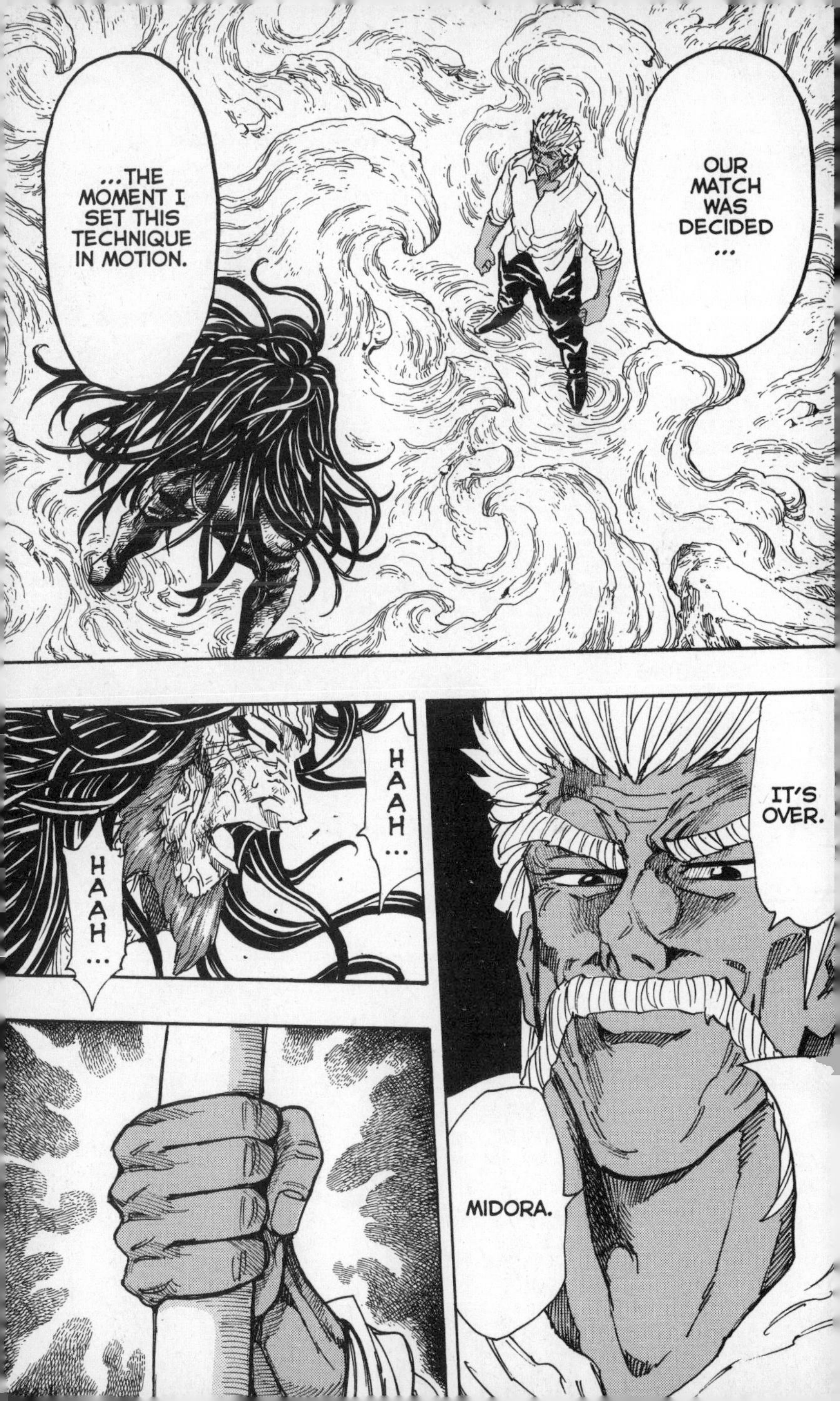
OUR MATCH WAS DECIDED ...
...THE MOMENT I SET THIS TECHNIQUE IN MOTION.
IT'S OVER.
MIDORA.
HAAH...
HAAH...

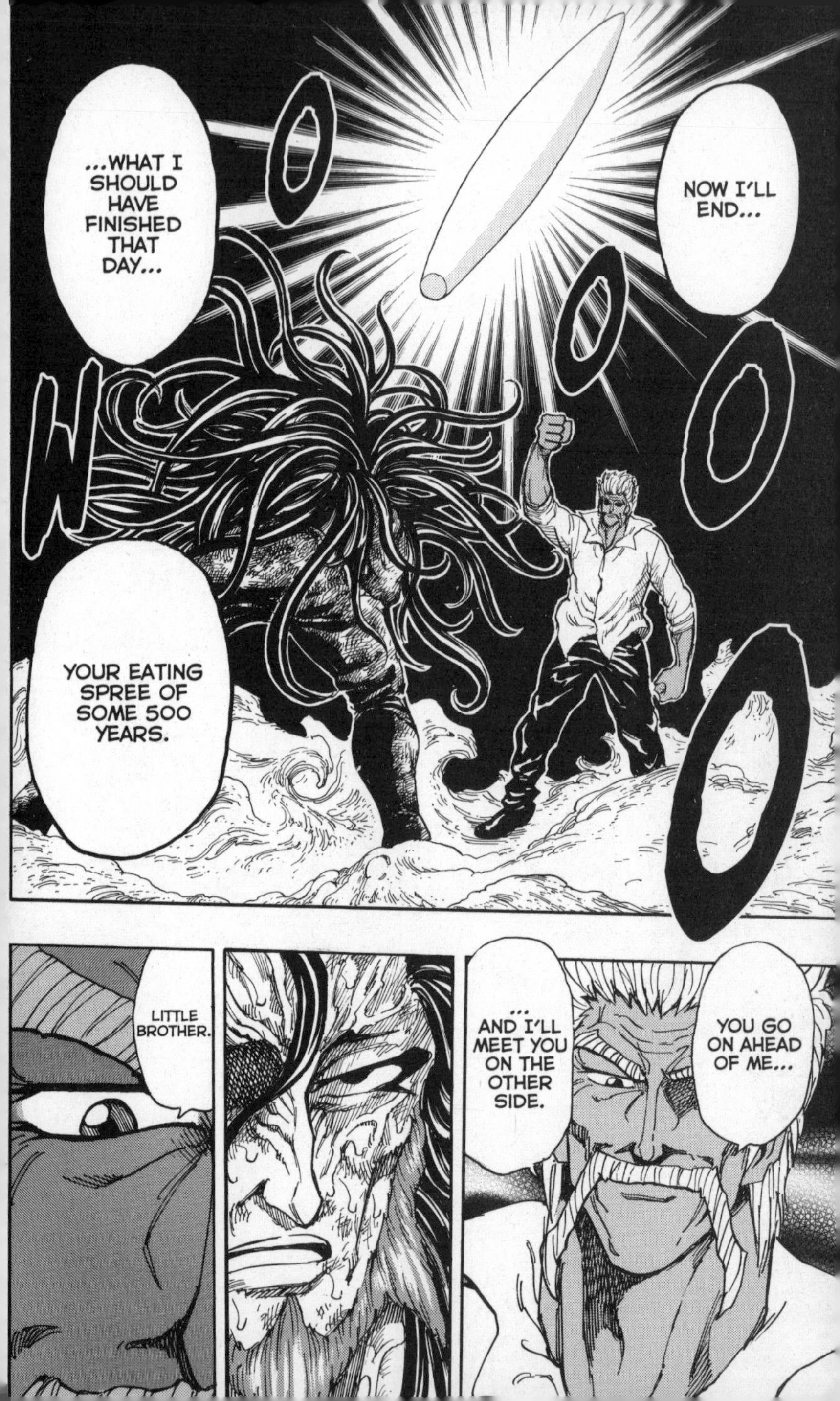
NOW I'LL END...
...WHAT I SHOULD HAVE FINISHED THAT DAY...
YOUR EATING SPREE OF SOME 500 YEARS.
YOU GO ON AHEAD OF ME...
...AND I'LL MEET YOU ON THE OTHER SIDE.
LITTLE BROTHER.

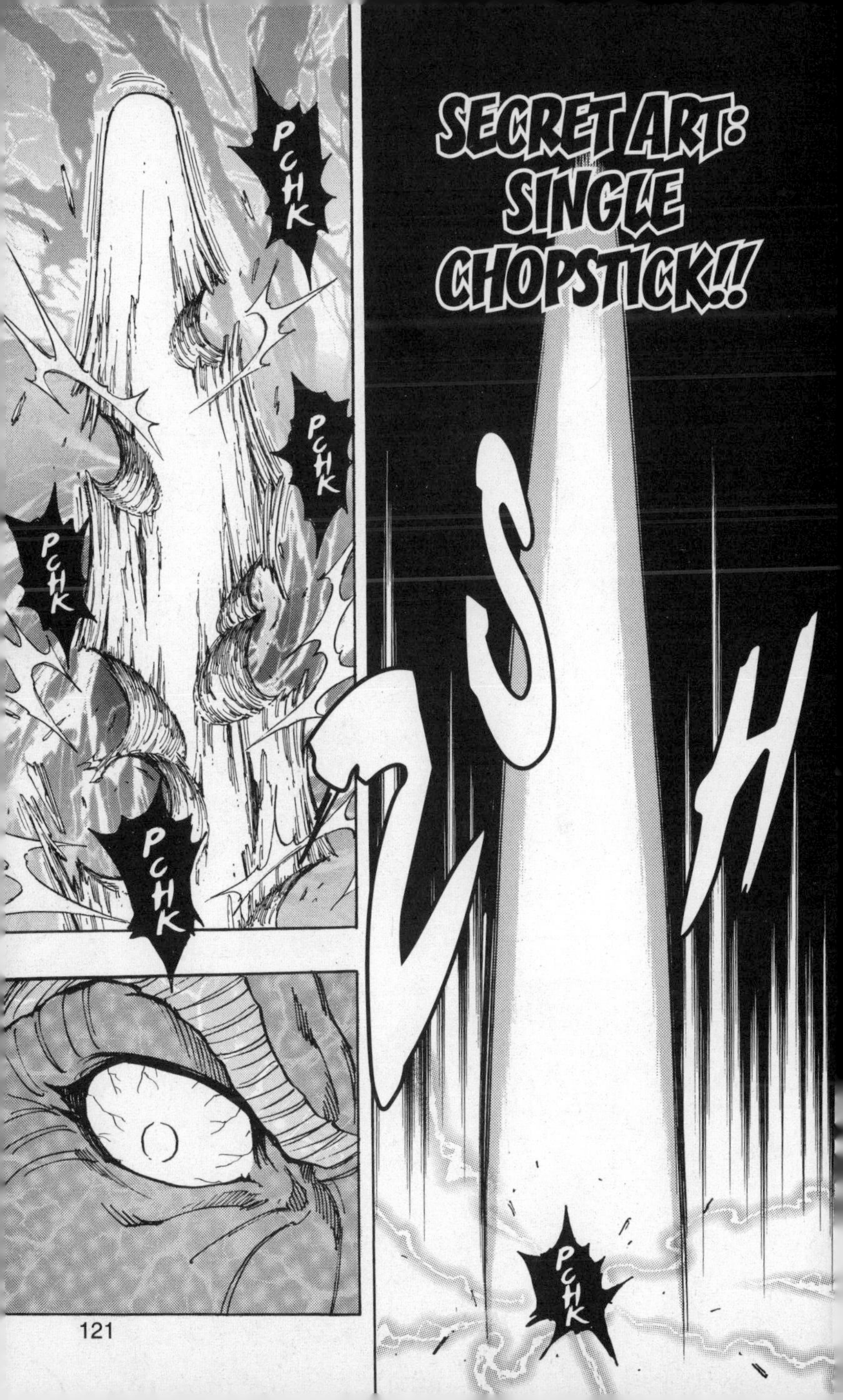
SECRET ART: SINGLE CHOPSTICK!!
ZSH
PCHK
PCHK
PCHK
PCHK
PCHK

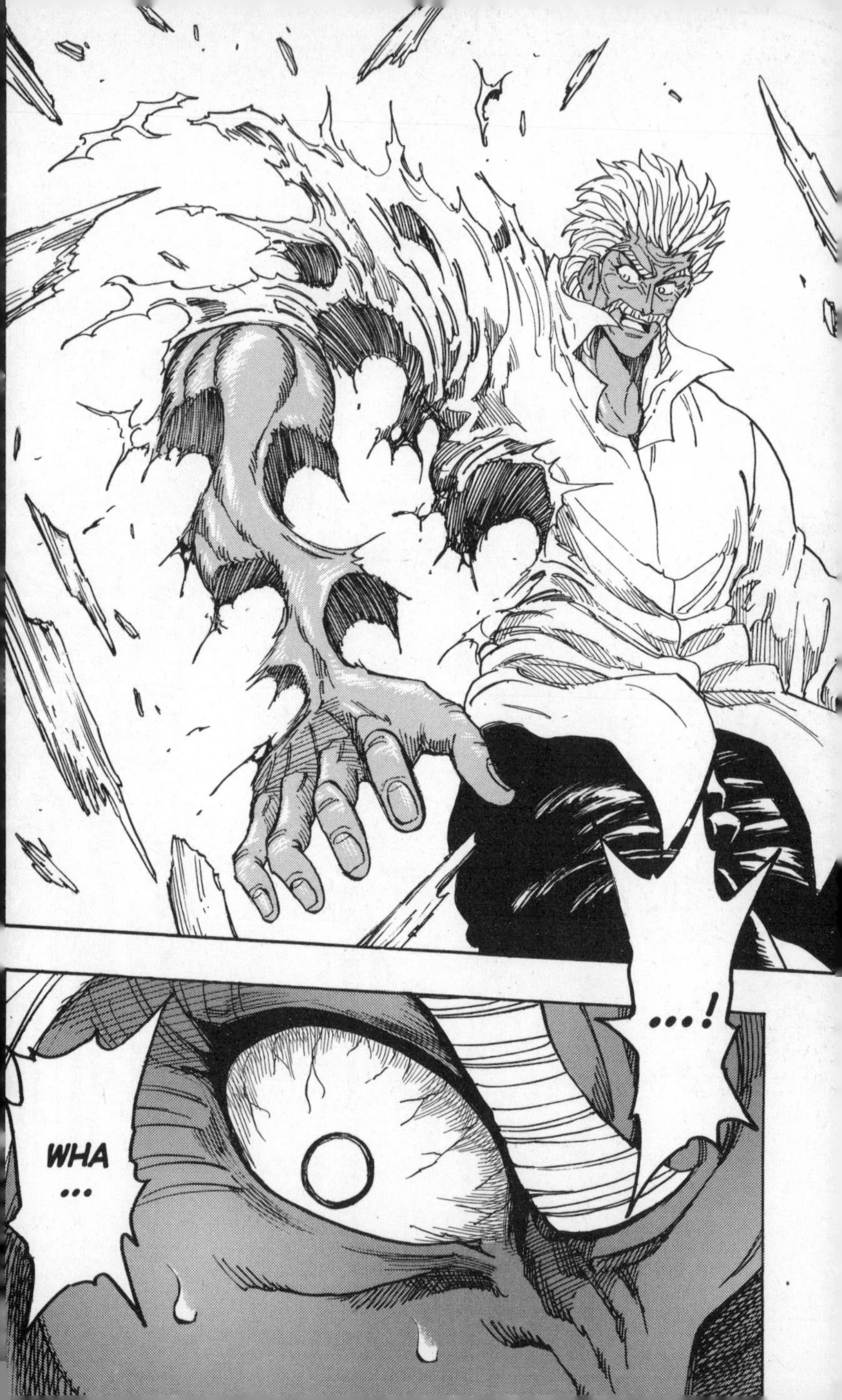
...!
WHA ...

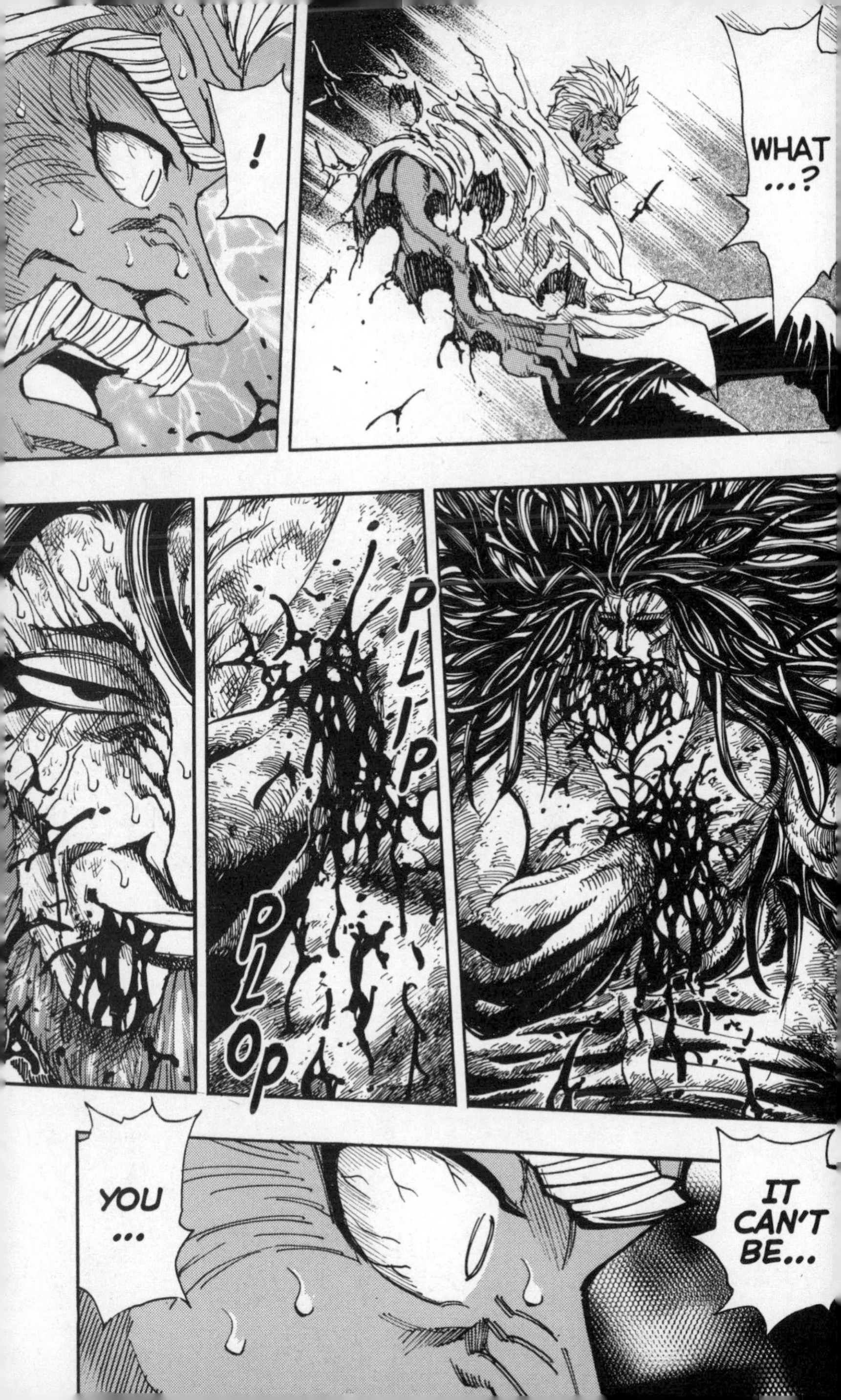
WHAT ...?
!
PLIP
PLOP
IT CAN'T BE...
YOU ...

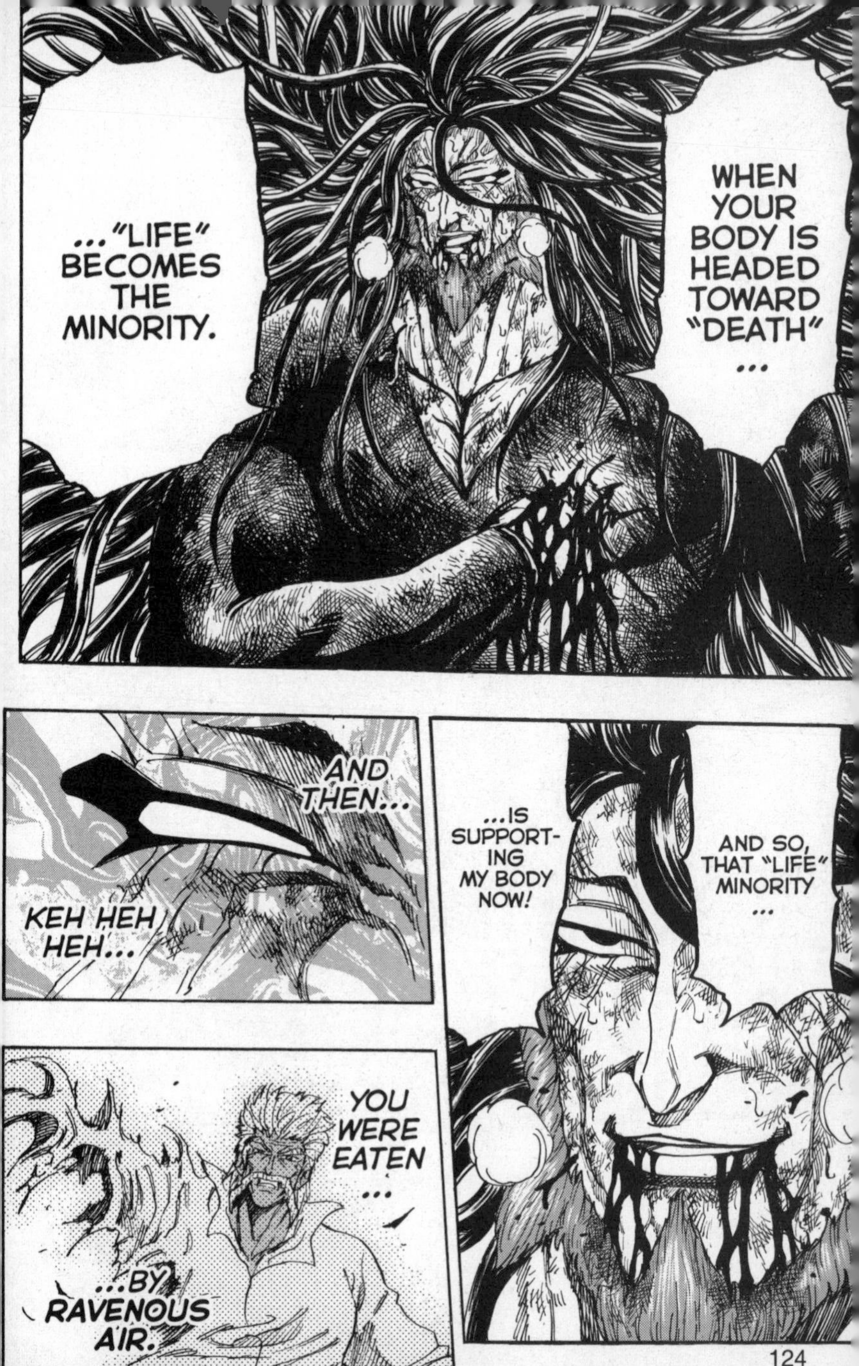
WHEN YOUR BODY IS HEADED TOWARD "DEATH" ...
..."LIFE" BECOMES THE MINORITY.
AND SO, THAT "LIFE" MINORITY ...
...IS SUPPORT-ING MY BODY NOW!
AND THEN...
KEH HEH HEH...
YOU WERE EATEN ...
...BY RAVENOUS AIR.

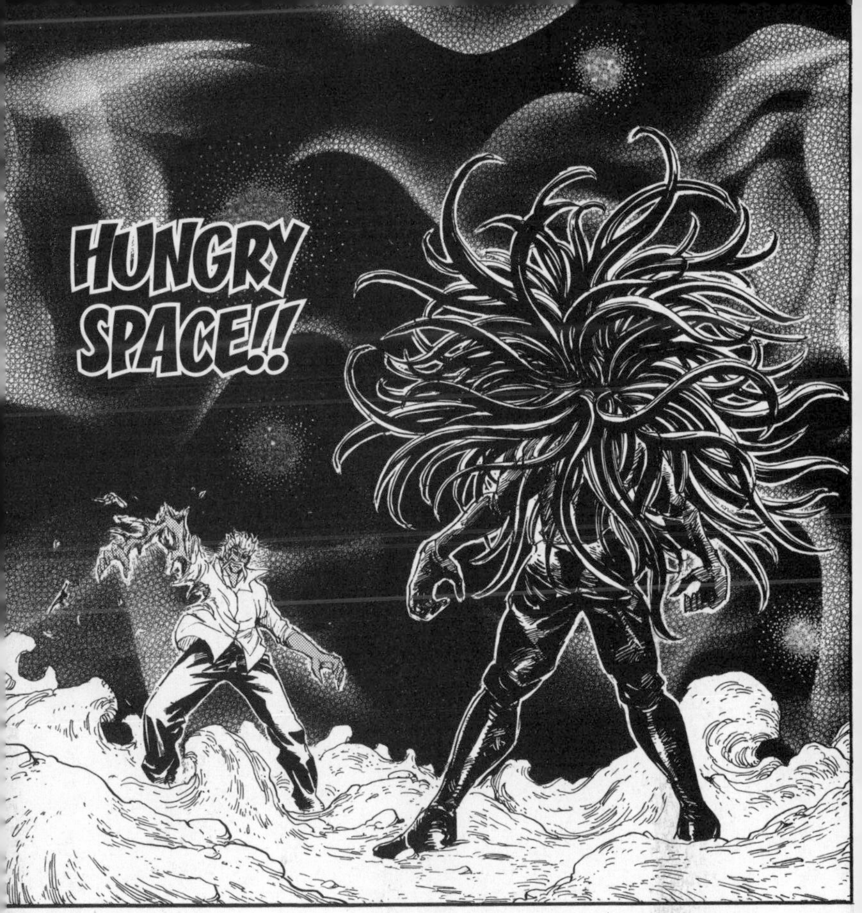
HUNGRY SPACE!!

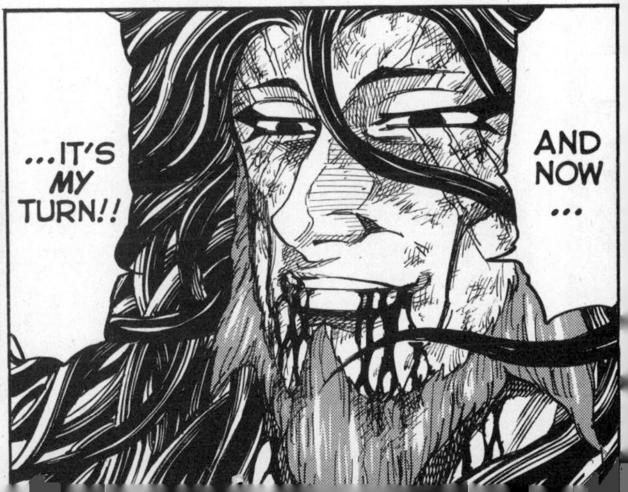
AND NOW ...
...IT'S MY TURN!!

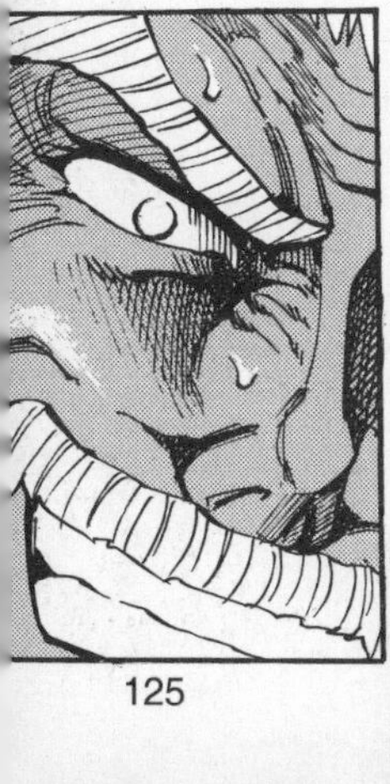

TORIKO

GOURMET CHECKLIST

Vol. 277

SAKE SALMON
(FISH)

CAPTURE LEVEL: 2
HABITAT: STEW POND
SIZE: 30 CM
HEIGHT: ---
WEIGHT: 3.5 KG
PRICE: 180,000 YEN PER FISH

A SAKE SALMON*
...

SCALE

A VARIETY OF SALMON THAT'S NATURALLY ALCOHOLIC. WHEN GRILLED, THE ALCOHOL WILL CATCH FIRE, SO SAKE SALMON IS OFTEN EATEN RAW AS SASHIMI. BOOZERS CAN'T RESIST THIS FOOD ITEM, THOUGH IT RARELY COMES ON THE MARKET. THIS HIGH-QUALITY FISH IS A FAVORITE OF CHIEF MANSOM'S.

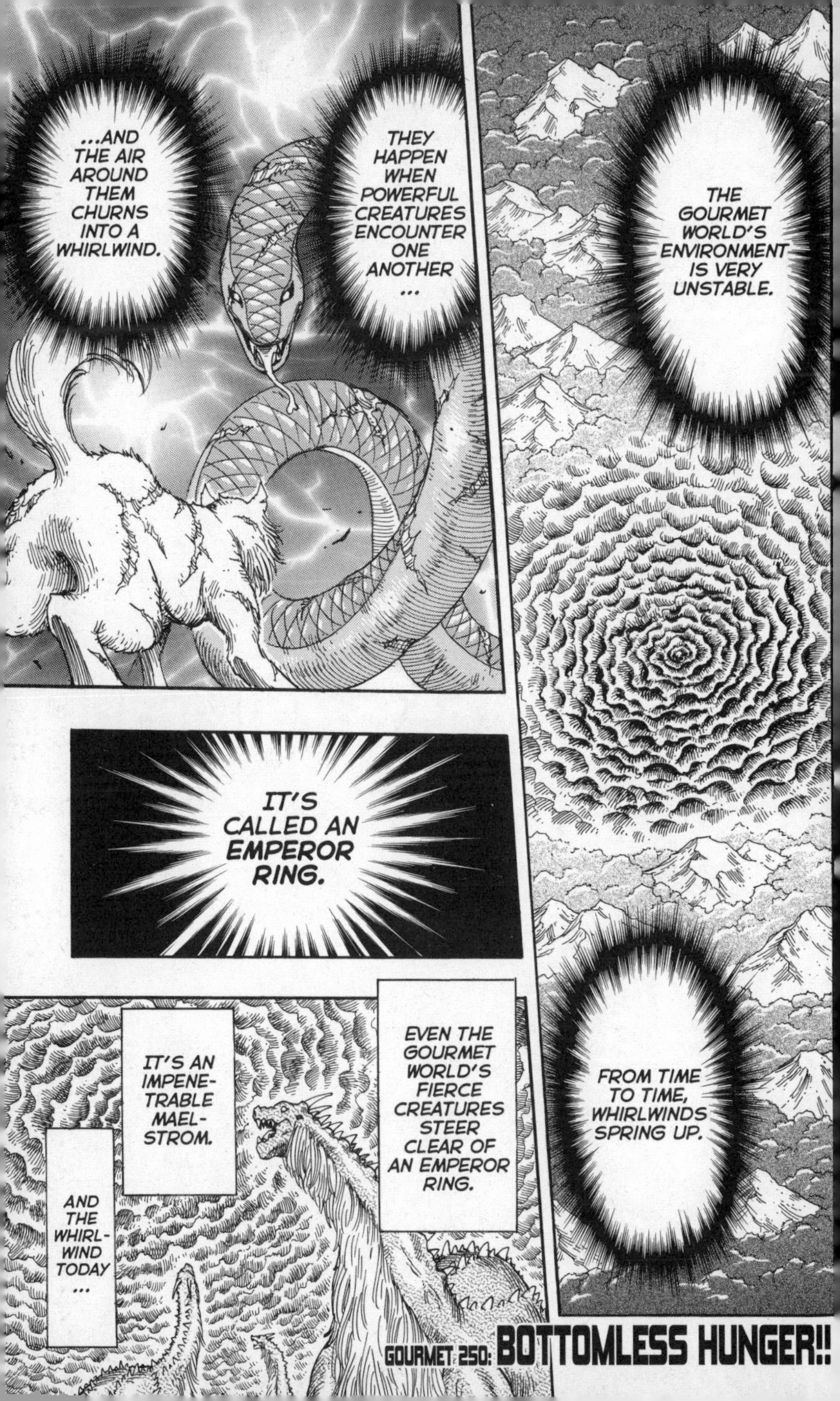
THE GOURMET WORLD'S ENVIRONMENT IS VERY UNSTABLE.
FROM TIME TO TIME, WHIRLWINDS SPRING UP.
THEY HAPPEN WHEN POWERFUL CREATURES ENCOUNTER ONE ANOTHER ...
...AND THE AIR AROUND THEM CHURNS INTO A WHIRLWIND.
IT'S CALLED AN EMPEROR RING.
EVEN THE GOURMET WORLD'S FIERCE CREATURES STEER CLEAR OF AN EMPEROR RING.
IT'S AN IMPENE-TRABLE MAEL-STROM.
AND THE WHIRL-WIND TODAY ...
GOURMET 250: BOTTOMLESS HUNGER!!

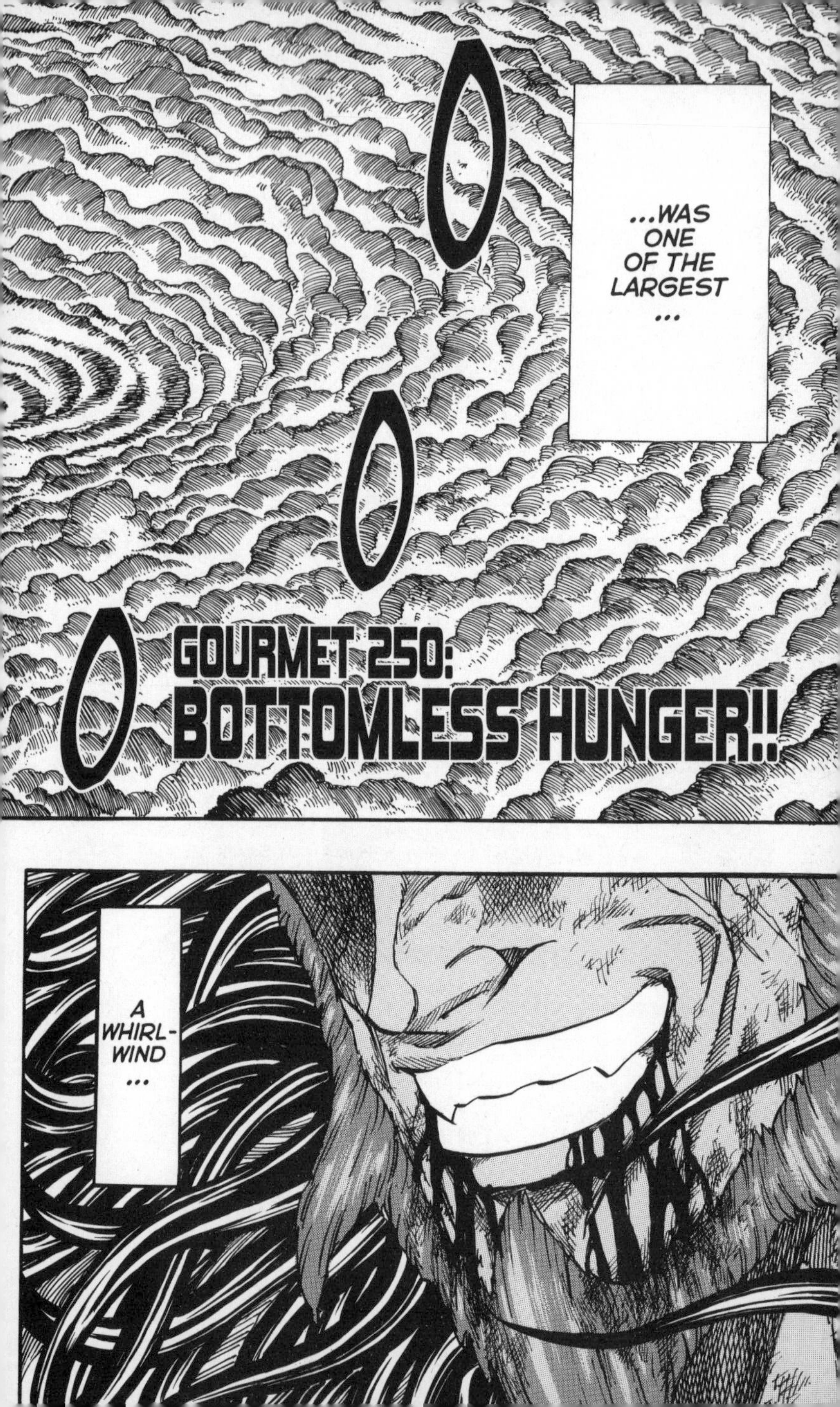
...WAS ONE OF THE LARGEST ...
GOURMET 250: BOTTOMLESS HUNGER!!
A WHIRL-WIND ...

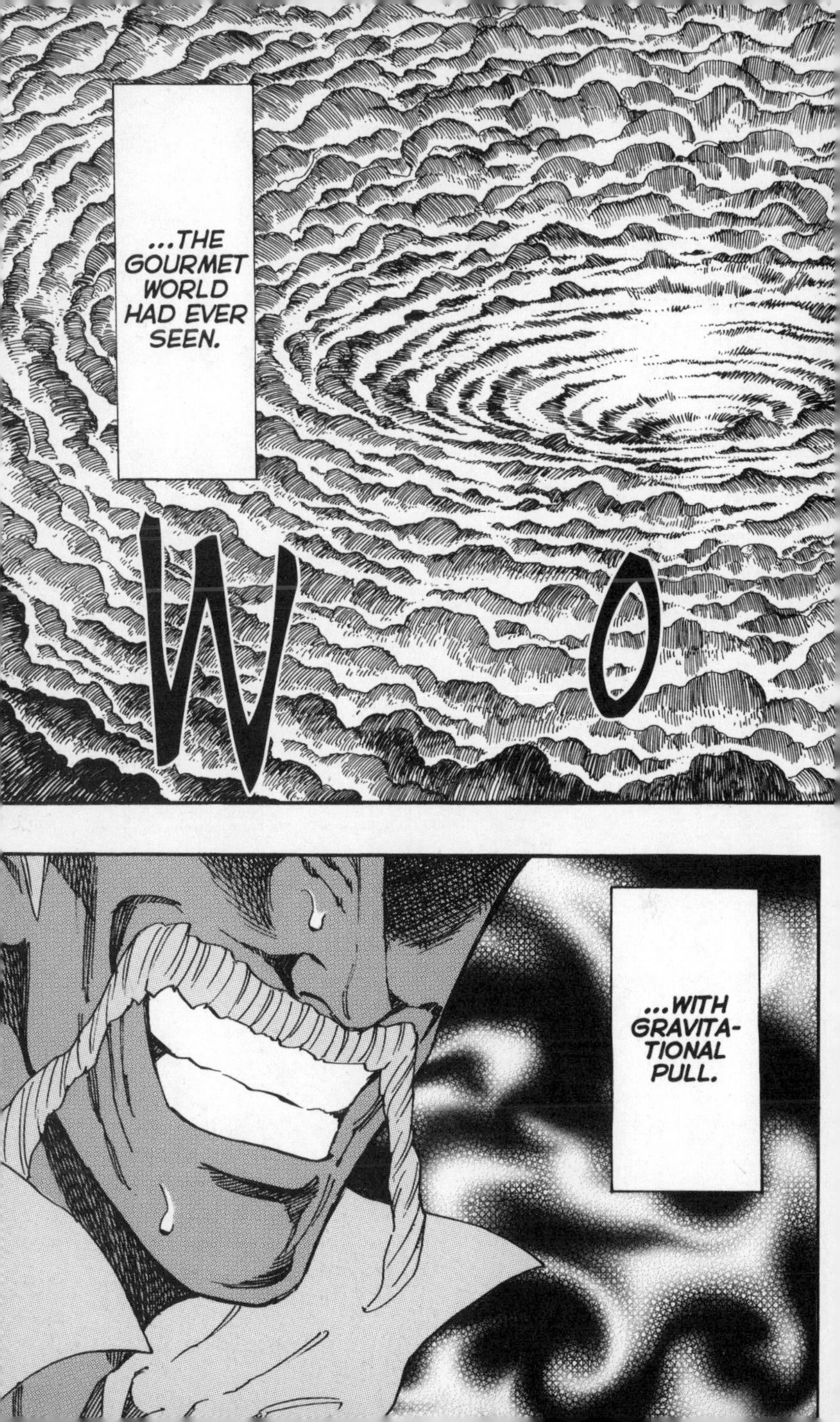
...THE GOURMET WORLD HAD EVER SEEN.
W
O
...WITH GRAVITA-TIONAL PULL.

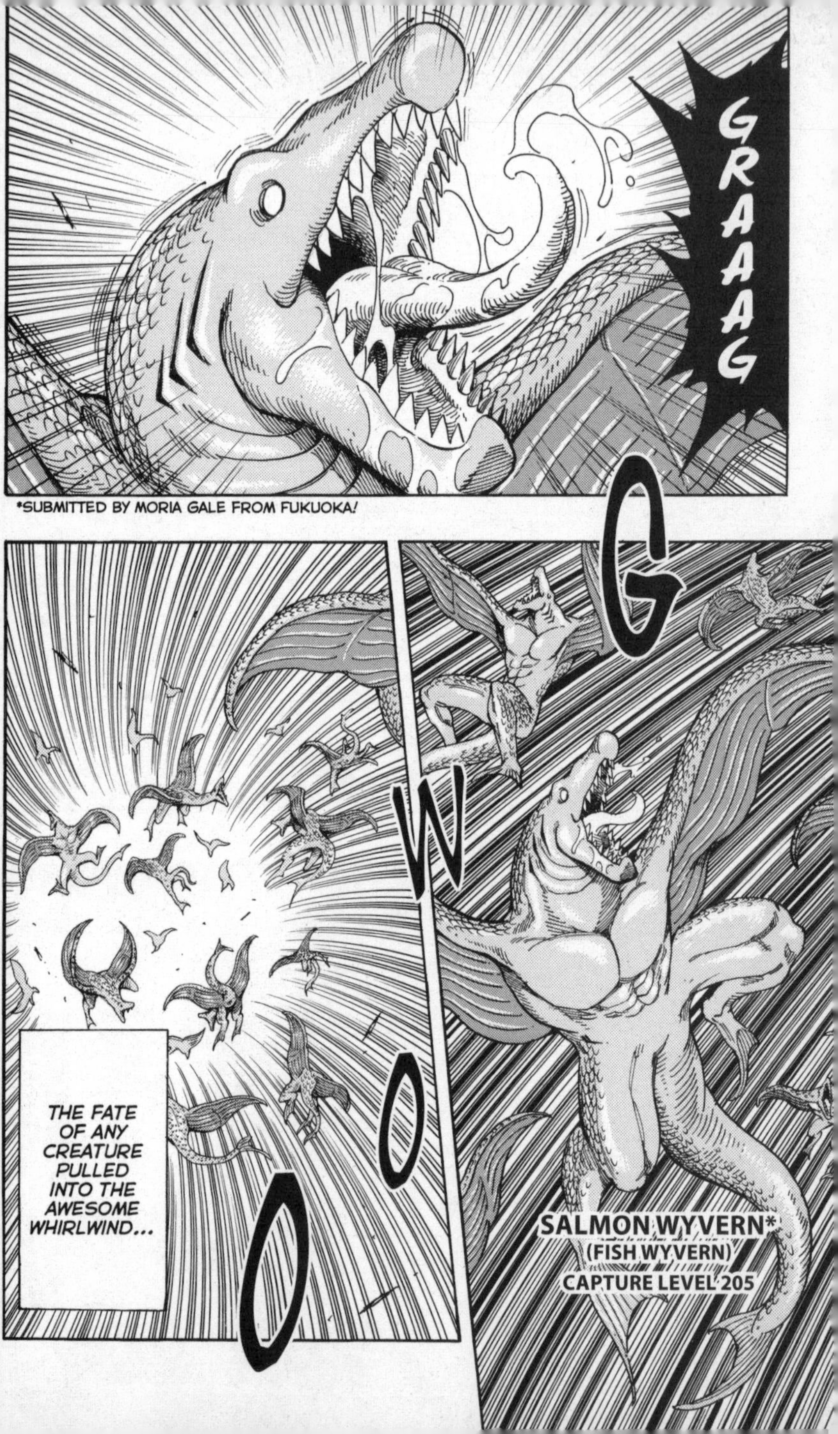
GRAAAAG
*SUBMITTED BY MORIA GALE FROM FUKUOKA!
GWOOO
SALMON WYVERN*
(FISH WYVERN)
CAPTURE LEVEL 205
THE FATE OF ANY CREATURE PULLED INTO THE AWESOME WHIRLWIND...

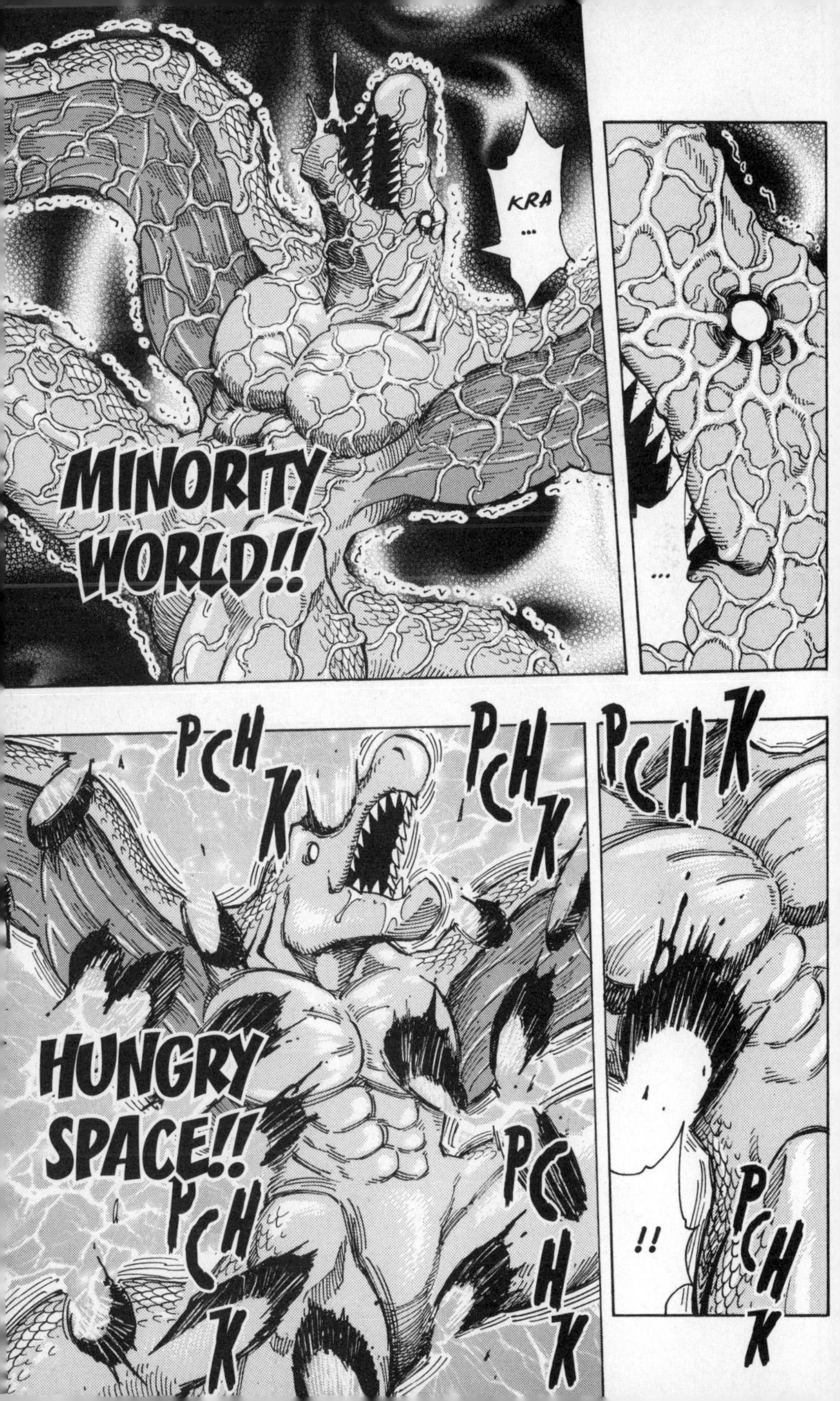
...
KRA ...
MINORITY WORLD!!
PCHK
!!
PCHK
PCHK
PCHK
PCHK
HUNGRY SPACE!!
PCHK
PCHK

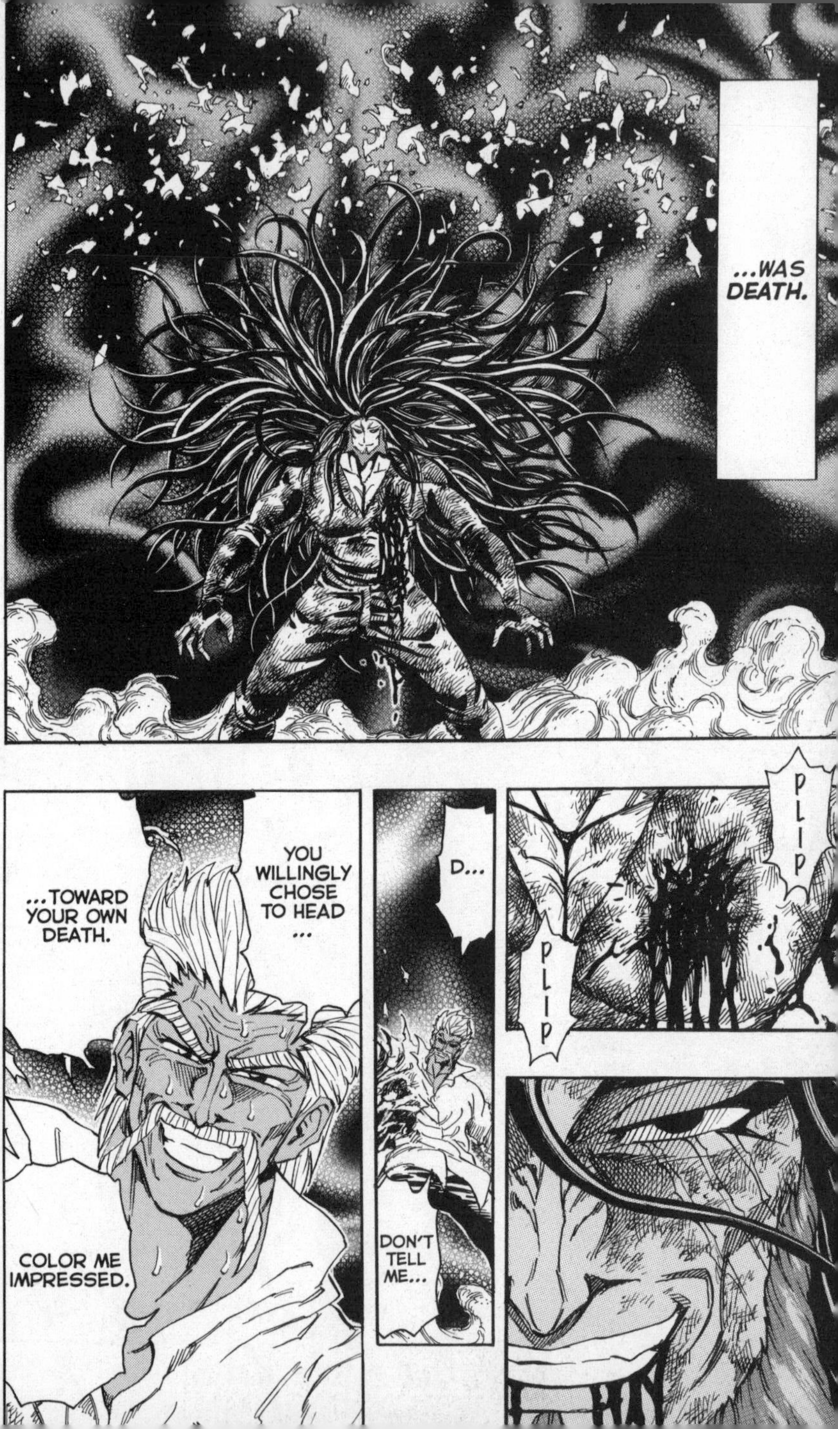
...WAS DEATH.
PLIP
PLIP
D...
DON'T TELL ME...
YOU WILLINGLY CHOSE TO HEAD...
...TOWARD YOUR OWN DEATH.
COLOR ME IMPRESSED.

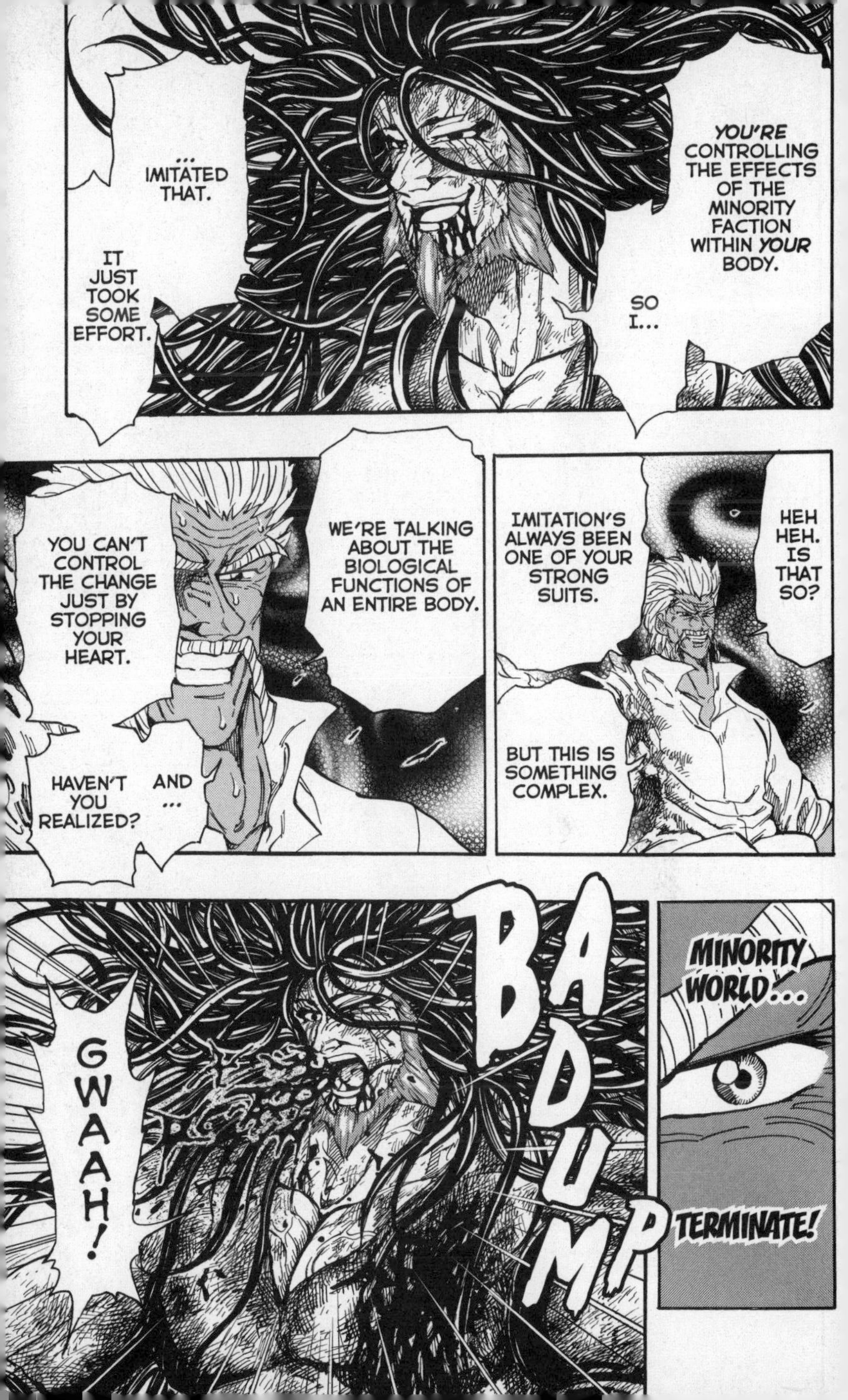

YOU'RE CONTROLLING THE EFFECTS OF THE MINORITY FACTION WITHIN YOUR BODY.
SO I...
...IMITATED THAT.
IT JUST TOOK SOME EFFORT.
HEH HEH. IS THAT SO?
IMITATION'S ALWAYS BEEN ONE OF YOUR STRONG SUITS.
BUT THIS IS SOMETHING COMPLEX.
WE'RE TALKING ABOUT THE BIOLOGICAL FUNCTIONS OF AN ENTIRE BODY.
YOU CAN'T CONTROL THE CHANGE JUST BY STOPPING YOUR HEART.
AND...
HAVEN'T YOU REALIZED?
MINORITY WORLD...
TERMINATE!
BADUMP
GWAAH!

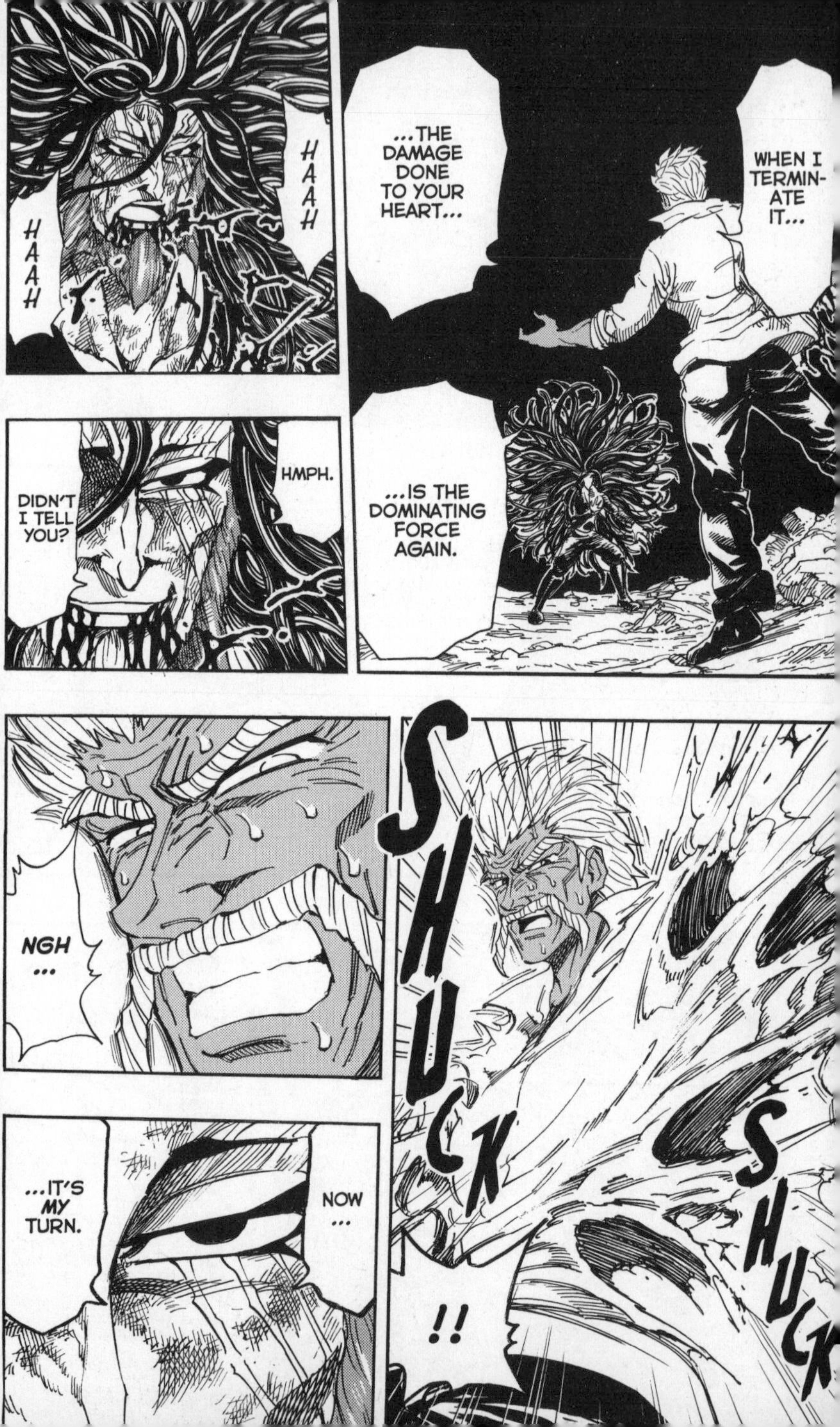
WHEN I TERMIN-ATE IT...
...THE DAMAGE DONE TO YOUR HEART...
...IS THE DOMINATING FORCE AGAIN.
HAAAH
HAAAH
HMPH.
DIDN'T I TELL YOU?
SHUCK
SHUCK
!!
NGH...
NOW...
...IT'S *MY* TURN.

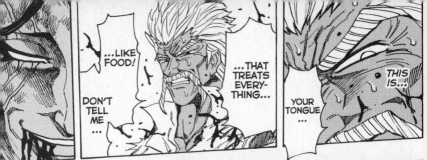

THIS IS...
YOUR TONGUE...
...THAT TREATS EVERYTHING...
...LIKE FOOD!
DON'T TELL ME...
MIDORA'S HUNGRY TONGUE WASN'T LIMITED TO EATING PHYSICAL OBJECTS.
IT COULD CONSUME THE VERY AIR.
THE VACUUM LEFT IN ITS WAKE...
...WAS AN UNSEEN MEAL FIT FOR A KING.
OTHERWISE KNOWN AS HUNGRY SPACE!
A SILENT KILLER, IT AMBUSHES ANY PREY THAT TOUCHES IT.
AND IT REMEMBERS THE TASTE OF ANY CREATURE IT'S TOUCHED!..

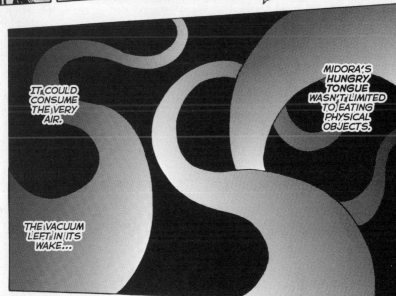

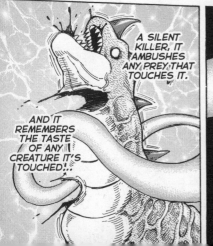

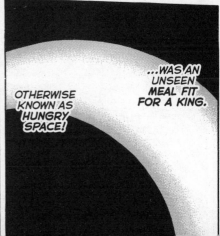

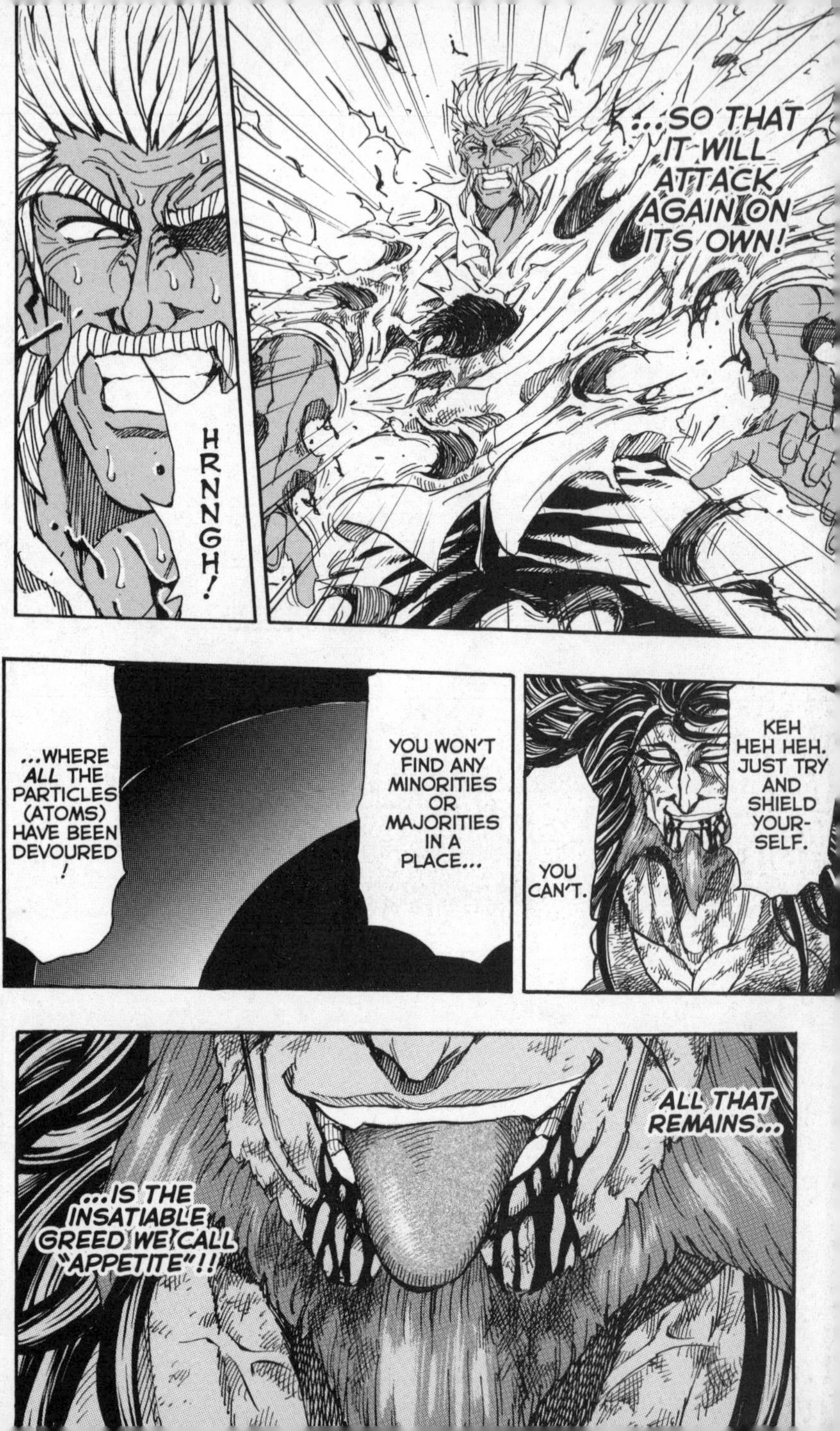
...SO THAT IT WILL ATTACK AGAIN ON ITS OWN!
HRNNGH!
KEH HEH HEH. JUST TRY AND SHIELD YOURSELF.
YOU CAN'T.
YOU WON'T FIND ANY MINORITIES OR MAJORITIES IN A PLACE...
...WHERE ALL THE PARTICLES (ATOMS) HAVE BEEN DEVOURED!
ALL THAT REMAINS...
...IS THE INSATIABLE GREED WE CALL "APPETITE"!!

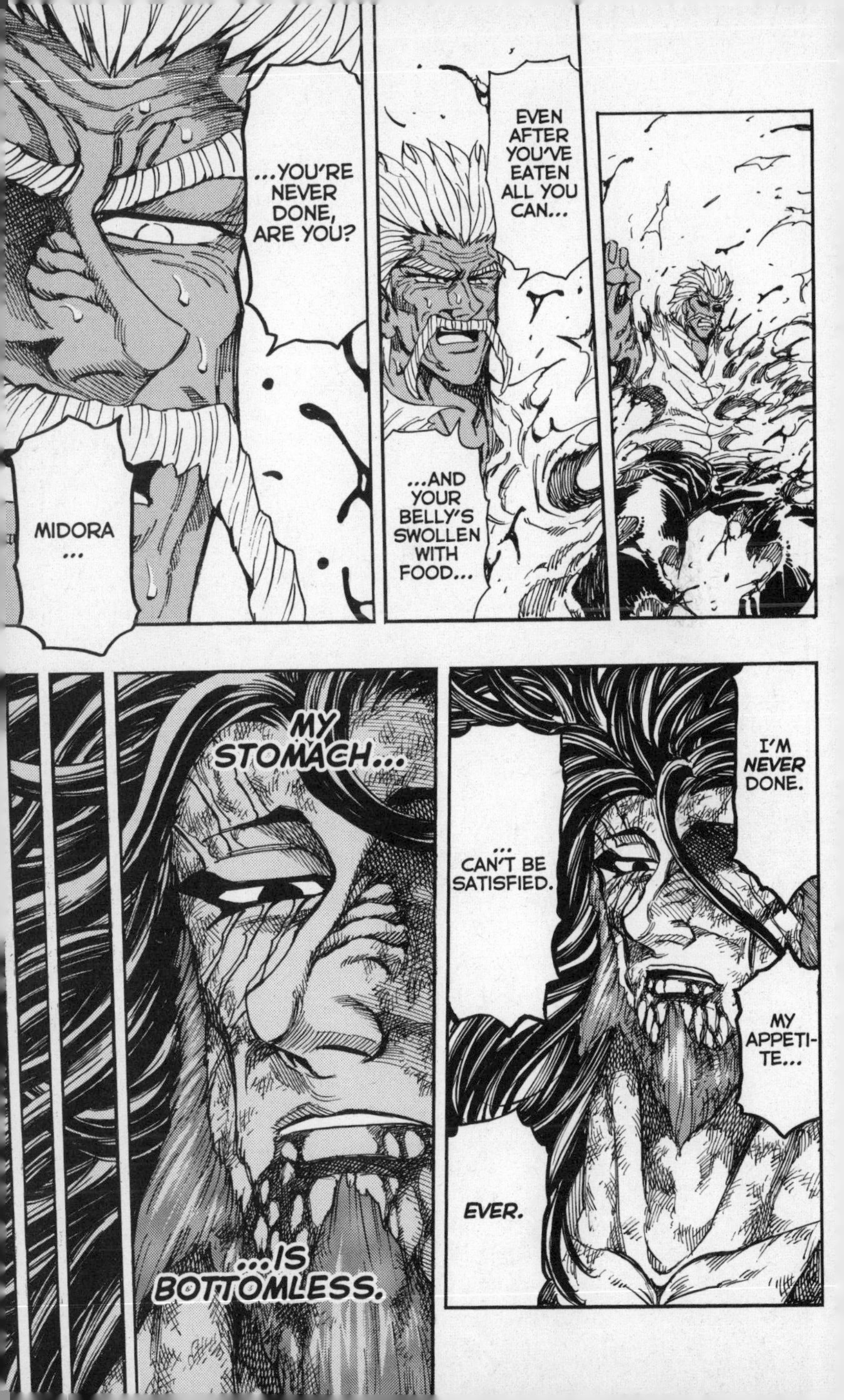
EVEN AFTER YOU'VE EATEN ALL YOU CAN...
...AND YOUR BELLY'S SWOLLEN WITH FOOD...
...YOU'RE NEVER DONE, ARE YOU?
MIDORA ...
I'M *NEVER* DONE.
MY APPETITE...
... CAN'T BE SATISFIED.
EVER.
MY STOMACH...
...IS BOTTOMLESS.

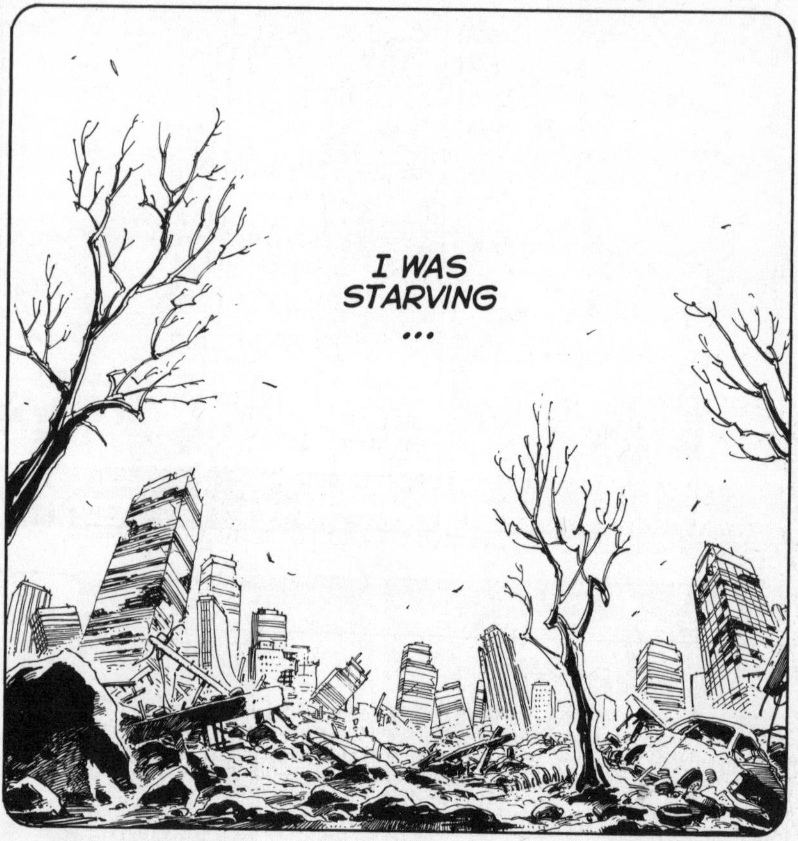
I WAS STARVING
...

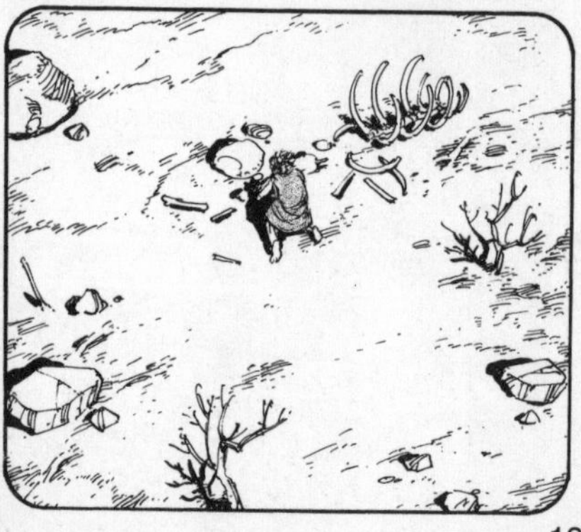

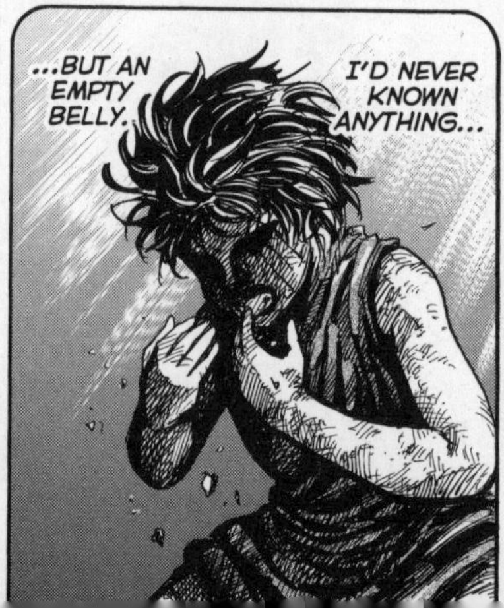
I'D NEVER KNOWN ANYTHING...
...BUT AN EMPTY BELLY.

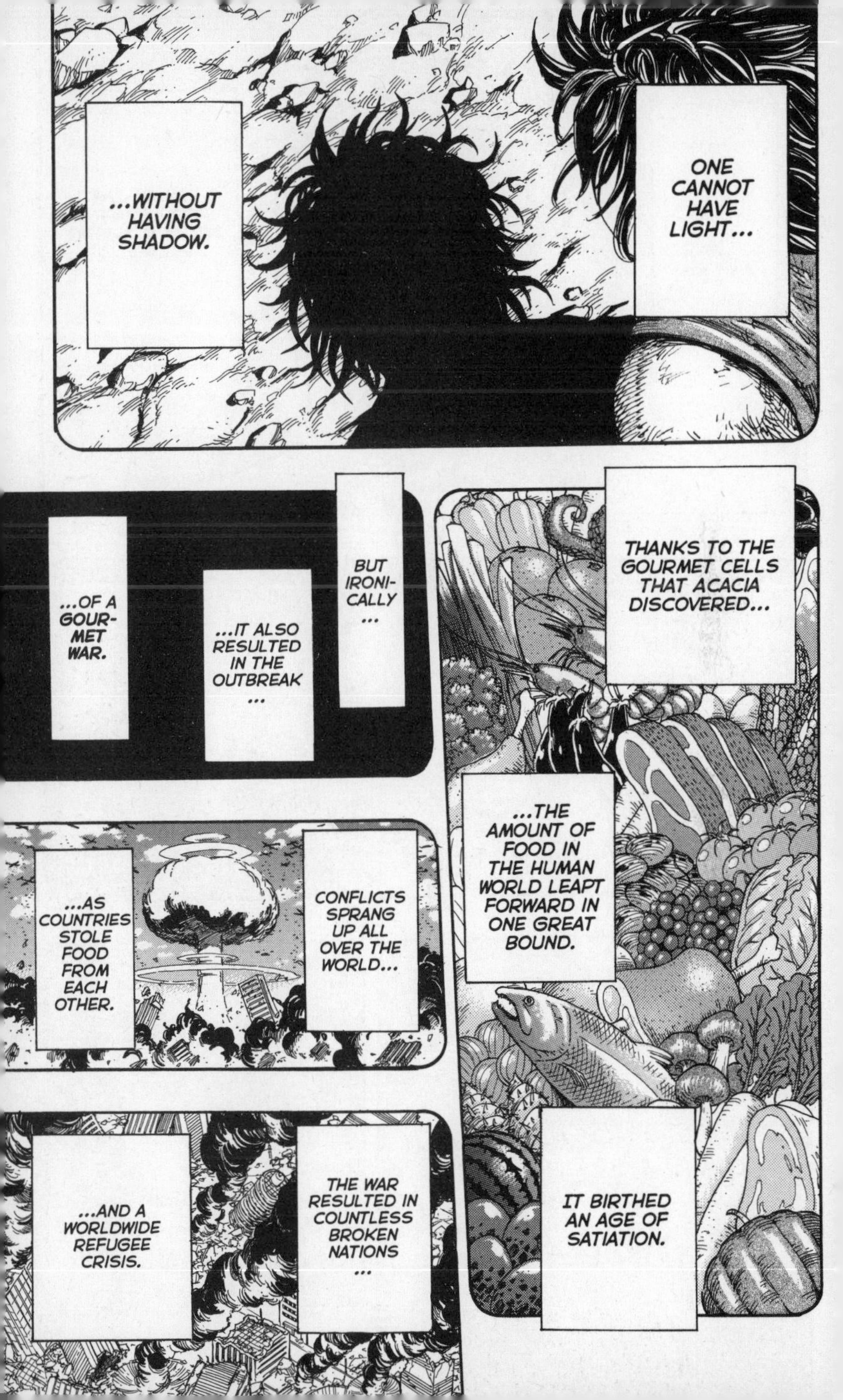
ONE CANNOT HAVE LIGHT...
...WITHOUT HAVING SHADOW.
THANKS TO THE GOURMET CELLS THAT ACACIA DISCOVERED...
...THE AMOUNT OF FOOD IN THE HUMAN WORLD LEAPT FORWARD IN ONE GREAT BOUND.
IT BIRTHED AN AGE OF SATIATION.
BUT IRONI-CALLY...
...IT ALSO RESULTED IN THE OUTBREAK...
...OF A GOUR-MET WAR.
CONFLICTS SPRANG UP ALL OVER THE WORLD...
...AS COUNTRIES STOLE FOOD FROM EACH OTHER.
THE WAR RESULTED IN COUNTLESS BROKEN NATIONS...
...AND A WORLDWIDE REFUGEE CRISIS.

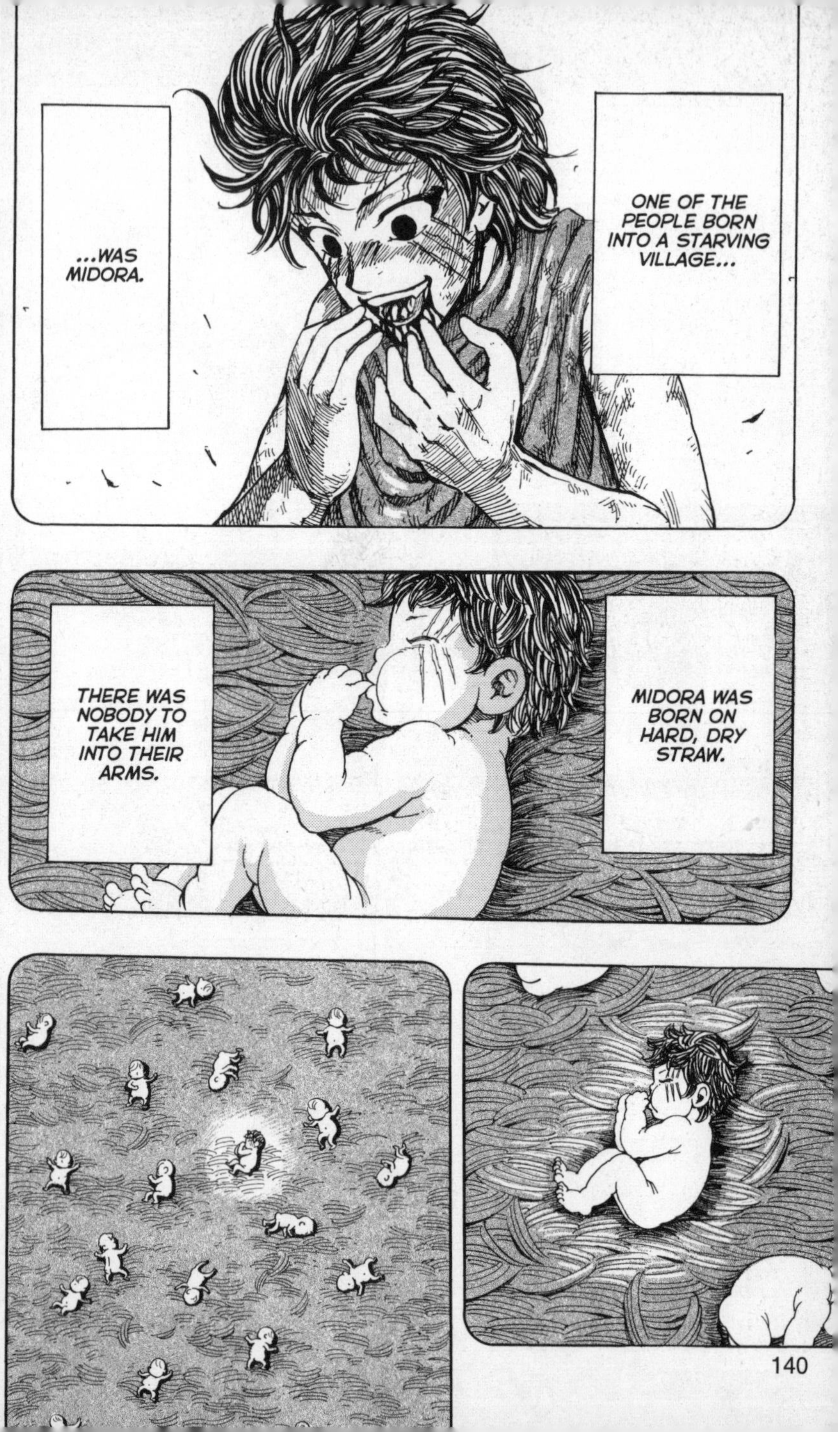
ONE OF THE PEOPLE BORN INTO A STARVING VILLAGE...
...WAS MIDORA.
MIDORA WAS BORN ON HARD, DRY STRAW.
THERE WAS NOBODY TO TAKE HIM INTO THEIR ARMS.

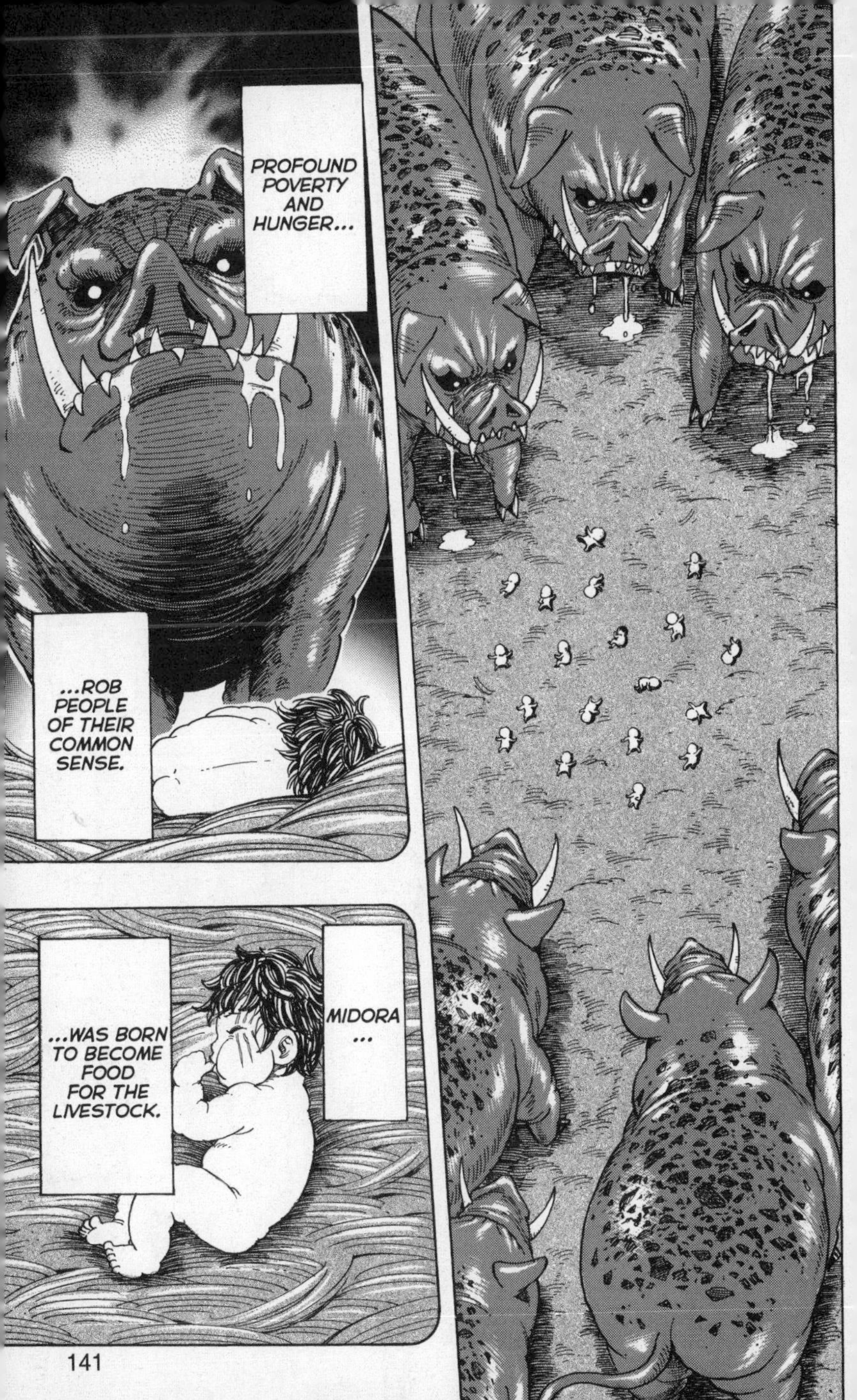
PROFOUND POVERTY AND HUNGER...
...ROB PEOPLE OF THEIR COMMON SENSE.
MIDORA...
...WAS BORN TO BECOME FOOD FOR THE LIVESTOCK.

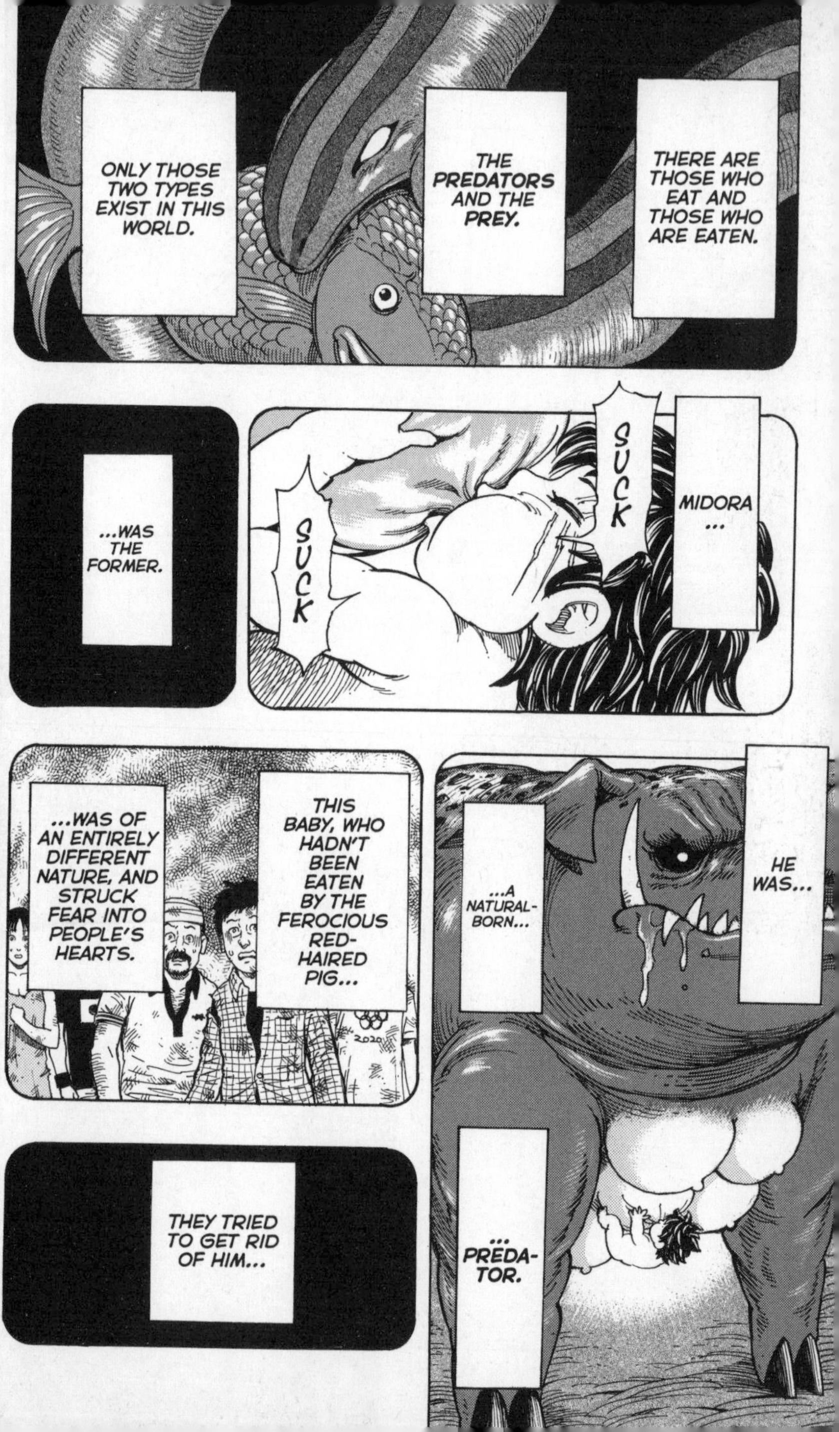
THERE ARE THOSE WHO EAT AND THOSE WHO ARE EATEN.
THE PREDATORS AND THE PREY.
ONLY THOSE TWO TYPES EXIST IN THIS WORLD.
MIDORA...
SUCK
SUCK
...WAS THE FORMER.
HE WAS...
...A NATURAL-BORN...
...PREDATOR.
THIS BABY, WHO HADN'T BEEN EATEN BY THE FEROCIOUS RED-HAIRED PIG...
...WAS OF AN ENTIRELY DIFFERENT NATURE, AND STRUCK FEAR INTO PEOPLE'S HEARTS.
2020
THEY TRIED TO GET RID OF HIM...

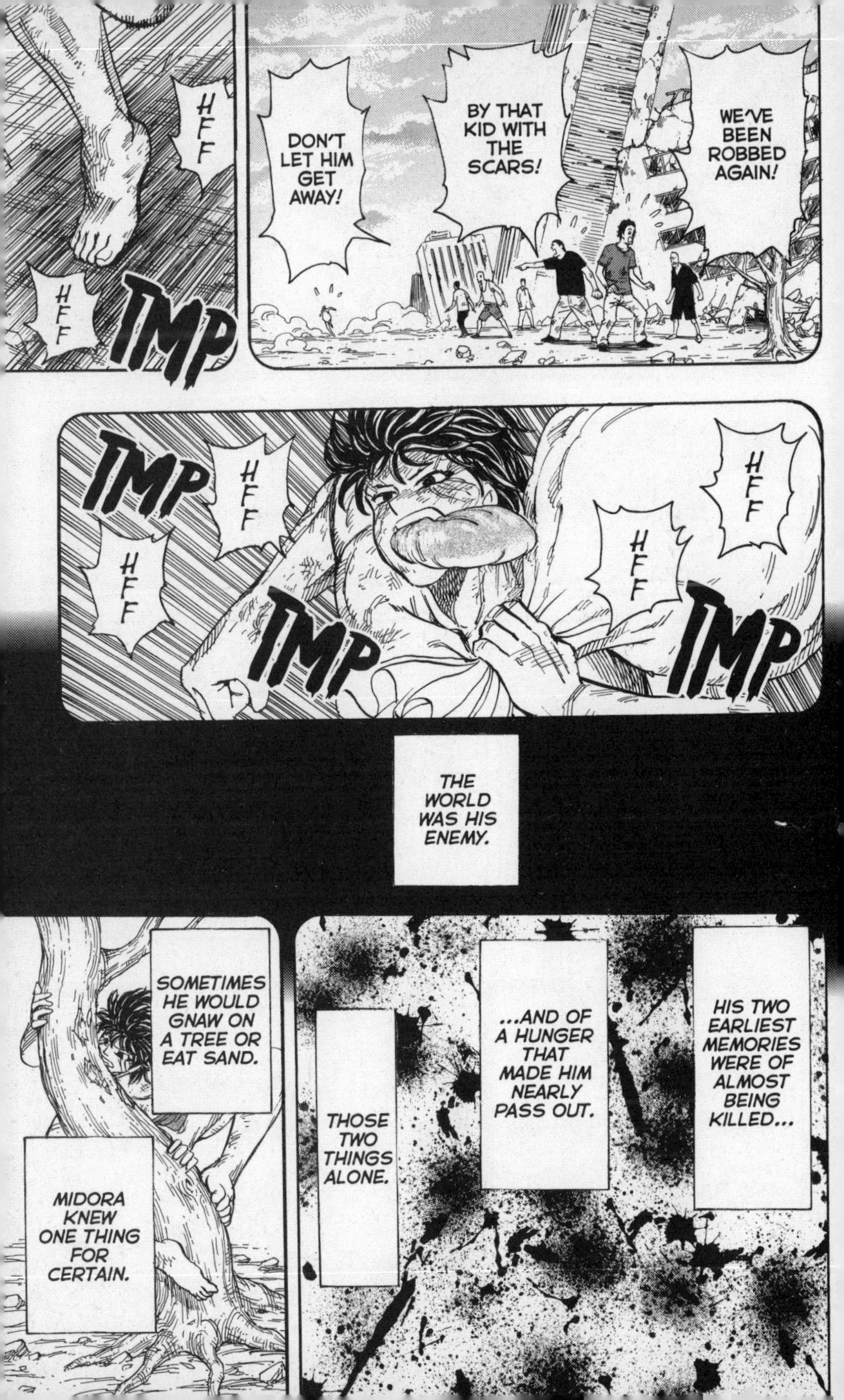
WE'VE BEEN ROBBED AGAIN!
BY THAT KID WITH THE SCARS!
DON'T LET HIM GET AWAY!
HFF
HFF
TMP
HFF
HFF
TMP
TMP
HFF
HFF
TMP
THE WORLD WAS HIS ENEMY.
HIS TWO EARLIEST MEMORIES WERE OF ALMOST BEING KILLED...
...AND OF A HUNGER THAT MADE HIM NEARLY PASS OUT.
THOSE TWO THINGS ALONE.
SOMETIMES HE WOULD GNAW ON A TREE OR EAT SAND.
MIDORA KNEW ONE THING FOR CERTAIN.

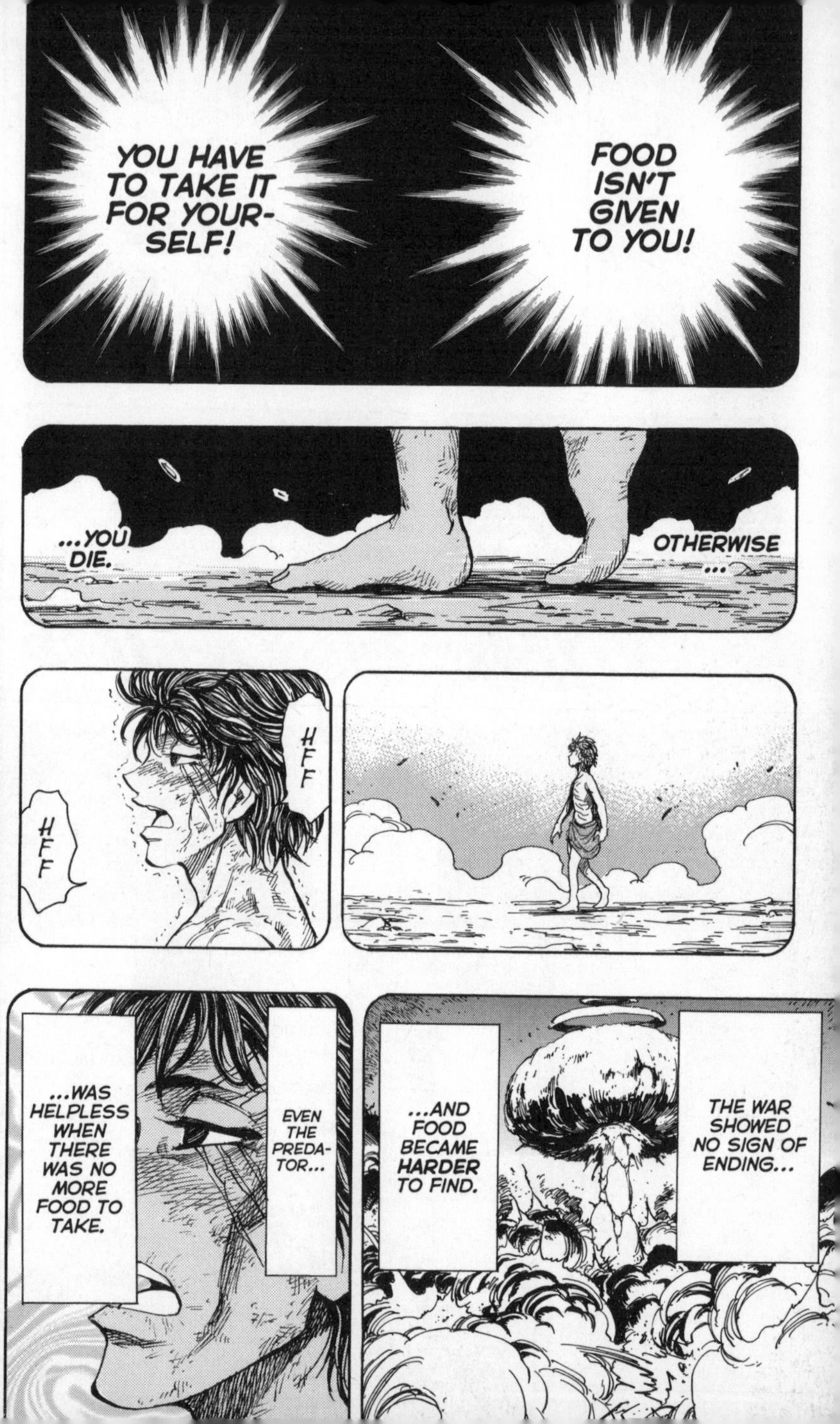
FOOD ISN'T GIVEN TO YOU!
YOU HAVE TO TAKE IT FOR YOUR-SELF!
OTHERWISE ...
...YOU DIE.
HFF
HFF
THE WAR SHOWED NO SIGN OF ENDING...
...AND FOOD BECAME HARDER TO FIND.
EVEN THE PREDA-TOR...
...WAS HELPLESS WHEN THERE WAS NO MORE FOOD TO TAKE.

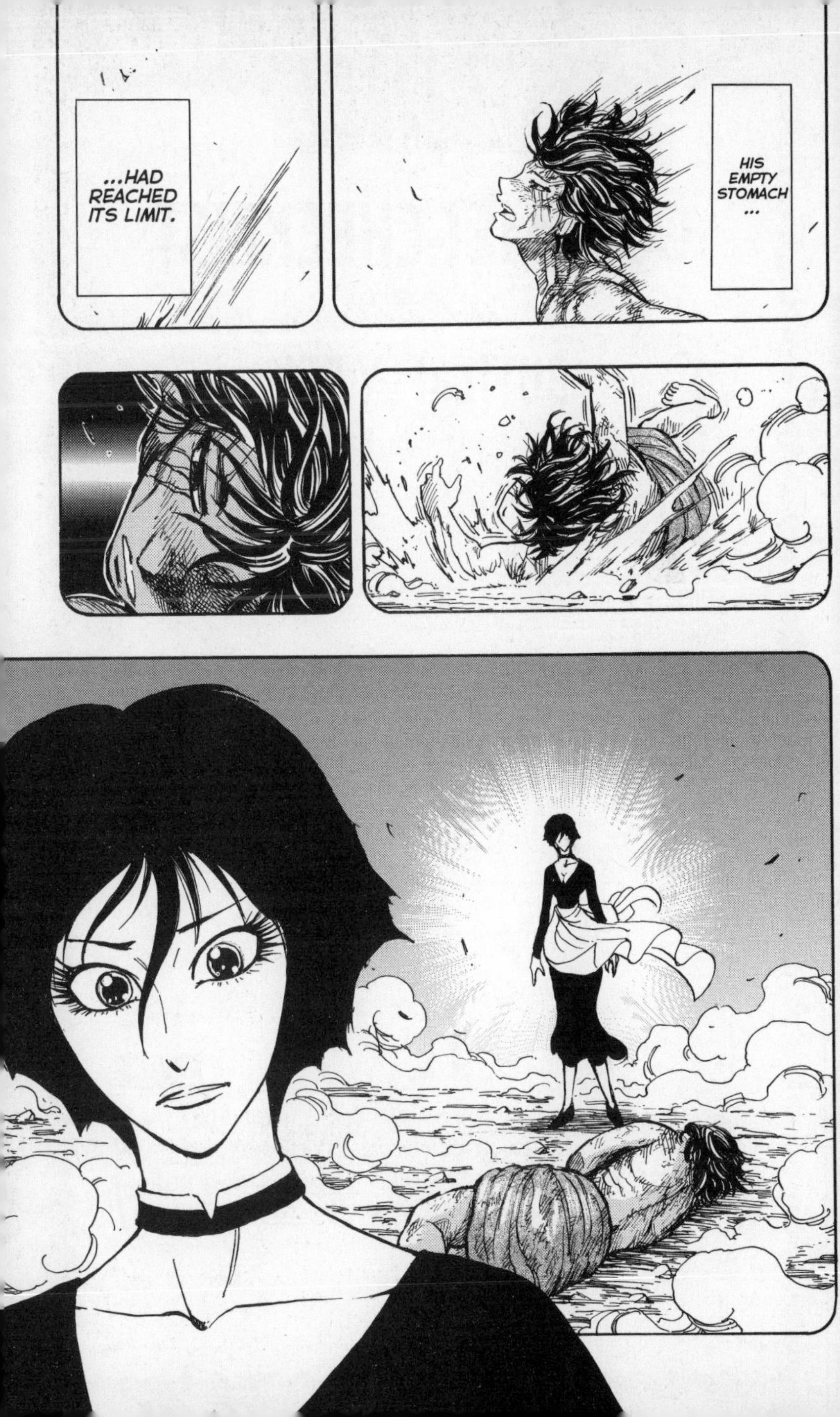
HIS EMPTY STOMACH ...
...HAD REACHED ITS LIMIT.

TORIKO

GOURMET CHECKLIST

Vol. 278

BUTTERFLY EEL
(FISH)

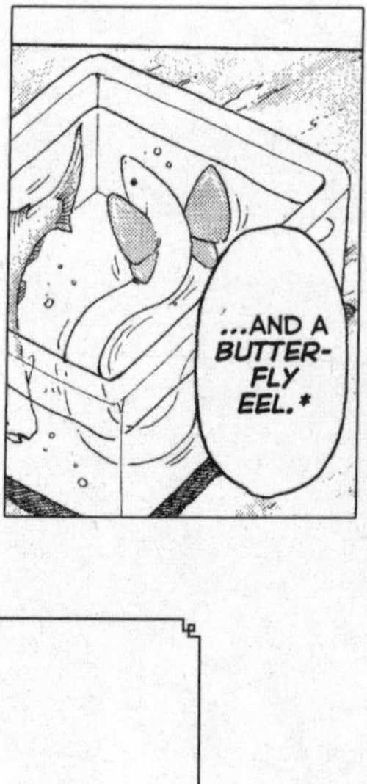
...AND A BUTTER-FLY EEL.*

CAPTURE LEVEL: 15
HABITAT: STEW POND
SIZE: 50 CM
HEIGHT: ---
WEIGHT: 3 KG
PRICE: 10,000 YEN PER FISH

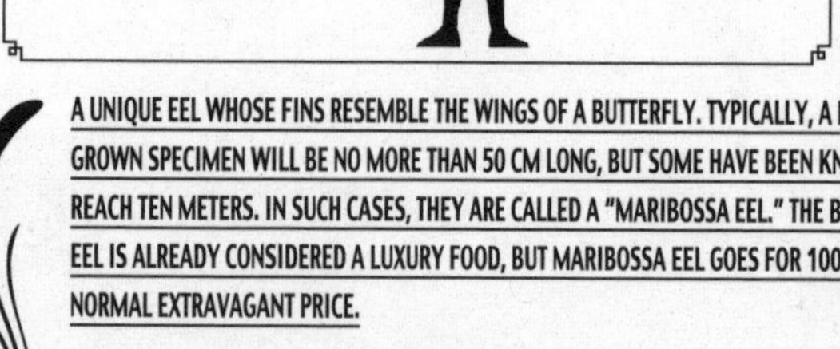

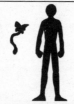

SCALE

A UNIQUE EEL WHOSE FINS RESEMBLE THE WINGS OF A BUTTERFLY. TYPICALLY, A FULL-GROWN SPECIMEN WILL BE NO MORE THAN 50 CM LONG, BUT SOME HAVE BEEN KNOWN TO REACH TEN METERS. IN SUCH CASES, THEY ARE CALLED A "MARIBOSSA EEL." THE BUTTERFLY EEL IS ALREADY CONSIDERED A LUXURY FOOD, BUT MARIBOSSA EEL GOES FOR 100 TIMES THE NORMAL EXTRAVAGANT PRICE.

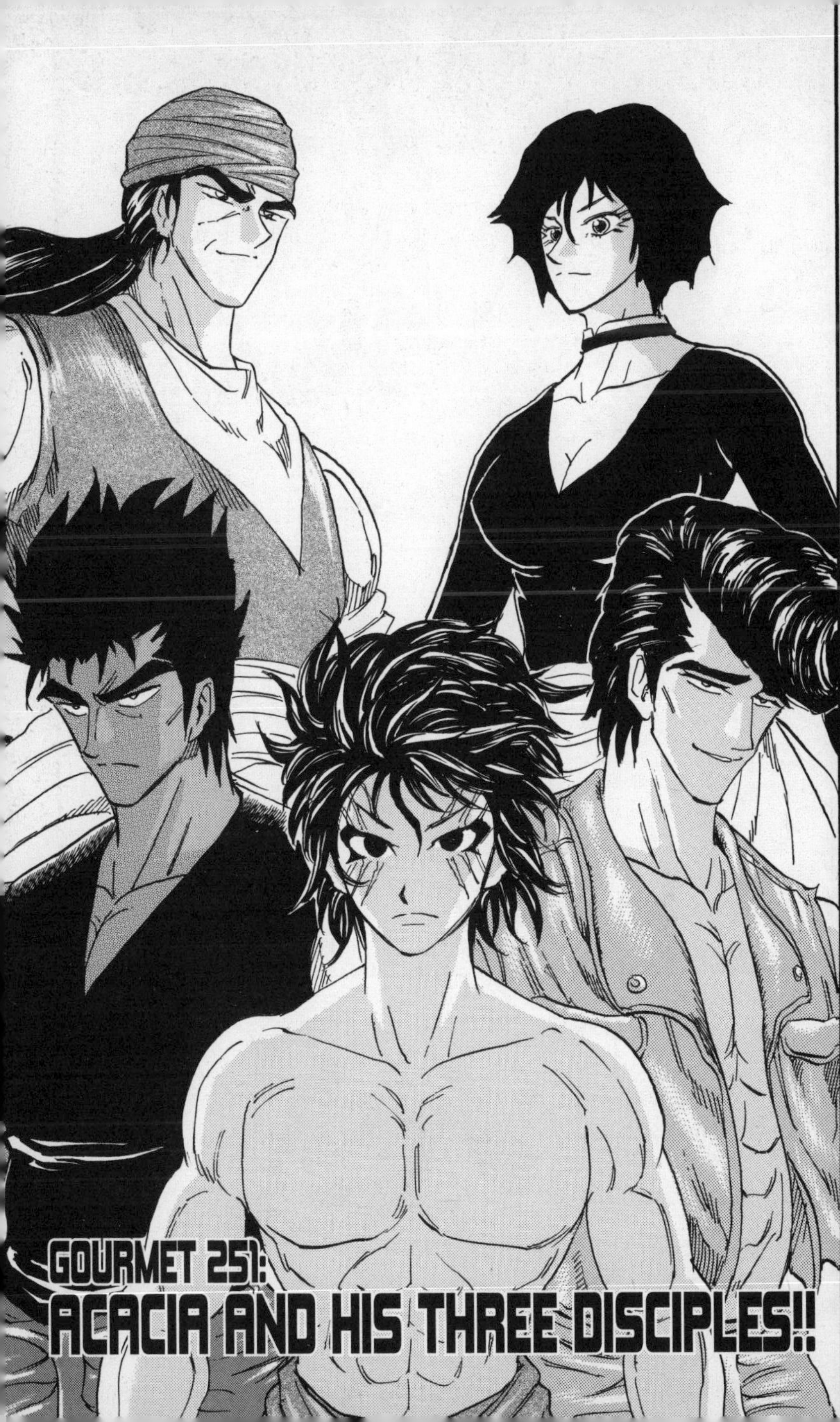
GOURMET 251:
ACACIA AND HIS THREE DISCIPLES!!

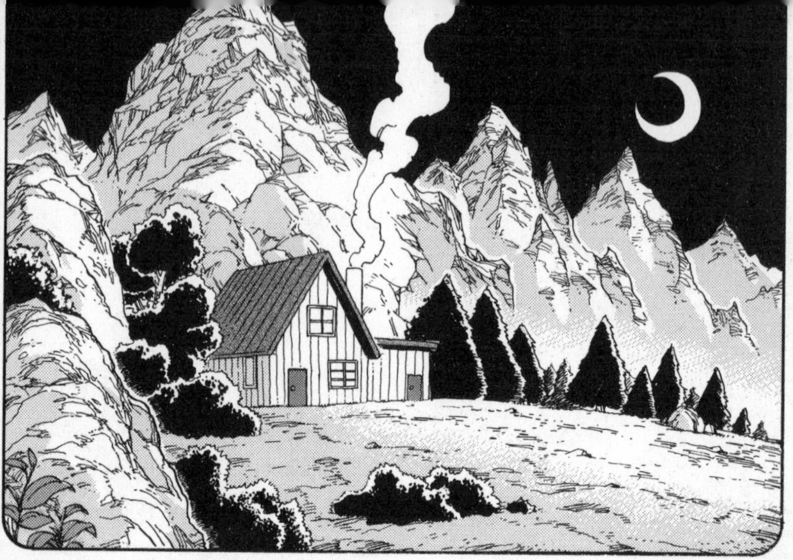

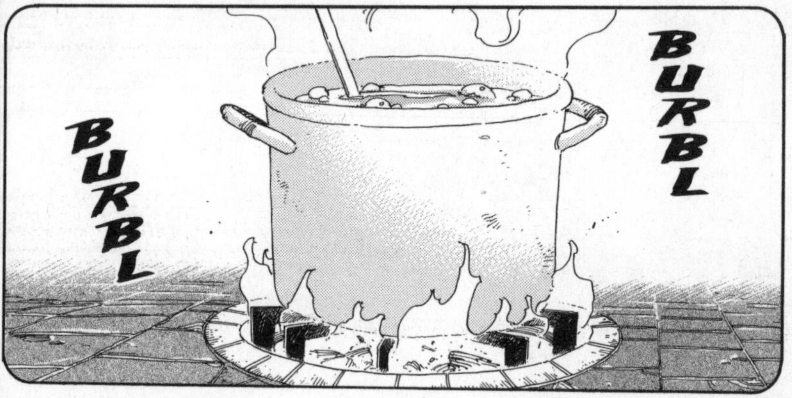
BURBL
BURBL

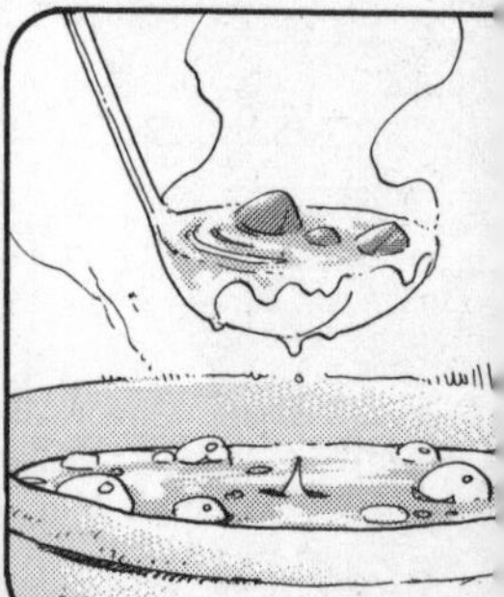

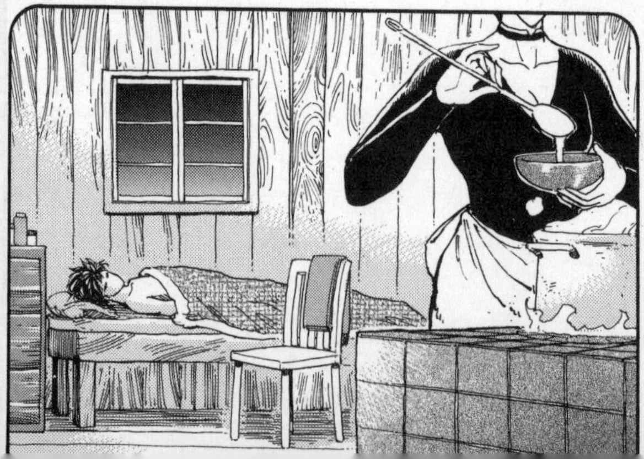

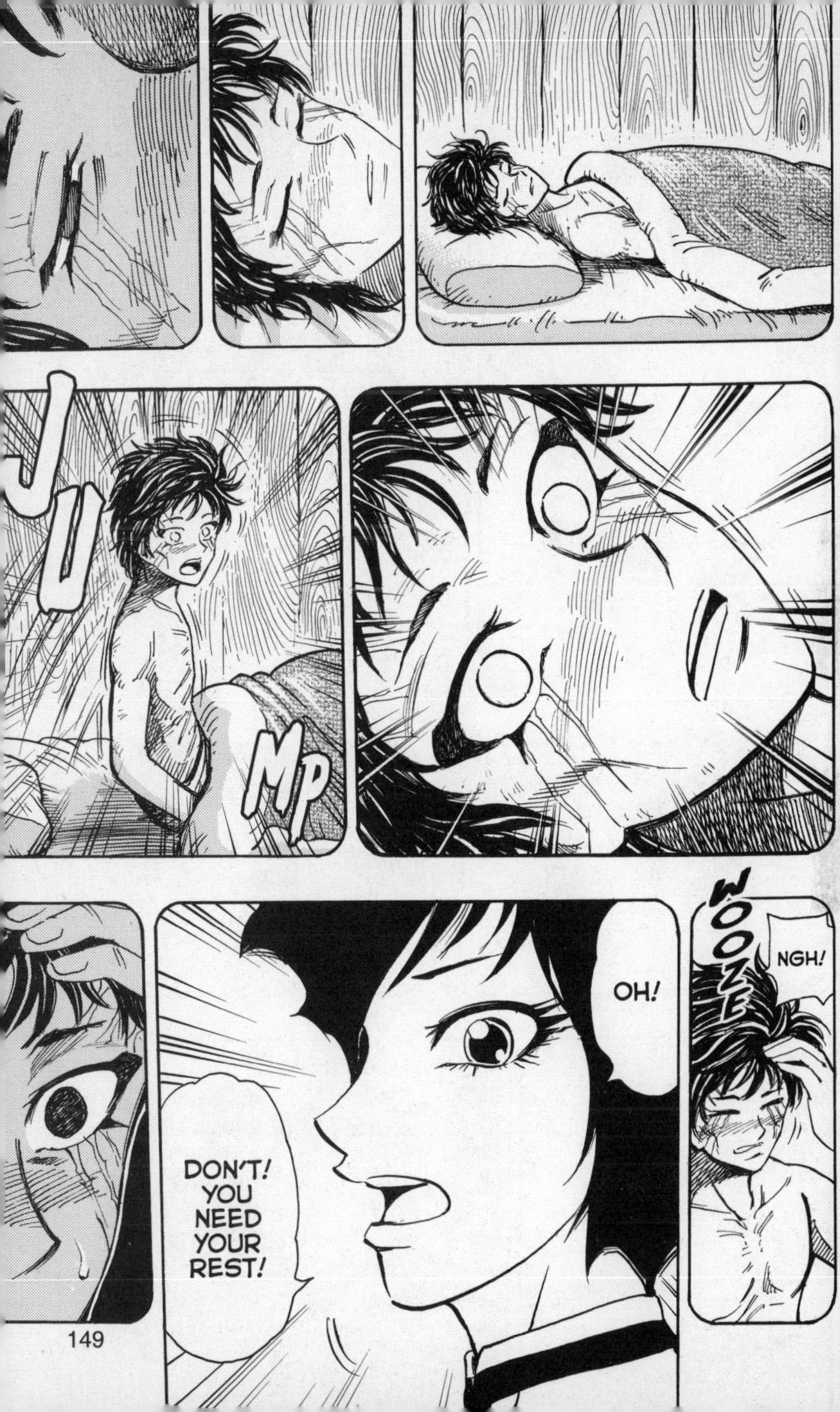
JUMP
WOOZE
NGH!
OH!
DON'T! YOU NEED YOUR REST!

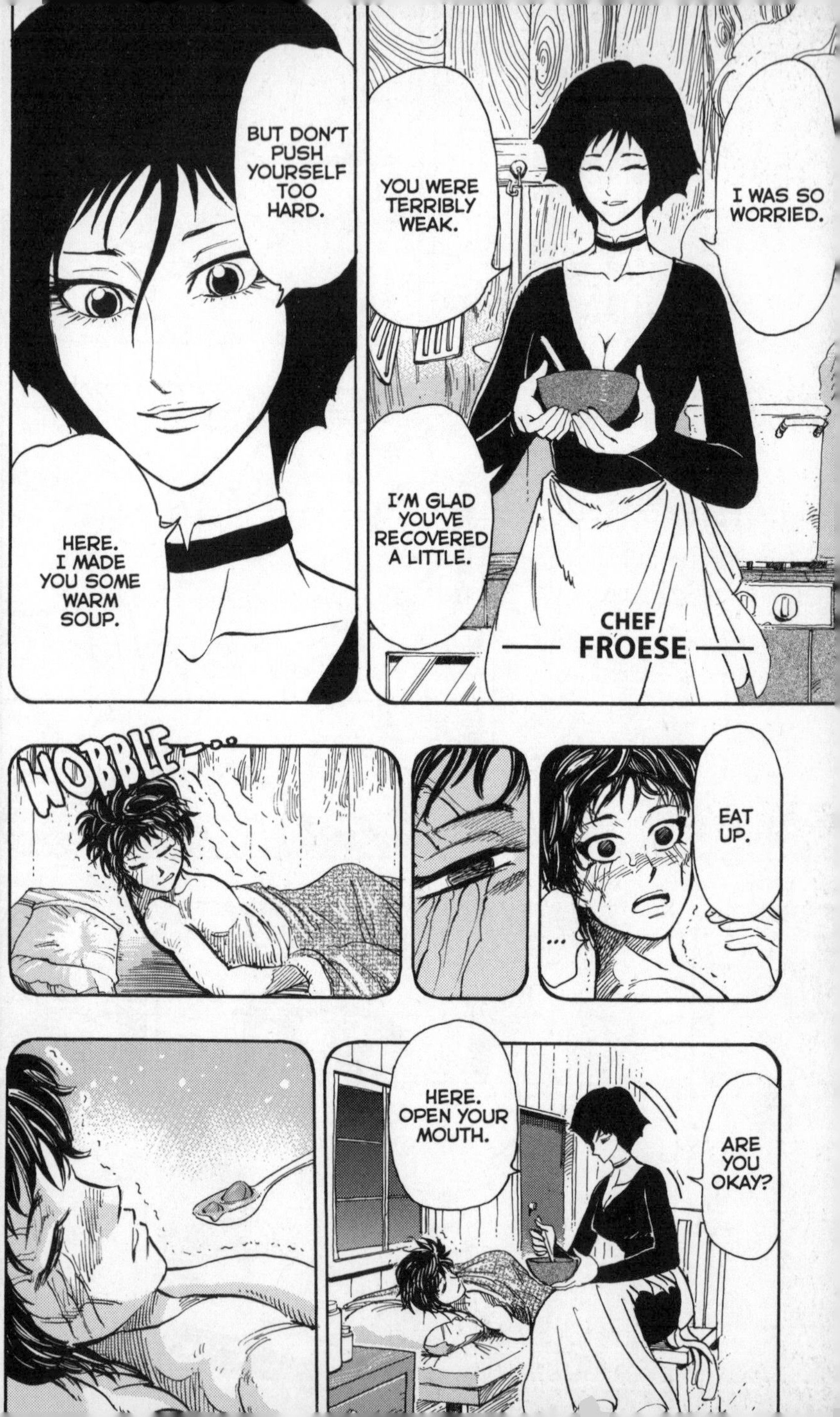
I WAS SO WORRIED.
YOU WERE TERRIBLY WEAK.
I'M GLAD YOU'VE RECOVERED A LITTLE.
CHEF — FROESE —
BUT DON'T PUSH YOURSELF TOO HARD.
HERE. I MADE YOU SOME WARM SOUP.
EAT UP.
...
WOBBLE...
ARE YOU OKAY?
HERE. OPEN YOUR MOUTH.

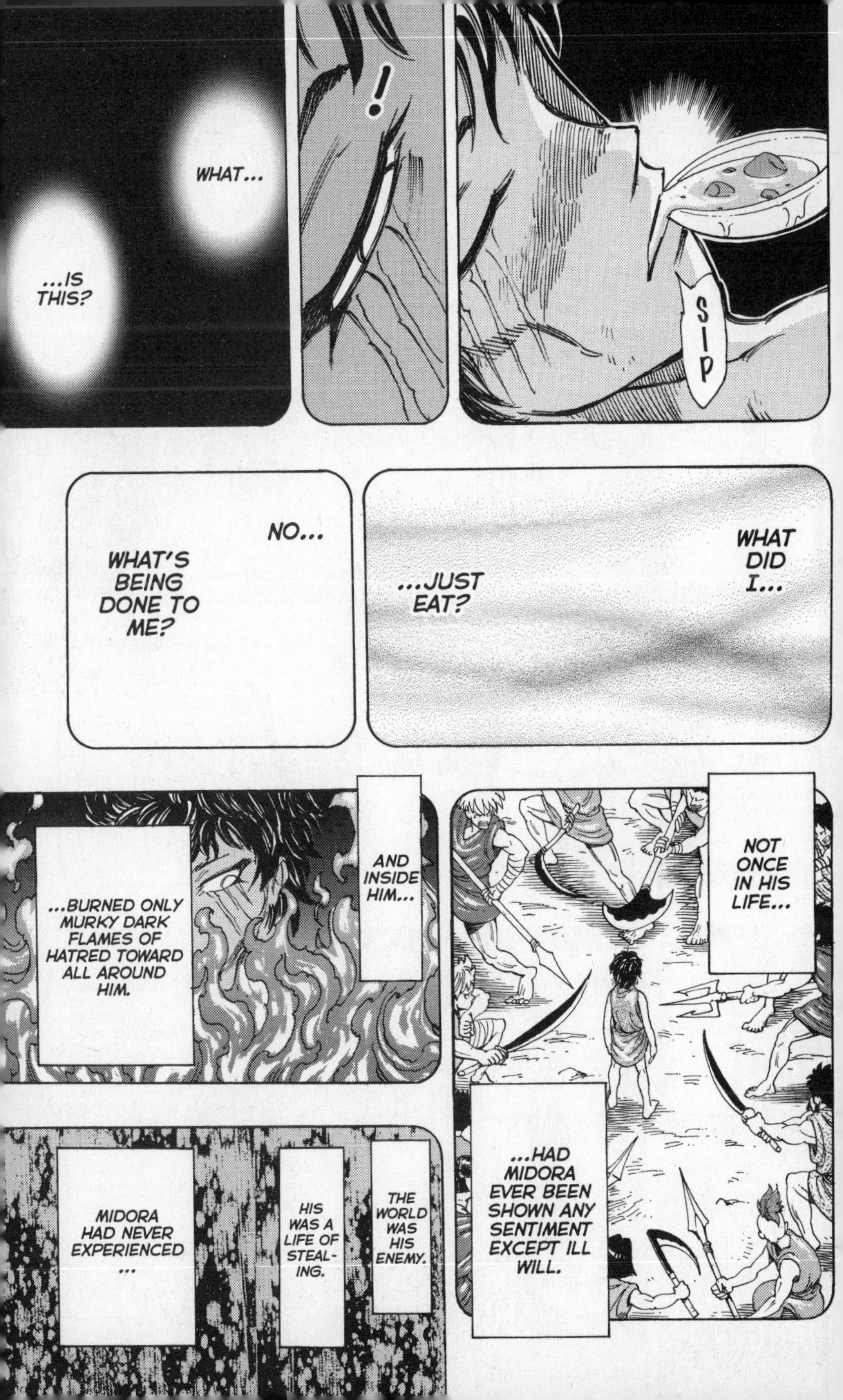
SIP
!
WHAT...
...IS THIS?
WHAT DID I...
...JUST EAT?
NO...
WHAT'S BEING DONE TO ME?
NOT ONCE IN HIS LIFE...
...HAD MIDORA EVER BEEN SHOWN ANY SENTIMENT EXCEPT ILL WILL.
AND INSIDE HIM...
...BURNED ONLY MURKY DARK FLAMES OF HATRED TOWARD ALL AROUND HIM.
THE WORLD WAS HIS ENEMY.
HIS WAS A LIFE OF STEAL-ING.
MIDORA HAD NEVER EXPERIENCED ...

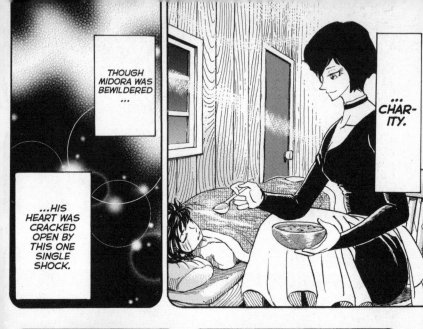

...CHARITY.
THOUGH MIDORA WAS BEWILDERED ...
...HIS HEART WAS CRACKED OPEN BY THIS ONE SINGLE SHOCK.
IT'S...
...DELICIOUS.
MIDORA'S CONSCIOUSNESS SLIPPED AWAY ...
...AS HE CHEWED OVER AND OVER AGAIN.
THAT LINGERING TASTE ON HIS TONGUE...
THE AROMA...
AND THE TEXTURE ...
HE DIDN'T WANT IT TO GO AWAY.
HE DIDN'T WANT TO FORGET.
HE DIDN'T WANT IT TO END.
SO HE CHEWED ...
... OVER AND OVER.

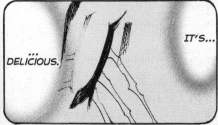

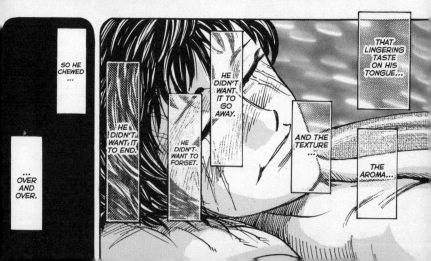

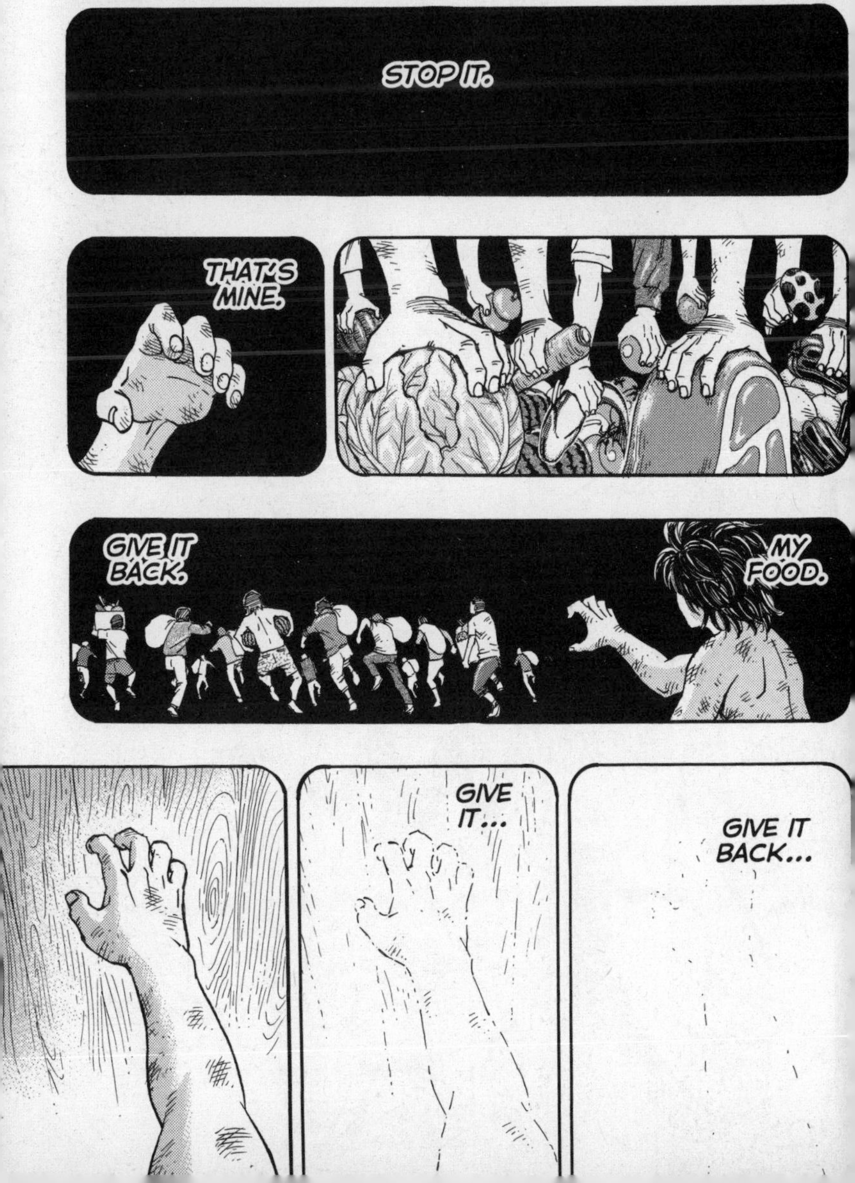
STOP IT.
THAT'S MINE.
GIVE IT BACK.
MY FOOD.
GIVE IT...
GIVE IT BACK...

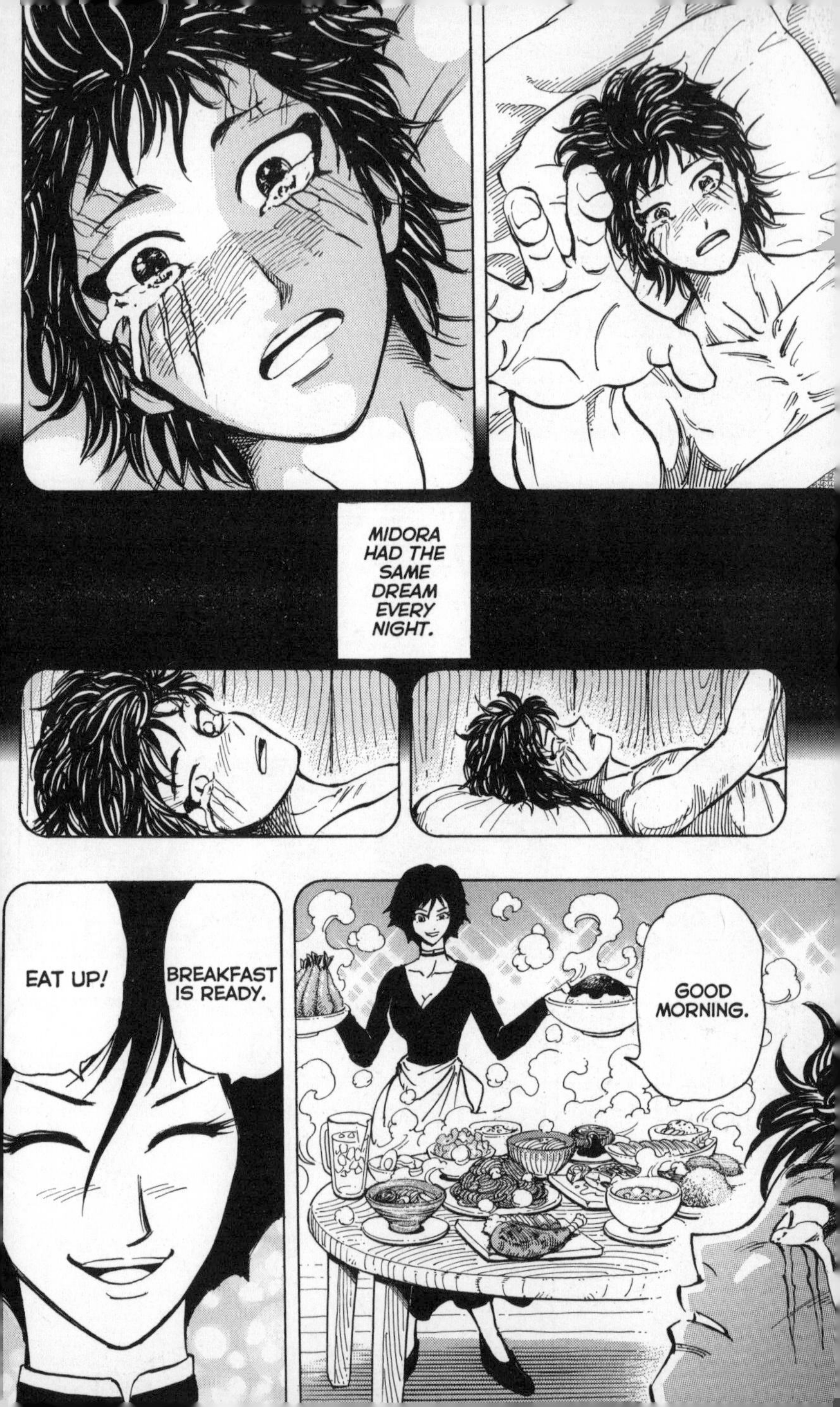
MIDORA HAD THE SAME DREAM EVERY NIGHT.
GOOD MORNING.
BREAKFAST IS READY.
EAT UP!

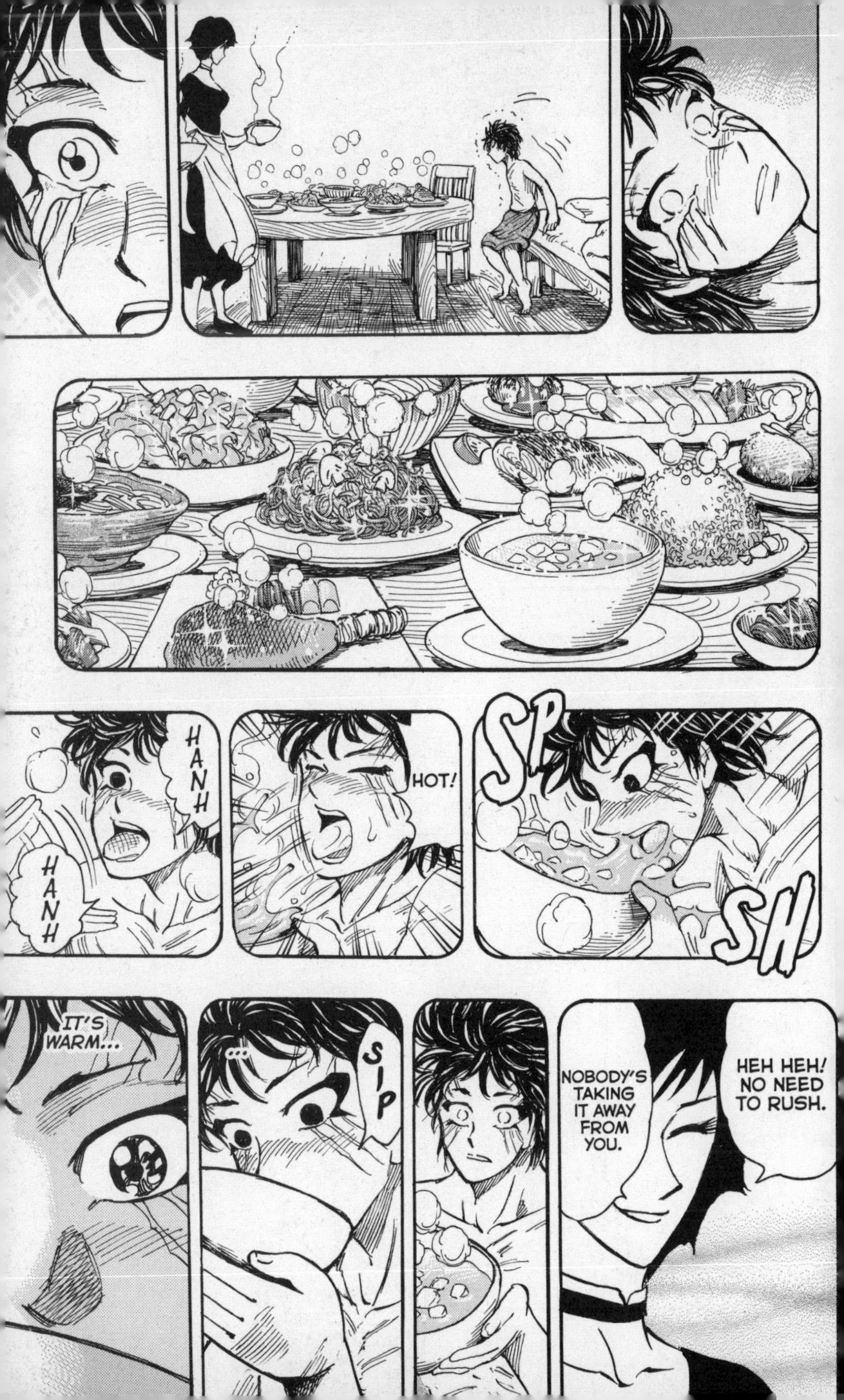
SP
SH
HOT!
HANH
HANH
HEH HEH! NO NEED TO RUSH.
NOBODY'S TAKING IT AWAY FROM YOU.
SIP
...
IT'S WARM...

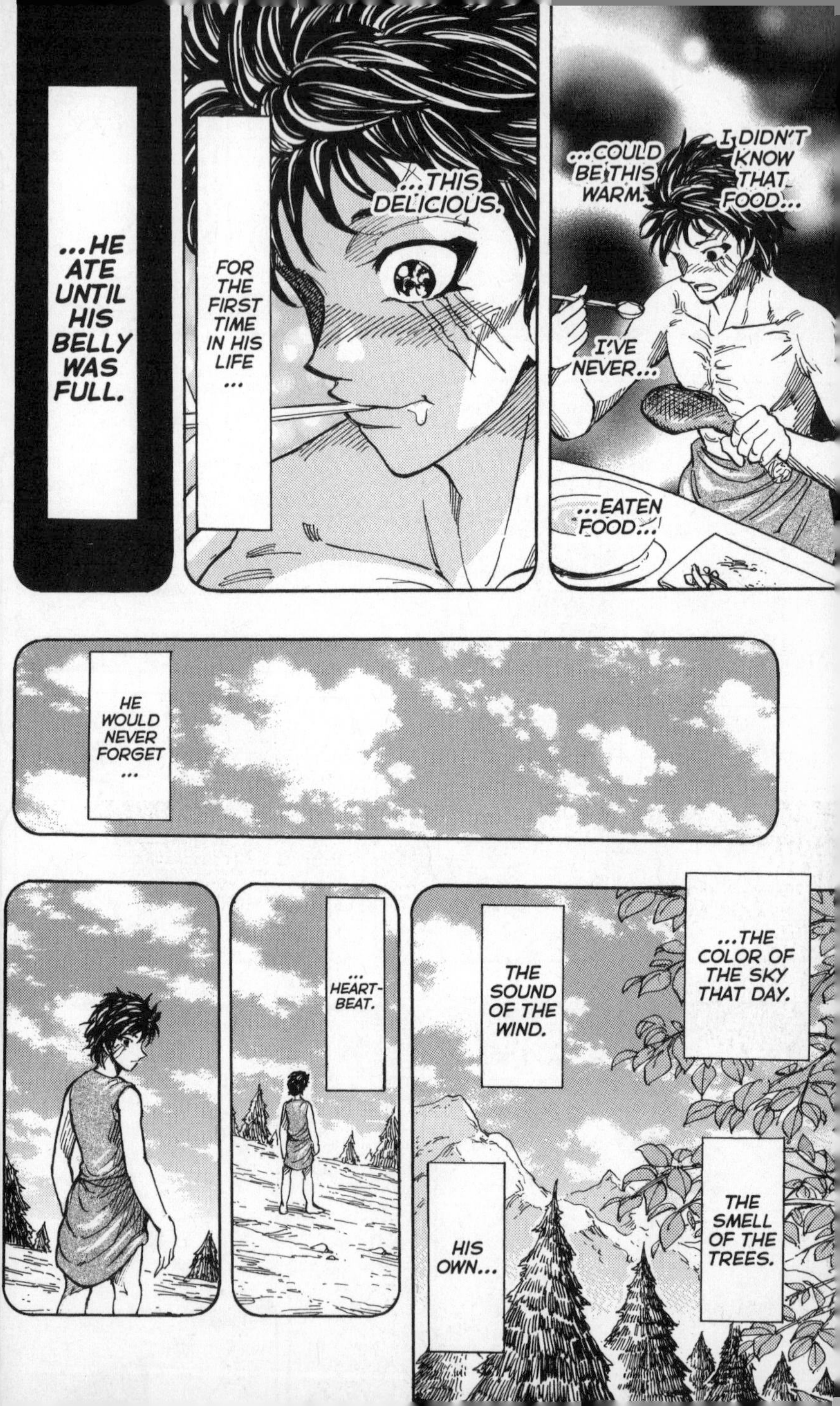
I DIDN'T KNOW THAT FOOD...
...COULD BE THIS WARM.
I'VE NEVER...
...EATEN FOOD...
...THIS DELICIOUS.
FOR THE FIRST TIME IN HIS LIFE...
...HE ATE UNTIL HIS BELLY WAS FULL.
HE WOULD NEVER FORGET...
...THE COLOR OF THE SKY THAT DAY.
THE SOUND OF THE WIND.
THE SMELL OF THE TREES.
HIS OWN...
...HEART-BEAT.

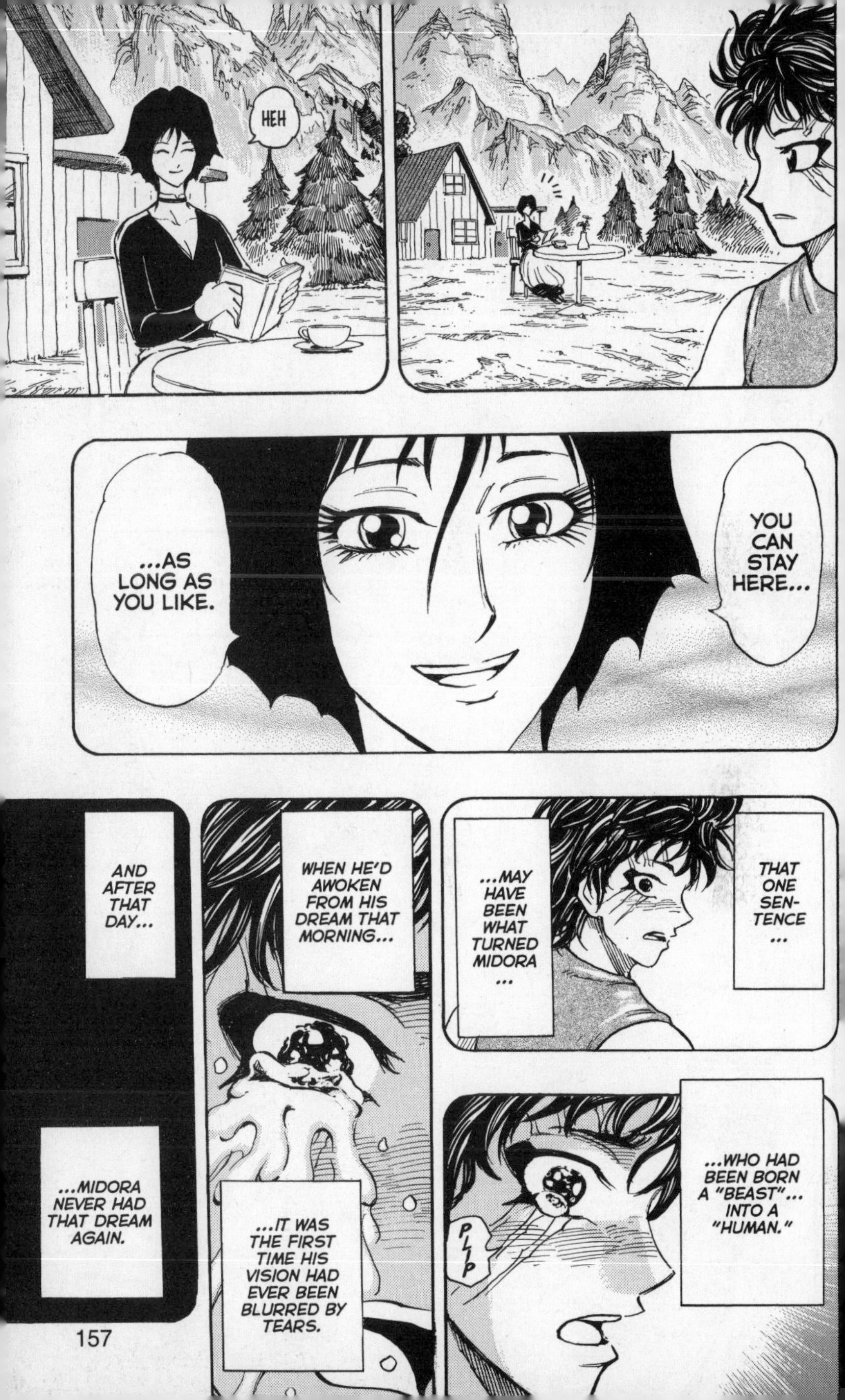
HEH
YOU CAN STAY HERE...
...AS LONG AS YOU LIKE.
THAT ONE SEN-TENCE...
...MAY HAVE BEEN WHAT TURNED MIDORA...
...WHO HAD BEEN BORN A "BEAST"... INTO A "HUMAN."
PLIP
WHEN HE'D AWOKEN FROM HIS DREAM THAT MORNING...
...IT WAS THE FIRST TIME HIS VISION HAD EVER BEEN BLURRED BY TEARS.
AND AFTER THAT DAY...
...MIDORA NEVER HAD THAT DREAM AGAIN.

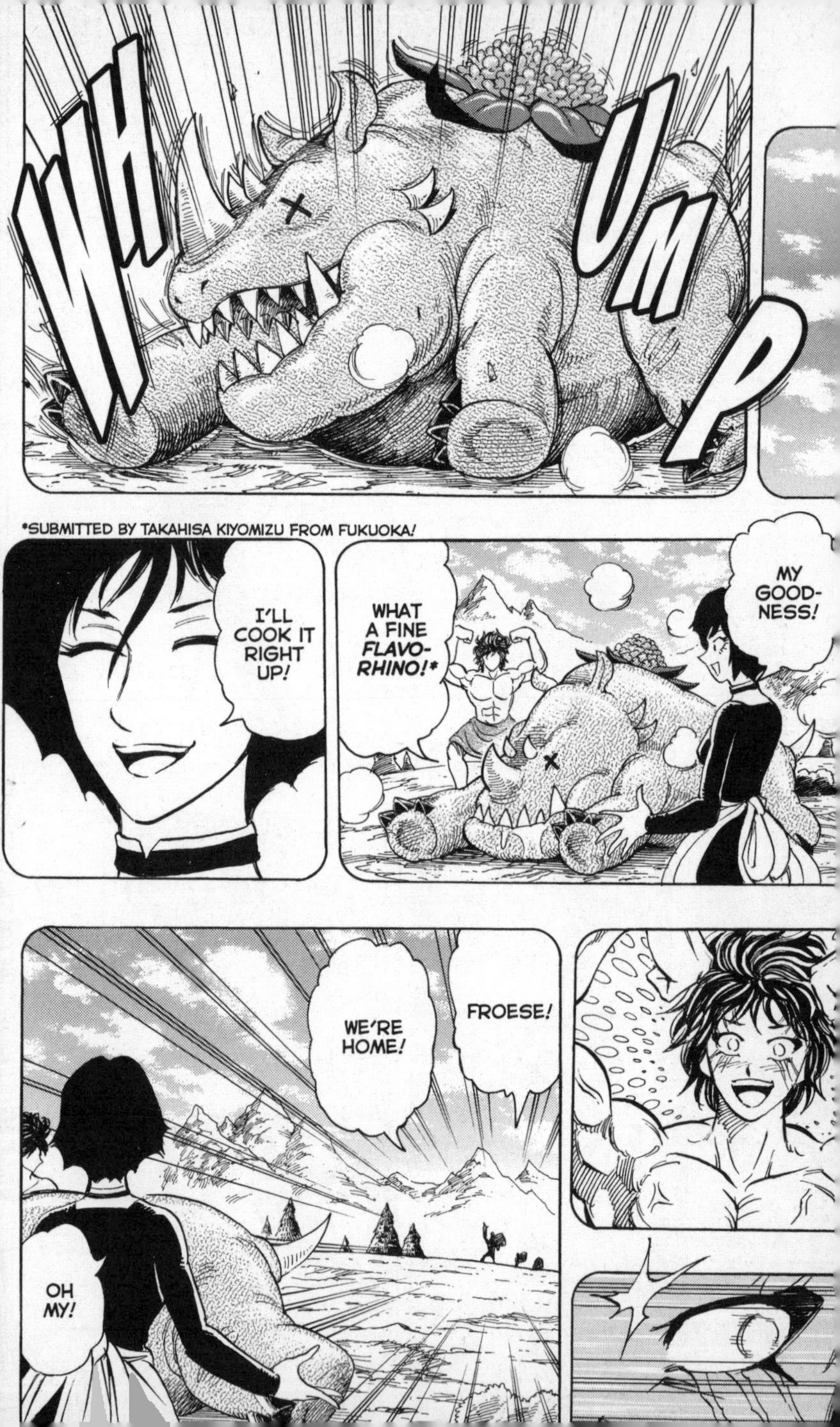
WHUMP
MY GOODNESS!
WHAT A FINE *FLAVO-RHINO!**
I'LL COOK IT RIGHT UP!
FROESE!
WE'RE HOME!
OH MY!

*SUBMITTED BY TAKAHISA KIYOMIZU FROM FUKUOKA!

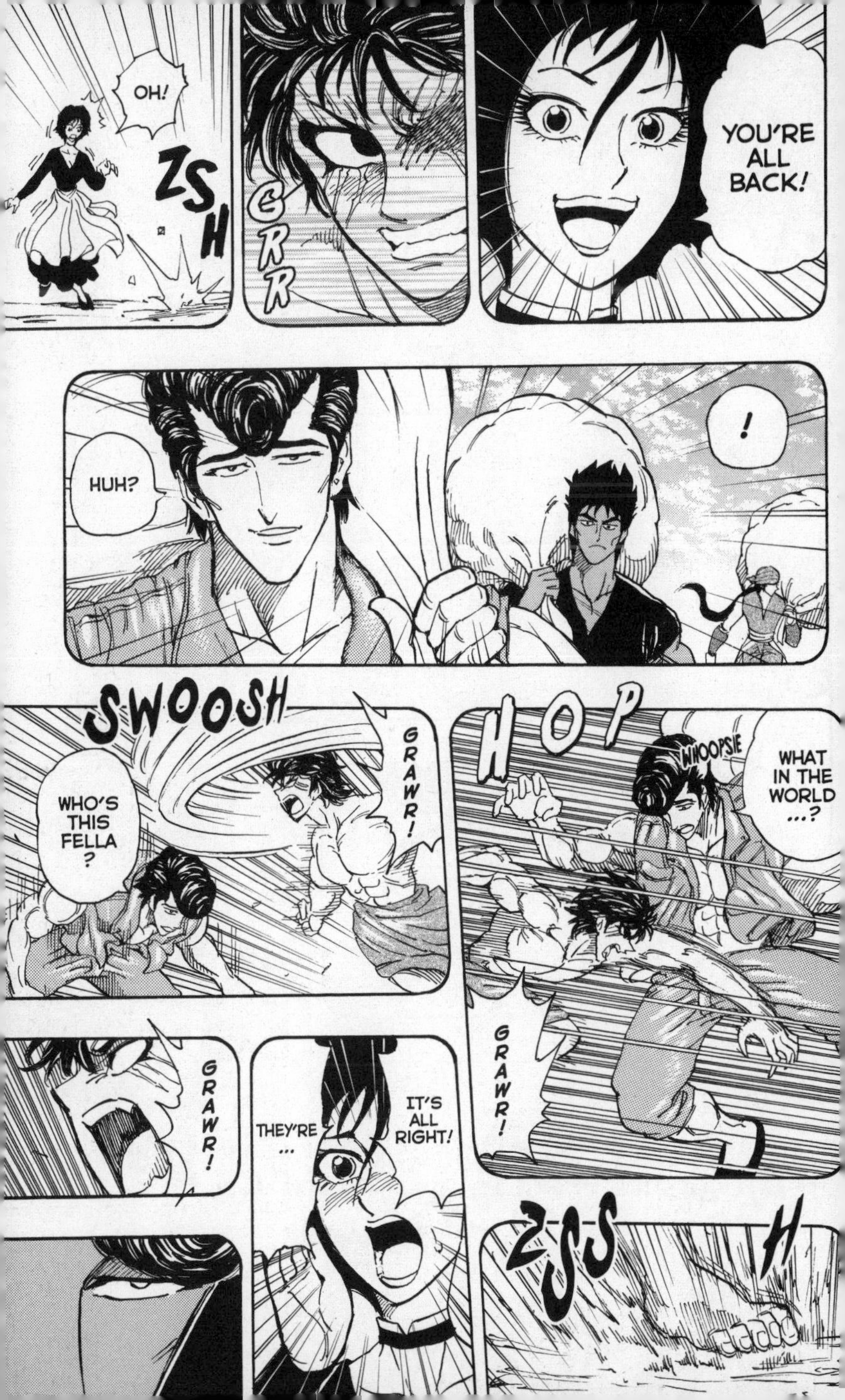
YOU'RE ALL BACK!
GRRR
OH!
ZSH
!
HUH?
HOP
WHOOPSIE
WHAT IN THE WORLD ...?
GRAWR!
SWOOSH
GRAWR!
WHO'S THIS FELLA ?
ZSSH
IT'S ALL RIGHT!
THEY'RE ...
GRAWR!

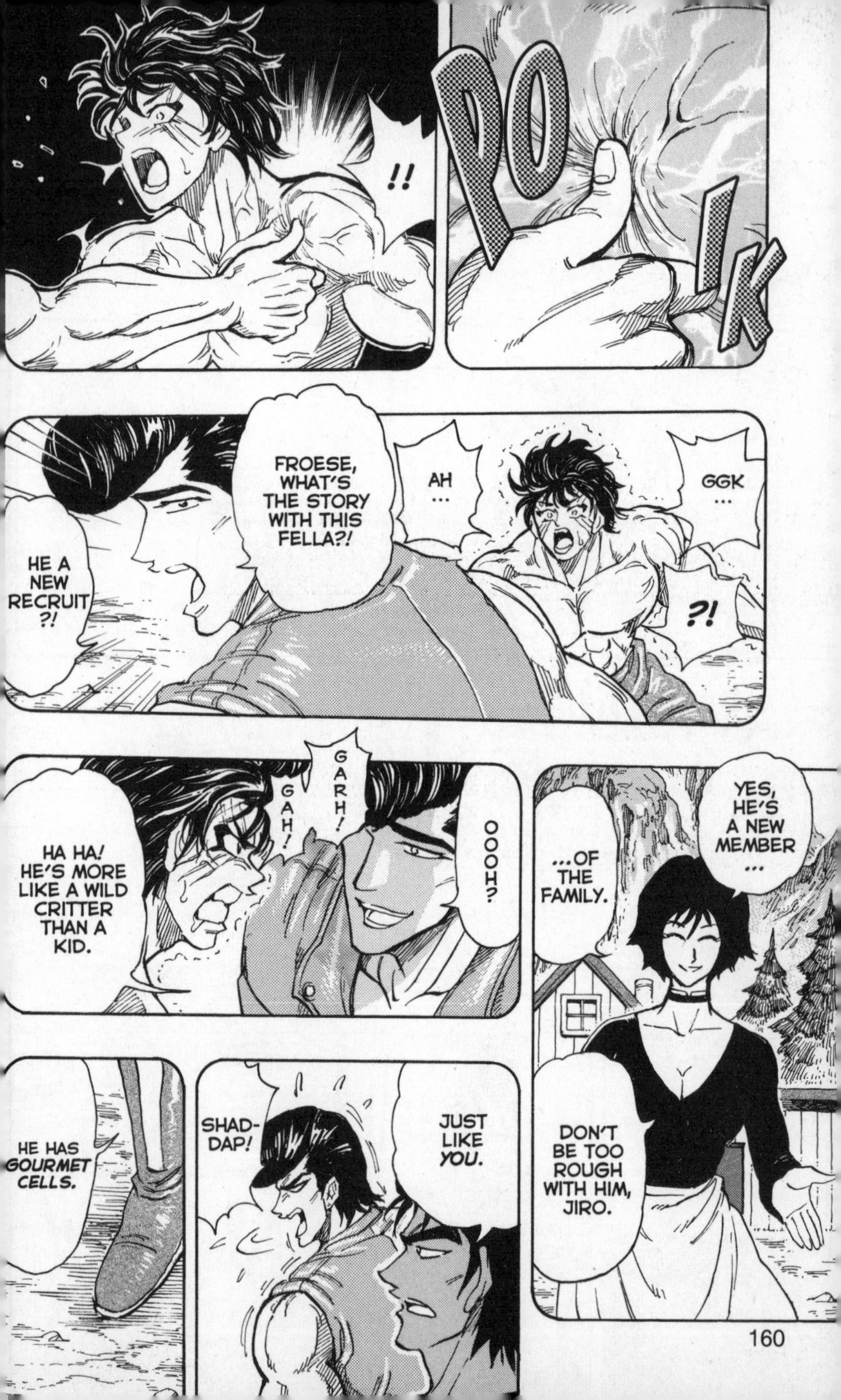
POIK
!!
GGK ...
?!
AH ...
FROESE, WHAT'S THE STORY WITH THIS FELLA?!
HE A NEW RECRUIT?!
YES, HE'S A NEW MEMBER ...
...OF THE FAMILY.
DON'T BE TOO ROUGH WITH HIM, JIRO.
OOOOH?
GARH!
GAH!
HA HA! HE'S MORE LIKE A WILD CRITTER THAN A KID.
JUST LIKE *YOU*.
SHAD-DAP!
HE HAS *GOURMET CELLS*.

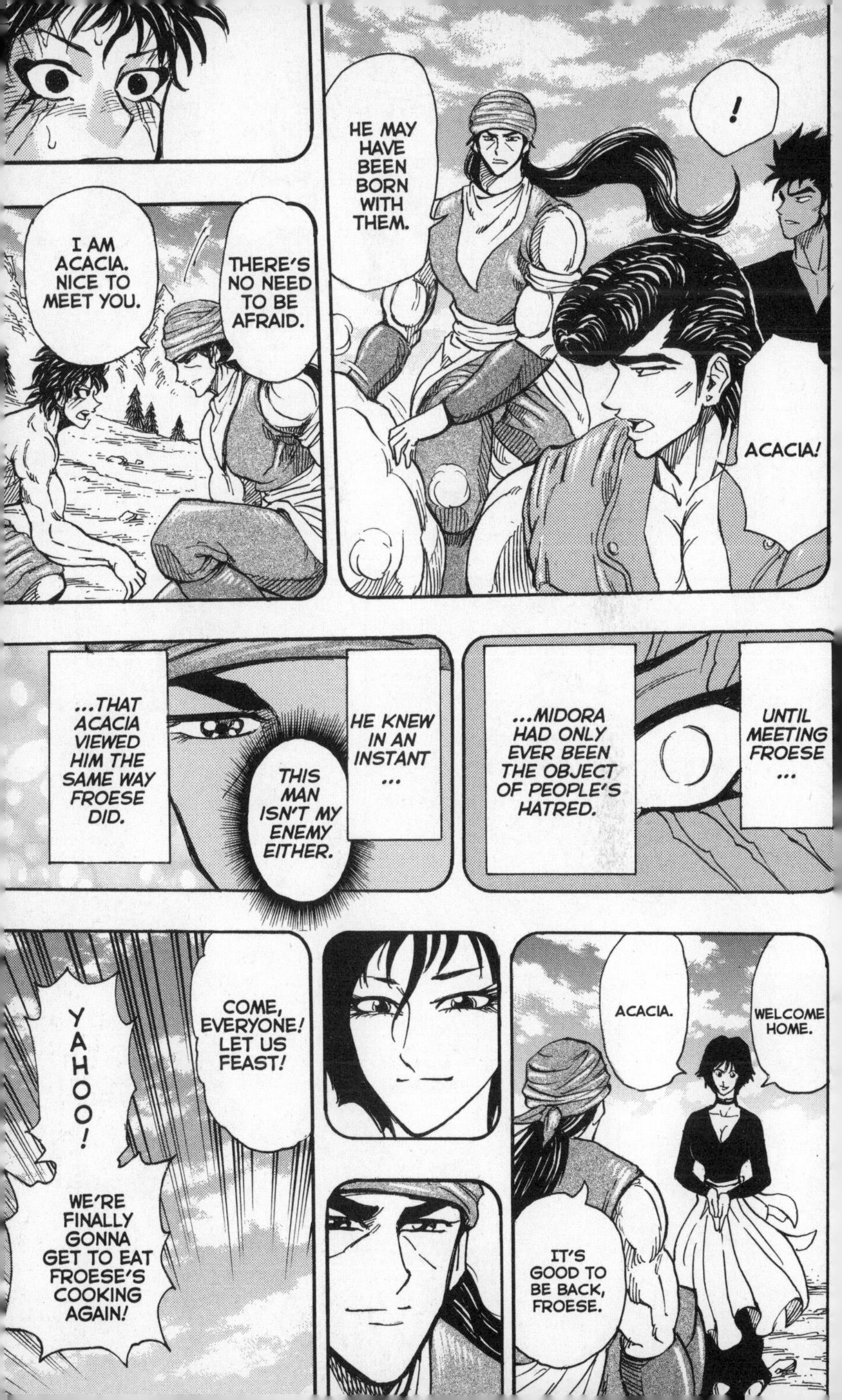

!
HE MAY HAVE BEEN BORN WITH THEM.
ACACIA!
THERE'S NO NEED TO BE AFRAID.
I AM ACACIA. NICE TO MEET YOU.
UNTIL MEETING FROESE...
...MIDORA HAD ONLY EVER BEEN THE OBJECT OF PEOPLE'S HATRED.
HE KNEW IN AN INSTANT...
...THAT ACACIA VIEWED HIM THE SAME WAY FROESE DID.
THIS MAN ISN'T MY ENEMY EITHER.
WELCOME HOME.
ACACIA.
IT'S GOOD TO BE BACK, FROESE.
COME, EVERYONE! LET US FEAST!
YAHOO!
WE'RE FINALLY GONNA GET TO EAT FROESE'S COOKING AGAIN!

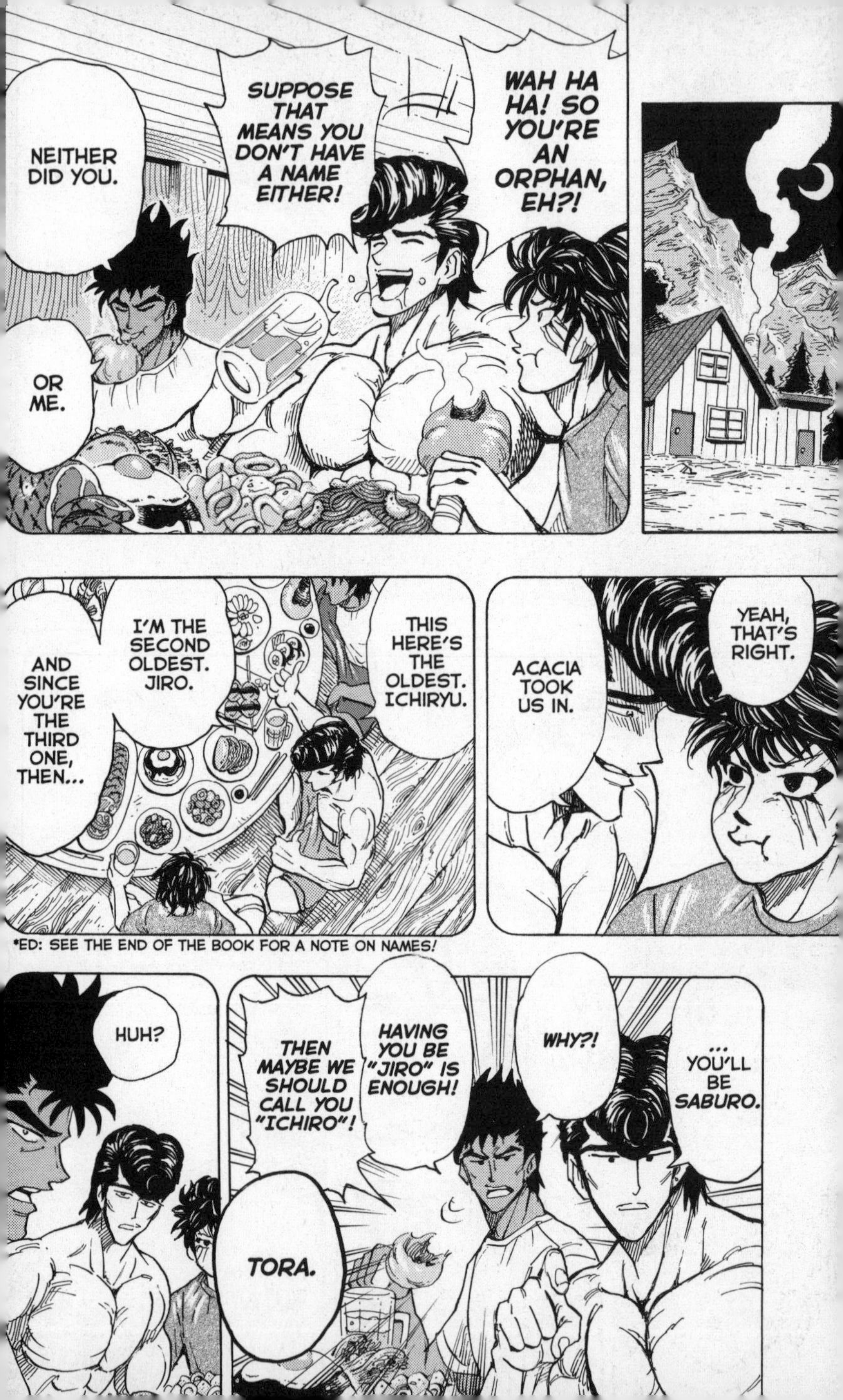
WAH HA HA! SO YOU'RE AN ORPHAN, EH?!
SUPPOSE THAT MEANS YOU DON'T HAVE A NAME EITHER!
NEITHER DID YOU.
OR ME.
YEAH, THAT'S RIGHT.
ACACIA TOOK US IN.
THIS HERE'S THE OLDEST. ICHIRYU.
I'M THE SECOND OLDEST. JIRO.
AND SINCE YOU'RE THE THIRD ONE, THEN...
... YOU'LL BE SABURO.
WHY?!
HAVING YOU BE "JIRO" IS ENOUGH!
THEN MAYBE WE SHOULD CALL YOU "ICHIRO"!
TORA.
HUH?

*ED: SEE THE END OF THE BOOK FOR A NOTE ON NAMES!

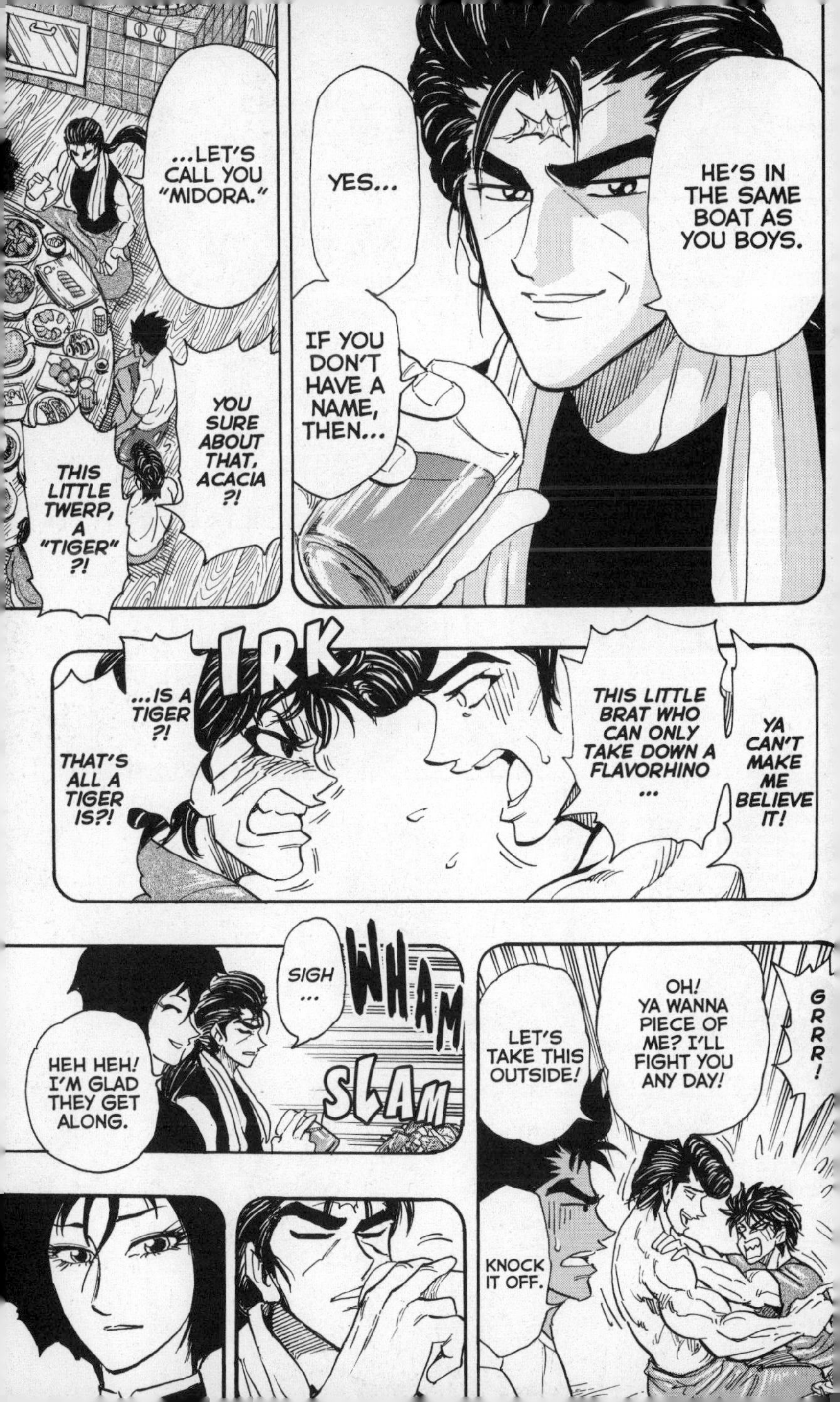
HE'S IN THE SAME BOAT AS YOU BOYS.
YES...
IF YOU DON'T HAVE A NAME, THEN...
...LET'S CALL YOU "MIDORA."
YOU SURE ABOUT THAT, ACACIA?!
THIS LITTLE TWERP, A "TIGER"?!
THIS LITTLE BRAT WHO CAN ONLY TAKE DOWN A FLAVORHINO ...
YA CAN'T MAKE ME BELIEVE IT!
IRK
...IS A TIGER?!
THAT'S ALL A TIGER IS?!
GRRR!
OH! YA WANNA PIECE OF ME? I'LL FIGHT YOU ANY DAY!
LET'S TAKE THIS OUTSIDE!
KNOCK IT OFF.
WHAM
SLAM
SIGH ...
HEH HEH! I'M GLAD THEY GET ALONG.

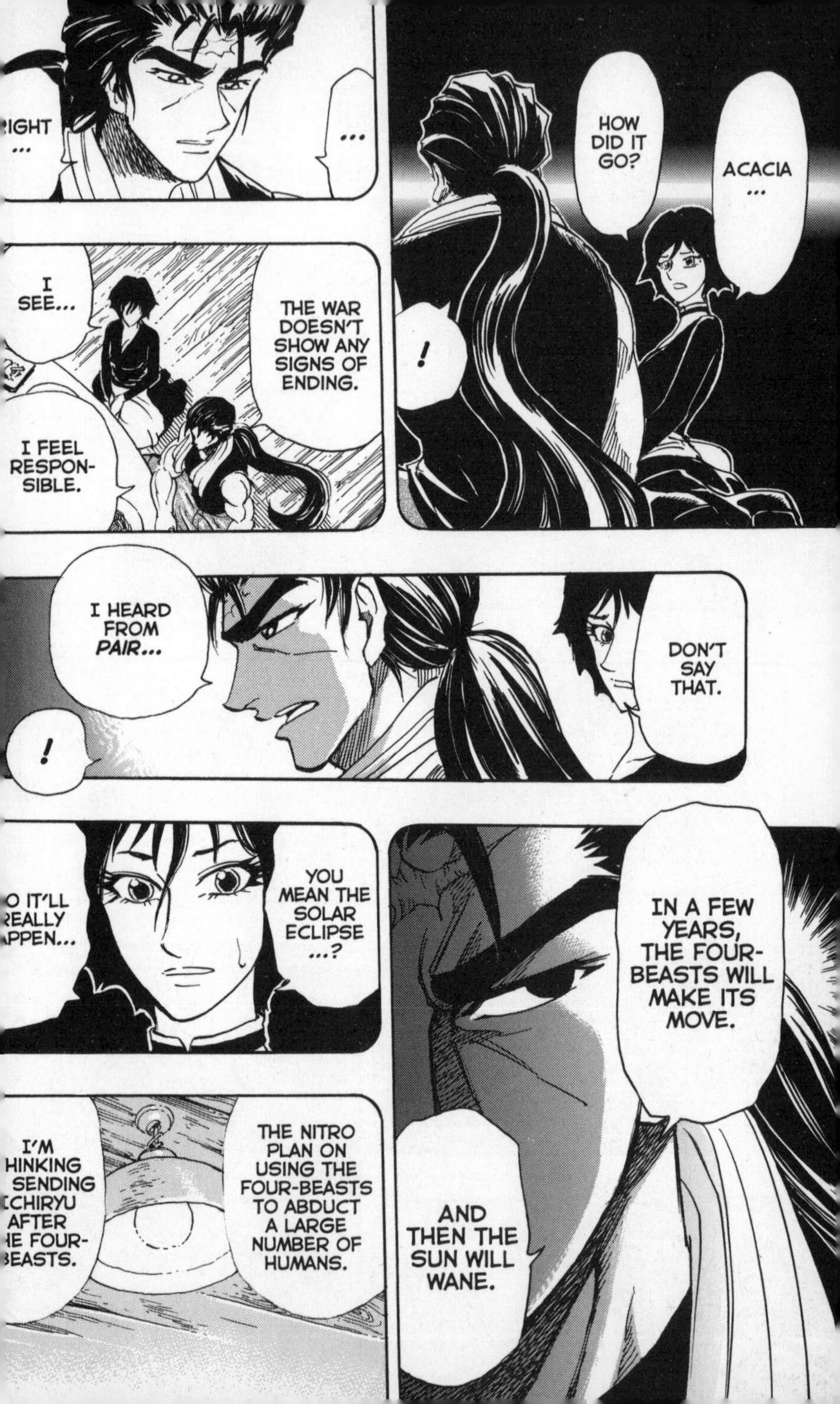
ACACIA ...
HOW DID IT GO?
!
...
IGHT ...
THE WAR DOESN'T SHOW ANY SIGNS OF ENDING.
I SEE...
I FEEL RESPONSIBLE.
DON'T SAY THAT.
I HEARD FROM *PAIR*...
!
IN A FEW YEARS, THE FOUR-BEASTS WILL MAKE ITS MOVE.
AND THEN THE SUN WILL WANE.
YOU MEAN THE SOLAR ECLIPSE ...?
O IT'LL REALLY APPEN...
THE NITRO PLAN ON USING THE FOUR-BEASTS TO ABDUCT A LARGE NUMBER OF HUMANS.
I'M HINKING SENDING CHIRYU AFTER HE FOUR-BEASTS.

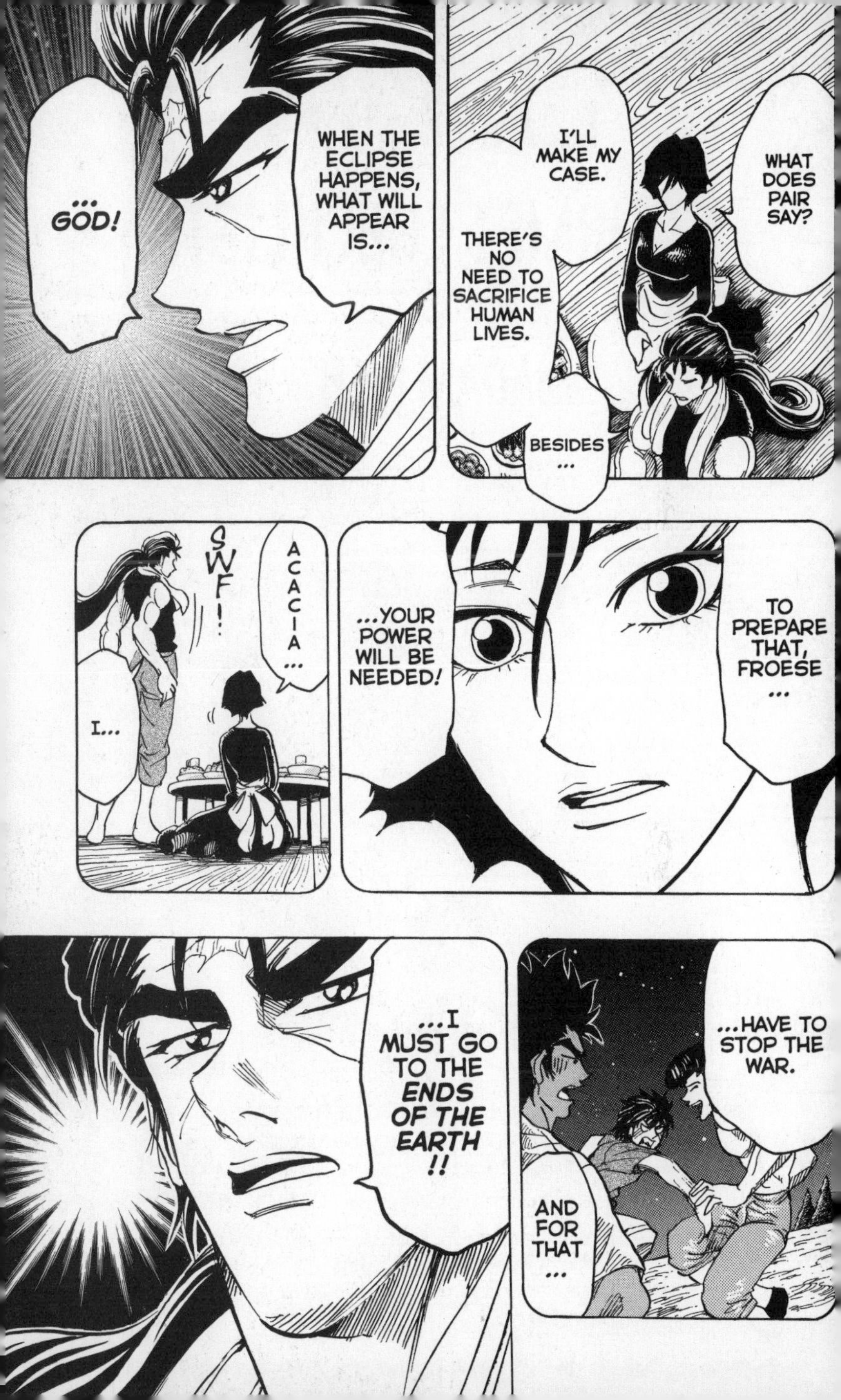
WHAT DOES PAIR SAY?
I'LL MAKE MY CASE.
THERE'S NO NEED TO SACRIFICE HUMAN LIVES.
BESIDES...
WHEN THE ECLIPSE HAPPENS, WHAT WILL APPEAR IS...
...GOD!
TO PREPARE THAT, FROESE...
...YOUR POWER WILL BE NEEDED!
ACACIA...
SWF!
I...
...HAVE TO STOP THE WAR.
AND FOR THAT...
...I MUST GO TO THE ENDS OF THE EARTH!!

TORIKO

GOURMET CHECKLIST

Vol. 279

MADAM FISH

(FISH)

CAPTURE LEVEL: 83

HABITAT: STEW POND

SIZE: 23 METERS

HEIGHT: ---

WEIGHT: 15 TONS

PRICE: 1 KG / 150,000 YEN

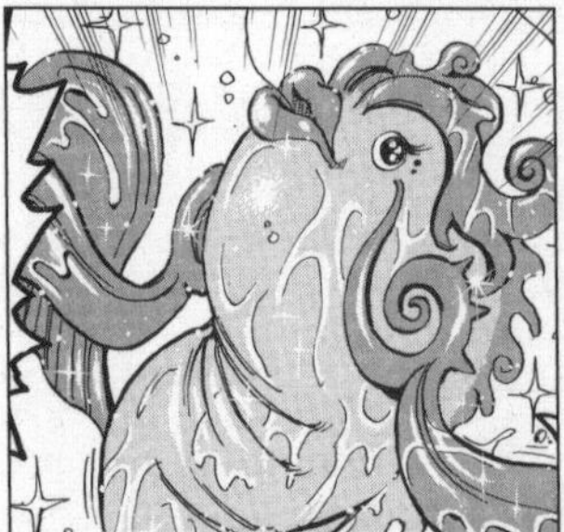

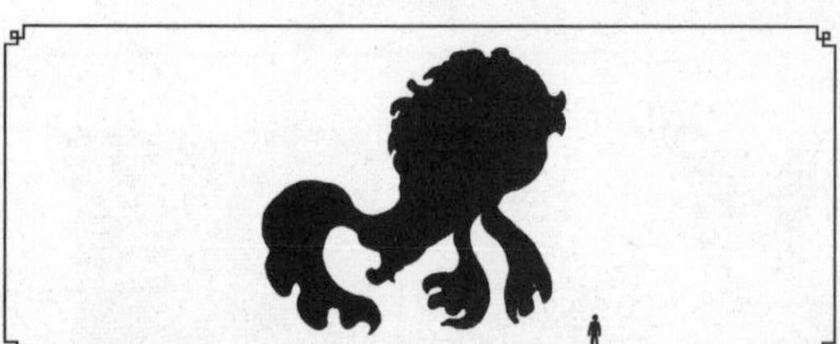

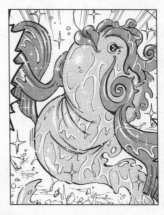

SCALE

THE REGENT OF STEW POND. THE BRILLIANT COLOR AND TASTE OF THIS MYSTERIOUS FISH MAKE IT AN ARISTOCRAT AMONG FRESHWATER FISH. THE MADAM FISH'S CAPTURE LEVEL IS HIGH, NOT BECAUSE OF ITS COMBAT STRENGTH BUT BECAUSE IT RARELY LEAVES ITS NEST. A MADAM FISH CAN SPEND DECADES IN ITS NEST. THE ONLY CHANCE OF CAPTURING ONE COMES WHEN THE SURFACE OF STEW POND IS FROZEN AND IT LETS ITS GUARD DOWN. SINCE THAT'S A ONCE-IN-A-LIFETIME EVENT, THE HIGH CAPTURE LEVEL IS UNDERSTANDABLE. MADAM FISH WAS ONE OF THE INGREDIENTS USED IN MONCHY'S FORTUNE ROLL FOR DIVINING THE LOCATION OF CHOWLIN TEMPLE.

GOURMET 252: ACACIA'S FAIRY TALE!!

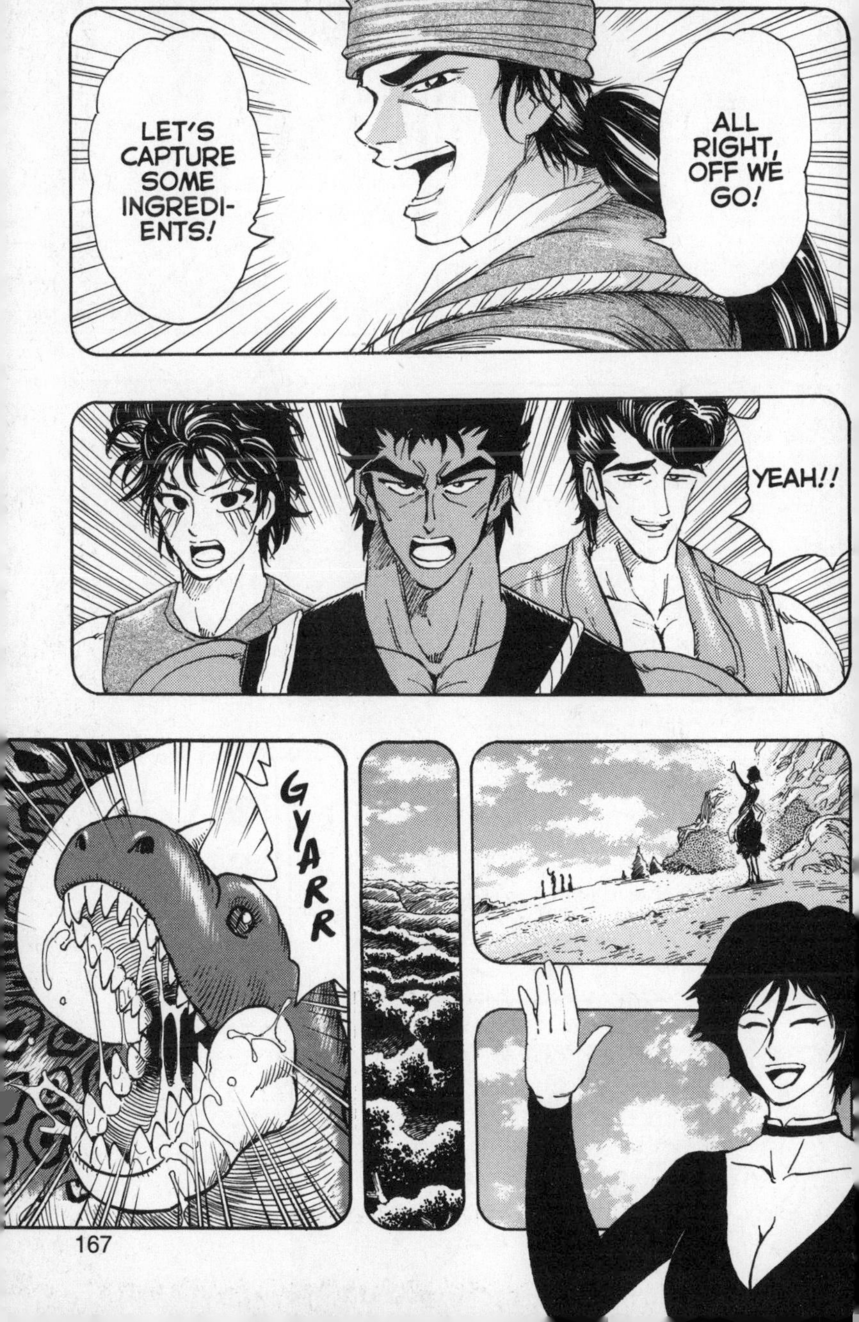
ALL RIGHT, OFF WE GO!
LET'S CAPTURE SOME INGREDI- ENTS!
YEAH!!
GYARR

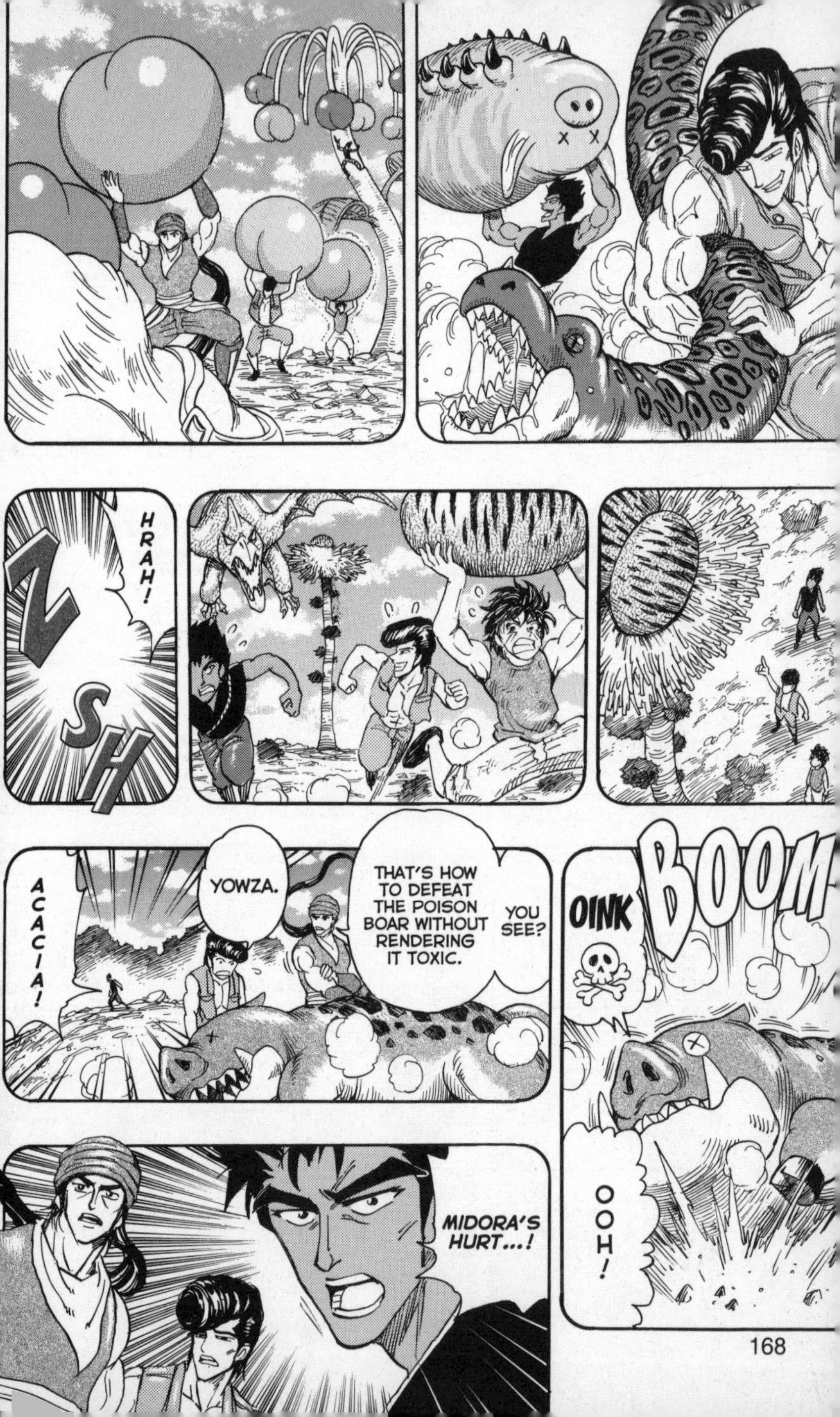

ZNSH
HRAH!
BOOM
OINK
OOH!
YOU SEE?
THAT'S HOW TO DEFEAT THE POISON BOAR WITHOUT RENDERING IT TOXIC.
YOWZA.
ACACIA!
MIDORA'S HURT...!

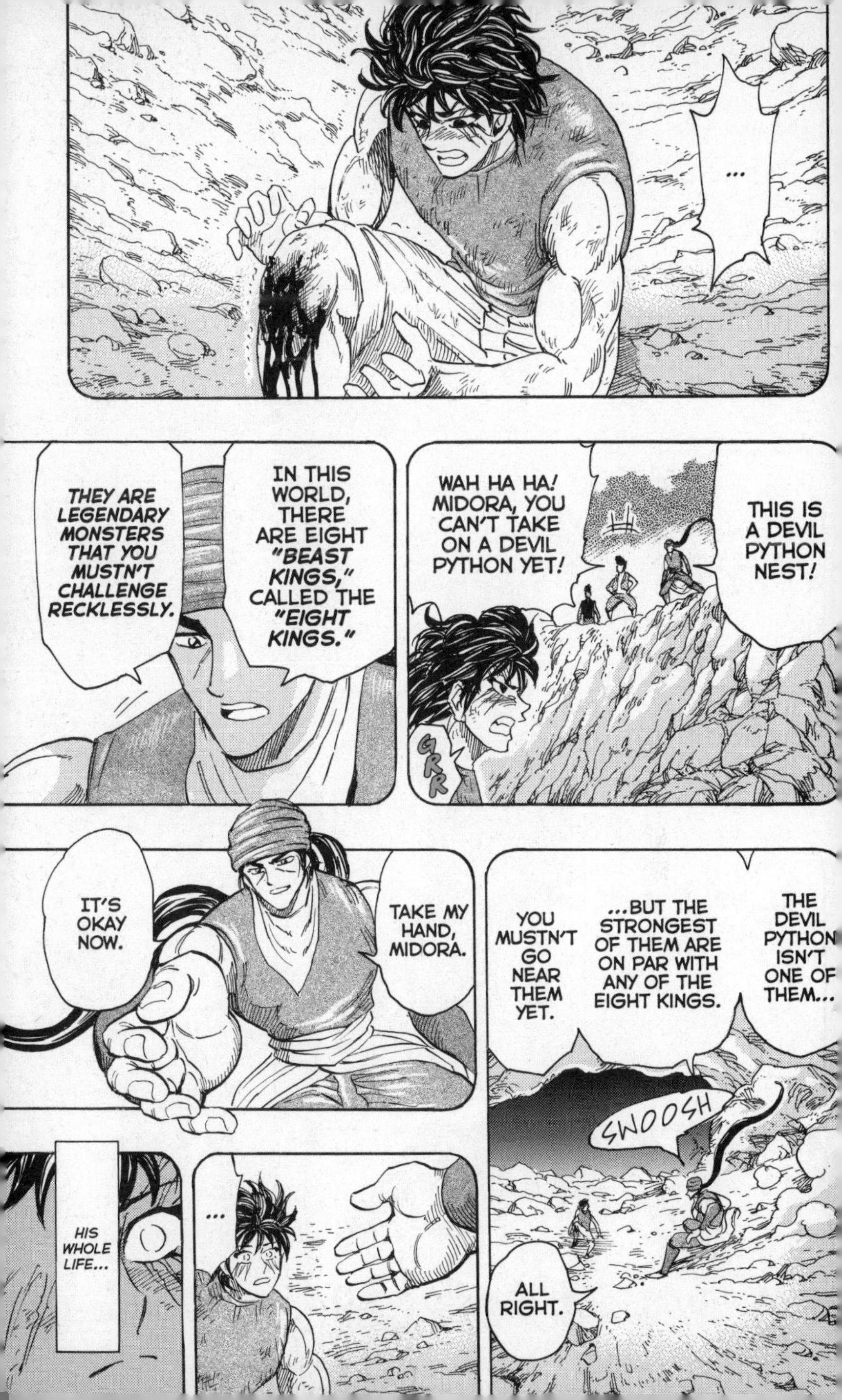
...
THIS IS A DEVIL PYTHON NEST!
WAH HA HA! MIDORA, YOU CAN'T TAKE ON A DEVIL PYTHON YET!
GRR
IN THIS WORLD, THERE ARE EIGHT "BEAST KINGS," CALLED THE "EIGHT KINGS."
THEY ARE LEGENDARY MONSTERS THAT YOU MUSTN'T CHALLENGE RECKLESSLY.
THE DEVIL PYTHON ISN'T ONE OF THEM...
...BUT THE STRONGEST OF THEM ARE ON PAR WITH ANY OF THE EIGHT KINGS.
YOU MUSTN'T GO NEAR THEM YET.
SWOOSH
ALL RIGHT.
TAKE MY HAND, MIDORA.
IT'S OKAY NOW.
...
HIS WHOLE LIFE...

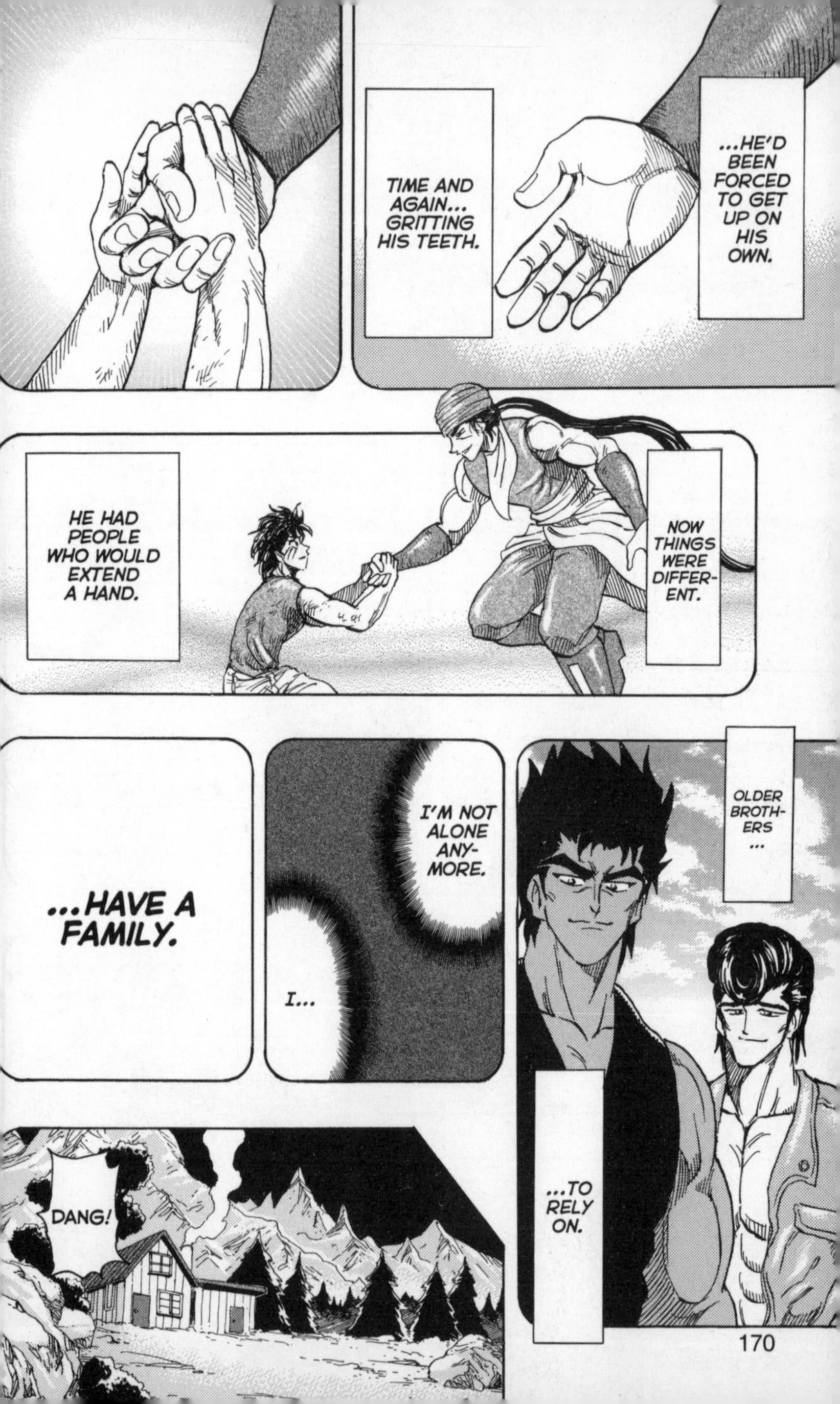
TIME AND AGAIN... GRITTING HIS TEETH.
...HE'D BEEN FORCED TO GET UP ON HIS OWN.
NOW THINGS WERE DIFFER-ENT.
HE HAD PEOPLE WHO WOULD EXTEND A HAND.
I'M NOT ALONE ANY-MORE.
I...
...HAVE A FAMILY.
OLDER BROTH-ERS ...
...TO RELY ON.
DANG!

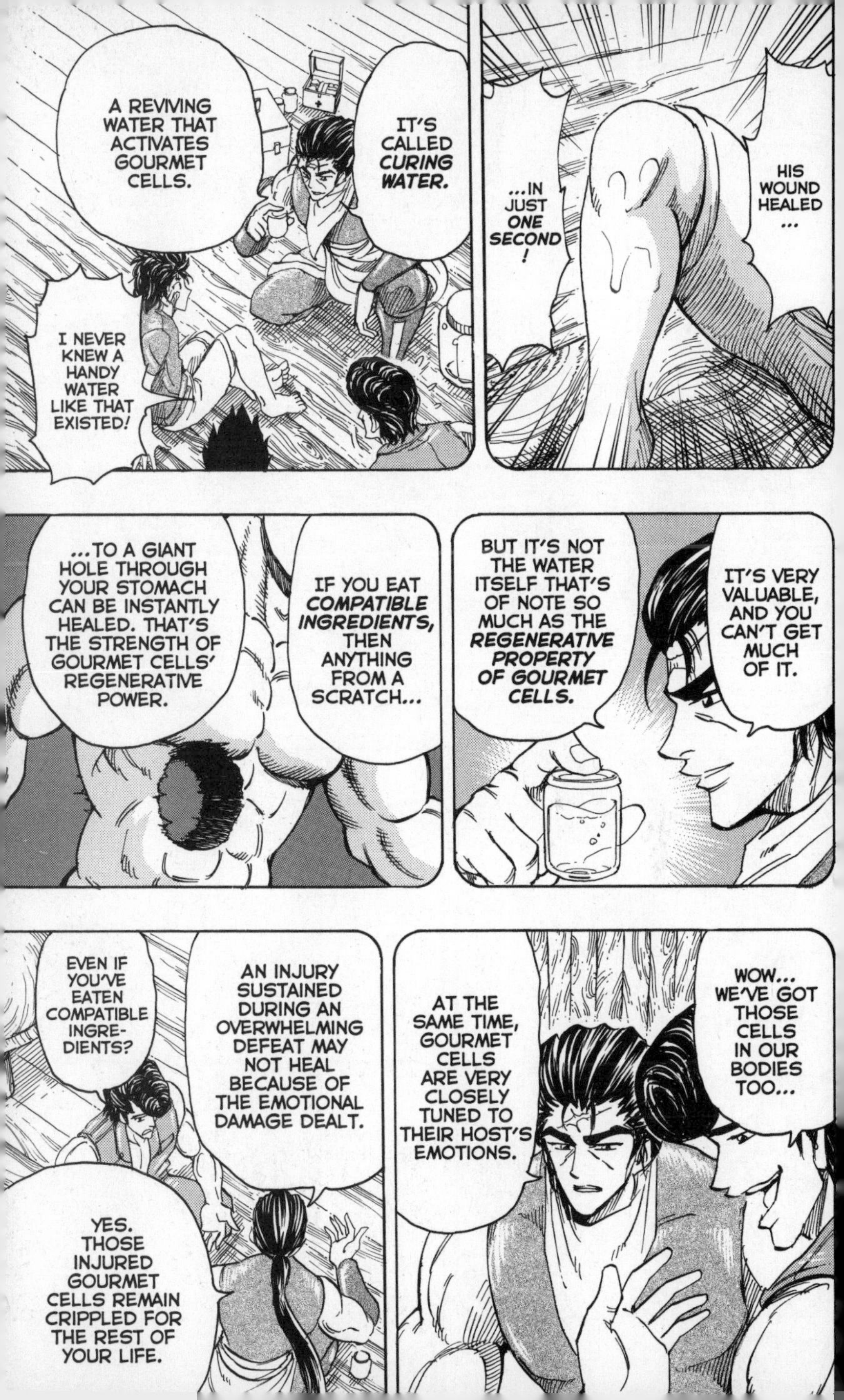
HIS WOUND HEALED...
...IN JUST ONE SECOND!
IT'S CALLED CURING WATER.
A REVIVING WATER THAT ACTIVATES GOURMET CELLS.
I NEVER KNEW A HANDY WATER LIKE THAT EXISTED!
IT'S VERY VALUABLE, AND YOU CAN'T GET MUCH OF IT.
BUT IT'S NOT THE WATER ITSELF THAT'S OF NOTE SO MUCH AS THE REGENERATIVE PROPERTY OF GOURMET CELLS.
IF YOU EAT COMPATIBLE INGREDIENTS, THEN ANYTHING FROM A SCRATCH...
...TO A GIANT HOLE THROUGH YOUR STOMACH CAN BE INSTANTLY HEALED. THAT'S THE STRENGTH OF GOURMET CELLS' REGENERATIVE POWER.
WOW... WE'VE GOT THOSE CELLS IN OUR BODIES TOO...
AT THE SAME TIME, GOURMET CELLS ARE VERY CLOSELY TUNED TO THEIR HOST'S EMOTIONS.
AN INJURY SUSTAINED DURING AN OVERWHELMING DEFEAT MAY NOT HEAL BECAUSE OF THE EMOTIONAL DAMAGE DEALT.
EVEN IF YOU'VE EATEN COMPATIBLE INGRE-DIENTS?
YES. THOSE INJURED GOURMET CELLS REMAIN CRIPPLED FOR THE REST OF YOUR LIFE.

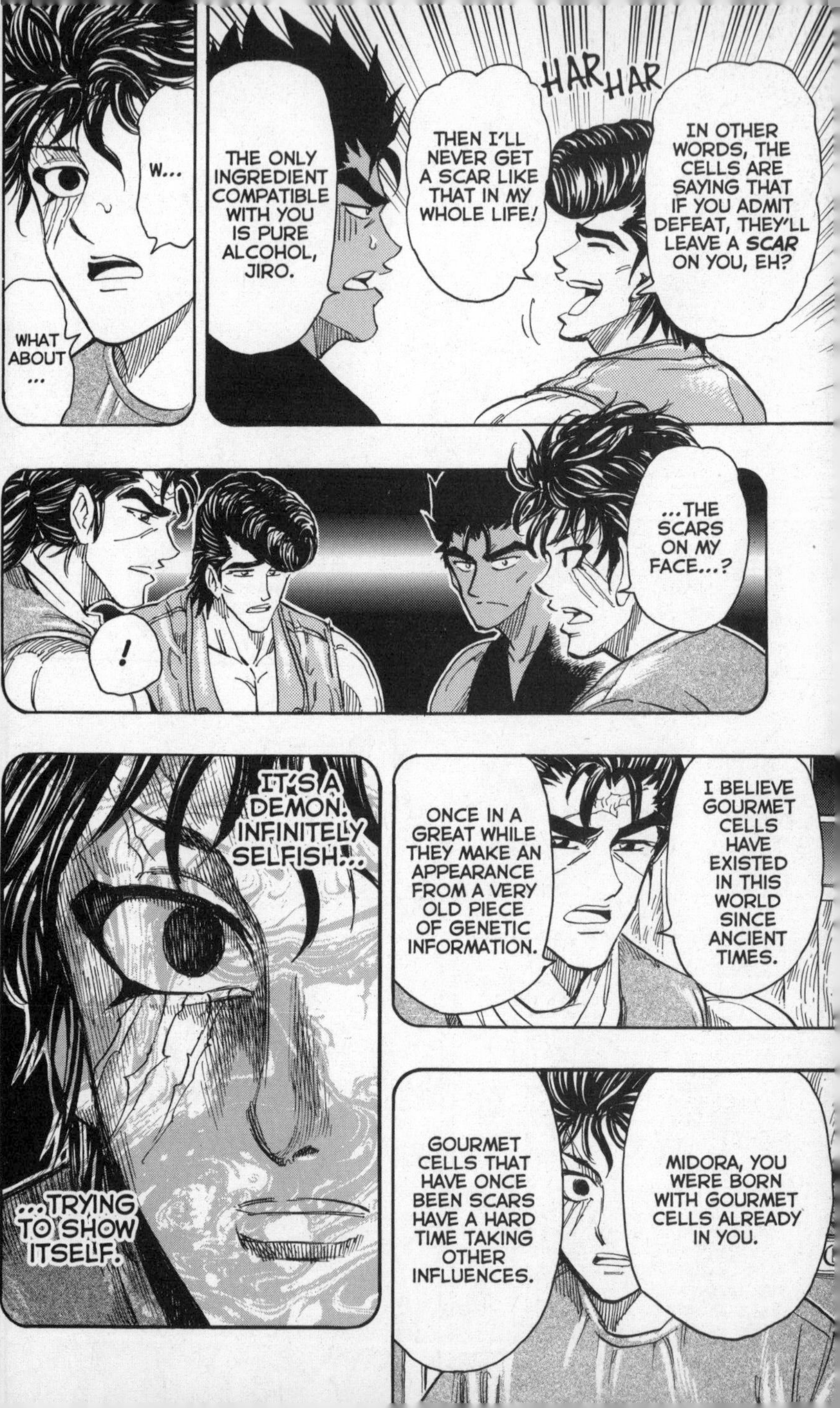
HAR HAR
IN OTHER WORDS, THE CELLS ARE SAYING THAT IF YOU ADMIT DEFEAT, THEY'LL LEAVE A **SCAR** ON YOU, EH?
THEN I'LL NEVER GET A SCAR LIKE THAT IN MY WHOLE LIFE!
THE ONLY INGREDIENT COMPATIBLE WITH YOU IS PURE ALCOHOL, JIRO.
W...
WHAT ABOUT ...
...THE SCARS ON MY FACE...?
!
I BELIEVE GOURMET CELLS HAVE EXISTED IN THIS WORLD SINCE ANCIENT TIMES.
ONCE IN A GREAT WHILE THEY MAKE AN APPEARANCE FROM A VERY OLD PIECE OF GENETIC INFORMATION.
MIDORA, YOU WERE BORN WITH GOURMET CELLS ALREADY IN YOU.
GOURMET CELLS THAT HAVE ONCE BEEN SCARS HAVE A HARD TIME TAKING OTHER INFLUENCES.
IT'S A DEMON. INFINITELY SELFISH...
...TRYING TO SHOW ITSELF.

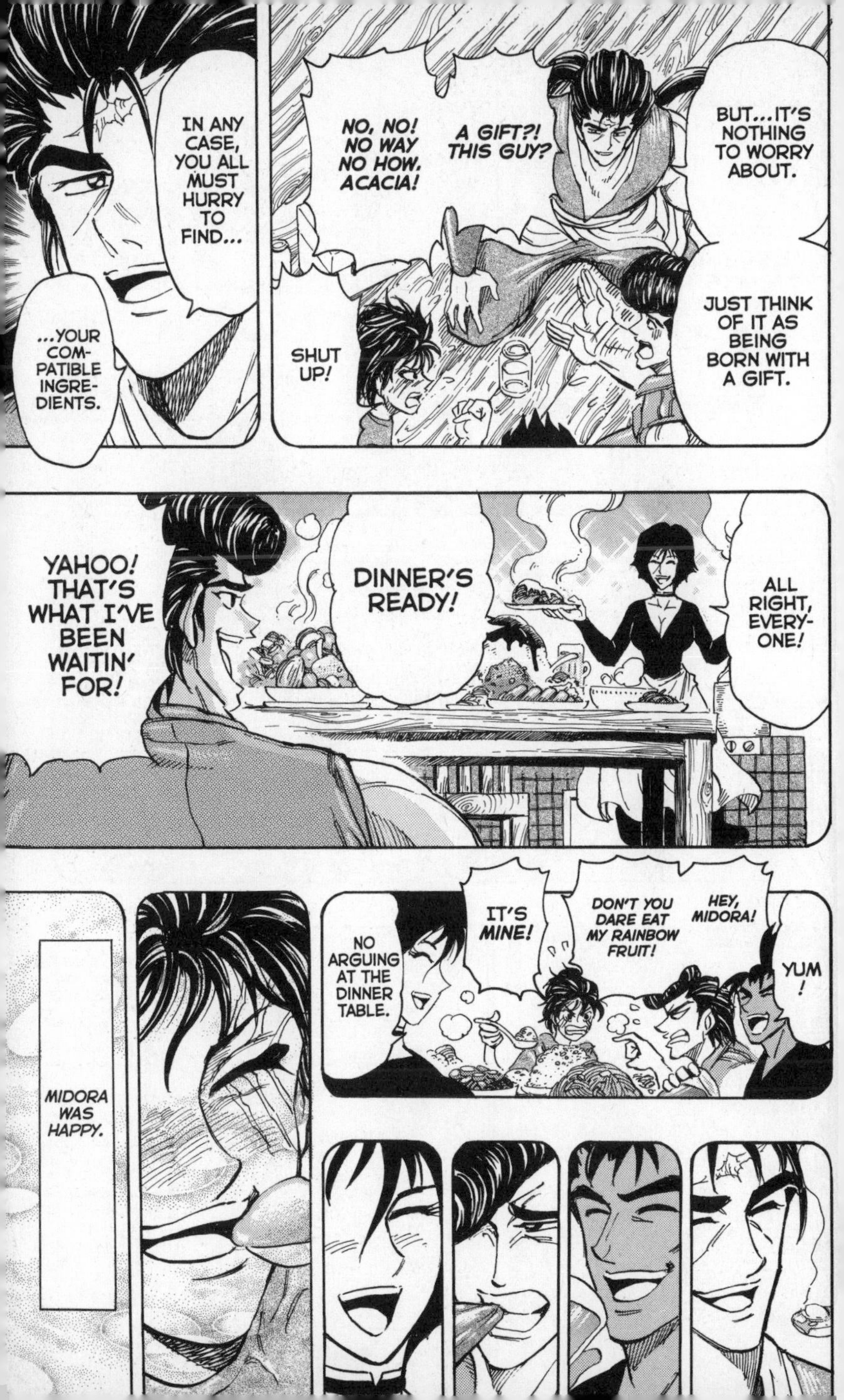
BUT...IT'S NOTHING TO WORRY ABOUT.
JUST THINK OF IT AS BEING BORN WITH A GIFT.
A GIFT?! THIS GUY?
NO, NO! NO WAY NO HOW, ACACIA!
SHUT UP!
IN ANY CASE, YOU ALL MUST HURRY TO FIND...
...YOUR COMPATIBLE INGREDIENTS.
ALL RIGHT, EVERYONE!
DINNER'S READY!
YAHOO! THAT'S WHAT I'VE BEEN WAITIN' FOR!
YUM!
HEY, MIDORA!
DON'T YOU DARE EAT MY RAINBOW FRUIT!
IT'S MINE!
NO ARGUING AT THE DINNER TABLE.
MIDORA WAS HAPPY.

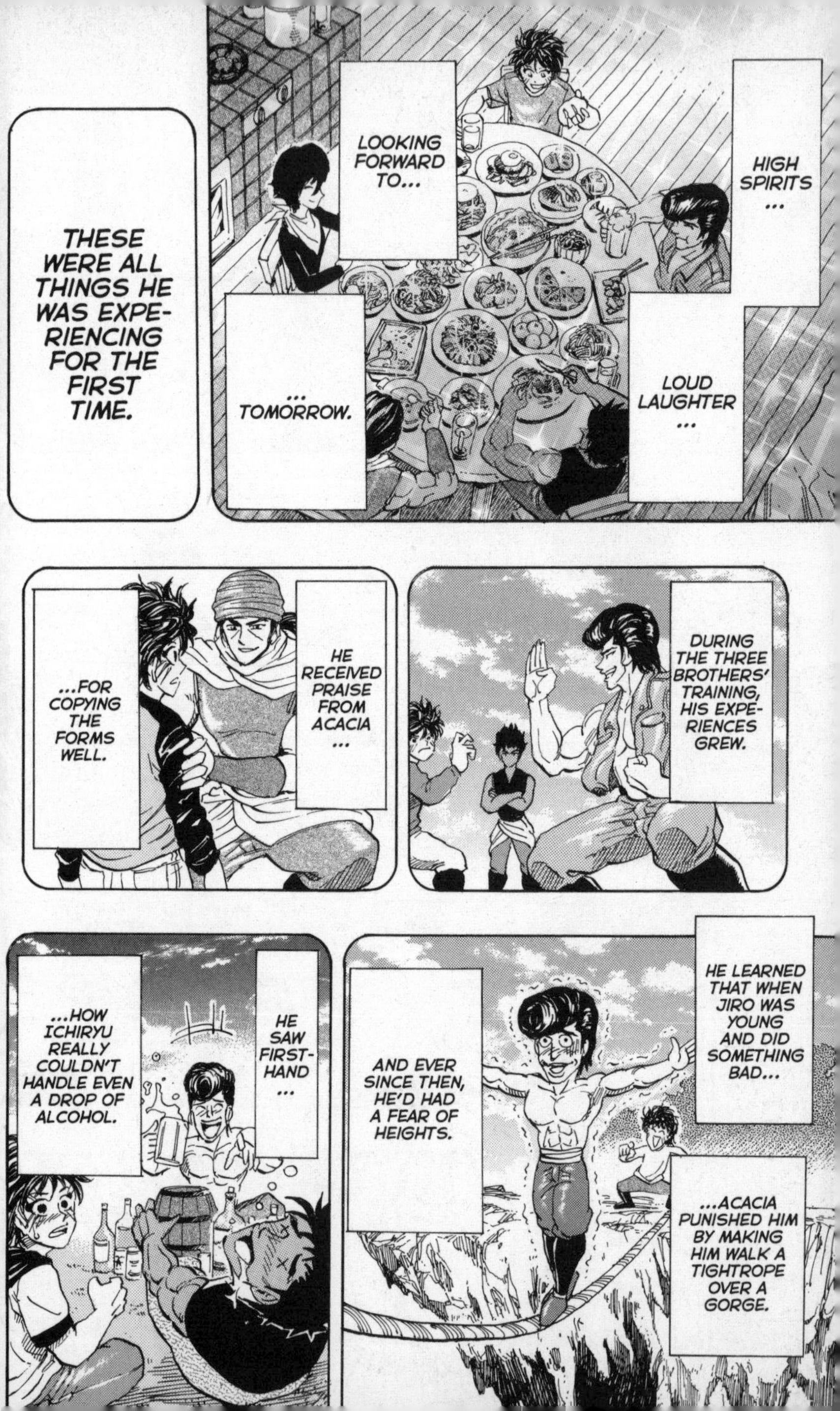
HIGH SPIRITS...
LOOKING FORWARD TO...
LOUD LAUGHTER...
...TOMORROW.
THESE WERE ALL THINGS HE WAS EXPE-RIENCING FOR THE FIRST TIME.
DURING THE THREE BROTHERS' TRAINING, HIS EXPE-RIENCES GREW.
HE RECEIVED PRAISE FROM ACACIA...
...FOR COPYING THE FORMS WELL.
HE LEARNED THAT WHEN JIRO WAS YOUNG AND DID SOMETHING BAD...
...ACACIA PUNISHED HIM BY MAKING HIM WALK A TIGHTROPE OVER A GORGE.
AND EVER SINCE THEN, HE'D HAD A FEAR OF HEIGHTS.
HE SAW FIRST-HAND...
...HOW ICHIRYU REALLY COULDN'T HANDLE EVEN A DROP OF ALCOHOL.

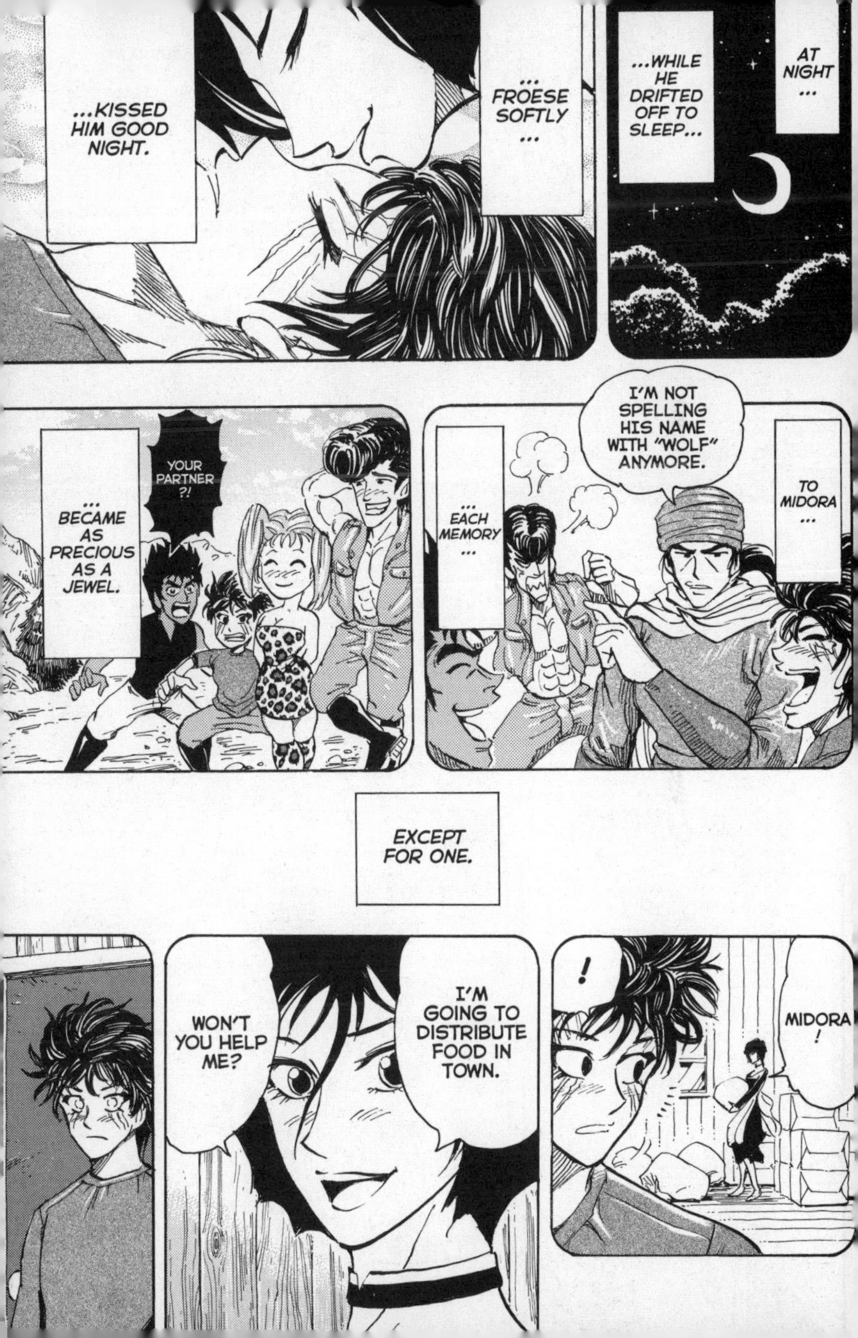
AT NIGHT...
...WHILE HE DRIFTED OFF TO SLEEP...
...FROESE SOFTLY...
...KISSED HIM GOOD NIGHT.
TO MIDORA...
I'M NOT SPELLING HIS NAME WITH "WOLF" ANYMORE.
...EACH MEMORY...
YOUR PARTNER?!
...BECAME AS PRECIOUS AS A JEWEL.
EXCEPT FOR ONE.
MIDORA!
!
I'M GOING TO DISTRIBUTE FOOD IN TOWN.
WON'T YOU HELP ME?

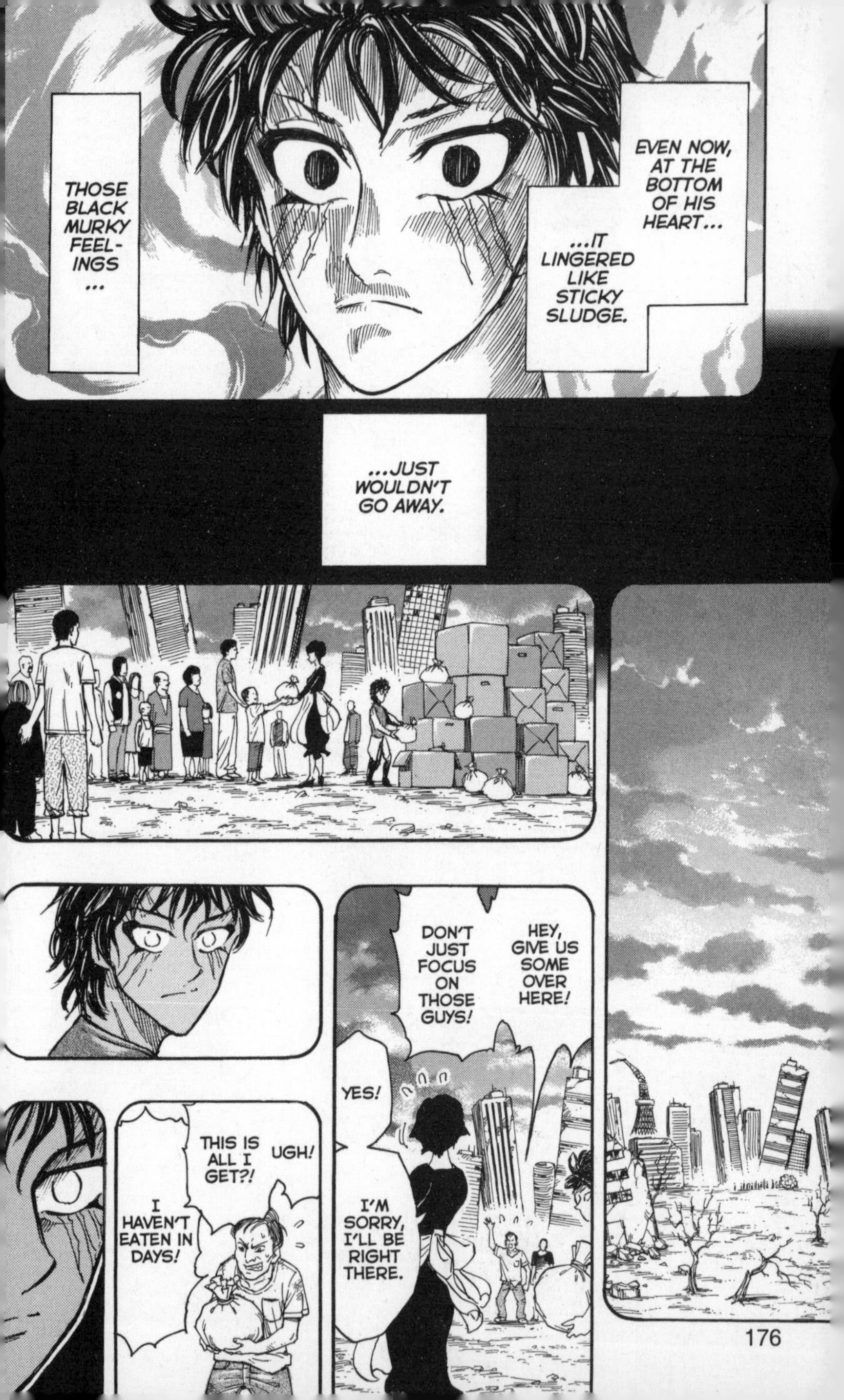
EVEN NOW, AT THE BOTTOM OF HIS HEART...
...IT LINGERED LIKE STICKY SLUDGE.
THOSE BLACK MURKY FEEL- INGS ...
...JUST WOULDN'T GO AWAY.
HEY, GIVE US SOME OVER HERE!
DON'T JUST FOCUS ON THOSE GUYS!
YES!
I'M SORRY, I'LL BE RIGHT THERE.
UGH!
THIS IS ALL I GET?!
I HAVEN'T EATEN IN DAYS!

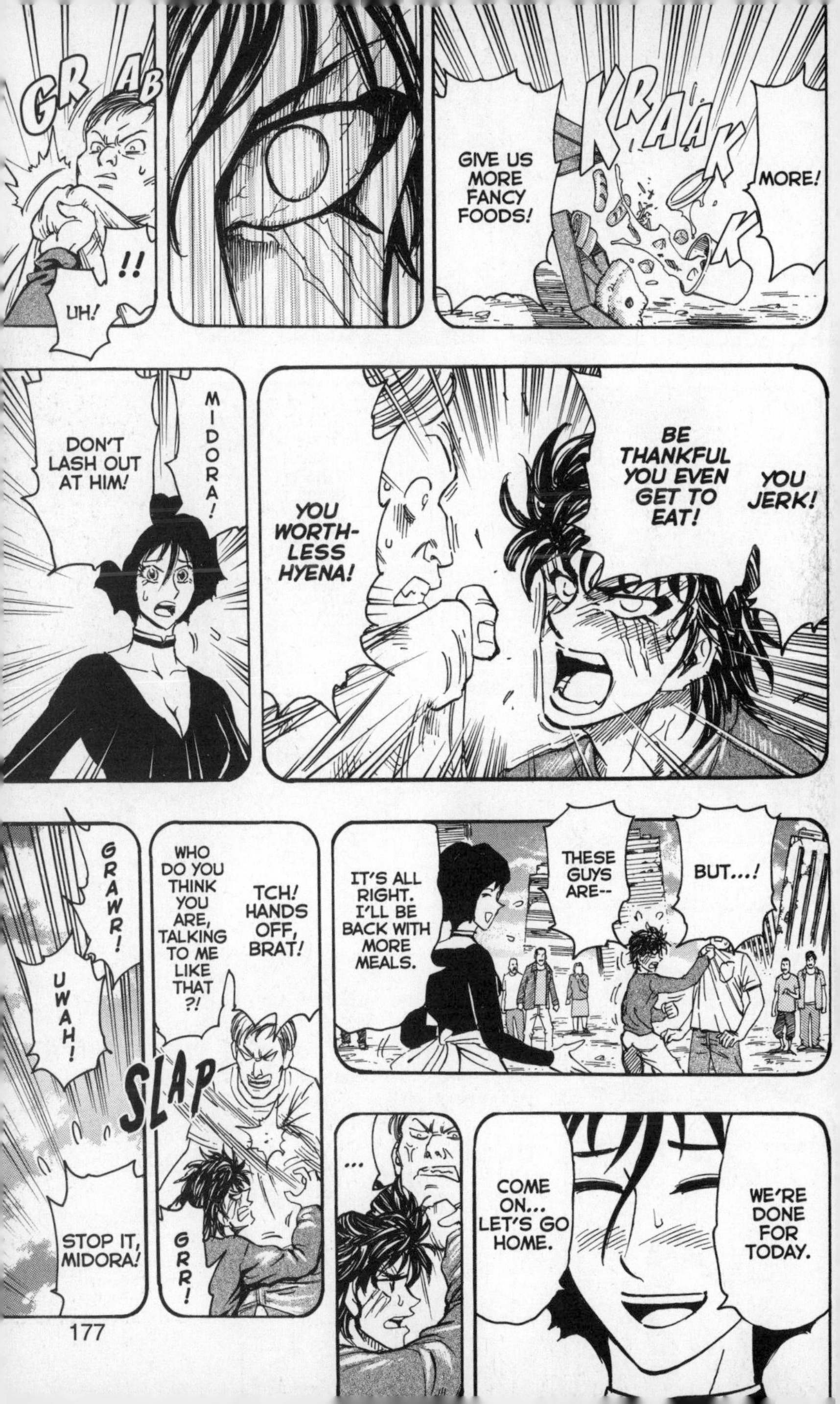
MORE!
KRAAAK
GIVE US MORE FANCY FOODS!
GRAB
!!
UH!
YOU JERK!
BE THANKFUL YOU EVEN GET TO EAT!
YOU WORTHLESS HYENA!
MIDORA!
DON'T LASH OUT AT HIM!
BUT...!
THESE GUYS ARE--
IT'S ALL RIGHT. I'LL BE BACK WITH MORE MEALS.
WE'RE DONE FOR TODAY.
COME ON... LET'S GO HOME.
...
TCH! HANDS OFF, BRAT!
WHO DO YOU THINK YOU ARE, TALKING TO ME LIKE THAT?!
SLAP
GRR!
GRAWR!
UWAH!
STOP IT, MIDORA!

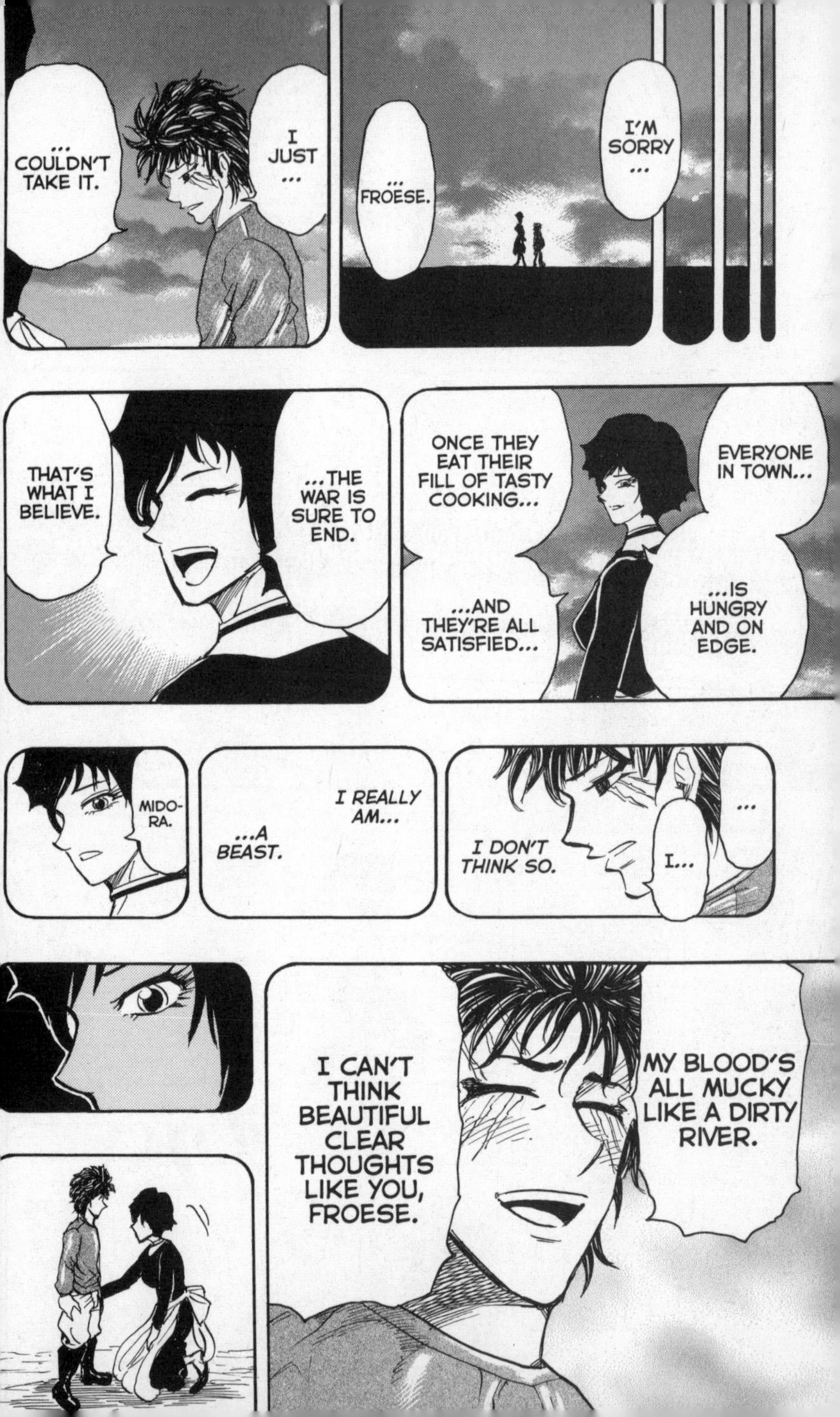
I'M SORRY ...
... FROESE.
I JUST ...
... COULDN'T TAKE IT.
EVERYONE IN TOWN...
...IS HUNGRY AND ON EDGE.
ONCE THEY EAT THEIR FILL OF TASTY COOKING...
...AND THEY'RE ALL SATISFIED...
...THE WAR IS SURE TO END.
THAT'S WHAT I BELIEVE.
...
I...
I DON'T THINK SO.
I REALLY AM...
...A BEAST.
MIDO-RA.
MY BLOOD'S ALL MUCKY LIKE A DIRTY RIVER.
I CAN'T THINK BEAUTIFUL CLEAR THOUGHTS LIKE YOU, FROESE.

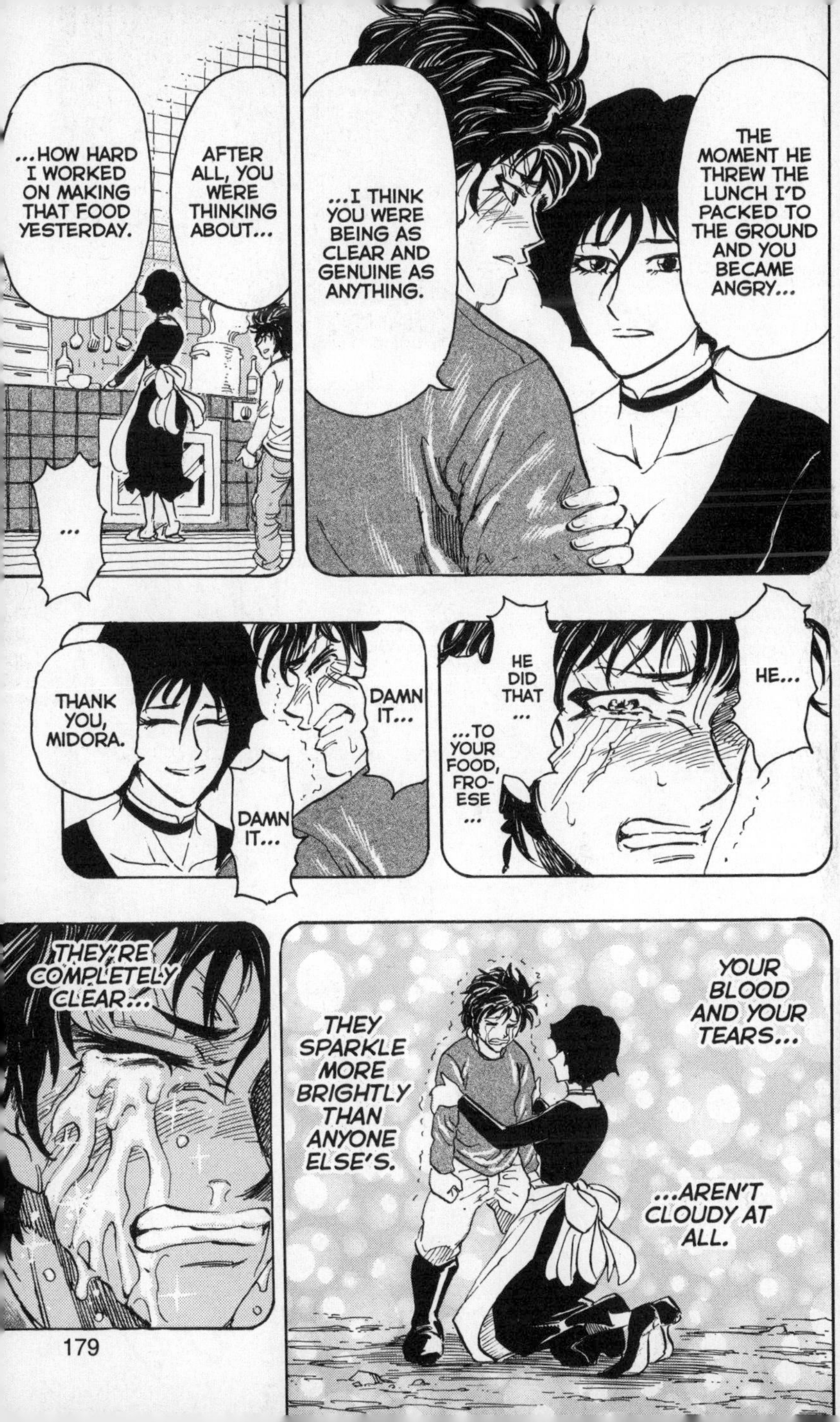

THE MOMENT HE THREW THE LUNCH I'D PACKED TO THE GROUND AND YOU BECAME ANGRY...
...I THINK YOU WERE BEING AS CLEAR AND GENUINE AS ANYTHING.
AFTER ALL, YOU WERE THINKING ABOUT...
...HOW HARD I WORKED ON MAKING THAT FOOD YESTERDAY.
...
HE...
HE DID THAT...
...TO YOUR FOOD, FRO-ESE...
DAMN IT...
THANK YOU, MIDORA.
DAMN IT...
YOUR BLOOD AND YOUR TEARS...
...AREN'T CLOUDY AT ALL.
THEY SPARKLE MORE BRIGHTLY THAN ANYONE ELSE'S.
THEY'RE COMPLETELY CLEAR...

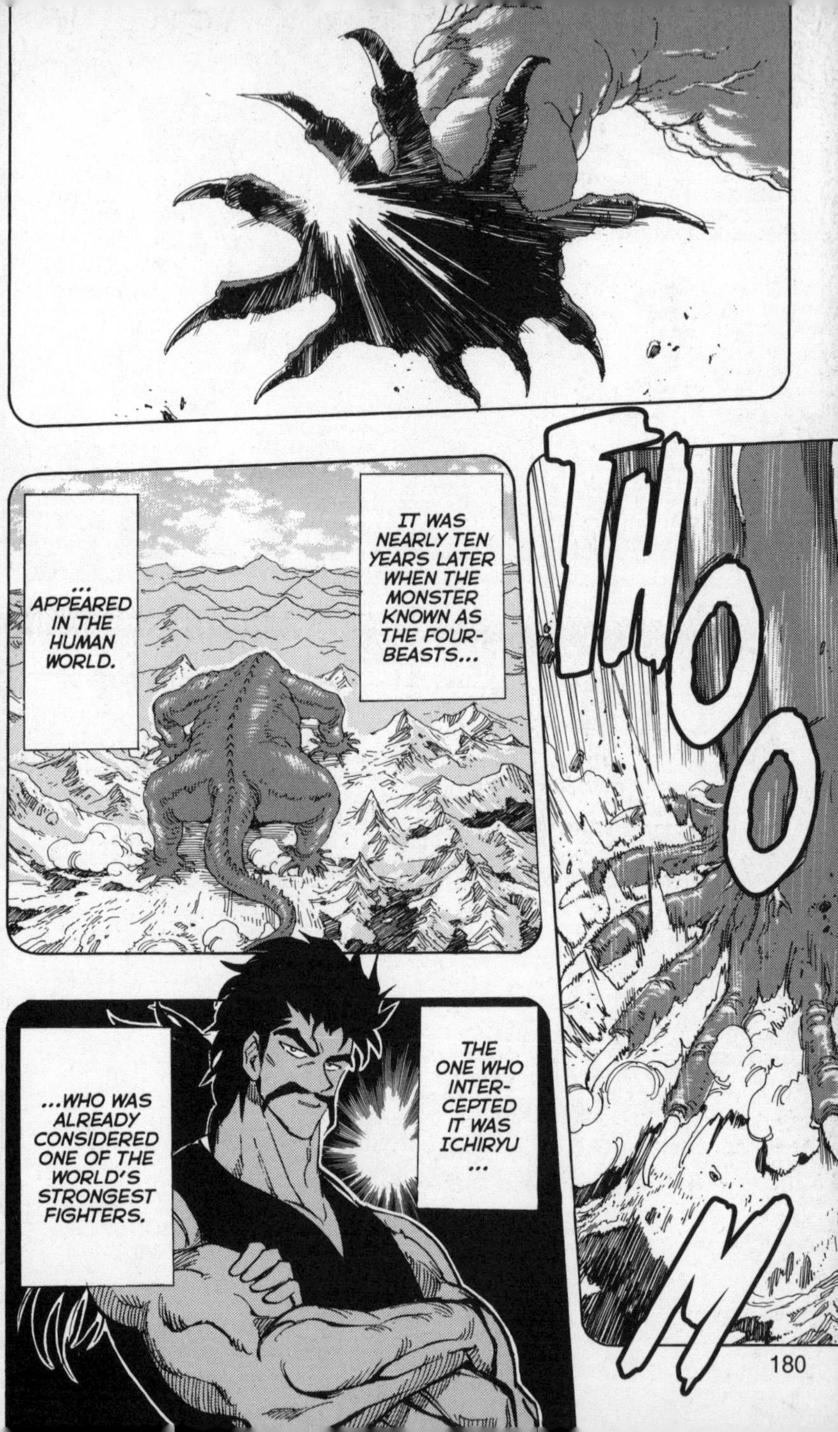
THOOOM
IT WAS NEARLY TEN YEARS LATER WHEN THE MONSTER KNOWN AS THE FOUR-BEASTS...
...APPEARED IN THE HUMAN WORLD.
THE ONE WHO INTERCEPTED IT WAS ICHIRYU...
...WHO WAS ALREADY CONSIDERED ONE OF THE WORLD'S STRONGEST FIGHTERS.

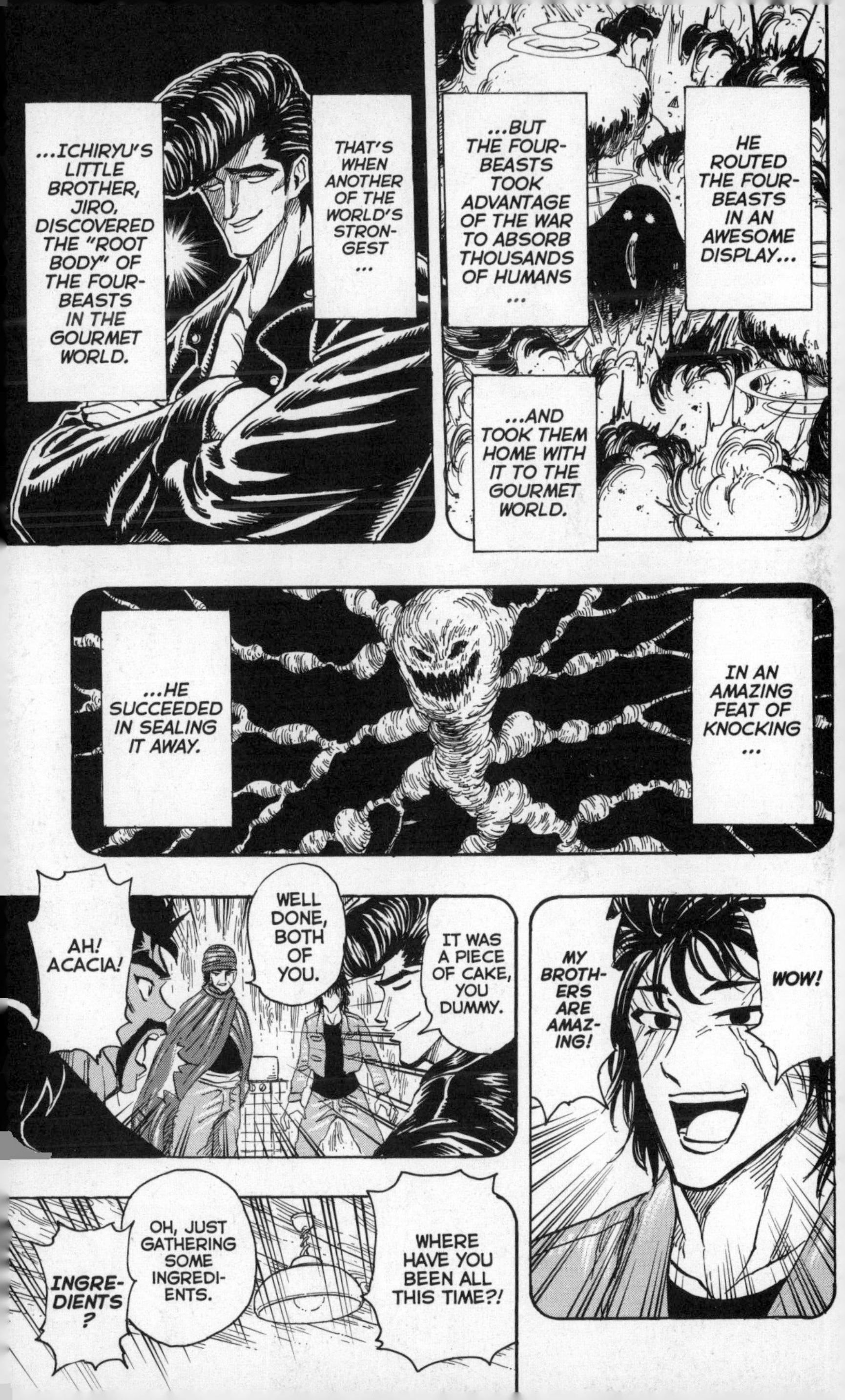
HE ROUTED THE FOUR-BEASTS IN AN AWESOME DISPLAY...
...BUT THE FOUR-BEASTS TOOK ADVANTAGE OF THE WAR TO ABSORB THOUSANDS OF HUMANS...
...AND TOOK THEM HOME WITH IT TO THE GOURMET WORLD.
THAT'S WHEN ANOTHER OF THE WORLD'S STRONGEST...
...ICHIRYU'S LITTLE BROTHER, JIRO, DISCOVERED THE "ROOT BODY" OF THE FOUR-BEASTS IN THE GOURMET WORLD.
IN AN AMAZING FEAT OF KNOCKING...
...HE SUCCEEDED IN SEALING IT AWAY.
WOW!
MY BROTHERS ARE AMAZING!
IT WAS A PIECE OF CAKE, YOU DUMMY.
WELL DONE, BOTH OF YOU.
AH! ACACIA!
WHERE HAVE YOU BEEN ALL THIS TIME?!
OH, JUST GATHERING SOME INGREDIENTS.
INGREDIENTS?

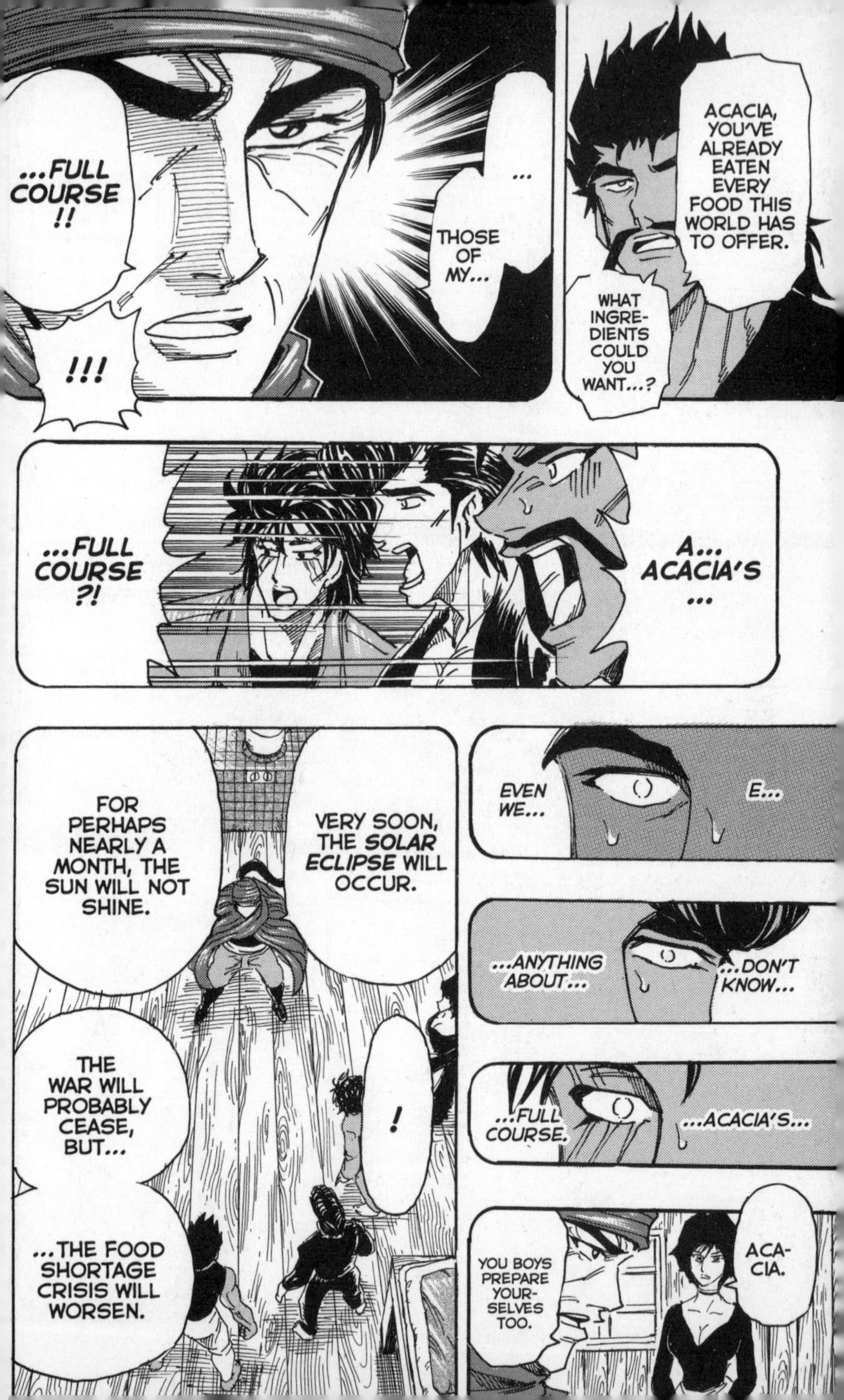
ACACIA, YOU'VE ALREADY EATEN EVERY FOOD THIS WORLD HAS TO OFFER.
WHAT INGREDIENTS COULD YOU WANT...?
...
THOSE OF MY...
...FULL COURSE!!
!!!
A... ACACIA'S...
...FULL COURSE?!
E...
EVEN WE...
...DON'T KNOW...
...ANYTHING ABOUT...
...ACACIA'S...
...FULL COURSE.
ACACIA.
YOU BOYS PREPARE YOURSELVES TOO.
VERY SOON, THE *SOLAR ECLIPSE* WILL OCCUR.
FOR PERHAPS NEARLY A MONTH, THE SUN WILL NOT SHINE.
!
THE WAR WILL PROBABLY CEASE, BUT...
...THE FOOD SHORTAGE CRISIS WILL WORSEN.

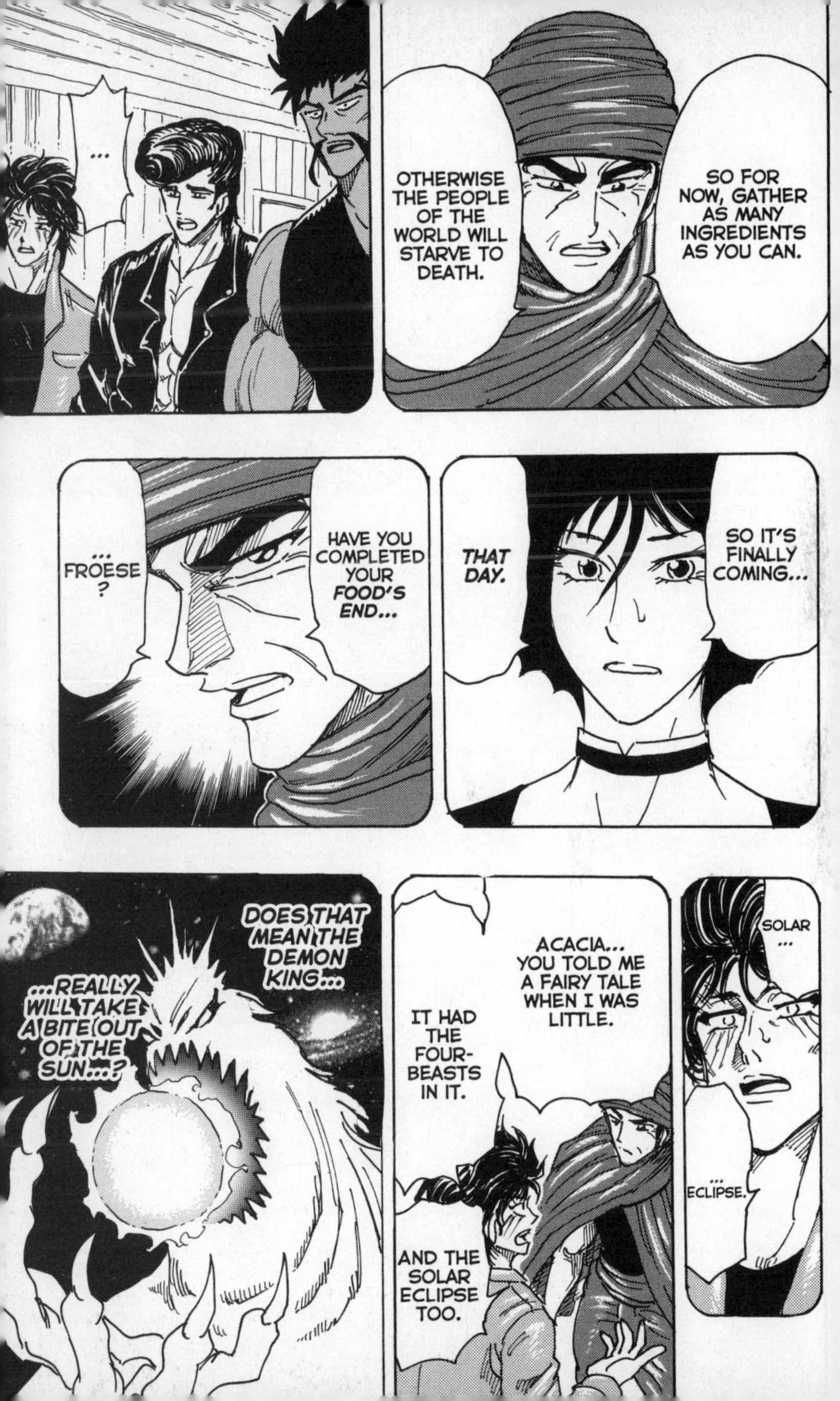
SO FOR NOW, GATHER AS MANY INGREDIENTS AS YOU CAN.
OTHERWISE THE PEOPLE OF THE WORLD WILL STARVE TO DEATH.
...
SO IT'S FINALLY COMING...
THAT DAY.
HAVE YOU COMPLETED YOUR *FOOD'S END*...
...FROESE?
SOLAR...
...ECLIPSE.
ACACIA... YOU TOLD ME A FAIRY TALE WHEN I WAS LITTLE.
IT HAD THE FOUR-BEASTS IN IT.
AND THE SOLAR ECLIPSE TOO.
DOES THAT MEAN THE DEMON KING...
...REALLY WILL TAKE A BITE OUT OF THE SUN...?

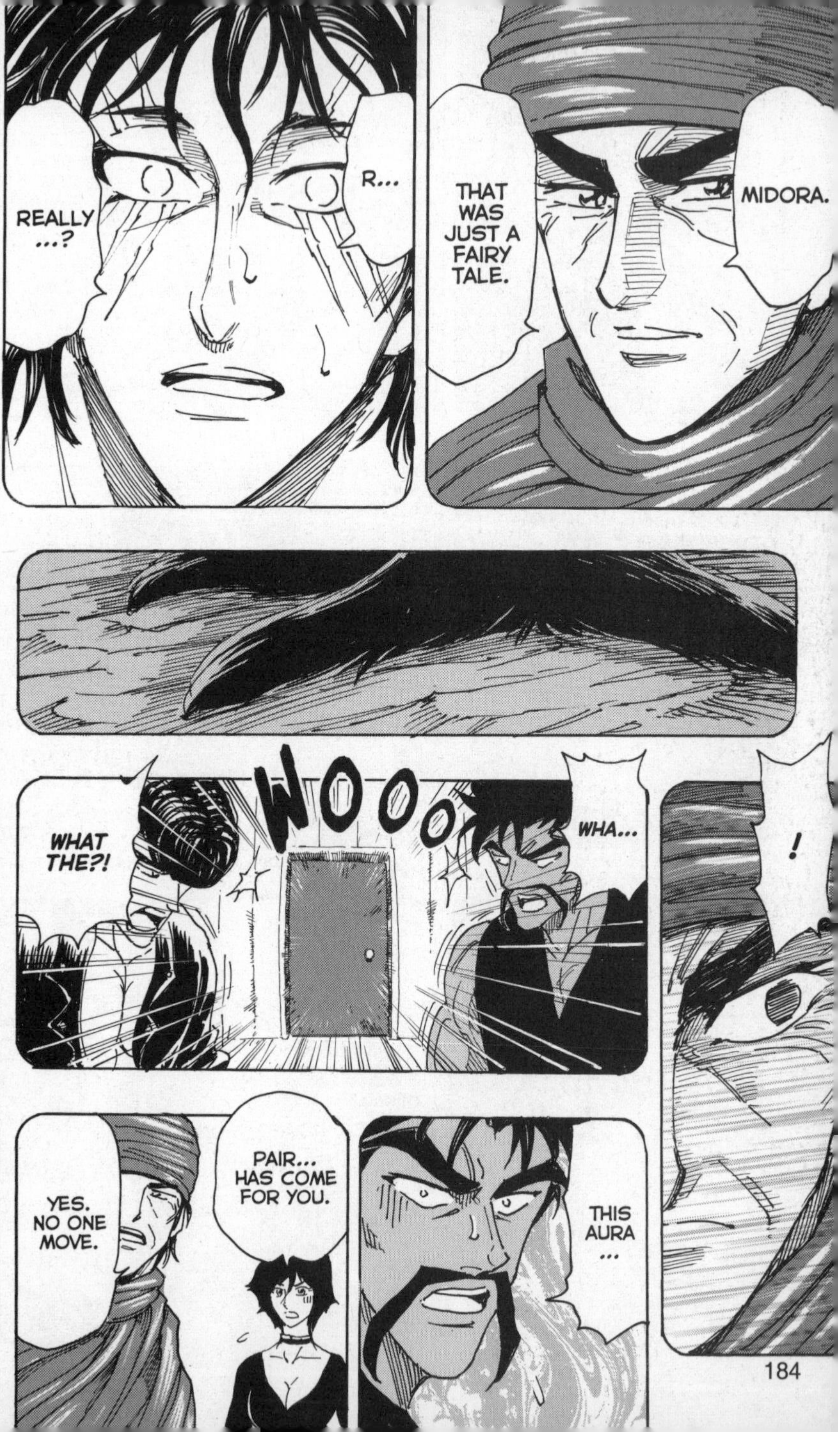

MIDORA.
THAT WAS JUST A FAIRY TALE.
R...
REALLY ...?
!
WOOO
WHA...
WHAT THE?!
THIS AURA ...
PAIR... HAS COME FOR YOU.
YES. NO ONE MOVE.

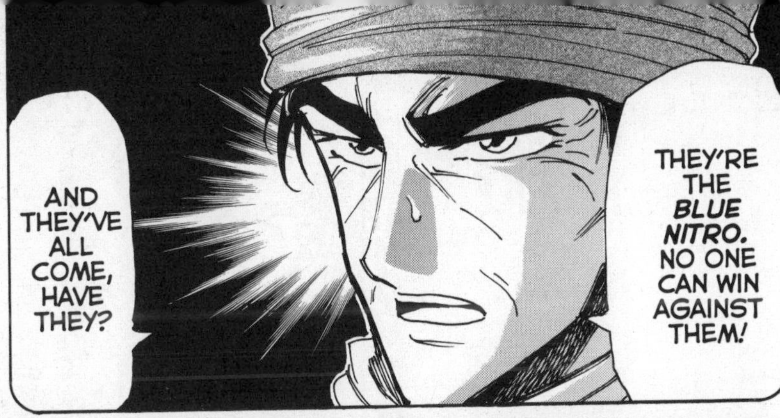
THEY'RE THE *BLUE NITRO.* NO ONE CAN WIN AGAINST THEM!
AND THEY'VE ALL COME, HAVE THEY?

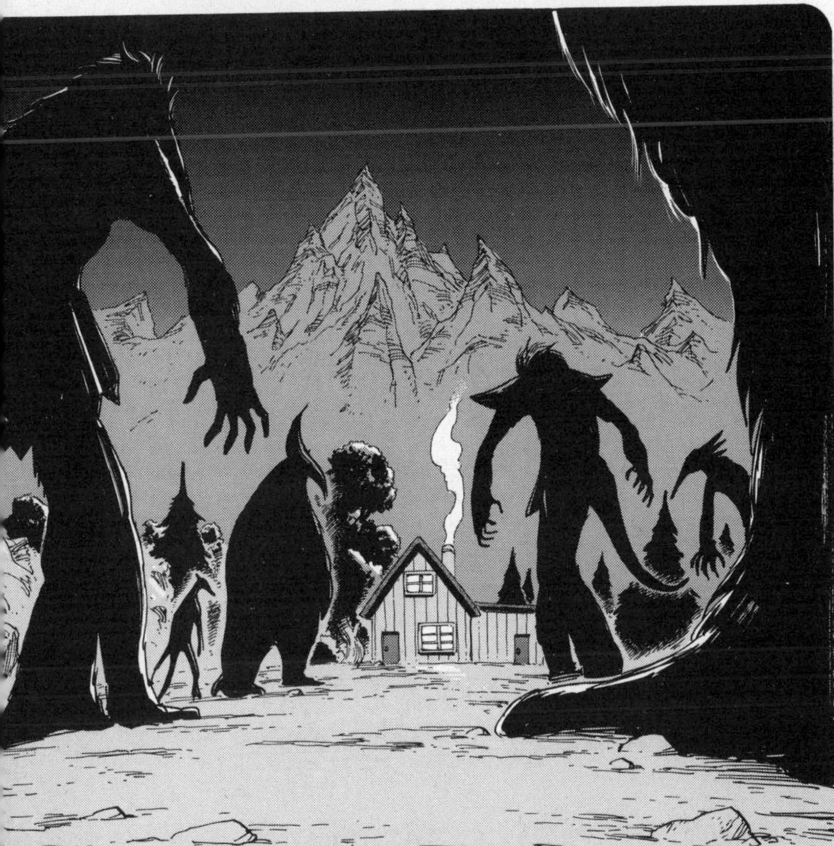

CHARACTER PROFILE

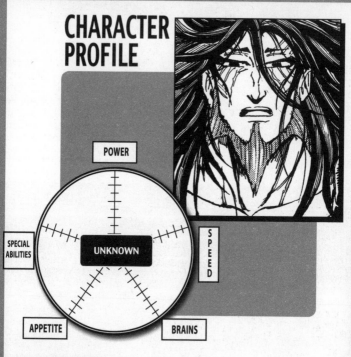

POWER

SPECIAL ABILITIES

UNKNOWN

SPEED

APPETITE

BRAINS

MIDORA

AGE:	UNKNOWN	**BIRTHDAY:**	MAR 3
BLOOD TYPE:	B	**SIGN:**	PISCES
HEIGHT:	265 CM	**WEIGHT:**	700 KG
EYESIGHT:	20/4	**SHOE SIZE:**	55 CM

SPECIAL MOVES/ABILITIES: • Hungry Tongue, Mountain Tongue, Machine Gun Tongue, Hungry Space, Mirror Neuron, Meteor Spice

The boss of Gourmet Corp. and Gourmet God Acacia's third disciple. He is in fierce competition with the IGO, Toriko and NEO for Acacia's Main Course of "God." He was born in a starving village, and hasn't forgiven humanity for abandoning him. After Froese's death, his hate only grew stronger. Is God really the only food that can satisfy this deeply miserable man?

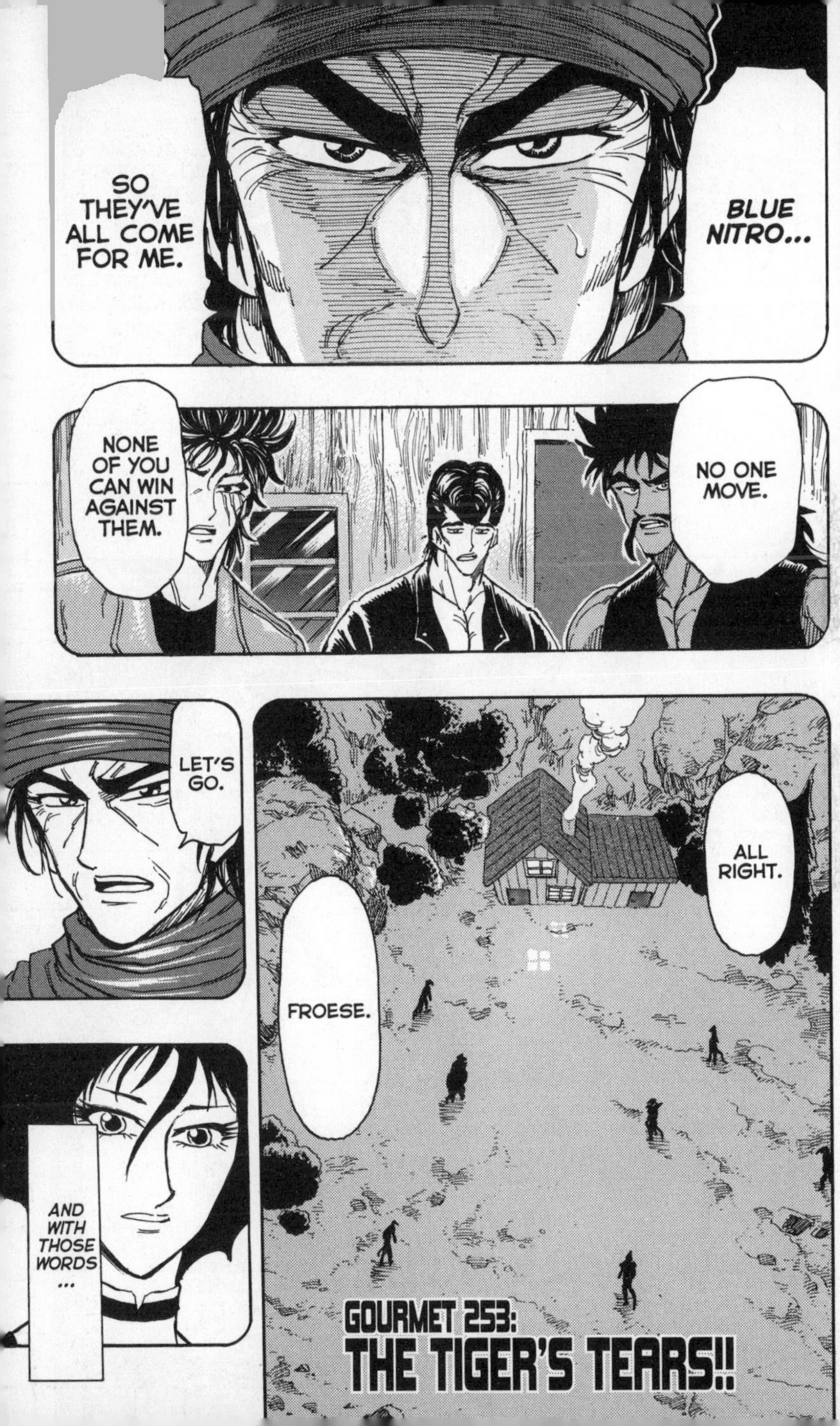
BLUE NITRO...
SO THEY'VE ALL COME FOR ME.
NO ONE MOVE.
NONE OF YOU CAN WIN AGAINST THEM.
ALL RIGHT.
FROESE.
LET'S GO.
AND WITH THOSE WORDS...
GOURMET 253:
THE TIGER'S TEARS!!

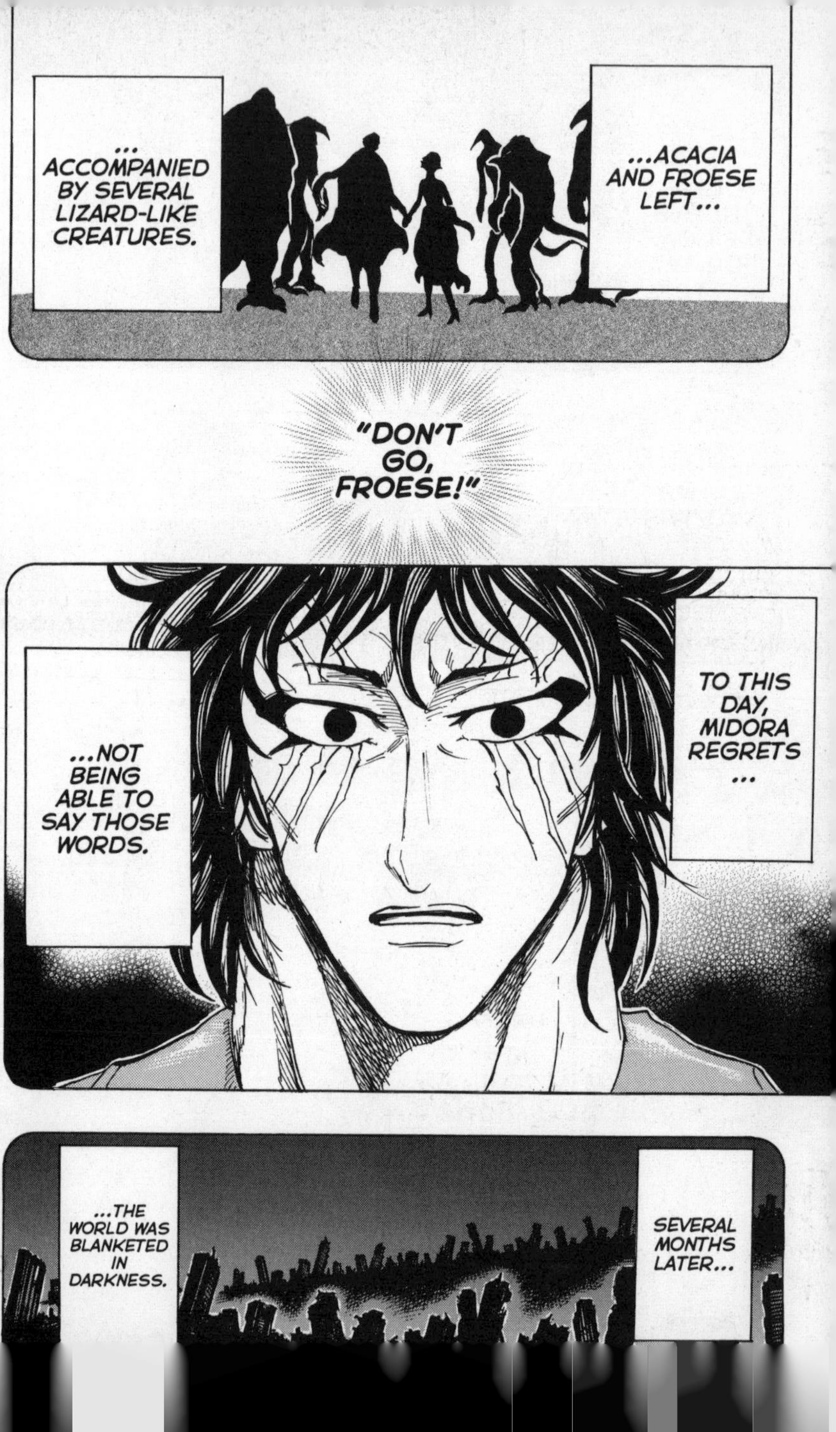
...ACACIA AND FROESE LEFT...
...ACCOMPANIED BY SEVERAL LIZARD-LIKE CREATURES.
"DON'T GO, FROESE!"
TO THIS DAY, MIDORA REGRETS...
...NOT BEING ABLE TO SAY THOSE WORDS.
SEVERAL MONTHS LATER...
...THE WORLD WAS BLANKETED IN DARKNESS.

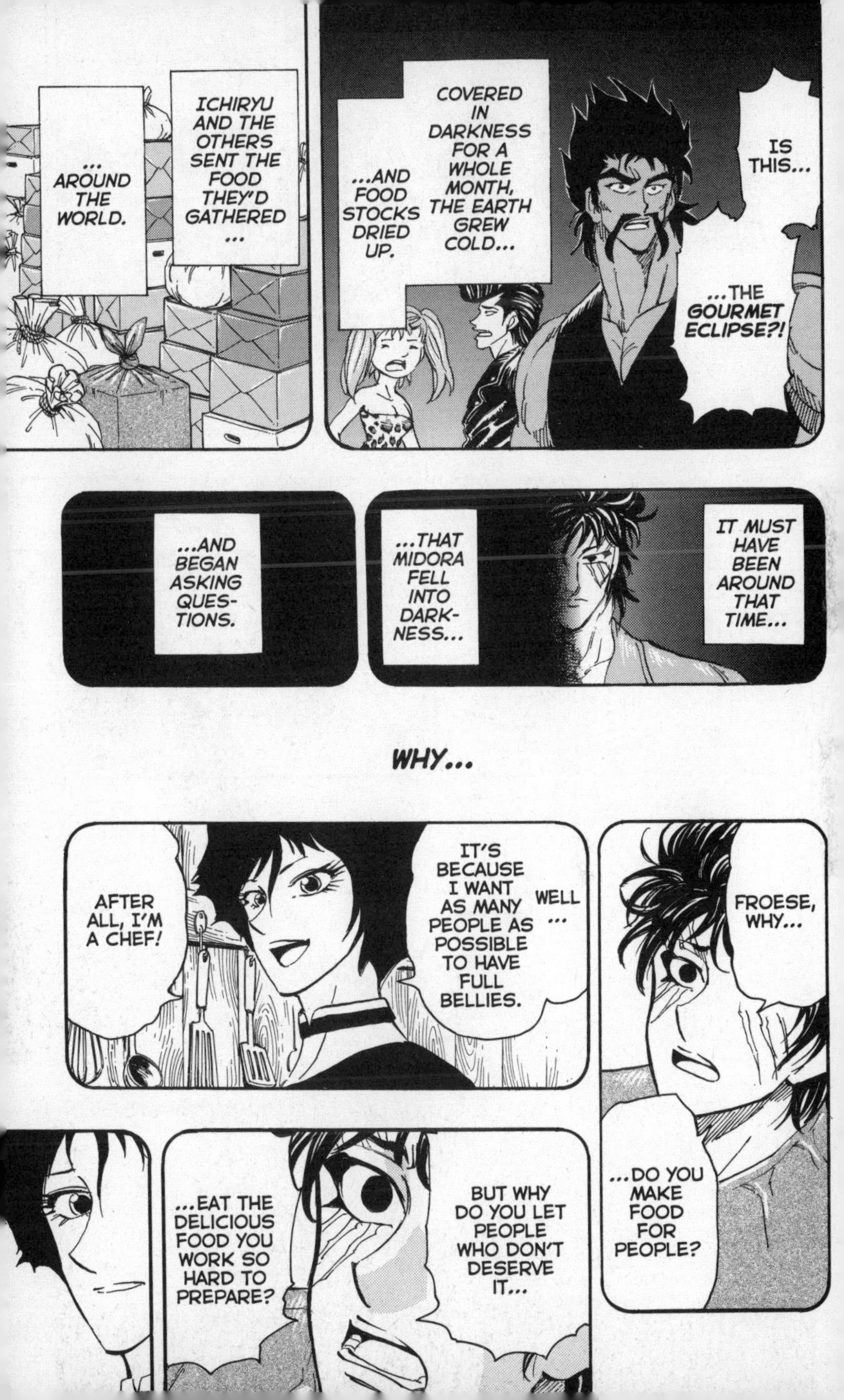
IS THIS...
...THE GOURMET ECLIPSE?!
COVERED IN DARKNESS FOR A WHOLE MONTH, THE EARTH GREW COLD...
...AND FOOD STOCKS DRIED UP.
ICHIRYU AND THE OTHERS SENT THE FOOD THEY'D GATHERED...
...AROUND THE WORLD.
IT MUST HAVE BEEN AROUND THAT TIME...
...THAT MIDORA FELL INTO DARKNESS...
...AND BEGAN ASKING QUESTIONS.
WHY...
FROESE, WHY...
...DO YOU MAKE FOOD FOR PEOPLE?
WELL...
IT'S BECAUSE I WANT AS MANY PEOPLE AS POSSIBLE TO HAVE FULL BELLIES.
AFTER ALL, I'M A CHEF!
BUT WHY DO YOU LET PEOPLE WHO DON'T DESERVE IT...
...EAT THE DELICIOUS FOOD YOU WORK SO HARD TO PREPARE?

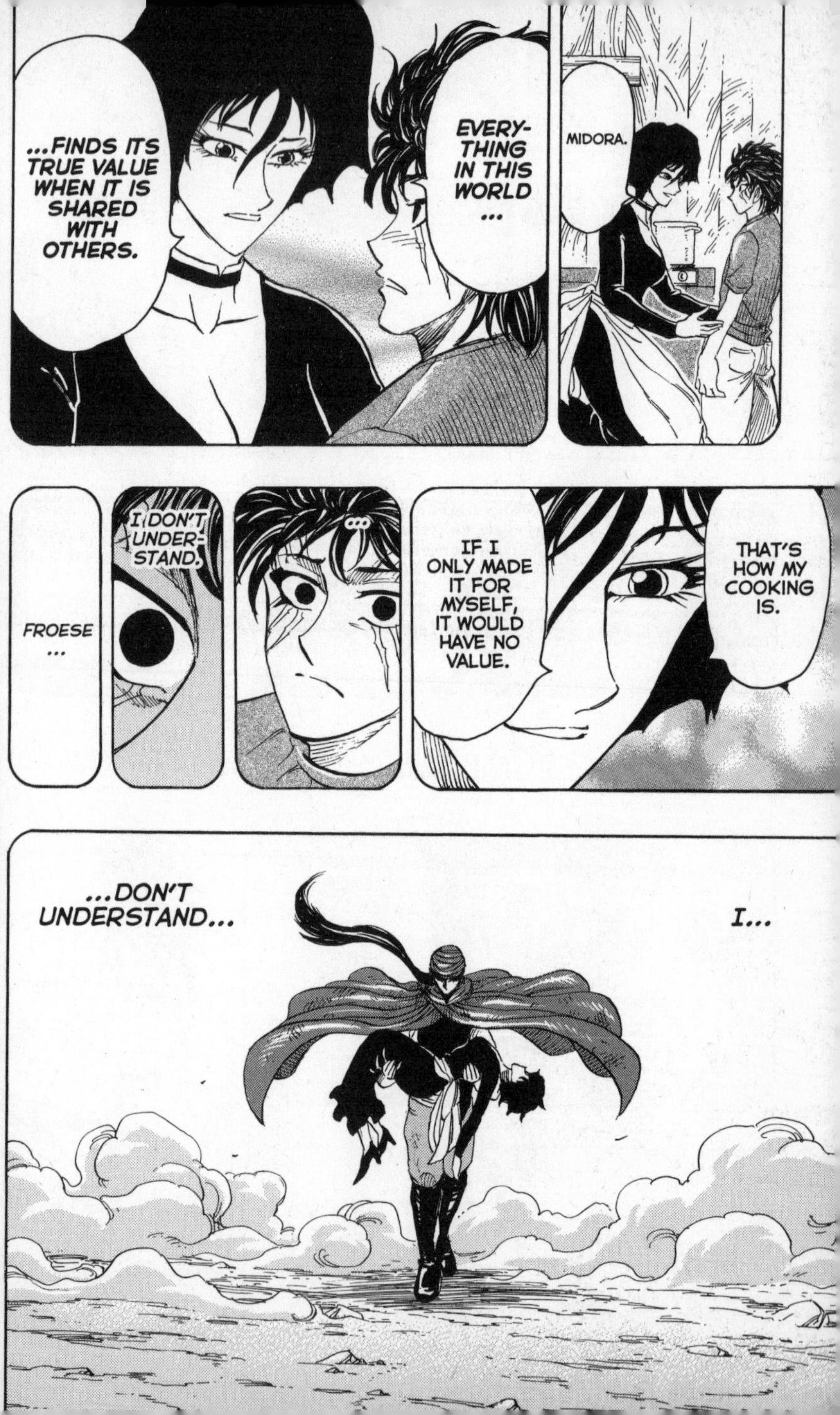
MIDORA.
EVERY-THING IN THIS WORLD ...
...FINDS ITS TRUE VALUE WHEN IT IS SHARED WITH OTHERS.
THAT'S HOW MY COOKING IS.
IF I ONLY MADE IT FOR MYSELF, IT WOULD HAVE NO VALUE.
...
I DON'T UNDER-STAND.
FROESE ...
I...
...DON'T UNDERSTAND...

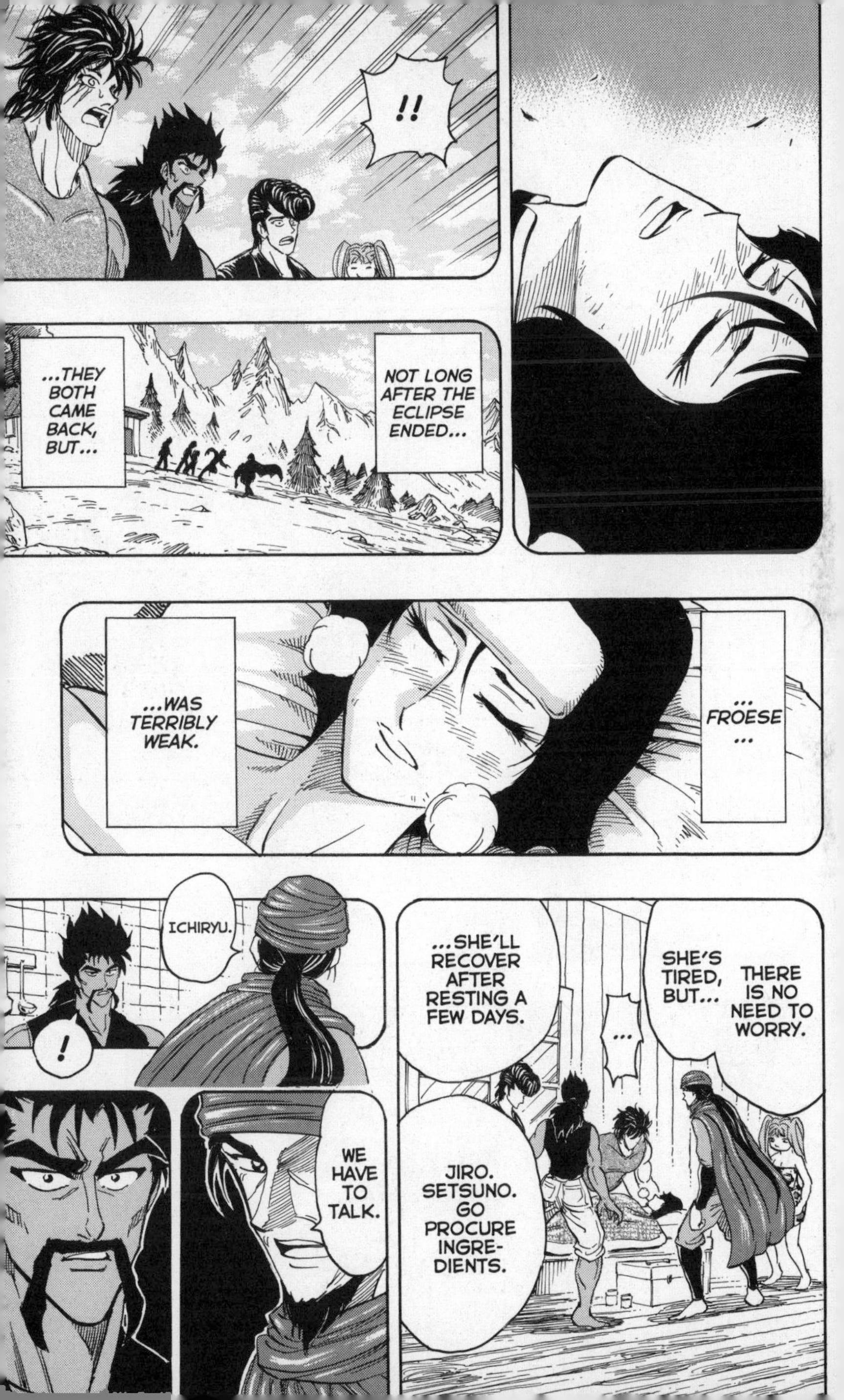
!!
NOT LONG AFTER THE ECLIPSE ENDED...
...THEY BOTH CAME BACK, BUT...
... FROESE ...
...WAS TERRIBLY WEAK.
SHE'S TIRED, BUT...
THERE IS NO NEED TO WORRY.
...
...SHE'LL RECOVER AFTER RESTING A FEW DAYS.
JIRO. SETSUNO. GO PROCURE INGREDIENTS.
ICHIRYU.
!
WE HAVE TO TALK.

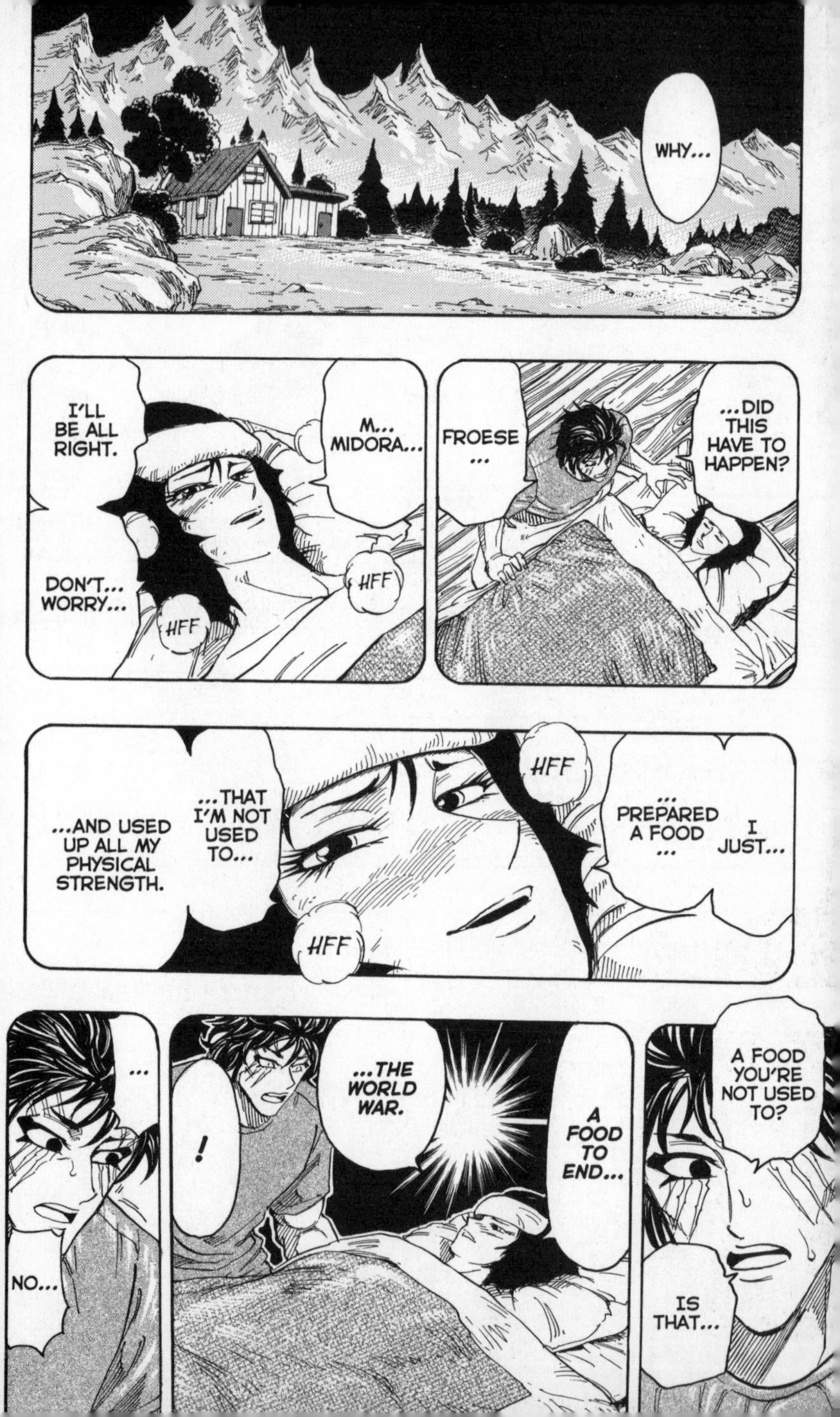
WHY...
...DID THIS HAVE TO HAPPEN?
FROESE ...
M... MIDORA...
I'LL BE ALL RIGHT.
HFF
DON'T... WORRY...
HFF
I JUST...
... PREPARED A FOOD ...
HFF
...THAT I'M NOT USED TO...
...AND USED UP ALL MY PHYSICAL STRENGTH.
HFF
A FOOD YOU'RE NOT USED TO?
IS THAT...
A FOOD TO END...
...THE WORLD WAR.
!
...
NO...

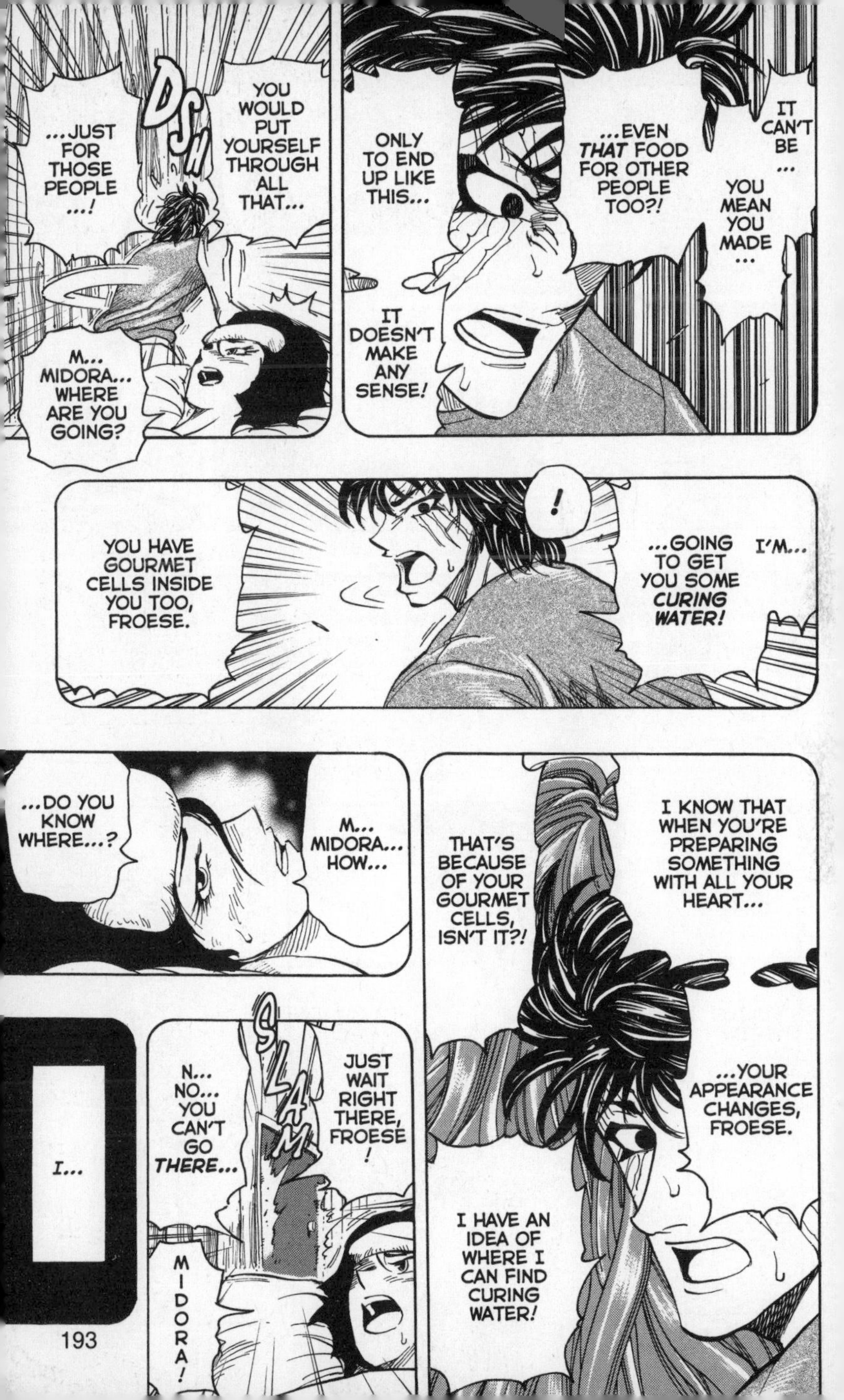
IT CAN'T BE ...
YOU MEAN YOU MADE ...
...EVEN *THAT* FOOD FOR OTHER PEOPLE TOO?!
ONLY TO END UP LIKE THIS...
IT DOESN'T MAKE ANY SENSE!
YOU WOULD PUT YOURSELF THROUGH ALL THAT...
DSH
...JUST FOR THOSE PEOPLE ...!
M... MIDORA... WHERE ARE YOU GOING?
!
I'M...
...GOING TO GET YOU SOME *CURING WATER!*
YOU HAVE GOURMET CELLS INSIDE YOU TOO, FROESE.
I KNOW THAT WHEN YOU'RE PREPARING SOMETHING WITH ALL YOUR HEART...
THAT'S BECAUSE OF YOUR GOURMET CELLS, ISN'T IT?!
...YOUR APPEARANCE CHANGES, FROESE.
I HAVE AN IDEA OF WHERE I CAN FIND CURING WATER!
M... MIDORA... HOW...
...DO YOU KNOW WHERE...?
JUST WAIT RIGHT THERE, FROESE!
SLAM
N... NO... YOU CAN'T GO *THERE...*
MIDORA!
I...

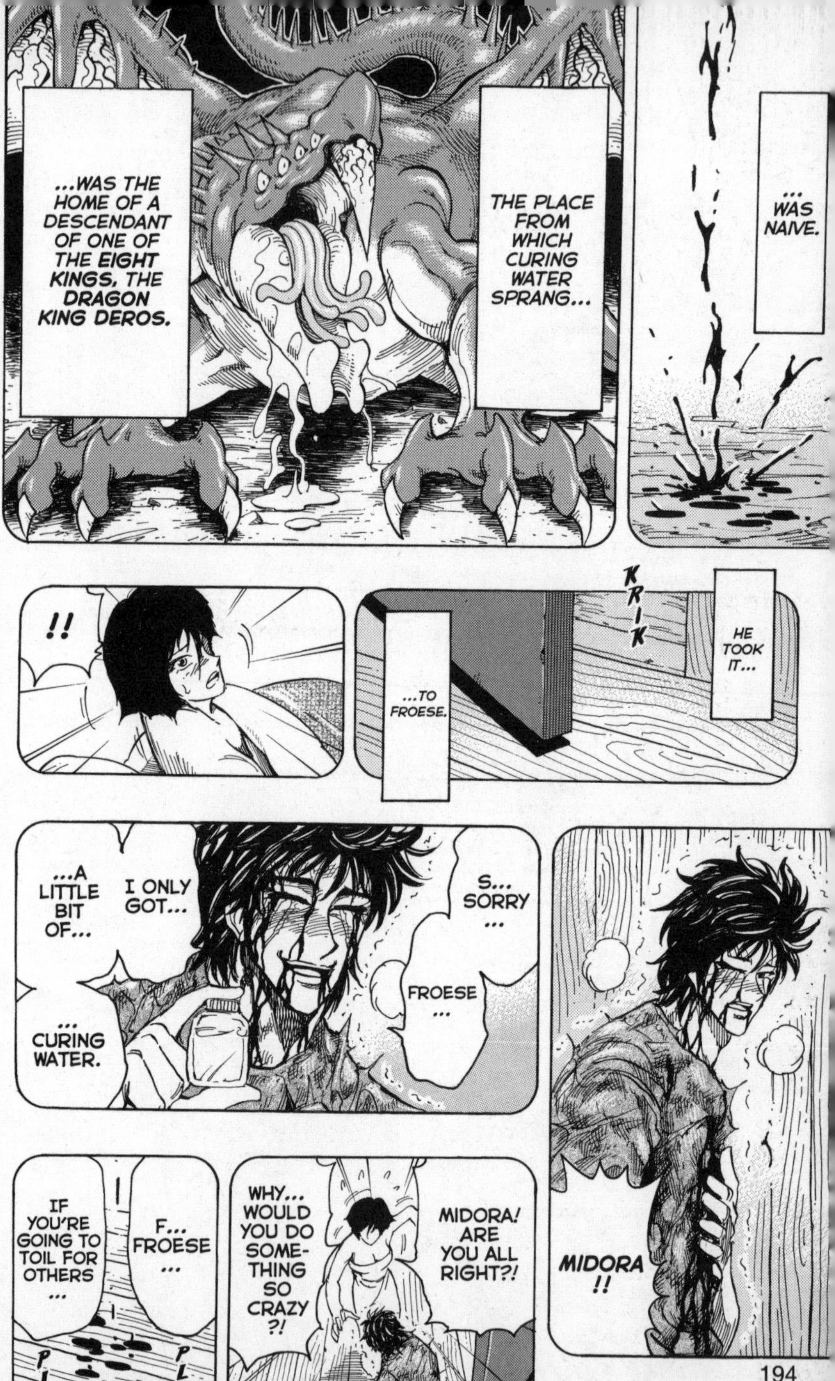

... WAS NAIVE.
THE PLACE FROM WHICH CURING WATER SPRANG...
...WAS THE HOME OF A DESCENDANT OF ONE OF THE EIGHT KINGS, THE DRAGON KING DEROS.
HE TOOK IT...
KRIK
...TO FROESE.
!!
MIDORA !!
S... SORRY ...
FROESE ...
I ONLY GOT...
...A LITTLE BIT OF...
... CURING WATER.
MIDORA! ARE YOU ALL RIGHT?!
WHY... WOULD YOU DO SOMETHING SO CRAZY ?!
F... FROESE ...
IF YOU'RE GOING TO TOIL FOR OTHERS ...
PLP
PLP

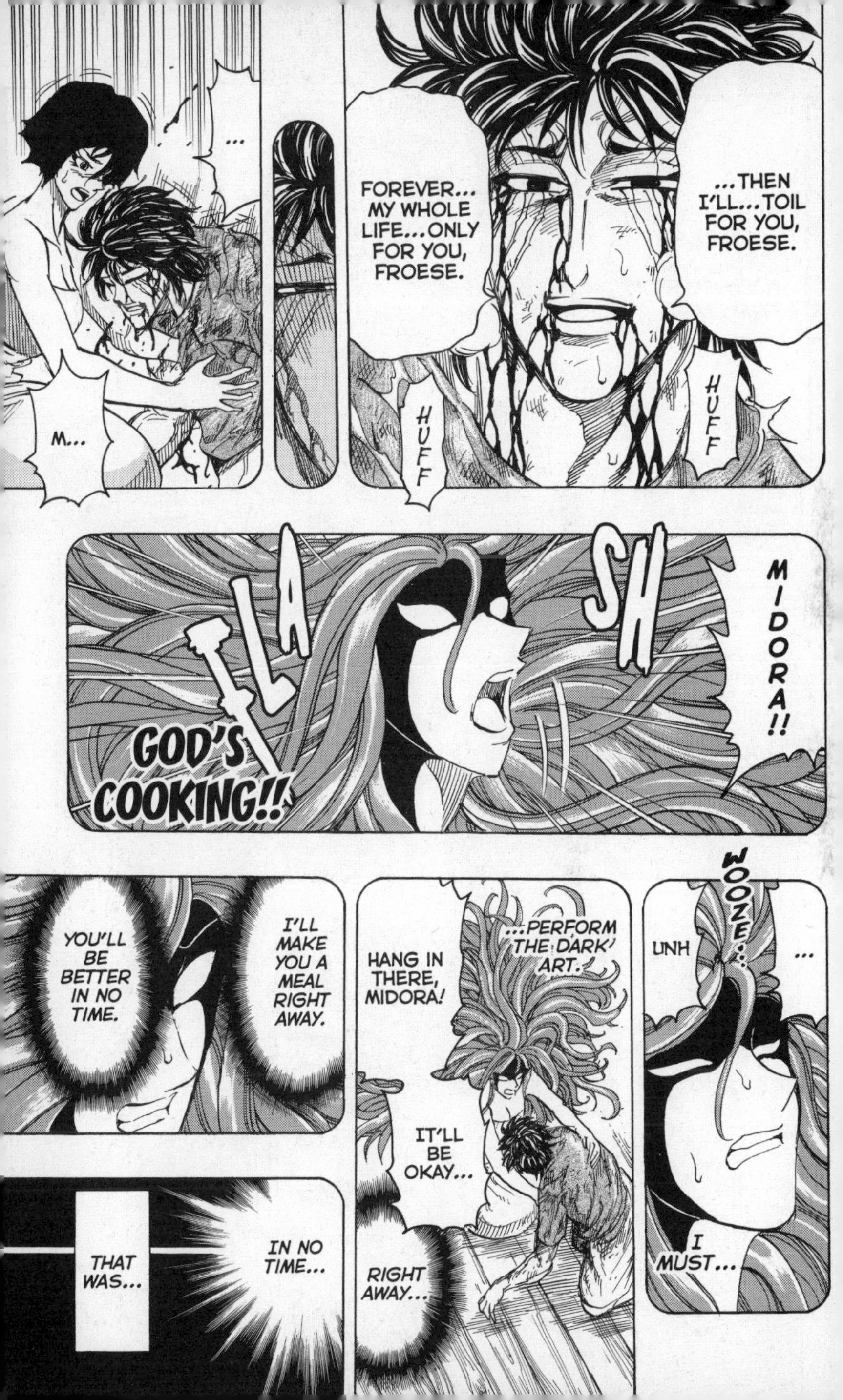
...THEN I'LL...TOIL FOR YOU, FROESE.
HUFF
FOREVER... MY WHOLE LIFE...ONLY FOR YOU, FROESE.
HUFF
...
M...
MIDORA!!
LA SH
GOD'S COOKING!!
WOOZE...
...
UNH
I MUST...
...PERFORM THE DARK ART.
HANG IN THERE, MIDORA!
IT'LL BE OKAY...
RIGHT AWAY...
I'LL MAKE YOU A MEAL RIGHT AWAY.
YOU'LL BE BETTER IN NO TIME.
IN NO TIME...
THAT WAS...

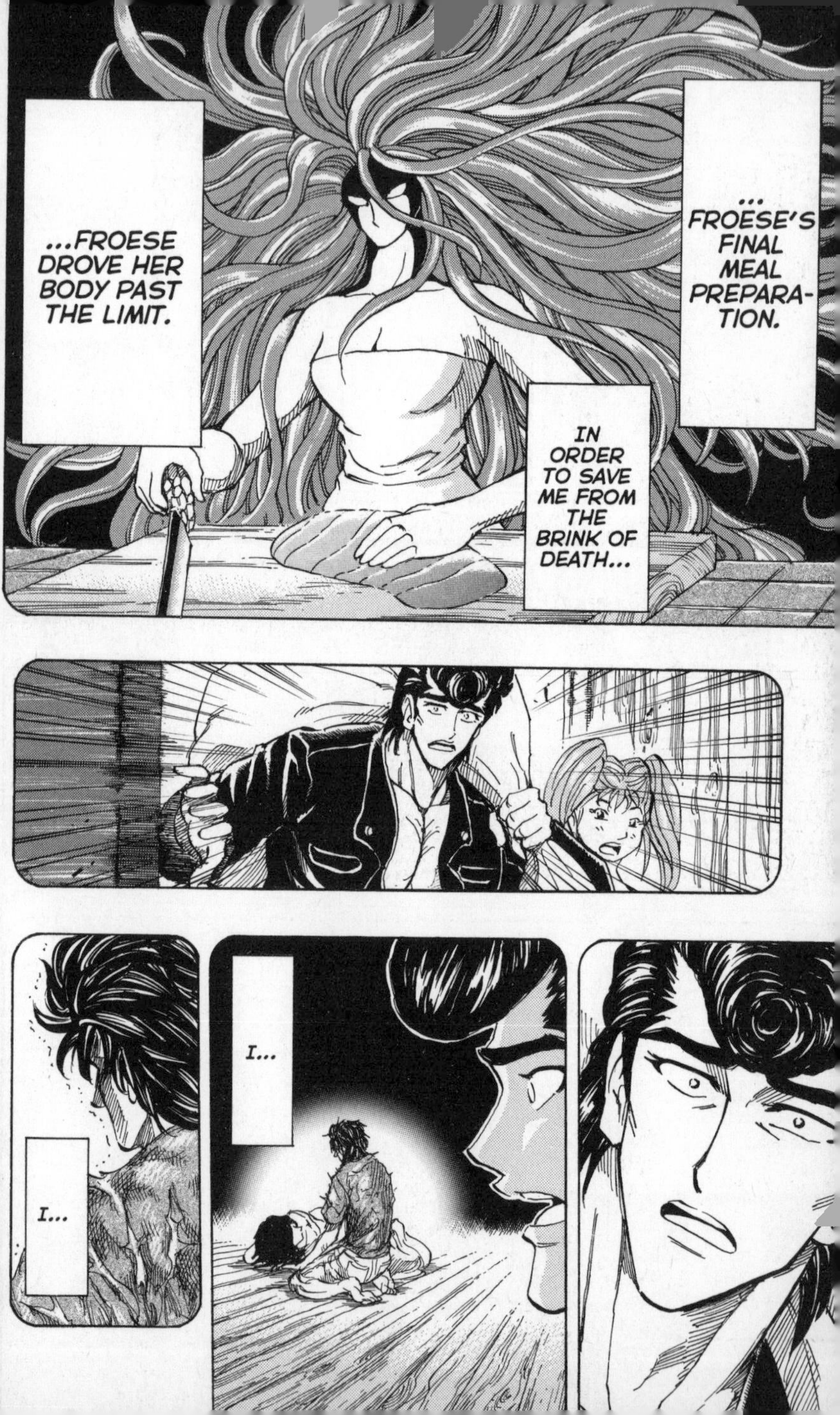
...FROESE'S FINAL MEAL PREPARATION.
IN ORDER TO SAVE ME FROM THE BRINK OF DEATH...
...FROESE DROVE HER BODY PAST THE LIMIT.
I...
I...

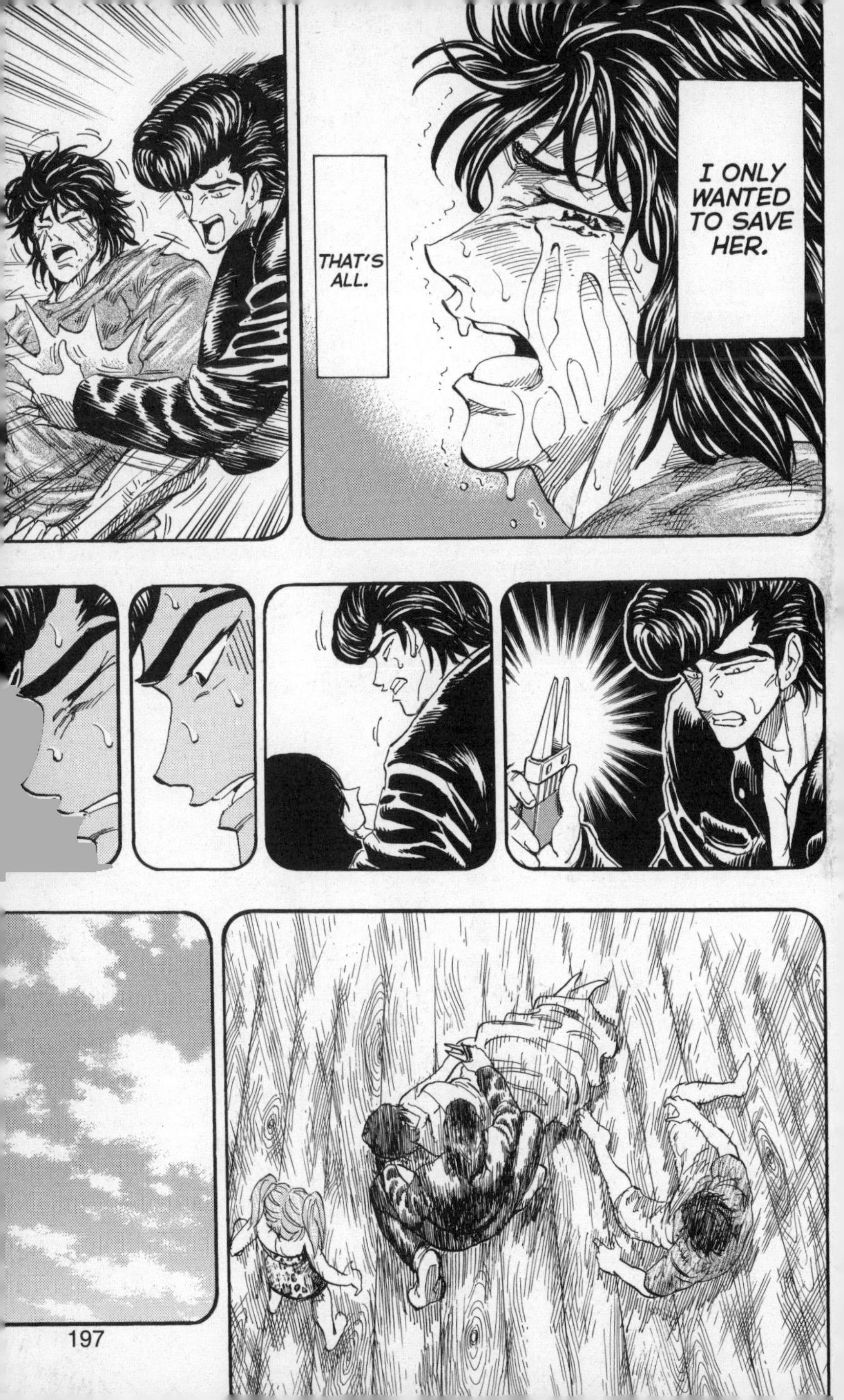
I ONLY WANTED TO SAVE HER.
THAT'S ALL.

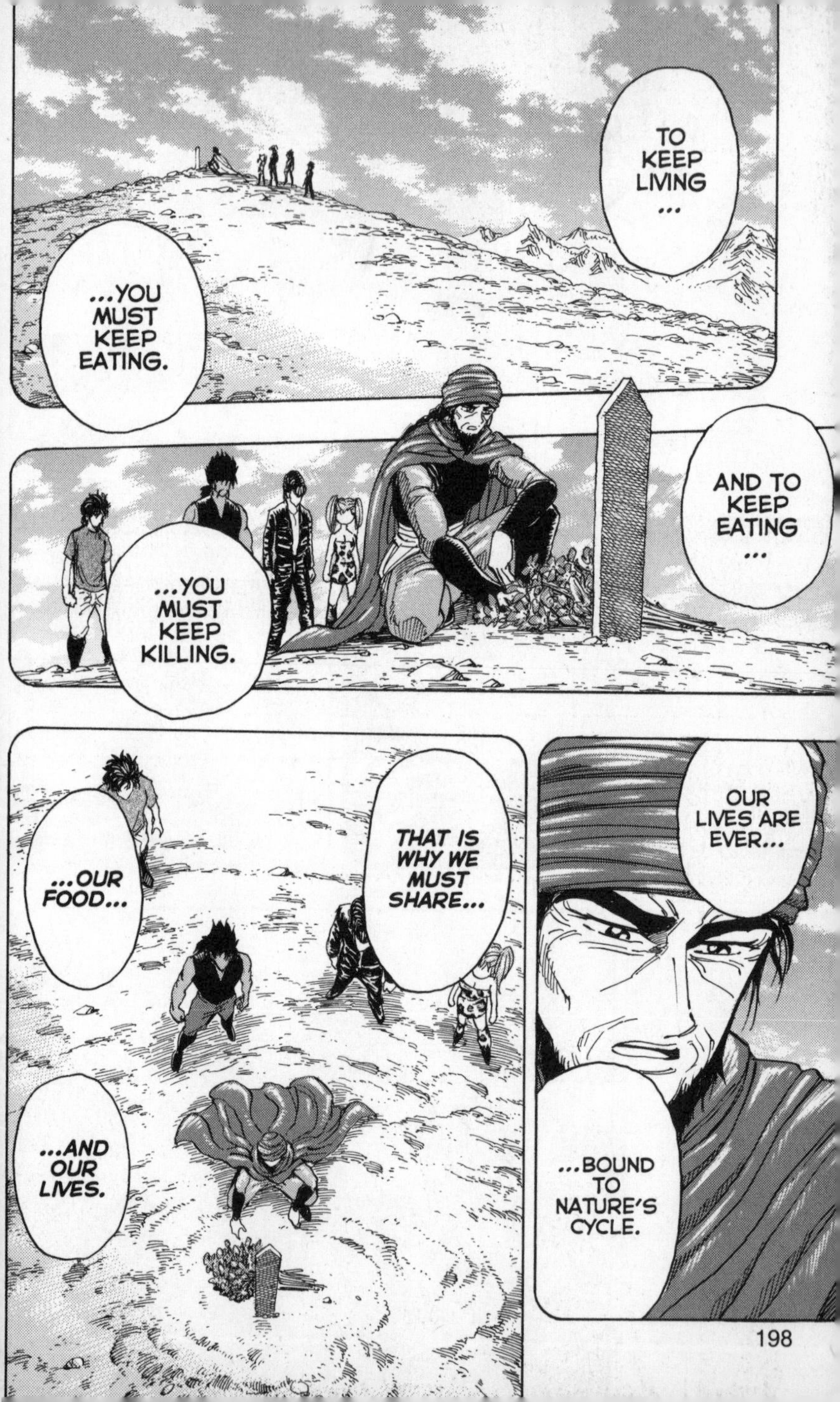
TO KEEP LIVING...
...YOU MUST KEEP EATING.
AND TO KEEP EATING...
...YOU MUST KEEP KILLING.
OUR LIVES ARE EVER...
...BOUND TO NATURE'S CYCLE.
THAT IS WHY WE MUST SHARE...
...OUR FOOD...
...AND OUR LIVES.

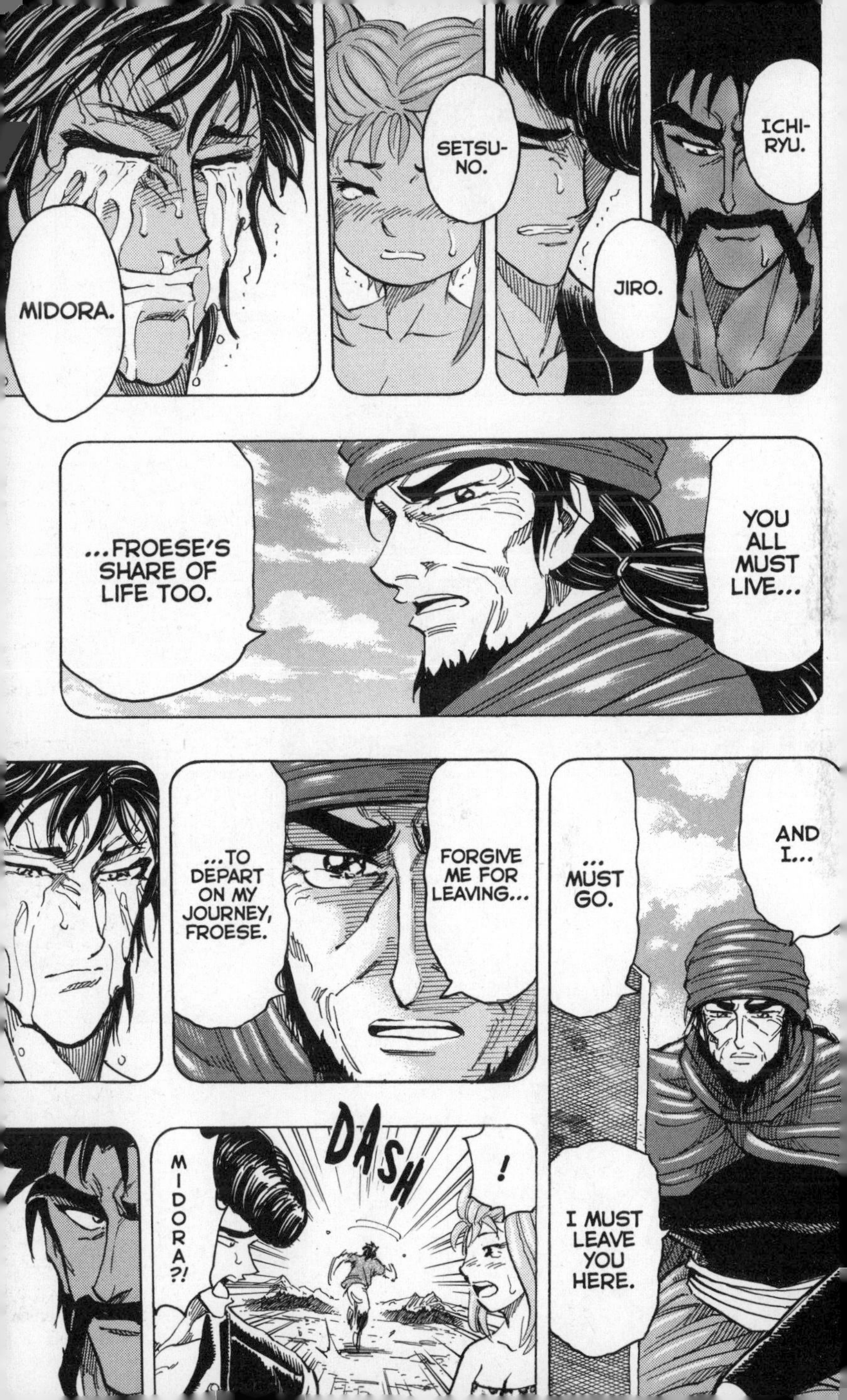
ICHI-RYU.
JIRO.
SETSU-NO.
MIDORA.
YOU ALL MUST LIVE...
...FROESE'S SHARE OF LIFE TOO.
AND I...
...MUST GO.
I MUST LEAVE YOU HERE.
FORGIVE ME FOR LEAVING...
...TO DEPART ON MY JOURNEY, FROESE.
DASH
!
MIDORA?!

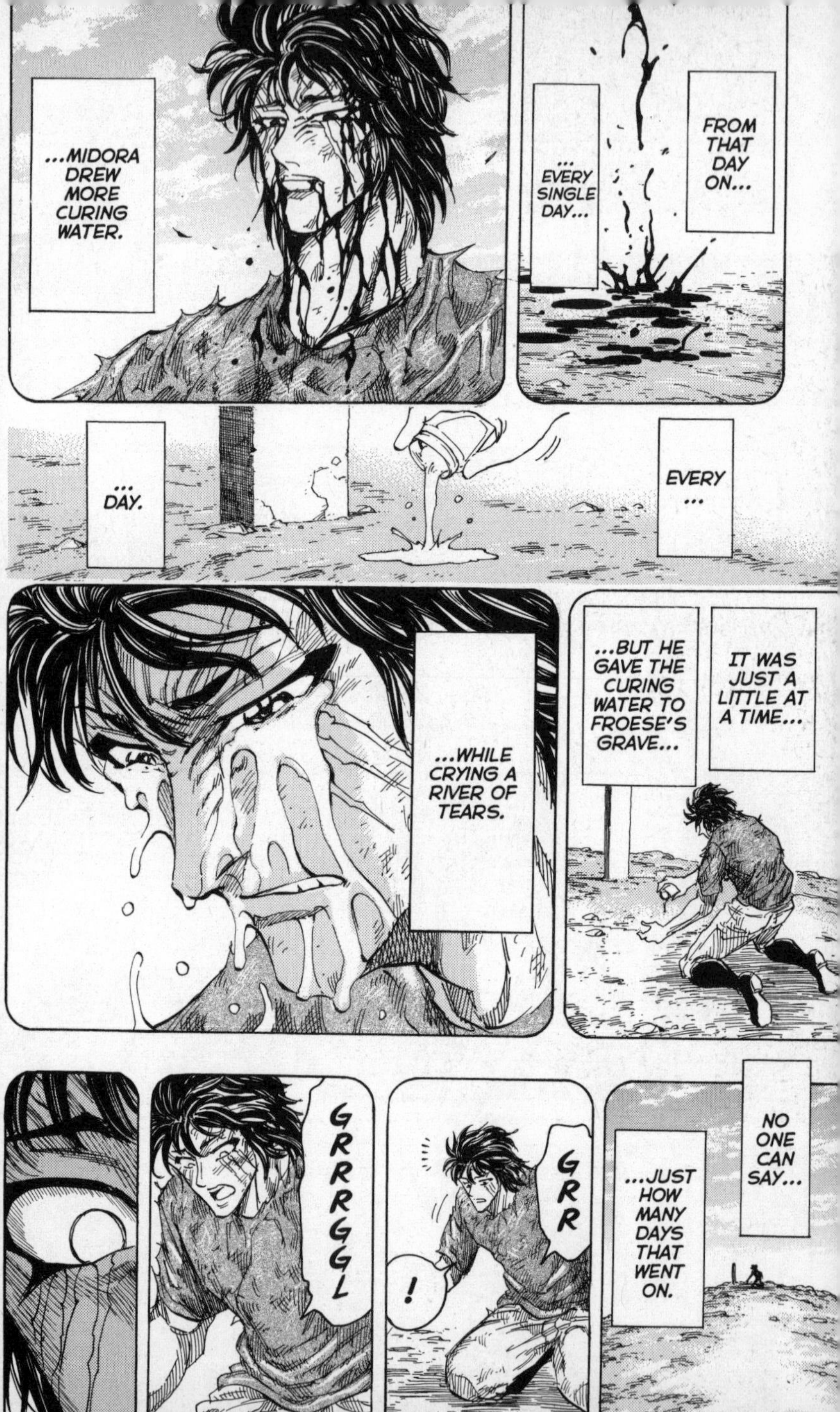
FROM THAT DAY ON...
...EVERY SINGLE DAY...
...MIDORA DREW MORE CURING WATER.
EVERY ...
... DAY.
IT WAS JUST A LITTLE AT A TIME...
...BUT HE GAVE THE CURING WATER TO FROESE'S GRAVE...
...WHILE CRYING A RIVER OF TEARS.
NO ONE CAN SAY...
...JUST HOW MANY DAYS THAT WENT ON.
GRR
!
GRRRGGL

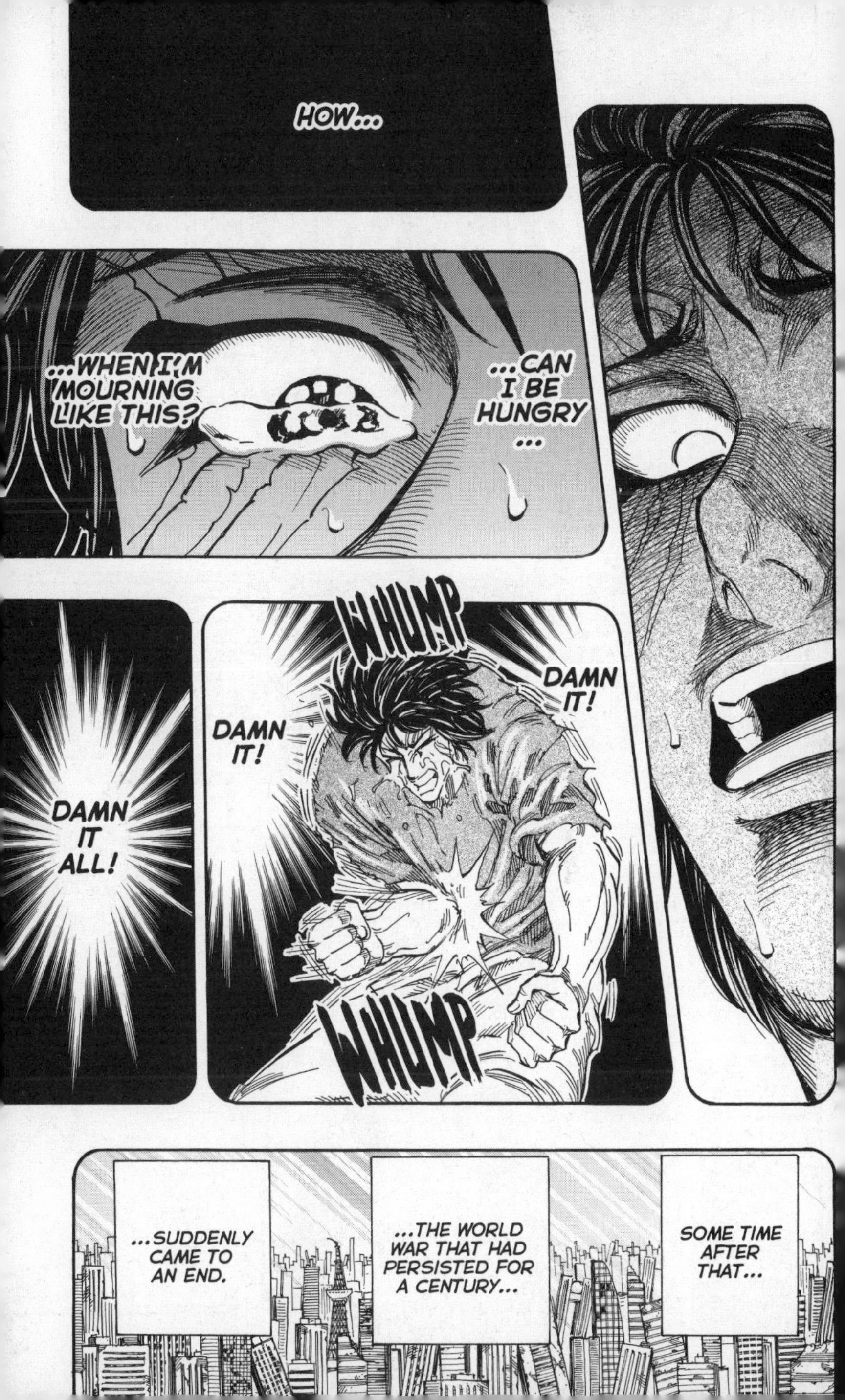
HOW...
...CAN I BE HUNGRY...
...WHEN I'M MOURNING LIKE THIS?
WHUMP
DAMN IT!
DAMN IT!
WHUMP
DAMN IT ALL!
SOME TIME AFTER THAT...
...THE WORLD WAR THAT HAD PERSISTED FOR A CENTURY...
...SUDDENLY CAME TO AN END.

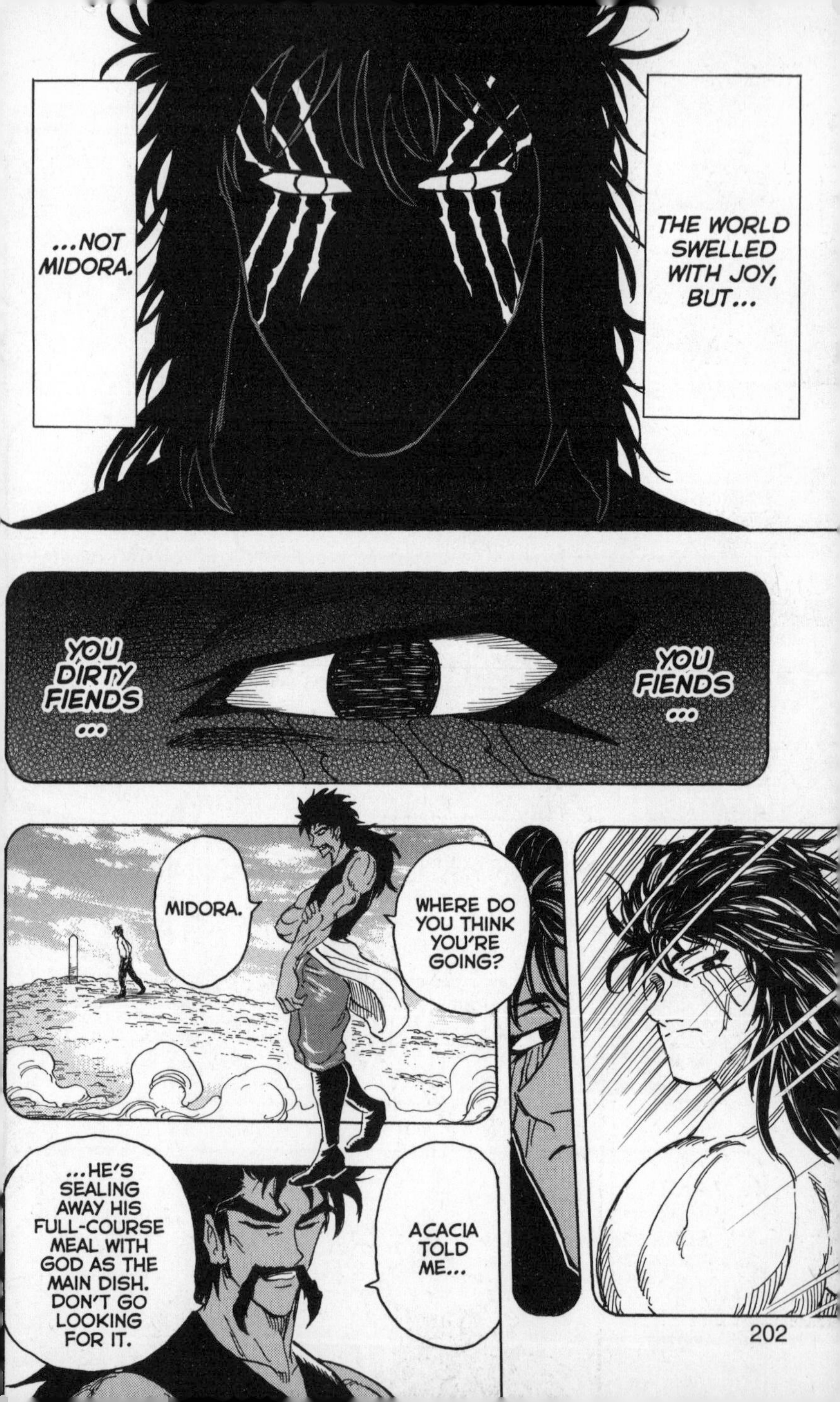
THE WORLD SWELLED WITH JOY, BUT...
...NOT MIDORA.
YOU FIENDS...
YOU DIRTY FIENDS...
MIDORA.
WHERE DO YOU THINK YOU'RE GOING?
ACACIA TOLD ME...
...HE'S SEALING AWAY HIS FULL-COURSE MEAL WITH GOD AS THE MAIN DISH. DON'T GO LOOKING FOR IT.

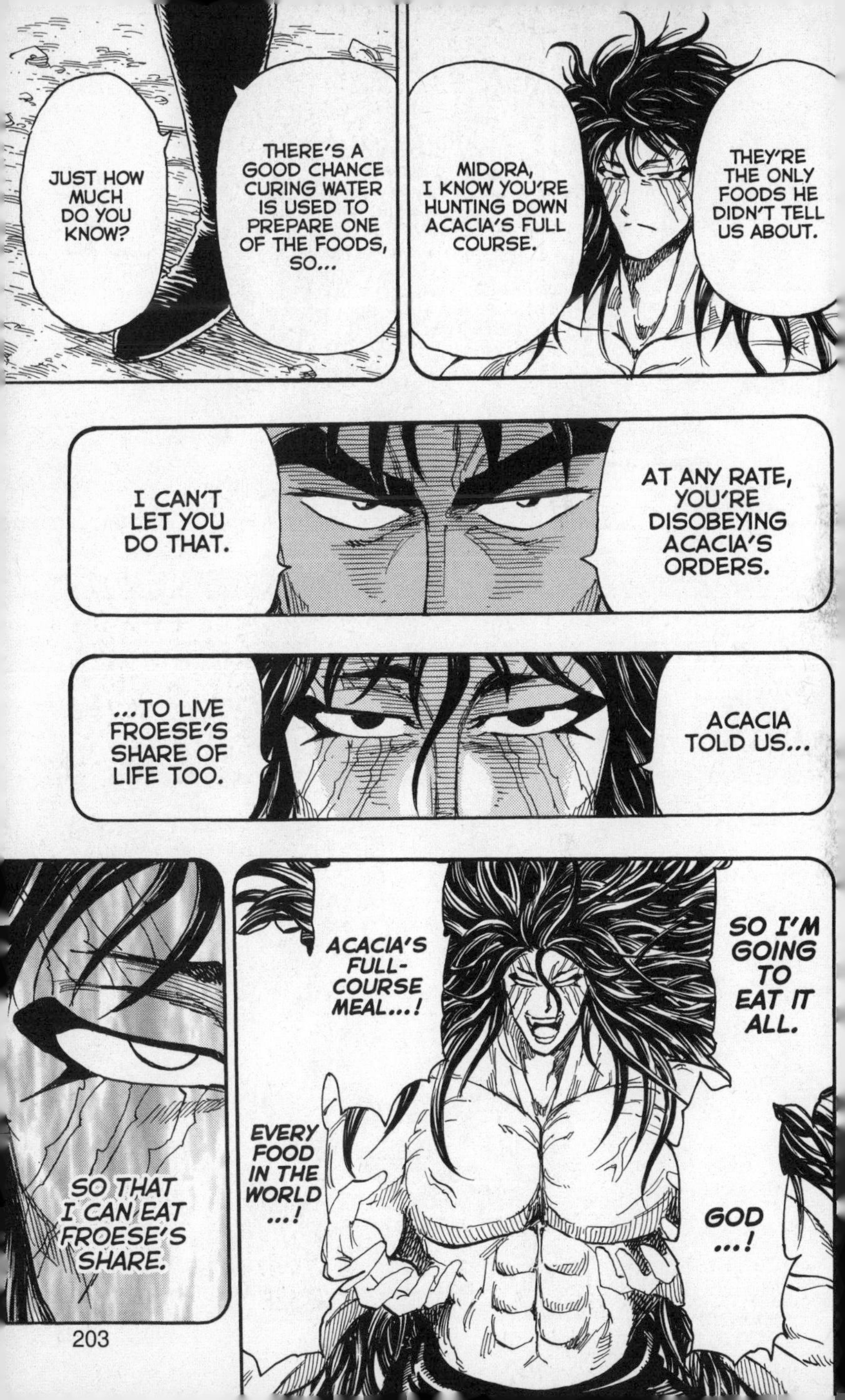
THEY'RE THE ONLY FOODS HE DIDN'T TELL US ABOUT.
MIDORA, I KNOW YOU'RE HUNTING DOWN ACACIA'S FULL COURSE.
THERE'S A GOOD CHANCE CURING WATER IS USED TO PREPARE ONE OF THE FOODS, SO...
JUST HOW MUCH DO YOU KNOW?
AT ANY RATE, YOU'RE DISOBEYING ACACIA'S ORDERS.
I CAN'T LET YOU DO THAT.
ACACIA TOLD US...
...TO LIVE FROESE'S SHARE OF LIFE TOO.
SO I'M GOING TO EAT IT ALL.
ACACIA'S FULL-COURSE MEAL...!
GOD ...!
EVERY FOOD IN THE WORLD ...!
SO THAT I CAN EAT FROESE'S SHARE.

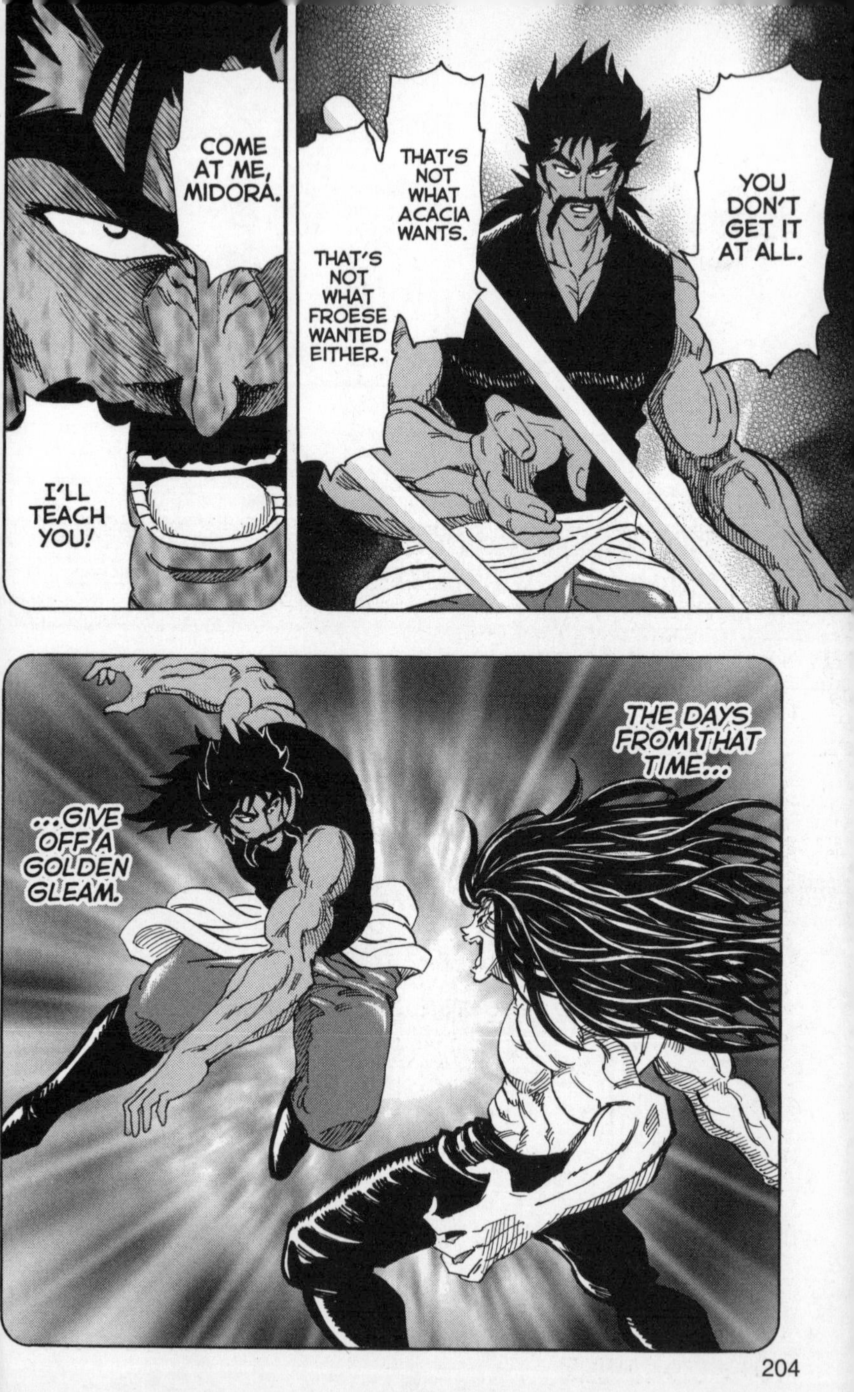
YOU DON'T GET IT AT ALL.
THAT'S NOT WHAT ACACIA WANTS.
THAT'S NOT WHAT FROESE WANTED EITHER.
COME AT ME, MIDORA.
I'LL TEACH YOU!
THE DAYS FROM THAT TIME...
...GIVE OFF A GOLDEN GLEAM.

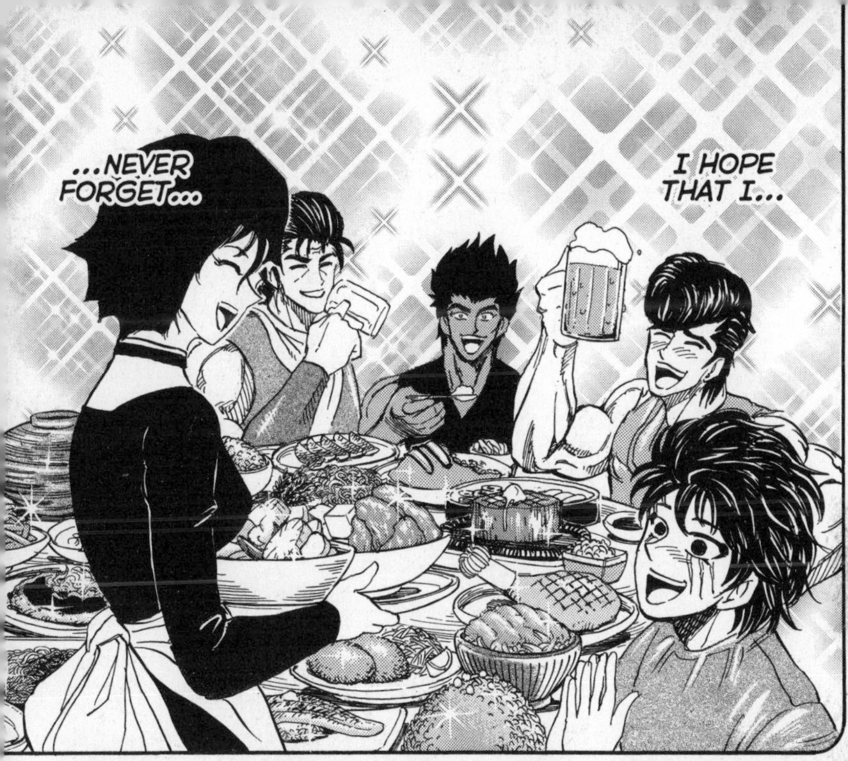
I HOPE THAT I...
...NEVER FORGET...

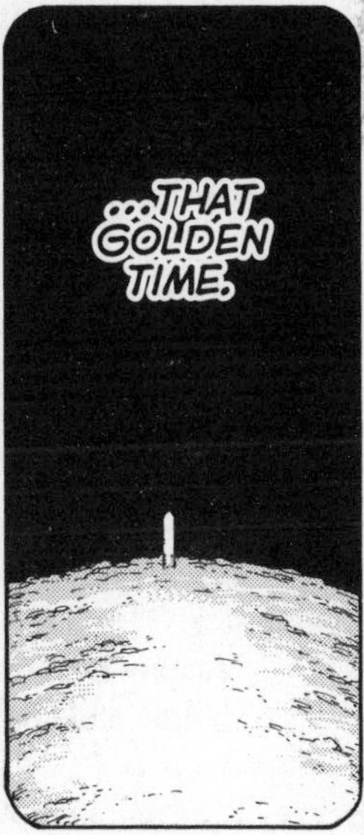
...THAT GOLDEN TIME.

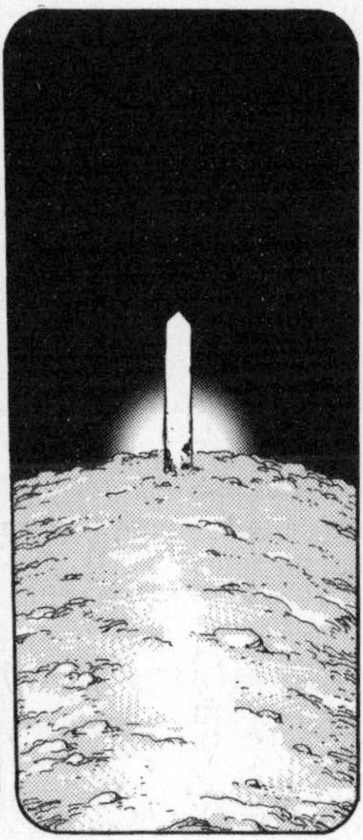

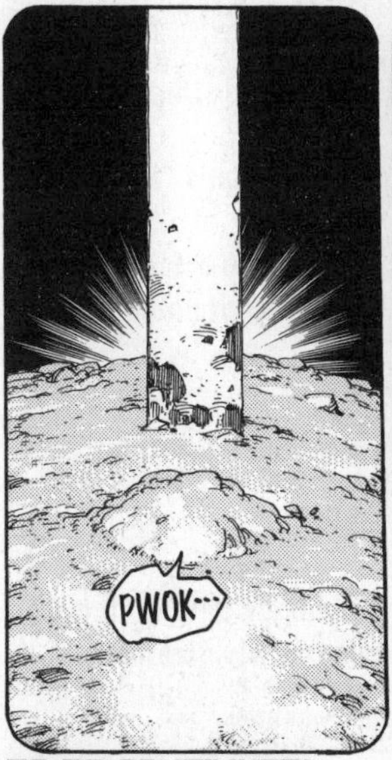
PWOK...

TO BE CONTINUED!

A NOTE ON NAMES

Acacia's disciples' names have special meanings in Japanese:

ICHIRYU - The character *ichi* means "one;" *ryu* means "dragon."

JIRO - The character *ji* means "second;" *ro* is a suffix for sons. However, Acacia initially spelled Jiro with different characters of the same sounds that mean "two" and "wolf" respectively.

MIDORA - The character *mi* means "three" and can also be read as *sabu* when combined with the *ro* for son. *Tora*, or *dora* in this case, means "tiger."

Acacia combined animal names with the common names "Ichiro," "Jiro" and "Saburo" to create unique names for his disciples.

-ED.

COMING NEXT VOLUME

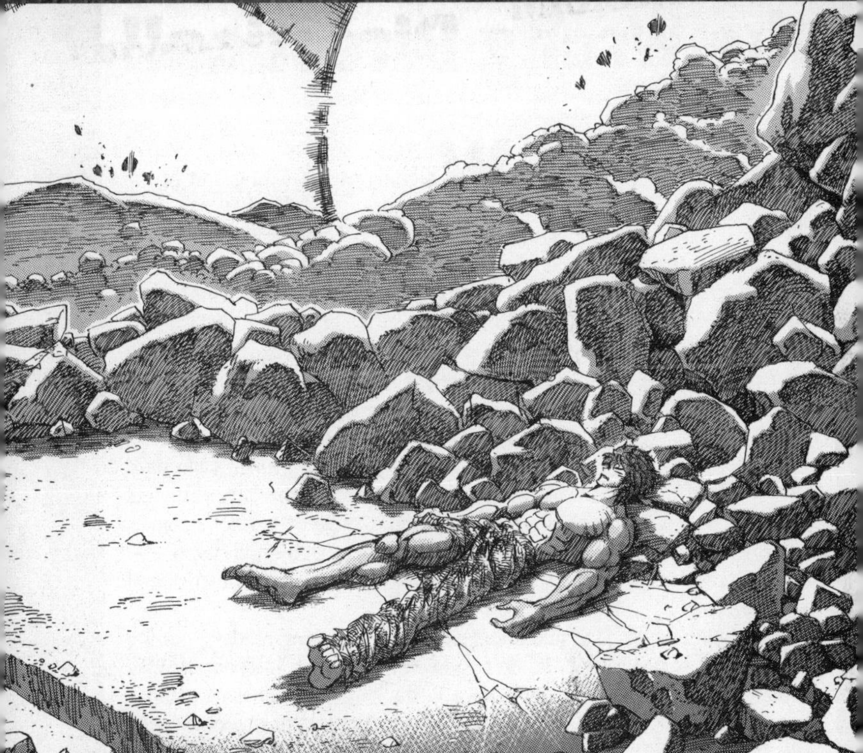

WORLD'S GREATEST GOURMET HUNTER

The horrific conclusion of the epic battle between the heads of rival organizations the IGO and Gourmet Corp. spells disaster for the entire world, and the sun sets on the Age of Gourmet. Having lost his appetite for life, Toriko wanders the world aimlessly. Meanwhile, Toriko's chef partner Komatsu finds a new purpose... at Gourmet Corp.!

AVAILABLE AUGUST 2015!

You're Reading the Wrong Direction!!

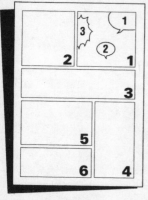

Whoops! Guess what? You're starting at the wrong end of the comic!

...It's true! In keeping with the original Japanese format, **Toriko** is meant to be read from right to left, starting in the upper-right corner.

Unlike English, which is read from left to right, Japanese is read from right to left, meaning that action, sound effects and word-balloon order are completely reversed... something which can make readers unfamiliar with Japanese feel pretty backwards themselves. For this reason, manga or Japanese comics published in the U.S. in English have sometimes been published "flopped"—that is, printed in exact reverse order, as though seen from the other side of a mirror.

By flopping pages, U.S. publishers can avoid confusing readers, but the compromise is not without its downside. For one thing, a character in a flopped manga series who once wore in the original Japanese version a T-shirt emblazoned with "M A Y" (as in "the merry month of") now wears one which reads "Y A M"! Additionally, many manga creators in Japan are themselves unhappy with the process, as some feel the mirror-imaging of their art skews their original intentions.

We are proud to bring you Mitsutoshi Shimabukuro's **Toriko** in the original unflopped format. For now, though, turn to the other side of the book and let the adventure begin...!

—Editor